A COUNTRY CATHEDRAL ORGANIST LOOKS BACK

A Country Cathedral Organist

Looks Back

1939-1978

David Gedge

Copyright © David Gedge 2005
Published by David Gedge 2009
Bridgend House
24 Bridge Street
Kidwelly
Carmarthenshire
SA17 4UU
First Published in 2005 by Serendipity

British Library Cataloguing-in-Publication data
A catalogue record for this book is available from the British Library
ISBN 978-0-95585-961-8

Printed and bound by CPI Antony Rowe, Eastbourne

Dedication

To Jane Brooks who as Organist of Ledbury Parish Church, was an inspiration; maintaining for so many years the last all - male church choir in Herefordshire.

Acknowledgements:

Thanks to Hugh Houghton, Kelvin Redford and Eileen Jones for typing and preparing this book, also to the countless number of people who have made music with me and made it such fun, not forgetting my wife, Hazel, who has been so very long-suffering and supportive.

Foreword

For many people, organised religion is not a necessity and for some it is positively to be avoided. For others, however, it has been, remains and always will be an intrinsic part of life. Within this latter group there are those for whom it is their life's work. Among these is David Gedge. Son of a South London Parish Priest, David grew up with the church, its daily round of worship and other activities as the norm. Open house, open church and the discipline of the church's music and liturgy were life itself.

It is, therefore, hardly surprising that David found himself drawn to music, and church music in particular, as a career option. Nor is it surprising that, having explored that option and made the choice to follow it, he developed a style and approach to his work which were reflective of his formative years. High standards were sought and more often than not achieved, but the approach was never, as far as I am able to discern, either exclusive or excluding. Nobody is turned away if they want to come and sing with us at Brecon where, in company with his wife Hazel as his assistant, David has been organist and Choirmaster for almost 40 years. There are no lines of social demarcation, no tests, simply a welcome and every possible subsequent encouragement to learn and sing and lead the worship of the Cathedral. The fact that in our Cathedral choir, all voluntary and with no choir school, and with choristers drawn from all walks of life, the attendance average is well above 95%, is ample testimony to the welcome, conviviality and sense of belonging that is created. It is not perfect, but it worked. In my five years as Dean, I have found it a valuable learning experience to watch David at work and coming to understand the enthusiasm which continues to motivate him.

Like all musicians and like all of us David, of course, has his own preferences and prejudices as well as his own firm opinions about what is good or less so, and what is desirable or undesirable. Like all of us he can be stubborn and even infuriating. Some modern developments, both liturgical and musical, as well as the ever increasing bureaucracy which (usually for good reason) impinges upon the church, grieve him rather that make him angry. For some who neither share his taste nor grasp what is the driving force behind his approach to his work, that has proved to be a frustrating problem, and relationships have not always been cordial. Some of this may be sensed or reflected in what is to be found in this volume in the personal outlook of someone whose gifts, energy and sheer love of his work I have come to value. I hope that it will be read with understanding.

John D.E. Davies - Dean of Brecon Cathedral
May 2005

I

A young priest stood in a Windsor hospital, praying over a dying old lady. Around the bed stood some relatives and friends all dressed in dark clothing. Among them was one woman younger than all the rest. When the priest had finished his prayers and everyone began to shuffle away, he darted round the side of the bed, caught the young woman by the arm and muttered quietly: "I can see you're not going to keep a straight face much longer: come to a dance tonight." So for the first time, my father met my mother. That evening in November 1929, they duly went to the dance and before the night was out they had become engaged. It seems that the young lady in question had run away from home to work as a secretary. Her clergyman-fiancé now, therefore, persuaded her to return to her parents. Her father, in gratitude, presented the young priest with a copy of "Love's Labours Lost" and inscribed the flyleaf with the words: "For Services Rendered"!

The wedding of the Revd Paul Gedge and Miss Gwendoline Middleton took place during the month of June 1930. It was a quiet affair at a church in an Oxfordshire village endowed with the unlikely name of Worminghall, where the Vicar was a friend. No parents were there. Indeed, afterwards, when they returned to Windsor to tell her parents what they had done, her mother rushed out of the house in a fury. On returning a little later, she apologized and explained that she had been upset by the news and had rushed down to the river meaning to throw herself in, only to change her mind at the last minute. At this her new son-in-law exclaimed: "Why did you not tell me? I would have given you a lift in the car!"

Part of the short honeymoon which followed was spent at the home of the bride's favourite uncle, Uncle Stan (as she called him), Hubert Stanley Middleton, Organist of Ely Cathedral. When nine months later (apparently the bridegroom's mother checked the number of months in her diary) a son was born to the young couple, they named the child Peter Stanley Gedge. Not long afterwards a child was born also to the bride's parents. This was only their second child, another daughter. What became obvious was that the parents of Wendy (as Gwendoline liked to be called) had never intended her to get away: rather, she was to stay with them to look after them in their old age. This second daughter, Janet, who was younger than Peter Stanley, never managed to get married. When in her mid-twenties she became engaged to be married, her mother suddenly "became ill" and Janet was expected to minister to all her needs, eventually to become disengaged. She never did marry and have a family of her own.

The Middletons were of Windsor origin, Wendy's grandparents living at 34 Temple Road. Her grandfather worked for up to ten hours a day, six days of the week, as a sheet metal worker at nearby Slough. Her grandmother also worked, doing washing and cleaning in other people's houses in order to swell her grandfather's meagre wages. Grandmother's money in particular paid the hire-purchase instalments on furniture bought so that their rented house could provide a more fitting place for their academically and musically brilliant son Hubert Stanley, the future cathedral organist, to entertain his friends.

There was another son who was musical, Frederick Cooper Middleton, and he had a special place in the family's heart. Frequently he would meet his mother on her way home from work in the late afternoon and take her hand in his. Then, after supper, he would often say to her: "Let's have a rest before we go to bed." Sadly, this lovable lad lived only fourteen years. Being an outstanding chorister in St. George's Chapel, Windsor Castle, where frequently he was called upon to sing solos, he attracted the attention of Prince Christian of Schleswig Holstein, a grandson of Queen Victoria, who lived at the castle and always took a great interest in the chapel music. Often the Prince would give young Fred a 5s 0d (25p) tip after singing a solo, which in those days was a considerable sum of money. This Fred always shared with his family so that perhaps they could eat much better for a few days, or pay off an outstanding debt, or even retrieve some valuable household item from the pawn shop. In due course Frederick won a scholarship to Westminster School, but before he could take it up, he was struck down by a mysterious illness. At first, tuberculosis was diagnosed and a long stay in a sanatorium on the Isle of Wight was prescribed – but how were the family to pay for this? Had Prince Christian been alive then doubtless he would have helped, but sadly he had died two years earlier. However, through the good offices of a local Vicar, the late Prince's Harley Street specialist was called in to give a second opinion. Sadly he diagnosed enteric fever, and within a few days Fred was dead. The disease which had carried him off along with three other people in the neighbourhood had been brought along by an Indian sailor "carrier". So Fred was laid to rest in Windsor cemetery on the outskirts of the town. At that time his grave must have appeared lonely, being close to the entrance, at the opposite end to the part of the cemetery by the chapel, which was being filled up first. Presumably this was done because of the filthy nature of the disease, in order not to endanger the health of the mourners and pall-bearers by carrying the coffin any further than was absolutely necessary. From that year on until the death of Fred's eldest and last surviving sister, Louisa, on January 5th 1940, a holly wreath was placed on his grave every Christmas Eve.

What Frederick Cooper Middleton might have achieved obviously remains a closed book, but not so his younger brother Hubert Stanley. Considering his poverty-stricken background his career was remarkable. He was born two years later, on May 11th 1890 and was sufficiently clever to win a place at the Imperial Service College, Windsor. In the course of his studies he had organ lessons with Walter Parratt, the renowned Organist of St. George's Chapel, Windsor Castle. Afterwards he went to the Royal Academy of Music before going up to Cambridge as a scholar of Peterhouse, reading classics and music. He took the degree of B. A. in 1916 and four years later, in 1920, not only acquired his M. A. and Mus. B., but was also appointed Organist of Truro Cathedral. Six years later he moved on to become Organist of Ely Cathedral, whereupon he resumed his connection with Cambridge as a fellow of Peterhouse, at the same time joining the staff of the Royal Academy of Music. He left Ely a year after Paul and Wendy visited him on their honeymoon, on being appointed Organist of Trinity College, Cambridge, in 1931, combining this position with a university lectureship in Music. Fifteen years later, in 1946, he had the distinction of being the first Organist of Trinity College to be appointed to a fellowship of the college. Meanwhile he had been awarded doctorates of music, by examination, at the universities of both Oxford (D. Mus. 1937) and Cambridge (Mus. D. 1943) which was then, and still is, a rare achievement. He is still remembered for the important part that he played in framing the syllabus for the music tripos instituted at Cambridge University in 1945. After his death on August 13th 1959, a tablet erected to his memory in the chapel of Trinity College pointed, in Latin, to the nature of his influence on music at Cambridge University, describing him as "one who furthered the course of music both within and without the University, and by his teaching and zeal sought to establish it in an equal place of honour among the other arts."

One of his distinguished pupils, the illustrious conductor, harpsichordist, composer and arranger Raymond Leppard, who had been a Choral Scholar at Trinity during the years 1948-1953, later paid him this tribute:

"The point about High Table was that you saw its members constantly around the college and could very easily see and speak with them more intimately whenever the need arose. They, almost all, felt an obligation to be available and take an interest in the undergraduates with whom, for one reason or another, they came in contact. Nor did they overdo it - they were just there and part of the place.

The ones I saw most of were interested in and involved with College music. Principal among them was Hubert Middleton, a much loved but underestimated man. I owe him and his wife, Dorothy, a very great deal. He directed my studies, but generally, in college, he was in charge of Chapel and College music, which he looked after with a wisdom and consistency of practice that taught us much beyond the events themselves, and helped to order and develop our various enthusiasms. He had been organist for many years before I met him, and only lately a Fellow of the College, which we felt did not reflect much credit on the Fellowship, though, it must be said, his modesty was as much reason for this late appointment as any lack of appreciation of his worth in the college. At home he and Dorothy were tireless in entertaining numbers of us to memorable evenings of talk, food and drink with, occasionally, a little music; but not often, for Hubert was a thinker about music with a marvellous ear and a warm enthusiasm for what was valuable. Its practice was something he loved to encourage in us, but was not good at himself. He was one of those people who said unforgettable things which influence you for the rest of your life. As a teacher, he had that greatest gift of all of making you feel that he thought you so much better than you knew you were; and you loved him, so you couldn't let him down by not being so."

Uncle Stanley was more of an academic than a practical musician, a fact born out by Raymond Leppard's less flattering but equally endearing description of the college choir during his time:

"I was a choral scholar, and this meant regular attendance at two weekday evensongs and one on Sundays – not an intolerable burden, even though it was a dreary business musically. Hubert went on valiantly but unenthusiastically with choir practices at which there was, irregularly, a motley collection of boys bribed in from the highways and byways. Some had been there so long they seemed biological miracles. It was all a sad echo of the days when Stanford and Alan Gray had a choir-school to draw from for a timetable of services that would have graced a cathedral."

Uncle Stanley composed some church music which to this day is still sung at divine services in the chapels of Trinity and St. John's Colleges.

Older than both Frederick Cooper Middleton and Hubert Stanley Middleton was Peter Middleton who was born in Windsor on March 9th 1886. Educated there at the National School, he went on to work in Wimbledon. During the First World War he served in the East Surrey Regiment as a Sergeant Instructor. Afterwards he moved to Watford to work as a Compositor with the Watford Observer. For a hobby he played double bass in a local amateur orchestra and later played flute in the Watford Philharmonic Orchestra, for a time serving on its committee.

It was while working in Wimbledon that Peter Middleton had met Alice Webb who was in service at a house nearby. Alice was the second of nine children whose father was a ploughman at a weekly wage of 8s 6d (42 p) living at Donnington, a small hamlet near to Stow-on-the-Wold in Gloucestershire. In addition to his usual farm labouring duties, her father also had responsibility on Sundays for the welfare of his employer's cart horses. This brought him a further 1s 6d (7 1/2p) each week, which was enough to pay the rent of the modest stone cottage in which the family lived. The cottage was semi-detached consisting of one main room downstairs in which there was a kitchen range to provide warmth and a means for cooking, and two bedrooms upstairs. Not being a "tied cottage" it belonged to a local landowner, Colonel Godman, who used to send his agent on each of the four "Quarter Days" each year to collect the rent. Obviously the colonel was a kind man because as he watched this young family increase by one child with great regularity every eighteen months or so, at his own expense and with no increase in the rent he enlarged the cottage, creating an extra room beyond the main living-room, which became a scullery, with an additional bedroom above. However, the Webbs were good tenants and despite their low income, the family was always held in high regard by the local people.

All but the eldest of the nine children were born in that cottage and all grew up to be strong children, all surviving healthily into adulthood, many living to old age. A mystery surrounded one of Alice's younger sisters, Fanny, a good-natured child, well-disciplined and always willing, kind and helpful. Apparently before she was born, her mother had been "badly frightened by a gipsy" (as it was quaintly put by a relative), so it was no surprise to anyone in the neighbourhood that she was such a dark-haired, olive-skinned girl. Indeed this affinity with the gipsies was even more emphasised when, as a schoolgirl, on her way home with several other local children one day, some gipsies tried to persuade her to join them, fully convinced that she was a Romany and belonged with them.

The school the children attended was in the nearby village of Broadwell, two miles away from Stow-on-the-Wold. Pupils started there at the age of three years, those between three and five years being allowed to drop off to sleep over their slates and desks just when they wished. Although Alice was the second child, having an older sister Annie Maria, it was Alice who had an innate sense concerning the welfare of her brothers and sisters and came to be regarded as a substitute mother. If, on her way home from school, she had been given a piece of bread and dripping, a jam tart or an apple by a villager, she usually waited to be joined by at least one or other of her brothers and sisters so that "the treasure" could be shared by them.

When Alice left school at the age of twelve years as was the custom, she went to work daily for the household of the baker at Broadwell. This entailed a walk of three-quarters of a mile from home each way, every day except Sundays. Although the duties she carried out for this household were mostly of a menial nature, she always carried them out in such a way that the baker and his wife were very pleased. An attractive-looking girl, she was fair-haired and blue-eyed and, when asked, always described the colour of her hair as being "the colour of corn", the word "blonde" holding no meaning for her. Being "as strong as an ox" and exceedingly trustworthy her mother often sent her on errands, especially when this entailed having charge of other members of the family.

There was such an errand to be carried out on Christmas Eve 1899. Her older sister, Annie Maria, was now in service and therefore spending her first Christmas away from home. So thirteen-year-old Alice was entrusted with the care of eleven-year-old Fanny and ten-year-old Will on the five-mile walk through Moreton-in-Marsh to the village of Batsford and Malcolm House, there to give a present to Annie Maria. When this uneven trio arrived at the gaunt common-wealth-style house they marched round to the tradesman's door, for they would never have dared knock on the front door. The door was opened by Annie Maria and she was allowed to spend a few minutes with them, just enough time to receive the gift of an apple saved from the harvest of her grandmother's apple tree, an orange, also a few hazelnuts gathered from the hedgerow during the previous autumn and saved to become a treat at Christmastime. The remainder of the children back at the cottage would receive exactly the same plus, possibly, one toy given by the lord of the manor to be shared between them. Poor Annie Maria was in tears at her first Christmas to be spent away from all her brothers and sisters. Alice, too, became upset at seeing her elder sister so distraught and also from the thought that, on returning back home with Fanny and William, she would have to relate to her parents how they had found her sister.

By the time the next Christmas came round, Alice herself was in service. She was now a kitchen maid in the household of Upper Slaughter Manor, a little further away from home, a distance of around seven miles. Her wages amounted to £4 per annum, paid in four instalments at the end of each period of three months worked, when she would be allowed just one day's holiday. This "holiday", however, did not start until after the breakfast dishes had been cleared away from the breakfast room and had been washed up to the satisfaction of the cook. Alice then had the seven miles to walk along the roads before reaching home, maybe having a lift for part of the way on the cart of some trusted carrier or perhaps having the company on foot of some other local servant acquaintance also travelling along the same way. Once home, she would not have many hours there as she would have to be back in her employer's house before nightfall.

Alice always gave her £1 wages to her mother to help support her brothers and sisters. However, this help came to an end two years later when at the age of sixteen years she secured a more senior position as Kitchen Maid at "Northdown", a small stately home near Broadstairs, where she was to become one of eleven indoor servants. Upon leaving her post at Upper Slaughter, she was presented with a leather-bound, gilt-edged copy of the Book of Common Prayer as both a memento and a testimony to the service she had given. But what was she to give to help her mother now? Furthermore, how could she help her grandparents, who had been living on Parish Relief for a number of years? Her grandfather had not worked since the time he had been involved in an accident in which his smock had been caught up in the flywheel of the threshing machine he had been cleaning. Afterwards he had been taken to the Radcliffe Infirmary at Oxford to have part of the injured leg amputated. Alice felt that she must contribute something really positive to all her family before leaving for her new post so far away. So this slim, sturdy teenage girl (who often boasted an eighteen-inch waist), ever practical, purchased a sow which was about to furrow. On presenting this large, handsome creature to her father, she said: "If you can't make any money out of these piglets, you never will!" Indeed, the bacon from the pig and the sale of all the piglets paid off all their existing debts to local tradespeople and helped them on their way to a brighter and slightly richer future. By then Alice was ensconced in "Northdown" where over the next three years she rose through the ranks from being a kitchen-maid to deputising competently for the cook, even to managing all the other servants when necessary.

Alice's final position was Cook at "Grange Lodge", 13 The Grange, Wimbledon, where to her joy she was joined later by her sister, Fanny, who became House-Parlourmaid. A Kitchen Maid completed the team of indoor servants, all of whom "lived in". There was also a daily gardener, a married man, who lived nearby. All of them were in the employ of Theresa Philo Bazalgette, whose father, Sir Joseph Bazalgette, had designed the Thames Embankment. The only free time they had was on a Sunday afternoon, after the washing-up had been completed, when they were allowed to enjoy an afternoon walk, maybe as far as Wimbledon Common, before returning to prepare afternoon tea. These periods on Sunday afternoons were much treasured by the girls and were always anticipated with eagerness, as also was their other period of free time on a Thursday afternoon, when they were allowed if they wished to receive a few approved visitors below stairs.

So while in Wimbledon, during the little spare time that she had, Alice Webb had met and fallen in love with Peter Middleton. Thus in March 1908 she finally turned her back on life in service, exchanging it for marriage with Peter. Then, within a surprisingly short time, on August 6th she brought into this world their first daughter, Gwendoline, to begin her own journey to her own wedding to the Revd Paul Gedge, twenty-one years later.

II

Wendy was elated by her new and unexpected life style. She wrote a fascinating letter to her favourite Aunt, her mother's youngest sister:

"My dear Auntie May,

No doubt you have already heard that I am married to a clergyman I met while I was at Windsor for Granny's funeral last November. He is now Assistant Chaplain to the Missions to Seamen in Buenos Aires. We don't actually live at the Mission but are having our letters addressed there as we have only taken this furnished flat for four months.

We had a very quiet wedding – I will describe it to you – it was great fun. I left the Universal Housing Co. on Saturday 3rd May about 2 o'clock (presumably to go to Windsor for the week-end and return Monday morning as I always did every other week), but really I rushed up to town to buy my "trousseau". This consisted of a few frocks and a beige two piece purchased in Berwick Market and some undies bought in Edgware Road. I quite expected Dorothy Perkins' shop in Oxford Street would be open and was at my wits' end when I discovered it was shut, so, as I absolutely had to get something, I went to Edgware Road which was the nearest place I could think of. I've never been in such awful shops in my life. I wanted to buy some crepe de chine sets but went into four shops without any luck and in the end had to put up with artificial silk. I actually managed to buy one crepe de chine nightdress (lavender colour), it was the only one they had in the place. While I was still in Edgware Road it came on to pour with rain. I wanted to catch the 6.30 from Waterloo to Windsor as Paul was meeting me then and still had some shoes and two hats to buy so I started off back to Berwick Market, of course I got absolutely soaked. At 6.15 I was buying my shoes in Oxford Street; while the girl packed them I hailed a taxi and got the man to pack all my parcels while I got in, the girl then flew out of the shop and chucked my parcel in with the rest and we drove off. I told the driver I simply must get to Waterloo by 6.25, we managed this and I then had to go to the cloakroom and collect my suitcase, leaving a porter to follow after me with my various packages. You would have laughed if you could have seen us rushing across the station; anyway I got into the train just before it started, and then proceeded to pack as many things as I could into the suitcase so that no-one I saw at Windsor would wonder whatever I had been buying so many clothes for and asking awkward questions. On Sunday Paul preached his farewell sermon at Windsor, and as usual we had about a dozen girls to tea; I pretended to be awfully sad because Paul was going away as the girls knew we were a bit friendly. Paul was going to hire a car and he arranged to pick Auntie Lou and I up at Datchet (about four miles out of Windsor) at 11 o'clock. As usual we got all behind and had to have a taxi to the station to catch the train. Well we arrived at Datchet and sat and waited for an hour. I got awfully worried at the thought he must have got run over. Eventually he arrived on the bus about 12 o'clock and said there had been a muddle over the car and his friend who had arranged it all for us was in town and wasn't expected back for about an hour, the manager of the shop was away and had left no instruction so the man left in charge wouldn't let him have a car. He said he was going back to Windsor again to see if Harry Wood had returned; if he wasn't back by 1.20 we were to take a bus into Slough and he would meet us there, so off he went. All this time I had been sitting on my suit case outside the station, Auntie Lou now went off to try and buy a paper (its [it's] such a hole she was unsuccessful) and I still remained seated; a workman came along and started talking to me. He asked me what was the matter, and because I couldn't really explain to him I told him we'd had a break-down. He said why didn't we go to Windsor for the day it was only a few miles away etc. etc. and started to describe all the beauties of the Castle and river to me. I listened and was too lazy to tell him we had just come from there, then Auntie Lou turned up again and he started on to her about Windsor, she just said "Oh we've just come from there" ... You should have seen his face - it was a picture. Well Paul didn't turn up so we caught the bus and as we arrived in Slough he arrived with the car, we all scrambled in and drove off as quickly as we could. This was about 1.30 and we had got about 40 miles to go. Auntie Lou was packed in the back surrounded with suitcases and parcels and I sat in the front feeding Paul with egg sandwiches. We went 53 miles an hour some of the way. Every time we went over one of those little bridges or a big bump in the road Auntie Lou got bounced right up off the seat and banged her head on the top of the car. She says she shall never forget our wedding day as long as she lives. Anyway we arrived safely at our destination and the ceremony was finished by exactly three o'clock. We were married by a Mr. Deacon at Worminghall Parish Church, Nr. Thame, Oxford. Auntie Louie, Mrs. Deacon and the Verger were the only people present. After the service we went back to the vicarage and had some tea, this took about two hours, we then asked Mrs. Deacon if she would like to come to Watford with us; she said she would and we all started off. We arrived there about 7.30 and just walked in and said we were married, I then packed up all my things and we left about 9 p.m. We had to stop at a garage and have the lights attended to and arrived in Windsor about 10 o'clock, dropped Auntie Lou, and then took Mrs Deacon back to Worminghall, we left there about 12 and proceed[ed] to an Inn near Kingston Blount which [we] were making our headquarters for a few days. We got there about 1 o'clock, then something went wrong with the clutch and Paul spent half an hour trying to get the car into the yard, in the end he gave it up and left it standing in the road. On the Wednesday we went to Broadwell with Mr and Mrs Deacon. Paul asked the lodge keeper if we could go and look over the place as I used to live there and he let us go through. It was great fun to look in all the old graneries [sic] (don't know how to spell it) and cowsheds, etc., we also went through Stow and down the road to the Station where the harebells used to grow. On Thursday we came to Watford, took China for a picnic in Munden woods (do you remember them), went home and also called on a few of my girl friends at the office to tell them I was married and going to South America. Needless to say they were astounded. On Friday we went to Southampton where Paul's mother is living with his brother who is a curate there, where we stayed until Tuesday. We went out from there every day to see his different relatives, who are scattered all over the South of England, none of whom I had seen before. It was an ordeal. On the Sunday he preached at the preparatory school he went to when he was a boy and where he taught for a short time before he was ordained. We had dinner afterwards with the headmaster and his wife. It was the first time I had ever been out to dinner, they had two maids flitting about and I was scared to death. We have been out several times since however and I am beginning to take it as a matter of course. We've got to dine with Sir Hilary Leng and his wife as soon as the old man gets well (he's just had a leg off). Paul says he's very nice but I'm scared stiff at the idea although I'd rather die than say so. It amuses me to think how I used to come and see you all when I was small and watch you dishing up all the grub. Paul hates eating a great meal and avoids it whenever possible. You'd laugh at our catering. We never cook anything but eggs. We've absolutely surpassed ourselves this week as his friend who is a schoolmaster at St. George's College, Quilmes, is staying with us. We've varied our menu with sardines and bacon. Usually we have tea, coffee, eggs, bread, butter, jam and fruit. Paul has done a lot of camp cooking so he does most of what is done, Green does nearly all the washing up, so I have an easy life. I usually make the bed. Its a ripping life. On Monday Paul made an omelette. We hadn't used the frying pan before so just put some fat in it and thought it would be alright; the pan turned out to be dirty, also we put too much fat in, by the time we finished it was simply poisonous, but we eat [ate] it. We have since cleaned the pan out and I made one today which was quite a success. I am staying in today as I have strained my foot a bit dancing too much, really we were to have gone to lunch on some ship (can't think of the name) and then on to a children's party at Flores, one of the suburbs where Paul preaches sometimes. I go round all the ships with him and have a lovely time. Last week we were on one that had two dear little black kittens. The captain said he would ask the officers if they would let me have one when they got bigger. Well yesterday they were sailing so we went down in the afternoon to enquire about them. We stayed on the ship about three hours, had two teas, one with the Engineer, who gave me a nice silver cigarette case which he'd had for about 15 years and never used, and umpteen magazines, and another with the Captain. In the end we forgot to enquire about the cat and that was what we really went down for. We were also supposed to go for lunch but got up so late that we couldn't get there in time. We never get to bed until two o'clock or later and get up about 10.30 or eleven. Quite a change from what I've been used to.

I seem to be getting this tale frightfully muddled up. I meant to tell you about our last two nights in England, but apparently forgot. Mid-day Tuesday we left Southampton, came up to town, dumped a lot of stuff at the Missions to Seamen office in the Strand, went to see Paul's Uncle at Crayford, from there to Tilbury to see an Aunt, back to Crayford to see his cousin who had been out when we called before, had a chat with her, left about 12.30, proceeded to Ely to see Uncle Stanley, had a puncture, arrived at Ely about 5.15 a.m., woke them up, had some breakfast, left about 10 o'clock, came up to town again to get our visa, did some shopping, proceeded to Windsor, said good-bye to a few of our friends there and informed them we were married, then arrived about 1.30 at Paul's friend's at Old Windsor where I stayed for the week-end in November when all the fuss was going on, stayed there the night, or rather until 4.30, when we all got up and went to Smithfield Market in the van to get the meat, Paul and I then stayed in town and did some more shopping. This was when we bought the typewriter. (I'm so glad we've got it as it will help me to keep up my speed.) The shopping kept us busy until it was time to catch the boat train. We sailed in the "Afric Star" from Victoria Dock at 2 p. m … She is a cargo boat and carried only three other passengers so we had a nice restful time which you can imagine we felt in need of after our strenuous time during the last 10 days. We went 1300 miles altogether in the car. We had a delightful voyage. I wasn't sea-sick. We should have gone direct from London to Buenos Aires but a man fell down the hold and broke his arm so we had to call at Madeira to land him. We were not allowed to go on shore.

We arrived here on June 4th – Canon Brady (Paul's chief) and his friend Green from Quilmes were there to meet us. At first we had to endure many welcomes and flash light photographs (which seems to be the favourite hobby of the B. A. newspapers), they take photographs of every single thing that happens at the Mission. For the first month we stayed with the hon. sacristan (don't know how to spell it but that's what it sounds like) and his wife. They have a large sixth floor flat in the road overlooking the docks, but on 9th July we moved into this small furnished flat we have taken for four months while the woman and her two children are in England. It consists of a bedroom, sitting room, bath room and kitchen, all of which open onto a nice verandah, it feels almost like been [being] on a ship and it's a great temptation to throw all our rubbish overboard as we used to on the sea, it also has a nice roof garden.

The programme at the mission every week is as follows:

Monday	Boxing
Tuesday	Officers Social (Bridge), whist drive for the men, and dancing for the apprentices. Tea and cakes for everyone.
Wednesday	Concert
Thursday	Apprentices social and whist drive for the men. Grub as above.
Friday	Boxing
Saturday	Dances for apprentices and grub.
Sunday	Communion 9.30, breakfast (eggs and bread and butter), Lunch 1 o'clock, about three football matches, tea at 5 o'clock followed by a sing-song of the Broadway Melody variety, service at 7.30 then dancing, bridge or billiards till midnight. After communion Paul and the Canon often have to dash off and help at the Cathedral or take a service at one of the churches in the suburbs.

I go to all the football matches and am the only lady at the boxing. I never wear a hat now, even to church. A number of the big passenger boats sail at 12.15 midnight and we often go down to see them start off or after everything is finished at the mission we make up a rubber and play until about 1 o'clock.

The Mission runs a football league to which about 70 ships belong of all nationalities. It's really comical to watch Paul refereeing sometimes when he doesn't know a word of either of the languages and has to do it all by signs.

I should have loved to come and see you all before we sailed but it was really impossible to squash any more in than we did. Won't it be funny in a few years' time if we go to England to see Kathleen and Edna going out to work.

Please give my love to everybody including Gerald.

With heaps of love
Gwen.
P. S. The Canon has christened me "Girlie" as he said he didn't like to keep calling me Senora.

Who was this young clergyman who had swept Wendy off her feet, driven her in a car round and round the Home Counties and then escorted her half-way across the world to Argentina?

Paul belonged to the Gedge family, which was supposed to have come to England from Scandinavia with the Vikings, way back in time. Gedges can be found in plenty in the counties of Norfolk and Suffolk. Indeed, in a recent Norwich and Norfolk telephone directory forty-seven such names were listed. Travel westwards, however, and the name dies out so that only one can be found in Wales. Being a clergyman was a family disease! Paul's maternal grandfather was the Revd. John Wycliffe Gedge who had died in 1918 at the grand old age of eighty-two years. For some of those, he had been Rector of Buriton in Hampshire and Inspector of Schools for the diocese of Winchester. An uncle on this side of the family, the Revd. Henry Theodore Sydney Gedge, had been a Vicar Choral at York Minster for twenty-nine years. As an undergraduate at Oxford University he had shown considerable prowess at sport, winning much-coveted Blues for rugby and athletics. As a clergyman he was famed for the fine quality of his voice, both singing and speaking, so that he was greatly in demand as a vocal teacher. To this day, there are elderly clergymen in Wales who still speak highly of the help he gave them at St. David's College, Lampeter, in both the sung and spoken portions of divine service.

Paul's paternal grandfather was another Gedge, the Revd. John Denny Gedge, who died in 1920 at the even greater age of eighty-three years. A Justice of the Peace for the county of Norfolk, he had also been Vicar of Methwold for twenty-nine years, where he was noted for his parish visiting and his interest in social reforms. One of the uncles on this side of the family was the renowned blind Canon Gedge, Rector of Gravesend for many years and an Honorary Canon of Rochester Cathedral. Another uncle was Vicar of Cothelstone in Somerset, a Prebendary of Wells Cathedral and also diocesan Inspector of Schools. Then there was the extraordinary Cousin Evelyn, who achieved some notoriety in the Church of England for her work as Organising Secretary to the Village Evangelists. In old age (she lived to be eighty-eight), she achieved still greater notoriety for the way she drove around the streets of central London in a red mini, clad in religious garb of some sort and frequently doing voluntary work, usually in the interest of St. Simon Zealot, Chelsea, the church where she worshipped.

That was not all! There was yet another relative, the Revd. Edmund Gedge, who was Vicar of Marden in Herefordshire for a number of years. Married to the sister of Bishop King of Madagascar, he fathered eight children but ended his days without an heir. Of his five sons, two died young and the other three were all killed in World War I. One was a priest and another was an ordinand, but it was the third who is of most interest: he was Fleet Paymaster Joseph Theodore Gedge, who had the misfortune to be on board H. M. S. Amphion when it was mined and sunk on August 6th 1914. He has the distinction of being the first British Officer to be killed in the First World War and the Gedge Medal in the Supply Branch of the Royal Navy was founded in his memory.

So Paul's mother and father were cousins of some sort! Although his mother was a good enough violinist to have obtained an LRAM diploma, even she was heavily involved in church affairs. She became Enrolling Member for the Mothers' Union, presumably at Havant in Hampshire, where she lived with her husband, Arthur Johnson Gedge, the much-loved local doctor. It seems that one of Doctor Gedge's failings was a reluctance to extract payment for treatment from his poorer patients and consequently there was never as much money around as there should have been. Even so, Paul and his brother Michael both attended Highfield, a preparatory school in nearby Liphook and then moved on to Charterhouse, the famous public school in Godalming. Paul excelled himself in Classics to the extent that occasionally, known only to himself and unknown to the master in charge, he did all the Latin or Greek homework for his particular set.

After Charterhouse the paths of the two brothers separated in more ways than one. Between leaving school and going up to Oxford, Paul became Assistant Scoutmaster of the church troop in Havant. During this time he had a religious experience which convinced him that God was calling him to give his life to the welfare of young people. At Keble College he spent most of his time rejuvenating or running scout troops in an area bounded by an arc seven miles round the north of the city. He also raised funds for their support. Sadly, however, after taking a Second in Mods, he had to come down from university owing to family poverty. Two years followed of being a prep-school master. Then, when he went up to St. Stephen's House in Oxford to prepare for ordination, he took the opportunity to complete his degree. Afterwards he was ordained first Deacon and then Priest in the diocese of Oxford, becoming Curate at St. John's Church, Windsor.

Paul's only sister, Alice, the youngest of the three children, also went to Oxford, where she won a Blue for lacrosse and captained the university team. Not being eligible for ordination (the Movement for the Ordination of Women was then not even a dream), she did the next-best thing and married a journalist who eventually became a priest.

Michael, however, eschewed the path that led to Oxford, believing it to belong unfairly to the privileged few. He chose instead to go to "red-brick" Leeds University. Here was a rebel in the making. After graduating in 1925, he went to Mirfield to train for the priesthood. Some time after ordination he became Charterhouse Missioner in Bermondsey, south-east London. Never able to tolerate nonsense, he refused ever to assent to the Thirty-Nine Articles of Religion, which meant that he could never have a parish of his own. The nearest he came to this was when he became joint Curate-in-Charge of Eythorne in Kent with a fellow clergyman. They attempted to combine the roles of priest and worker by sharing both parish duties and a daily shift in a coal mine, even down to taking an active part in union business. The experiment put intense pressure on both of them, especially his colleague, whose marriage rocked a little under the strain of maintaining the dual role of miner and parish priest. The Archbishop of Canterbury, Geoffrey Fisher, stepped in and put a stop to this novel and revolutionary experiment, but not before Michael had persuaded the S. P. C. K. to publish a book that he had written anonymously concerning "The Priest Workman in England". So Michael may have got there ahead of the Roman Catholic Church, which was experimenting with this sort of work in France.

In the end, however, it was the Roman Church which claimed him. Apparently, he read a book entitled "Why I am not a Roman Catholic" and promptly became one. Three years in Rome was followed by ordination again and fifteen years as a parish priest at Fawley, near Southampton. This was not far from home and was a cunning move by the Roman Church as it presented Michael to the many family and friends who had known him of old as a sheep that had been lost, now returning to the fold. At Fawley, Michael designed his own church with a clear glass screen at the West End, so that mothers with babies or toddlers could watch Mass being celebrated and feel part of the action without causing any distraction. Fr. Michael was an unbending Roman Catholic. When a member of his family telephoned to ask if he could bring his wife and children to visit him one Sunday morning, his immediate reply was "Yes, but I cannot give you communion". When invited to share with them in a sumptuous picnic, he declined, saying that he had not eaten such food for a long time and was not going to start now.

Not long after this, a motorway was built linking Southampton to Portsmouth, and he noticed that at one entering point there were no signs forbidding cyclists. Immediately he returned to his clergy house, took out his bicycle and promptly cycled down the motorway. When the inevitable happened and he was stopped by the police, he told them they couldn't and took them back to show them why. In retirement, he went to live among the homeless, sleeping rough, determined to reveal what he believed to be discrepancies in the Vagrancy Laws. His health began to suffer, so he was taken into care by some Sisters and acted as their Chaplain. Finally, he retired to his birthplace, Havant, and continued an active ministry until his death at the age of ninety-one.

Meanwhile, Michael's older brother Paul had worked quite happily as a priest in the Church of England - since he was prepared to pay lip service to the Thirty-Nine Articles! Stories of strange goings-on showed that he too was an eccentric. He had written a play about King Neptune searching for a bride and played Neptune himself, while the remaining parts were played by scantily-clad parish maidens. Then, noticing how the Vicar always raised his biretta whenever the words "Jesus", "Christ" and "Lord" were uttered, he preached a sermon using them as often as possible until in the end the desperate Vicar removed his biretta altogether and placed it upon his lap.

Life with Paul Gedge could never be dull, as Wendy had by now discovered.

III

Much as Paul and Wendy were having the time of their lives in Argentina, they were not able to remain there long, because their first child was soon on the way. They returned to England, to what was then a slum area of Southampton where Paul, like his brother Michael before him, began his work as a Curate in the Church of England. There Peter Stanley Gedge was born on March 31st 1931, to be joined three years later by Daphne Margaret on January 12th. Then tragedy struck. Towards the end of the following October, Wendy went upstairs to attend to the baby only to find her dead, having suffered what is now called a "cot death". Wendy and Paul were devastated, yet, as they so often did, they bounced back and on August 3rd 1935 a replacement was born, Daphne Elizabeth. Shortly afterwards Paul and his family moved to London, to the parish of Rotherhithe close to London Docks, living at 114 Amos Estate.

This move was, presumably, no accident. According to his brother Michael, Paul was modelling his ministry on that of Fr. Wainwright, a famous Vicar of St. Peter's, London Docks, who had died only a few years before. From an early age, Lincoln Stanhope Wainwright had been fascinated by Wapping in the East End of London on the opposite side of the River Thames to Rotherhithe and had long harboured an ambition to work there. When this was realised, he very soon settled down and entered into the life of the parish even though at first he felt rather overawed by the High Church ritual. In those days Wapping was an island bounded on one side by the River Thames and on the other side by the docks. It was crowded with warehouses, tenements, narrow alleys and little courts full of small houses. There was the constant noise of ships and also the clatter of horses' hooves as the heavy carts rumbled along the narrow streets to and from the docks. In the evenings, the pubs were crowded with people of every nationality sharing each other's joy and sorrow, poverty and occasional moments of prosperity. At the heart of the parish was the beautiful church of St. Peter which at that time had a great reputation of caring for its people body and soul. For many, the church was the most beautiful home they ever knew. The ceremonial and colour of the services lifted them out of the drabness in which they lived, whilst the numerous societies and clubs attached to the church provided a welcome alternative to the pub for many.

Fr. Wainwright had been instituted Vicar of St. Peter's back on January 16th 1884 and spent the remainder of his life there, seldom being away for a night, let alone for a holiday. Each and every day started at the altar, where he gained the strength to face whatever the day might bring. After a breakfast of tea and toast he spent the remainder of the morning dealing with correspondence and matters arising therefrom. He never had a midday meal, realising that to understand hunger you had to be hungry. He made it his business to ensure that the children at school had a good hot dinner even if he had to beg money for those that could not pay for it. Each afternoon he went visiting in the parish and as he made his way around the streets he always had time to talk to anyone he met. At 5.30 p.m. he had his second meal of tea and toast. During the early evening he was at home to anyone, whether the help they needed was spiritual or material. His generosity knew no bounds and no-one was ever turned away. He gave the shirt from his back to a man who needed one to obtain work, he gave coal from his own scuttle to a family who had none, he gave blankets from his own bed for a man who was sick. If he ran out of money, food and clothes as he sometimes did, he never ran out of love. Later in the evening he would visit the hospitals, often not returning to his clergy house until midnight or later. Only then would he eat the main meal of the day which his housekeeper had left warming by the fire.

Fr. Wainwright's clergy house was served by an assorted bunch of Dickensian characters. When a curate, feeling his position, called them servants, he said quietly to him "I have no servants, only friends". He loved children and sometimes on cold winter evenings would gather them under his cloak and take them back home with him for food and warmth by the fire. Small wonder that when he died, on February 6th 1929, countless of his parishioners flocked to see his body. Burly dockers with cap in hand, women from the tenements, little children clutching posies all filed up the uncarpeted stairs of the clergy house into the sparsely fur-nished room where he lay. When his funeral procession wound its way through the mean streets that had been so dear to his heart, passing shops and tiny houses where every curtain was drawn, it was followed by hundreds of working folk. At the graveside they all sang the hymn "Rock of Ages" and men who had never been known to cry, wept.

If this was the priest who inspired Paul it would account for the invariable pat-tern of the life which he adopted. Every conceivable moment of time which could be spared from more humdrum parochial routine, including the whole of his hol-idays, he now occupied with camps, theatrical performances (he wrote his own plays) and expeditions of all kinds: indeed, any activity for and with his young parishioners. While at Rotherhithe, he even taught on every school day in one of the several church schools in the parish. He only differed from Fr. Wainwright in that he had a wife and children to care for in addition to his flock, but even they were gradually drawn into the pattern of his ministry.

Paul remained at Rotherhithe for four years, with special responsibility for the nineteenth-century church of St. Paul, which was later destroyed in the Second World War. This was especially sad because the building was distinguished by having all its woodwork created out of the remains of the "Fighting Temeraire", a ship immor-talised by the famous Joseph Mallord William Turner who painted a picture of her shortly before she was broken up in a dock nearby. If any thought of war was but a dream at the start of his ministry in Rotherhithe, when the time came to move on in 1939, that dream gave every sign of becoming a reality. Paul harboured thoughts of working as an Army Chaplain, but the Bishop of Southwark had other ideas. He appointed him Vicar of Holy Trinity, Lambeth, just at the time when I arrived into this world at 114 Amos Estate. Not long afterwards, the family moved once again.

The new parish, enclosed by Westminster Bridge Road, Lambeth Road, Archbishop's Park and St. Thomas's Hospital was full of two-up, two-down terrace houses, a few gaunt Peabody Buildings, one of which had so little in the way of san-itation that it was smelly from a considerable distance, and some dark, dismal roads through dimly-lit arches beneath the main Southern Railway lines that carried around two thousand trains daily into Waterloo Station. Although many trains were powered by electricity, the filth was still unbelievable as steam trains to Southampton, Bournemouth and Weymouth, or Basingstoke, Salisbury, Exeter and deepest Devon belched filthy smoke throughout the parish. To this was added a variety of smells which issued forth from the profusion of small private industrial works that existed beneath the remaining arches and also the steaming dung that was deposited by the massive council cart-horses as they hauled the dust carts around the narrow streets, not forgetting the contribution left by the more glamorously-attired horses that hauled the brewery's dray, carrying barrels of beer to the Royal George across the road from the church. It was an area full of character that defied description.

It was obvious to my father that when war did break out, his parish would become a sitting target to German bombers, as the main railway line from London to the docks at Portsmouth and Southampton ran right through the middle of it. So he set about creating a shelter in the vicarage garden. This involved digging a hole some fifteen feet deep and big enough for there to be a general living and sleeping room complete with fireplace and chimney, a small bedroom for the baby – me, a lavatory and an entrance stairway along with an escape hatch at the far end. The entire construction was lined with wood and lit by electric light. It was remarkable and so well-built that it lasted until long after the war had ended.

The Vicarage itself was an enormous soot-covered Victorian brick building with twenty-one rooms spread over three floors. Downstairs, a green baize door led to the service rooms, comprising kitchen, scullery, larder, pantry, lavatory and a two-roomed cellar. A back door opened into a yard where there were sheds for coal and storage for such items as bicycles. Originally, the green baize door was the dividing line between servants and family. Presumably, the servants' living quarters were situated high up in the attic, which left ten rooms on the ground and first floors for the Vicar and his family. The three large rooms on the ground floor all included huge fireplaces with elaborate mantelpieces on which were carved such texts as "Give Attention To Reading" and "Fear God, Honour The Queen". The largest of these was the sitting room, known during the time of Paul and Wendy as the Blue Room, because most of the furniture was covered in blue fabric. During much of my childhood this room was kept locked and the key hung out of my reach, because I could on occasion be just a little destructive in my games! A bay window in this room looked out onto the large garden, an oasis of green in an urban jungle.

Of the two remaining rooms one, lined with cupboards and books and containing a small billard table in the middle and a table with a typewriter on it, was Paul's study. The other, also lined with shelves, although these contained a motley collection of toys, and a large table, which sometimes did service as a ship's deck, was a play room. All three rooms opened into a substantial hallway from which a small stairway led down to the garden door, while a door on the other side led into a porch which opened into the lane. In one direction, this led to the church primary school and in the other was the church, beyond which was Carlisle Lane. A larger staircase led from the hallway to the first floor of the vicarage, where there were five bedrooms, a bathroom and a cloakroom containing a lavatory and a wash-basin. My bedroom overlooked the railway so that whenever I was ill I would have my bed moved to the window to enable me to collect the numbers of the engines. As it was, I quickly learnt to tell the time by the departure of express trains.

Such pursuits were a little way off, however, as the war years intervened. Of these I remember little. My first recollection is of being wrapped up in a blanket one night and taken to nearby St. Thomas's Hospital. Apparently, I had ear trouble, double mastoids, and for almost two years I regularly had horrible yellow dressings put into my ears. I was three years old when all this began and I was subjected to four operations. Because of the war, patients requiring such treatment were taken to an emergency hospital at Hydestile near Godalming in Surrey. Obviously I failed to enjoy the experience, because when the time arrived for the fourth and final operation and I was being put on a special bus outside St. Thomas's Hospital, I made a run for freedom up Lambeth Palace Road. I was pursued by a laughing nurse who duly caught me and put me back on the bus. When it came to the actual operation, the anaesthetic did not work, so I was wheeled into the operating theatre still conscious and given a dose of gas which did the trick but left me with a fear of anaesthetics for many years.

At some stage of the war I was evacuated to Dorchester in the Thomas Hardy country of Wessex. After a little while, I returned home to be with my mother and sister as company for my father, my brother being in Torquay with his school. The war was a depressing experience for my father as he was forced to watch his parishioners suffer. One night he was particularly upset when he returned to the vicarage, having watched a small block of flats go up in flames. With an oil shop underneath, the human suffering must have been terrible. I got used to the barrage balloons hanging in the sky above Waterloo Station, an obstacle to enemy bombers and fighter planes, but my young and simple mind experienced problems at working out which were our British planes and which were German. One day it was explained to me that the German planes were the ones with puffs of smoke around them, but not until long after the war did it dawn on me that this was because British anti-aircraft guns were being fired at them!

Air Raids were a frequent hazard, especially at night time. On one occasion, when Grandma Gedge was staying at the Vicarage, the Air Raid Siren sounded, whereupon we all leapt out of bed, raced down the stairs into the garden and down into the shelter. Not so Grandma. She went the other way and locked herself into the cloakroom. My father had to break open the door, pick her up bodily from the lavatory and carry her downstairs screaming. As he carried her past the window on the stairs she grabbed the curtains and hung on to them, bringing them down with her into the shelter!

Towards the end of the war, the "doodle-bugs" (as we called the V-1s) became a menace. Providing these could be heard there was no danger, but when the engine stopped there was half a minute to reach the shelter before the unmanned craft hit the ground and exploded. One morning as we were sitting around the kitchen table enjoying our breakfast, we heard a "doodle-bug" approach. Suddenly there was a deafening silence as its engine cut out. We all leapt up, ran down the passage, through the green baize door, across the hall, down the steps into the garden and down again into the shelter. The explosion was enormous. When we came back out of the shelter, our home had no roof, doors or windows. From out of the remains of the kitchen window came our black cat, Dicky, covered with dust and dirt. As for my breakfast, I was devastated to find that the blue willow-pattern bowl which contained my porridge now also contained part of the ceiling.

Throughout the war my mother remained a tower of strength to my father, doing her best to keep up some semblance of a home in the vicarage, but it was an uphill task. With Waterloo Station such an obvious target for German bombers it seems strange that it was never put out of action. Instead, it was the surrounding areas that suffered. One casualty was Field's soap factory close to the vicarage. All that remained was a huge crater and a tall chimney: little by little the hole filled with water, whereupon someone added a few fish which in due course multiplied to provide a welcome amenity for local youngsters. They would arm themselves with home-made fishing rods, sit upon flimsily-constructed rafts made out of timber from ruined buildings and embark upon riotous fishing trips to while away many a happy hour.

Holy Trinity Church itself was another casualty, although it was never struck by a bomb. Like the vicarage, it was affected adversely by bomb blasts, with the result that its weakened structure had to be supported inside by scaffolding. It was not a pretty sight.

When the war came to a welcome and satisfactory conclusion, my mother slept, so I was told, for two days. This, I suppose, was a quaint way of telling me that she had suffered a breakdown. She was sent to Littlehampton on the Sussex coast, to rest. When she returned she tried to bring normality back to the Vicarage. The War Damage programme allowed it to be repaired and decorated after a fashion. Three colours were allocated for the interior woodwork: blue, brown and green! She was brilliant at creating something special out of nothing. As Christmas approached she found a shop in St. George's Road, close by the Roman Catholic Cathedral, which had for sale some simple, colourful paper chains and we went and purchased a few which we hung all over the Vicarage. If this was the Christmas when Grandma Gedge gave her famous presents (one pound to my brother, five shillings to my sister and a bar of soap to me), so what? Suddenly and unexpectedly a huge parcel covered in white linen arrived from Canada, packed with all sorts of goodies: a wonderful gesture from Canadian sympathisers. For me, pride of place was taken by what is now called caramel instant whip (or suchlike), as I had never tasted the like before. It was truly delicious!

On Christmas Eve there was a knock at the door and, when my father answered it, there stood a soldier. He needed somewhere to stay over the festive season, so in he came. Not long afterwards he took my mother down to The Cut, a popular local market, and lavished a lot of money on goodies to give us the best Christmas we had ever had. On the evening of Boxing Day we were all in the Blue Room with a lovely fire burning in the hearth, playing Cops and Robbers, when we were interrupted by a loud knock on the door. My father, wearing an imitation policeman's helmet, opened the door saying: "Open up in the name of the law!" To his amazement he was confronted by two real policemen. One said, "We believe you have a soldier in there who we want". And so it was. Apparently, all the money the soldier had lavished on us had been stolen.

Another person who took refuge in Holy Trinity Vicarage at around this time was a middle-aged lady who had escaped from a mental institution. As she seemed fairly normal to my father, who knew that if she could remain undiscovered for twenty-eight days she could not be forced back to an asylum, he gave her sanctuary and allowed her the use of the small spare bedroom above the porch. Imagine her consternation one morning when she overheard a policeman at the front door in the porch below making enquiries about her. She needn't have worried as Paul denied all knowledge of her, leaving her to complete the statutory twenty-eight days and melt away into society.

Not very long after this there was a crippling train strike which brought the railway service to a virtual standstill and more strangers to spend a night at the Vicarage. Young as I was, I was sent up to Waterloo Station in the evenings to bring home anyone who was stranded and in need of a bed. It must seem bizarre now that an eight-year-old boy could be sent to wander around a major London railway station offering a free bed to anyone who wanted one, but it was so. After all, not long before, I had been given a front-door key and a bicycle by my free-minded parents and told to get on with my life! One person that I picked up was a young, pretty, Swiss girl who appeared to get more and more agitated as I led her down into the dingy streets of Lower Marsh (the historical name for that part of Lambeth) and through the long, gloomy arch on Carlisle Lane. The relief that lit up her face on reaching the safety of the Vicarage was indescribable and reward in itself. I also picked up Leonard and Rose Welton. Although they owned the London Music Shop, their home was at Exmouth in Devon. As a result of this encounter, my sister worked in their Weymouth Street shop when she was a student and in need of extra money, by which time I was purchasing all my musical needs there also. More than fifty years later, I still correspond with Rose, who is now a widow and living near her daughter on the outskirts of Bristol.

So Holy Trinity Vicarage became an open house with an interesting assortment of people, both rich and poor, influential and without rank, foreign and British, coming and going in great numbers. Saturday mornings were the worst times. My father trained the Church of England Primary School soccer team in the field that separated the Vicarage garden from Archbishop's Park. Whenever there was a home game on a Saturday morning, the players would assemble in the Vicarage study, change into their football gear, descend the steps into the garden, cross the field, pass through the private gate into the park and walk to the soccer pitch. Afterwards they would return to the study, strip off their now filthy kit, go up the main staircase leaving a trail of mud and down the passage into the bathroom, where all eleven would have what amounted to their weekly bath. The mess left for my mother to clear up was beyond description – water upstairs, mud downstairs! The achievements of that football team were also beyond description. Suffice it to write that during the three seasons in the years 1947-1950 it won the league without losing a game, it won the cup without having a goal scored against it and seven of its players were members of the South London Primary Schools XI.

Life was never dull and at the centre of it all was Holy Trinity Church. Built in 1839, one old picture hanging on the wall of the vicarage kitchen showed it in its original glory soon after it had been built, with elegant, well-dressed ladies clutching their parasols, their partners meticulously attired with top hat in hand arriving for divine service. Another picture, hanging alongside, showed its wonderfully coloured interior, the ceilings of red and blue covered with many tiny white stars. A light green wooden screen cut the church in two, separating the chancel and Lady Chapel from what passed for a nave. In the chancel were some low choir stalls, then the altar rails and finally some carpeted steps which led up and added prominence to an elaborate High Altar. Above this stood a massive plaster figure of Jesus Christ, flanked by six tall candles, three on one side and three on the other, which added a touch of splendour to the gorgeous but faded interior. On the left of the sanctuary was the tiny Lady Chapel, dimly lit, full of colour and atmosphere, so obviously a house for God. The entire set up was unique; I have never seen anything quite like it anywhere else. The smell, however, was certainly not unique, because Sunday by Sunday this house was filled with the smoke of incense, lots of it, hanging in the air like a real pea-souper of a London smog, only this one lingered throughout the entire week and I loved it. The ritual was what, I suppose, in Anglican circles, is called Roman (as opposed to English or Sarum) and it surely must have been an echo of what Fr. Wainwright used to have at St. Peter's, London Dock.

The youngsters from the parish loved it too. They made the church their spiritual home and were transported out of the ordinariness of their lives outside in the drab and dirty streets. Upwards of forty children came to church each Sunday. They served at the altar, they acted as acolytes, they "sang" in the choir hymns from the English Hymnal along with John Merbecke's immortal music for the service of Holy Communion. On major Festivals there were processions to mark that day as special, with still more incense. Routine ceremonial sometimes took up a lot of time, especially the ablutions after the distribution of the bread and wine, in which case the hymn would be sung twice. Those youngsters who could not find useful employment as servers or choristers sat on pews in the nave. Sermons never exceeded seven minutes and were delivered by my father from memory, usually winding and unwinding his handkerchief through his fingers as he spoke, always full of good, sound, theological teaching and in such a way as to be understood by all present, both young and old. When it came to leaving the church after Mass, the only difference between the generations was that the youngsters were given a stamp bearing a relevant picture for that particular Sunday which they could stick in a special book they had been given to help them remember that day and its significance.

The organ in Holy Trinity Church stood on a gallery situated on the south side of the chancel overlooking the choirstalls. It was the work of August Gern, a Belgian organ builder who had worked for the famous French firm Cavaillé-Coll, but who had decided to settle in England and set up in business in 1866. It was built in 1894 and was still making pleasant noises after being in regular use for more than fifty years. My mother acted as Church Organist but not always with much enthusiasm. In the winter the church was so cold that she had difficulty in getting her hands and fingers to work properly. So my father, who was something of a Do-It-Yourself electrician, was instructed to install a point to enable my mother to switch on an electric fire by the organ. Another day when, as often happens, relations between the Vicar and Organist had become somewhat strained, she threatened not to play the organ any more unless another electric point was installed, this time in the little room further along the gallery that housed the organ blower, in order that she could boil a kettle of water to brew up a cup of tea during the sermon! When this was done all went well for a little longer until they had their next disagreement, whereupon she resigned.

My father now had to find a new Organist. He advertised in the Church Times, offering an annual salary of £52, which was no mean sum in those days. The number of replies he received was surprisingly large but, not being a practical musician and being too pig-headed to take advice from his retiring organist, my mother, he did not know what to do next. Suddenly he had an idea. He wrote down on a sheet of paper the names of all the applicants and picked up a pin, shut his eyes and stuck the pin into the list. In this way Mr. Steptoe, a dance band pianist, was appointed Organist of Holy Trinity, Lambeth, even though he had a wooden leg! He was a great hit with the congregation, always playing jolly voluntaries at the end of Mass. Even in the solemn season of Lent, it was not unknown for the assembled congregation to be regaled with a Chopin waltz. When Mr. Steptoe resigned because of pressure of work, he gave my mother and father a mahogany stationery box which he had made in the shape of an upright piano and very beautiful it was too. My father now set about finding a new Organist using exactly the same procedure as before. This time the pin selected a long distance lorry driver ...!

IV

Paul was not only interested in drawing young people into his church. He was interested also in their everyday existence, always endeavouring to give them the time of their lives. Summer holidays in particular were eight weeks of continual lovely sunny days and balmy nights in the most beautiful English countryside. At least that is how it seemed to me, looking back through the rosy spectacles of time. After all, we lived in a grimy, sooty part of London where smog proliferated and dirt and filth were commonplace.

The first camp I remember was on the edge of Windsor Great Park soon after the war had finished. To a Londoner used only to plane trees, the great majestic oaks which abounded in this park had magical qualities. At night time, when darkness really was darkness and not a street lamp shone through the fog, these trees took on an additional, eerie quality after we were told the most grisly ghost story by my father. Suddenly, from out of the forest, we would hear the most blood-curdling cries and frightening screams. So terrifying would this be that we would pull our sleeping bags over our heads and snuggle closer together in our tents in a vain attempt to try to sleep. Next morning, naturally, we would talk about nothing else. There never was a dull moment as we traversed the countryside, climbed trees, dammed streams, played games or explored new places like Windsor. We were in heaven!

A land camp on the same site can eventually become monotonous, however, so a pattern soon emerged. The first seven weeks of the summer holidays came to be spent on the River Thames, not stuck in the same place doing the same things day after day, for the river was fluid and different. No! Each week, six or seven different boys and girls would join Paul on the boat that he had bought. They would meet up at the vicarage, travel by train down to Richmond, bundle everything they needed into the boat and be off. According to Paul, the first time you go by boat from London to Lechlade it is an odyssey, the second time an adventure, the third time, and thereafter, Green Content. The most attractive aspect about a river journey is the prospect of going a long way slowly and seeing new places. Then, as the river claims you by its gentle wooing and incorporates you into its smooth, timeless calm, there grows a sense of deep-lying contentment.

Over the years, boatload after boatload of youngsters from Lambeth rowed from Richmond to Lechlade and back, enjoying one hundred and thirty miles of ever-changing scenery stretching out on either side of the river, as well as the opportunity to camp somewhere different each night. The camping sites were important, because it was not unknown for these Cockney kids to discover an orchard nearby and promptly empty it. The most sensible course of action then was to row swiftly away! Actually, the most cosy place to sleep was on the boat itself, snug and warm, with no draught possible below the level of the gunwhale (otherwise the water would come in with it). However, my father had boys and girls to look after and, having been born in 1903, had different ideas from those prevalent today about the morality of shared sleeping accommodation. That was the reason why he insisted on carrying a tent for the girls to sleep in on the bank, away from the boys in the boat.

So they rowed from London to Lechlade, past a landscape of green trees and gently flowing streams, through delicate and picturesque country so different from Lambeth. The further up-river they rowed, the lovelier the shades of green in the meadows, woodlands and hills, the lovelier the willow, beech and poplar trees, the more plentiful the campsites, all removed from the haunts of man. For a week these young boys and girls lived a completely different life. The sun was their clock. Early in the mornings they would wake to rising mists hanging on the water with promises of another roasting day. Then, while the cheery sun dispelled the haze they would make use of the unlimited supply of soft water that flowed around them, some washing, some shaving, some even diving straight in to become part of the magical river. Away from the busy streets, the cinema, the loud noises, even money, they would live out the day. When the sun lay low on the horizon, they would seek a pitch for the night. Finally a candlelight yarn as they settled down in their blankets would end the day. Bliss!

What about the eighth week? That week was dedicated to the Parish Church School soccer team. For many years now, on their wedding anniversary, Paul and Wendy had made a pilgrimage to Worminghall where they had been married. It was on one of these visits, while walking through the nearby village of Ickford, that they saw for sale a small field in which stood a derelict single-decker bus. Paul promptly bought this and made it a land base for more camps. Ickford, on the border of Buckinghamshire and Oxfordshire, was a typical English village. It had a green, a manor house, a cricket pitch and also a lovely old mediaeval church. This contained a scatty Vicar, who had been a Choral Scholar in an Oxford College many years before and who drove an equally old car in a most perilous manner. Four miles away was the ancient town of Thame, which is reputed to have the widest High Street in England. Nearly two miles away was the old Great Western Railway station, Tiddington, on the branch line from Princes Risborough to Oxford. That great university city, of course, was ten miles away, home to the Morris car factory, not forgetting the River Thames.

The old bus, which quickly became known as the Caravan, was conveniently sited more or less in the centre of the village, opposite the village shop which, despite its tiny size, seemed to contain absolutely everything that could be needed. Inside the caravan Paul nailed one of those old gramophone horns to the wall behind the driver's compartment, attached one end of a pipe to it and buried the other end in the ground underneath, thereby providing a urinal for those people who slept in the caravan! It was highly unhygienic, but no-one seemed to suffer unduly. Thus, in the final week of the school holiday, the week before the new term began, the church school soccer team moved onto the site to train. They were the élite. They worked in the adjacent field, barefooted, oblivious to the thistles and undaunted by the vast quantities of cow dung which lay around. No wonder that team succeeded!

What of the remaining weeks in the year? In his two parishes, Paul had always encouraged drama and produced an endless stream of plays for his protégés. He wrote these himself, believing that many published plays were beyond the powers of humble performers. Furthermore, he believed that to import leading actors from outside the confines of the parish would rob a play of its spontaneous charm and take away the proper pride of a genuine home product. Paul had another theory, that the freshness and originality of the storyline were essential to the success of a play, because so many youngsters were so used to going every week to the "pictures" (as the cinema was called) that if they saw a standard Nativity or Passion play, they would think that they had seen it all before. Thus it was essential to seek for new ideas if the interest of youngsters was to be retained. So he wrote a continual stream of short plays which were intended for performance in church halls, rather than churches. First of all, he would produce them in his own church hall, the "Institute" as it was called in Lambeth, and then take them out and about throughout the diocese of Southwark, always acted by his youngsters. In this way money was raised for foreign missions, for hard-pressed parishes and even for the building of new churches to replace those destroyed during the war. The amount of fun generated by these modest productions was unbelievable. I have memories of being part of a monster and falling back through the trap-door which was supposed to represent the lake from which the monster had risen! Truly, there was no time for boredom.

In 1946, Paul had written "A New Three Hours' Devotion, based on The Seven Words and the Seven Sacraments", which was published by A. R. Mowbray & Co. Ltd ... Now, in that same year, he persuaded Frederick Muller to publish "Four Simple Parish Plays". Included in the dedication were:

> *The children of Amos Estate*
> *The "Lambeth Lambs"*

and

> *Wendy the Unwearying*

all of whom had been central to his life's work. Interestingly, this book had brought him into contact with a gentleman by the name of Eric Crozier, which had fascinating consequences. It fell to Eric to read the plays for the publisher to assess their commercial value. As a result, he and Paul became good friends.

Eric Crozier was not unlike some of Paul's protégés, He, too, had struggled out of an impoverished and bitterly unhappy London childhood, but in his case had worked his way into the professional theatre. At this time he was working for Sadler's Wells Opera Company and was actually staging his first production for the company: Bedrich Smetana's "The Bartered Bride". Just at this time, moves were also afoot for Sadler's Wells to stage Benjamin Britten's new opera "Peter Grimes". Although they were keen, the venue remained a problem. The actual Sadler's Wells theatre in Islington had been closed since the Blitz with the result that the company had been forced to give its London season in cramped West End theatres. Peter Grimes needed more space and also a lot of work, as both the soloists and chorus were experiencing difficulty with the music which, incidentally, was not quite completed. It also needed a young lad for the non-singing, small, but pivotal part of the apprentice, John. The opera begins with the words: "We are here to investigate the death of your apprentice", so it was important to have the right lad. This is where Paul became useful to Eric Crozier,

It was over a cup of tea on the Vicarage lawn that Eric Crozier met fourteen-year-old Leonard Thompson for the first time, liked him and offered him the part. Leonard was nonplussed at this turn of events. He asked my father why he'd been recommended, only to be told that he wasn't quite as big a fool as some of his friends! Previously Leonard had endured the loss of two houses by bombing and two spells of evacuation from London, all of which had combined to leave him with a very independent outlook at so tender an age. He had left school aged four-teen and obtained his first job as a telegram boy, complete with bicycle and pill-box hat. His entire social life, however, had revolved around Holy Trinity, his local church, and he had spent a lot of time acting in the plays. Indeed it was my father who had seen that he had no future in his job and had arranged an appren-ticeship for him with a printing company, which in those days was a much-prized plum. He therefore had to exchange that apprenticeship for the one in "Peter Grimes" without causing undue hard feeling. As soon as this was accomplished, Leonard could put his mind wholly on the opera.

On the following Monday morning he took the train alone to Wolverhampton, found the Civic Hall and immediately joined in a rehearsal, as "Peter Grimes" was being put together wherever the company happened to be performing. Leonard had no idea of what he was to do, but had no need to worry: Eric Crozier explained it all in a couple of sentences."You're a little boy who's been brought from a work-house to come and work for this big, brutal man who treats you very roughly. You're very frightened of him." That night Leonard heard his first opera, "The Bartered Bride". Benjamin Britten found the time to give him a potted history of this music and its composer, as well as indicating which highlights to look for.

Despite the tensions at rehearsals, with many of the chorus near rebellion at the difficulty of the music, with the renowned Joan Cross having problems learning the intricate part of Ellen Orford, with Peter Pears faring little better as Peter Grimes and many other associated problems, Leonard, however, had a wonderful time as he became the darling of the company. Although the first season at Sadler's Wells in peacetime included such operas as "Madam Butterfly", "La Bohème", "The Bartered Bride", "Così Fan Tutte" and "Rigoletto", it was "Peter Grimes" which had been chosen for the first performance. When the big day arrived, there in the stalls were Ralph Vaughan Williams and William Walton, as well as Yehudi Menuhin; among the orchestral players was the future conductor Edward Downes playing trombone. Benjamin Britten at the back of the stalls stood for three hours, too nervous to sit down; nerves were still bad backstage and Leonard was experiencing his first attack of butterfly tummy. The house lights went down to be followed by applause for the conductor, Reginald Goodall, whereupon Leonard's butterflies were stirred into frantic activity. The performance went smoothly enough apart from the chorus's Drinking Song and then came Leonard's first entrance. Joan Cross saved his day. She was calmness itself. As he was tucked under her cloak, she gave him a quick squeeze and with a quiet "Good Luck, Leonard", they were on.

When the performance ended there was an interminable silence and then the applause began, becoming more and more enthusiastic with each curtain call. When Benjamin Britten bounded onto the stage there was pandemonium and ecstatic applause. Leonard lost count of the curtain calls once the number exceeded ten, but he had no doubt that he had been part of one of the most important occasions ever in the history of English opera. He knew that it was something special and for the privilege of being there he could thank Paul. In due course, Paul received thanks from an entirely unexpected source: two years later Benjamin Britten produced another opera, "Albert Herring", which was set in East Anglia. There among the characters was "Mr Gedge, the Vicar". My father had been immortalised in gratitude for his help.

Paul was a great lover of opera and ballet. His favourite music, which he played over and over again on his ancient record player in the Blue Room, was the Easter Hymn from Pietro Mascagni's opera "Cavalleria Rusticana". Tchaikovsky's ballet "Swan Lake" was another favourite, especially when Margot Fonteyn was dancing. Sometimes he would take a few of his parish youngsters with him to performances at Sadler's Wells and Covent Garden. Always he would pay, but then so much of his money went on subsidising parochial activities. His brother, Michael, told of an occasion when a tradesman knocked on the Vicarage door and requested payment for a bill. Michael called for Wendy but there was no reply. He went to look for her, but failed to find her, not realising that she was hiding in the shed, embarrassed because she had no money. Clearly this could not go on, so my mother began to give violin lessons to earn some money of her own. She also began to make a conscious effort to protect her children from over-exposure to parish activities. Sometimes she would take my sister and me out for a long ride on our bicycles through the streets of central London and out to a park in the suburbs. This could be quite an adventure because of the heavy traffic, especially at the traffic lights, not forgetting the wretched tram lines. If we were going camping we would load up with pannier bags on either side of the back wheel, which made us even more unsteady on our bicycles. We camped one night in Highgate Wood only to discover on the next morning that we shouldn't have done this.

One August my mother took me by train to Wool in Dorset. Her bicycle came too! She rode around the countryside during the daytime while I enjoyed myself riding around on the railways with the aid of a "Runabout" ticket. Corfe Castle fascinated me. At Swanage, nearby, I tasted my first peppermint ice-cream. Another holiday took us to Gloucestershire and Herefordshire, the land of her forefathers on her mother's side. While she visited relatives at Broadwell, Stow-on-the-Wold and Ross-on-Wye, I again spent most of my time travelling on railway lines which are now no more.

Paul, meanwhile, was writing about his experiences on the River Thames. This was not to be a guide book, as there were plenty of those. Rather, it was to be about camping. In this book he wanted to share with his readers the fun that he had experienced with his parish urchins - and perhaps he also wanted to earn some more money to spend on them! Writing this book took up a lot of his time, particularly at night, when he would type away in his study until the early hours of the morning. "Thames Journey" was published by George G. Harrap and Co. Ltd. in 1949. It was not a bestseller, but sales were good enough for one shop in Reading to make a special window display out of the book. It was copiously illustrated with photographs that he had taken over the years, as photography appeared to be the one luxury in which he indulged himself.

However, the writing was on the wall for the old life and he was becoming cantankerous. On receiving a telephone bill, he deducted some money for poor service, sent a cheque for the balance, was sued by the G. P. O., fought them in court defending himself and lost the case. This was not his only brush with the G. P. O … A copious letter-writer, my father used to do much of his correspondence in the early evenings because, in those good old days, the last post was collected at 9 p. m … The letter box could not have been nearer, since it was sited in Carlisle Lane at the end of the Vicarage Lane, close by the church. The problem arose when he arrived at the letter box at 9 p.m. only to find that it had already been emptied. Naturally, he would return to the vicarage, telephone the G. P. O. to complain – and there was always the possibility that he was in the right, because the chimes of Big Ben were clearly audible in the house. In the end, a cat-and-mouse game developed. The G. P. O. van would wait round the corner with its driver noisily revving up its engine. Then, as Big Ben began its preparatory quarter chimes my father would trundle down the lane, so that as the great clock sounded the first chime of nine o'clock he would be posting his letters just as the G. P. O. van rounded the corner to collect them.

Sadly, more and more of these letters were being written in defence of his church and parish. He had taken his plays around the diocese of Southwark to raise money for the Bishop's emergency fund for new churches to replace those destroyed in the war and now his own parish and church were in danger of being made redundant because the population there had almost halved in number. He himself did not help matters by writing often to his bishop in letters which began:

"My dear Lord Bish.,
May I point out to you that your initials are B. F …"

And so they were, yet in more normal circumstances, Paul would have realised that his bishop, Bertram Fitzgerald Simpson, was actually a very lovely, gentle person. It was just that Paul was fighting for his parish and his church, his life's work. He cared deeply for his parishioners and did not want to see their interests swept aside for the sake of a financial equation. Most of these people were poor and underprivileged and needed a special ministry. For the Church to desert them now would be a sin. The plan was to amalgamate the parish of Holy Trinity Lambeth with that of St. Mary's Lambeth, but the trouble was that the two congregations were incompatible. One was a poor, working-class, High Church parish, while the other was basically middle-class white-collar workers in a safe middle-of-the-road church which included Lambeth Palace and the Archbishop of Canterbury in its parish. It was a Dives and Lazarus situation and the gulf between the two parishes was exceedingly wide.

Paul had enlisted a huge amount of support for his campaign to save Holy Trinity and there was also a massive petition. He even had the matter raised at the House of Commons, where the member of Parliament for Lambeth was sympathetic to his cause, but to no avail. A committee of six declared his parish redundant and in the final issue of the church magazine, each member of this committee was ridiculed in a poem which began:

"Canon Brown

is a clown..."

There were some final twists to the tale. On the day before the parish ceased to exist, Paul sat down at the table in his study and wrote out a number of cheques, all made out to charities. The next day, when the Vicar of St. Mary's Lambeth arrived at the vicarage to collect the church keys and the cheque books, he discovered that all the money left in the church bank account would cover the outstanding bills and no more. He was not pleased! Some time after this, the up-and-coming organ builder, Noel Mander, arrived to take away the organ.

The final episode was tragic. Paul found the church open one day. Vandals had forced their way into the building and pushed the enormous, colourful figure of Jesus from off the altar onto the floor beneath, where it lay in large chunks. My father was devastated and remarked that even Hitler had failed to accomplish this. Sadly, it was a sign of the times as more and more local youngsters who in past years had frequented the church now began to frequent the juvenile courts. For Paul, however, there were no more books, no more parishes. He was offered that of St. Matthew's, near the Elephant & Castle, on the Old Kent Road, but declined it, saying that he could not hear Big Ben from there. In truth, he was a lost soul, a rebel without a cause. Now, when asked, he helped clergy in other churches. Otherwise, he sat around in the Vicarage, dreaming dreams. It was a sad sight.

V

From an early age my mother did all she could to nurture any musical talent that I had. She taught me to play the piano, she also taught me to play the violin but on a minute instrument. When she had string quartet sessions with friends in the Blue Room, she made me sit next to her and let me join in, which could have been quite upsetting for the other three players had they not been so good natured. Truth to tell, I found the violin much more fun to play and consequently, to my sorrow now, I practised the piano but little.

The crunch came when I was eight years old. My mother wanted me to join Southwark Cathedral choir; so did I. I was sent along for an audition at the Cathedral one dark and dismal autumn evening and given a few notes to pitch which I did incorrectly because I was distracted by a vestry full of eavesdropping choristers, including my highly-embarrassed older brother, Peter. I was sent home having been accepted as a probationer largely on account of both my mother's persistence and my brother's prowess as Head Chorister.

The following Sunday, for the first time, instead of attending Mass at Holy Trinity Church, I was off to the Cathedral for the day. Just as I was about to leave the Vicarage, I heard the most almighty row going on between my mother and father. My father was furious that I was forsaking Holy Trinity for the Cathedral, shouting out: "No man can serve two masters." When my mother pointed out that one day I might make a living out of church music, he retorted: "No son of mine will earn his living as a church musician; he should do it for the love of God." At this my mother shrieked back at him: "Try keeping me on the love of God and see how long I stay!" whereupon I melted away and set off for Southwark Cathedral. When I returned later that day my mother had gone. She had run away. Someone broke to me gently that she had taken refuge in the home of a very dear old (to me, then) lady named Miss Pittis, who looked after the older inhabitants of some almshouses a little further down Carlisle Lane, not all that far away.

However, my mother had won and Southwark Cathedral became my second home. I loved it and its music and also everyone connected with the place. The Cathedral is one of London's best-kept secrets. Its nave, built in the 1890s and completed in 1897 was the work of the eminent architect son of a famous Bishop of London, Sir Arthur Blomfield who, I learned many years later, was also the architect of St. Mary's Church, Swansea. The remainder of the great building is gloriously mediaeval. On the floor alongside the choirstalls lies the tomb of Edmund Shakespeare, brother of William: the Globe Theatre was not far away - indeed the public house nearest the cathedral is reputed to be built in the same shape. Best of all is the whitewashed retrochoir, perfection in the gothic style of architecture: four lovely, graceful, white chapels, each with its own distinctive altar. When the monks were turned adrift from the Priory in 1539, this Retrochoir became a Consistory Court. Here commissioners sat in judgement on their fellow Christians by order of Parliament. In particular, they tried for heresy six prominent clerics including Bishop Ferrar of St. David's and Bishop Hooper of Gloucester and

Worcester and sentenced them all to be burned at the stake. The Organist of St. George's Chapel, Windsor, John Merbecke, was also tried here. He too was sentenced to death, but was reprieved, so legend has it, because King Henry VIII liked his music.

When religious persecution died its own death, the Retrochoir was leased and let out to a baker to become a bakehouse. Later, it was also used as a hog-sty! Beyond the Retrochoir was originally another chapel, but this was demolished, possibly to make way for a new London Bridge, the one that was eventually taken down and shipped stone by stone to the U. S. A. where it was re-erected. This London Bridge, which was opened by King William IV in 1831 was on a higher level than the one before, which had many arches beneath and many houses above it, and resulted in the Cathedral being around fifteen feet below the level of the approach road to the bridge, the Borough High Street. Not many years later the railways arrived and encompassed the south of the Cathedral with mammoth viaducts and subjected it to a daily bombardment of noise. It was on this very approach to London Bridge that one American tourist was overheard saying to another, while looking down on this great mediaeval pile, "What a stupid place to build a cathedral!"

True, the Cathedral was surrounded on all sides by industry. Between the Cathedral and the River Thames stood dirty old Hay's Wharf with its tall warehouses: in those days, the Pool of London nearby was still active as a port. The enormous wooden gates leading to Hay's Wharf were situated next to the door that opened onto the steps that led down to the Cathedral Choir vestry. On Sundays up to twenty milk bottles were left outside for the milkman to take away. Unfortunately, before Sunday morning choir practice, some of the choirboys who arrived early used to while away time by lining up these bottles against the gates and practise taking penalty kicks with a tennis ball to see how many could be smashed. On the other side of the Cathedral was the Borough Market where, on every day of the week except Sunday, fruit and vegetables were sold from little trading areas which were enclosed within wooden or metal fences. Twice weekly, all the fruit and vegetables which had become rotten were left out in the evening for the dustmen to collect the next morning. However, those were two of the evenings, Tuesday and Thursday, when we choirboys sang Evensong, with the result that afterwards we would rush out of the Choir Vestry, split up into two sides and have "bad fruit fights", hurling evil smelling missiles at each other with great delight, having a riotous time.

Playing cricket here was a hazard, because anyone who hit the ball hard enough for it to land in one of those fruit and vegetable storage areas had to climb over the fence to retrieve it. Just occasionally the boy concerned climbed back unknowingly into the arms of patrolling policemen, the other boys having scarpered. Football was played on a small stretch of pavement situated at the side of the steps leading from the Borough High Street down to the Cathedral. One of the goalposts had the misfortune to be a telephone box. This sometimes led to disaster, as it was not unknown for choirboys to put a hand through one of the glass panes and have to visit nearby Guy's Hospital to be patched up. One Sunday lunchtime, while enjoying a game of football there, one boy kicked the tennis ball into a tomb at the side of the Cathedral and while climbing over the surrounding railings to retrieve it, lost his footing and ended up dangling by a foot. He too was carted off to Guy's Hospital for treatment and returned with his leg in plaster.

Inside the Cathedral there was just as much fun. Sometimes after Evensong choirboys, if unsupervised (which was rare) remained behind in the dingy choir vestry to enjoy hassock fights. Again boys divided into two sides and hurled hassocks (kneelers) at each other across the room until, in the heat of the moment, a lightbulb might be hit and smashed, whereupon everyone would vanish out into the night. Occasionally, however, Woody (a term of endearment for Mr. Wood, the third Verger) would chase the boys out, beating with a broom handle those he was quick enough to catch. It was not unknown in services, while kneeling supposedly in prayer, for one choirboy to tie together the surplice sleeves of two other boys. Then at the end of the service when the choir processed out in two orderly lines, one of these boys would drag the other out after him in anything but a dignified manner. Best of all was when Guy Fawkes' Day happened to be a Sunday. As the choirboys left the Choir Vestry for lunch, they stuffed lighted bangers into the Cathedral letterbox and ran off. When they returned after lunch they found the door of this letterbox hanging open, supported by one hinge only, and the wicked deed blamed upon local youths.

Such high-spirited pranks provided a welcome relief from the more serious side to musical affairs at Southwark Cathedral. In charge of these was the legendary Dr. E. T. Cook who had been Organist since 1909. Now approaching three-score years and ten, he was entering the twilight of a long and distinguished career. Born in 1880 in the city of Worcester, by the age of thirteen he was organist of St. Oswald's Church, then, five years later, organist of St. Leonard's Church at Newland near to Malvern. Here was a small choir school attached to an equally small church built not long before alongside a group of almshouses. It was in the fourteenth-century style, having coloured walls and marble decoration throughout and windows filled with stained glass. In keeping with this mock-mediaeval creation, monastic plainsong reigned supreme at services sung within the walls of this church.

Young Edgar Tom Cook also spent a considerable amount of time at the Cathedral, one of the homes of Britain's oldest musical festival, the Three Choirs Festival, which encompassed Worcester, Hereford and Gloucester Cathedrals. This was important to the young musician, because in the days before radio, television, record and compact disc players, it exposed him to making music with orchestras and big choirs. There was the added bonus of living and working close to Edward Elgar and witnessing the excitement that surrounded the first performance of the "Enigma" Variations and the controversy that dogged the early productions of "The Dream of Gerontius".

For four years, Edgar Tom Cook was also Assistant Organist at Worcester Cathedral and heavily involved in the day-to-day running of the Cathedral services. In those days the cathedral choir sang Matins and Evensong daily, which required singing an enormous amount of music. The Organist, Ivor Atkins, had some interest in early music. He produced new editions of the great J. S. Bach Passions according to St. Matthew and St. John. Furthermore, he encouraged his cathedral choir to sing music of the Tudor era, including the Short Service by a sixteenth-century Organist of Worcester Cathedral, Nathaniel Patrick. Eventually, when this was published, it became known as "Nat Pat by Ivor At".

Not surprisingly, therefore, when E. T. Cook was appointed Organist of Southwark Cathedral in 1909, he brought with him a love of plainsong, a love of Tudor Church Music and a love of the great choral works of J. S. Bach and Edward Elgar. His love of plainsong resulted in its being used for Office Hymns in Southwark Cathedral as well as for parts of the Ordinary of the Mass and for the singing of the Passion Story during Holy Week. In 1928, he published a useful, short book entitled "The Use of Plainsong".

Shortly before this, E. T. Cook began to achieve notoriety for his weekly broadcasts of organ music on Mondays from 2LO, the London radio station. These started in 1924 and lasted until December 16th 1935, when the organ's action gave way, causing that day's recital to be transferred to the London Church of St. Mark, North Audley Street, and the long-running series to be terminated. This was not before Dr. Cook (he was awarded a Lambeth Mus. D. in 1934) had distinguished himself by including a lot of French organ music in his programme. He also was among the first to propagate the organ works of his friend Sigfrid Karg-Elert, particularly the Op. 65 Chorale Improvisations, which he proudly possessed in a bound copy duly inscribed by the composer himself.

Dr. Cook also achieved notoriety for the training of his choirboys. He used only three exercises: scales, always sung descending then rising by a semitone, to extend the range of the voice; singing the five vowel sounds on one note, then rising by a semitone again, to get the correct formation of words; counting numbers on one note, rising higher each time, to improve breath control. In this way not only did he develop head tone in his boys' voices but he appeared to produce a line of trebles who continued singing until well into their teens, although some observers claimed that the oldest boys were singing falsetto. So my brother sang treble until he was at least sixteen years old. Indeed, when I joined the Cathedral Choir the top eight boys were all aged between fourteen and sixteen years old. Consequently the sound was big and mature and also benefited from the more intelligent musicianship that comes from age and experience. It is a well-documented fact that one of Dr. Cook's "boys", Harry Coles by name, sang treble in the choir at the Coronation of King George VI in Westminster Abbey in 1937 at the age of nineteen. Other trebles are reputed to have knocked out their pipes before choir practice, another to have requested time off to get married! Certainly, there was never any shortage of choirboys, One of the Sunday bass lay-clerks, Albert Frisby, requested a place for his nephew, a boy of exception musical talent gifted with an extraordinary voice. Sadly, there was no vacancy and the boy went elsewhere, to the Temple Church. His name was Ernest Lough, the boy who became famous for his recording of Mendelssohn's "Hear My Prayer", which includes "O for the wings of a dove".

Before the Second World War nearly all the choirboys attended St. Olave's, an old foundation grammar school that dated back to the days of Queen Elizabeth I, which was half-a-mile away down Tooley Street towards Tower Bridge. By the time I joined the Cathedral Choir in 1947, the 11+ examination decided whether or not a child attended a grammar school. Now any choirboy who failed went to Archbishop Temple's Secondary Modern School close to Lambeth Palace and St.

Mary's Lambeth, near to Lambeth Bridge. However, although around two miles away from the Cathedral, these boys could board a number 10 or number 44 bus from outside the school and be at London Bridge within ten minutes. Actually Dr. Cook liked boys to join the choir long before this, preferably at the age of around eight so that they could develop vocally in their own good time.

The weekly routine for the choir began on Sunday at 10 a.m. with a fully choral Matins but with no sermon. This left enough time for a short practice before Choral Eucharist which was the best-attended service of the day. Afterwards the choristers walked across London Bridge, down the steps on the other side to the church of St. Magnus the Martyr, along Fish Street, where the smelly Billingsgate Fish Market could be found, to Tower Hill for lunch at the nearby Toc H building. The quicker we ate our lunch, the more time we had to play football on our strip of pavement alongside the steps down from the Borough High Street to the Cathedral. Sometimes Dr. Cook would come out to watch us to make sure that we did not shout and thereby strain our delicate voices. At two o'clock we were in the choir stalls wearing our black cassocks, ready for a full choir practice. At three we would sing Evensong and endure a second sermon, but there was always something "big" in the musical line which brightened the proceedings. One Sunday afternoon the choir was due to sing an anthem by Edward Elgar. There was a long organ introduction, but when a certain chord was reached, there was a very loud cipher (a note sticking). Immediately Dr. Cook switched off the organ, then switched it back on and started again. When he reached that same chord the cipher came back on again. Great were our expectations when, after switching the organ off and on again, he started for a third time. We were not to be disappointed, as the loud note stuck for the third time. While we stood there wondering what would happen next, Dr. Cook appeared beneath the tower with his back against the large Steinway grand piano, red in the face, pushing it with all his might towards the choir stalls. Having reached his destination, he sat down and proceeded to play the introduction followed by the accompaniment to the remainder of the anthem.

On another Sunday afternoon, when the choir was singing the extrovert musical setting of the Magnificat and Nunc Dimittis in C by Stanford, we suddenly became aware of a tall, thin, balding, middle-aged gentleman in the congregation who was daring to join in the singing, and at the top of his voice as well. The problem was that not only did he have a very loud and strident voice, but he also paid no attention to the correct length of the notes. When it came to the loud Gloria the performance turned into a comedy show, especially when the final chord was ended but his voice continued ringing around the cathedral with its three-second echo, for some considerable time. We choirboys were in hysterics, stuffing our surplice sleeves into our mouths in a vain effort to silence our laughter. Unfortunately, in the Nunc Dimittis this Gloria is repeated, so we were not disappointed as once more this voice rang out loud and long after we had finished. Not surprisingly, the monotoned Creed that followed was rather a disaster. Later we learned that this gentleman belonged to an evangelical Protestant organisation which was an avowed opponent to such niceties as Choral Evensong in Cathedrals.

On a Sunday afternoon at Evensong the anthem was followed by prayers and a hymn which preceded the sermon. This provided certain members of the choir with the weekly opportunity to observe the following scenario. During my early days in the Cathedral Choir, the organ console was situated in the South Choir Aisle, behind the choirstalls. The Assistant Organist always accompanied this hymn and, while he was so doing, Dr. Cook would put on his overcoat, don his trilby hat and make his way to an outside door in the aisle where Mrs. Thomas, his secretary/helper, would be waiting to give him his umbrella and case so that he could set off immediately for London Bridge Station. Then, as we endured the sermon, he would be on the train to Chipstead where he lived with his devoted wife and daughter in a house called Newlands, which had a beautiful garden and revolving summer house, as Dr. Cook was a keen gardener. By the time we had sung the hymn after the sermon and the Assistant Organist had played the final organ voluntary, Dr. Cook would most likely be walking home from the train, about to enjoy his tea.

There was an equally endearing routine for Dr. Cook on a Sunday morning when he travelled to Southwark Cathedral, which I witnessed several times later when staying with the family of a chorister friend who lived at Tattenham Corner, a few stations on from Chipstead. The train often arrived early at Chipstead and as it stood still by the platform, a porter would hold open the door of a compartment and wait. Just one minute before the train was due to depart, the small figure of Dr. Cook would be seen scurrying across the passenger bridge and down the stairs. As he entered the compartment, he would raise his trilby in a gesture of thanks and say "Good Morning" to the porter, who would shut the door and wave the train away. On arriving at London Bridge Station and leaving the train, Dr. Cook used to walk straight through the barrier, raise his trilby to the ticket-collector and again say "Good Morning". Never once did I see him show his season ticket!

Unlike a parish church, choir wasn't just for Sundays – it was much more of a commitment than that. At Southwark Cathedral on Monday and Tuesday evenings at 5.15 p.m., the choir sang Evensong, as it did on Thursday and Friday evenings; on Mondays and Fridays the singing was done by the trebles only, but on Tuesdays and Thursdays they were joined by the alto, tenor and bass lay clerks, two of each. For the boys there was a practice on each of these days after school at half-past four. Wednesday was a free evening. Dr. Cook's wisdom lay in withdrawing the boy probationers from the choir for Choral Evensong on Tuesdays and Thursdays, leaving them with the Assistant Organist in the choir vestry, to do nothing but sight-reading exercises with the aid of old-fashioned tonic sol-fa. Not surprisingly, by the time these boys became choristers they could read at sight almost any music put in front of them. When I joined the choir, evensong was sung also on Saturday afternoons, but this was abandoned as a result of a petition sent in by the choirboys' parents. My mother was the only parent who refused to sign, on the grounds that anyone joining the choir knew what the commitment was and should not expect to change it to suit themselves. She and my father had many strong principles; indeed, my father would never allow me to sing at any Cathedral weddings during Lent. However, having made his point to the Cathedral authorities concerning the correct observance of the solemn season of Lent, he did not allow me to suffer and always gave me the equivalent fee of five shillings from his own pocket.

In addition to this heavy workload, choristers were expected to take part in school games if selected. I, for example, played in school rugby teams and took part in the long jump for the school athletics team. Furthermore, there was plenty of homework to be done and the masters at St. Olave's School made sure that this was completed. Failure to produce the work on time could result in Saturday morning detention from nine until eleven at the school. The amount of homework ranged from one hour nightly for year one pupils, aged eleven, to three hours nightly for year five pupils, taking what used to be called 'O' (Ordinary) level examinations. The full workload therefore, choir plus school, was exceedingly heavy, but we choirboys learned to cope.

Yet there was still more, because choristers used to assist Southwark Cathedral Special Choir with some of its music-making. Dr. Cook himself as a youngster had experienced at first hand the work of the Three Choirs Festival chorus at Worcester Cathedral, singing great choral works with symphony orchestra accompaniment. When he arrived at Southwark Cathedral, one of his priorities was to start a choral society there. So Southwark Cathedral Special Choir was born and it did such good musical pioneering work in South London that whenever there was a concert the audience would wait in a queue that stretched back to half-way across London Bridge. The choirboys did their bit too in all this, singing the *ripieno* part in the opening chorus and the chorales of J. S. Bach's "St. Matthew Passion". By the time I was taking part in these performances, many other similar choirs had sprung up in London with the result that audiences for Dr. Cook's concerts were smaller in number. Nevertheless there was still the same enthusiasm among the members of his Special Choir. He had also raised his own orchestra to accompany the performances. So I too came to know the great Passions of J. S. Bach, Handel's "Messiah" and Elgar's "Dream of Gerontius" and these works made a great impression on me despite my young age.

One musical event which was of more than special interest to me in my early days in the choir was the first London performance of Benjamin Britten's "St. Nicolas". This took place in Southwark Cathedral and was given by a visiting choir and orchestra conducted by the composer himself. Peter Pears sang the part of the older St. Nicolas, three of the senior choristers were the Pickled Boys that St. Nicolas saved, while I sang the part of the young Nicolas. It long remained a mystery to me why I had been given this part to sing, but presume now that it must have come about through the connections between my father, Eric Crozier, Peter Grimes, Benjamin Britten and "Albert Herring"; after all, at that time I was way down the order in the ranks of the Cathedral trebles. For me, however, it meant half a day off school, making music in such exalted company, seeing Queen Mary the Queen Mother sitting in the front row of the audience only a few feet away from me and receiving five shillings for my pains. I was elated!

It was about this time that the Cathedral's fine T. C. Lewis organ, which had been built around fifty years before, was rebuilt at last by Henry Willis, the firm which had taken over the original builders. Unfortunately the ideas of the two firms did not match and furthermore Henry Willis III was quite a formidable character, in contrast with Dr. Cook's gentleness. So the organ builder "persuaded" the Organist to modernise the instrument far more than he might have done. Notably, the louder brassy reed stops were made to sound more forceful and a lot of electrical gadgets were added. One in particular fascinated the choirboys: a column of lights which gradually lit up as the organist played louder and louder until "Full Organ" hit the jackpot! This we named "The Blackpool Illuminations!" Even so, Dr. Cook was delighted with the end result and duly had his photograph taken a number of times seated at the organ. At last, after so many years of being completely unreliable, his Cathedral Organ was now in tip-top condition. Many of his choristers and admirers purchased copies of these photographs and I had my copy framed and hung on a wall back at home in the Vicarage. Many, many years later I acquired a second photograph, in Bristol (of all places), and the two now hang side by side.

Dr. Cook was fast becoming an old man, yet never did he let up in his efforts to produce great music. In the year 1949 he was created a C. B. E., and not before time. Stories about him abounded, such as how he played Johann Sebastian Bach Chorale Preludes on the organ from music which had not two but three different clefs, transposing the music into another key "just to keep his eye in"; or how, at one practice in the vestry, seated at the old Broadwood grand piano totally absorbed in the music being performed, he failed to be aware of a fly landing on his bald head and a spider descending at lightning speed from the light above to catch it; or how he composed a Communion Service which Oxford University Press published, but when he found an error in the printed copy, he made the firm withdraw all the ten thousand copies and do the job again; or how when the choir were rehearsing the anthem in the Cathedral one Sunday afternoon for Choral Evensong, Basil Harwood's "O How Glorious is the Kingdom", which has a fiendishly difficult organ part, he stopped the proceedings to bark at the Assistant Organist: "Play it a semitone lower"!

On Thursday morning, March 5th 1953, Dr. Cook set off from home as usual, bound for London on the train from Chipstead Station. All day he taught at the Royal College of Music as he had done for many years to supplement his Cathedral Organist's salary. Afterwards he moved on to Southwark Cathedral where he rehearsed the boys, played the organ for Evensong and took the weekly practice of his Special Choir. Finally, he walked up to London Bridge Station, caught the train back to Chipstead, walked back home, sat down, and died. He was a few days short of his seventy-third birthday. The next morning at school the choirboys were told about his death. I cried.

VI

I didn't cry often: chiefly when my father gave me a good hiding with a walking stick or when my mother did likewise with an ebony hairbrush, which really did sting! However, they belonged to a generation that saw nothing untoward in meting out such treatment to miscreants. My father had gone through the very traditional preparatory and public school system when floggings were considered normal. The Headmaster of St. Olave's Grammar School, where most of the Southwark Cathedral choirboys were educated, Dr. Roger Cecil Carrington, also subscribed to this way of thinking. He ruled with a rod of cane! On one famous occasion I remember him caning an entire class of twenty-eight pupils because they had been excessively noisy while waiting for the teacher (called "master" in those days) to arrive to take the next lesson. His system for caning involved lining up the culprits on the gallery in the main hall outside his room, then one by one they would file into his room, receive their punishment and walk or hobble through another door which led into the library and then out. I was working in the library on this occasion and heard him give twenty-seven of the unfortunate culprits four of the best, reserving six for the Form Captain because he had failed to keep order. That added up to a total of one hundred and fourteen strokes of the cane.

Dr. Carrington had been a high flier. His doctorate from Oxford had been the result of research at Pompeii. Afterwards he taught for a few years at Dulwich College before being appointed Headmaster of St. Olave's at the unbelievably young age of twenty-nine. Here his career foundered and sank, probably on account of his exploits with the cane, although he had some other strange foibles. He had no time for opposition. A kindly deputy headmaster, who nevertheless possessed a mind of his own, dared to disagree with him and was summarily demoted. A head of the Physical Education department, while enjoying his cup of tea during a break, was requested to sign a piece of paper only to discover that he had signed his own resignation. My mother persuaded him to allow her to give violin lessons in the school, but I never did discover why her appointment was terminated so abruptly, as he did not know one end of the violin from the other. Her replacement was a disaster, an elderly gentleman who made his pupils hold a book under their right arm as they played their violins. This completely restricted the freedom of their bowing arm.

Yet the tragedy was that, in a strange way, Dr. Carrington was an exceedingly good and far-seeing man: it was just that he also seemed to be a sadist. Twice daily there was a school assembly at which pupils sang good, traditional hymns from, firstly, the Olavian Hymnal, and then when these books wore out, from the radical Songs of Praise. Twice weekly, what constituted a school orchestra accompanied the singing of the hundred-strong four-part choir that stood on the gallery outside his room, in the great hall, around the small but fine two-manual T. C. Lewis organ that supported the musical noises. Woe betide the remainder of the school's pupils if they did not sing lustily in the morning, because if that happened they would all be summoned back to the hall at break to sing the hymn again. Not surprisingly, the singing at the second assembly, at the end of the day, was inevitably lusty and strong so that there would be no delay about going home. Once a week at morning assembly there would be a musical item, which usually consisted of the Music Master playing a solo on the grand piano or on the organ, thereby exposing pupils to a weekly dose of culture.

Far more exciting, however, was the assembly on Friday mornings which always ended with Dr. Carrington reading from a hard-bound exercise book the names of all pupils who had committed any misdemeanour that week which was considered serious enough to warrant their attending school from 9 a.m. to 11 a.m. on Saturday. Perhaps homework had been done badly, perhaps it hadn't been done at all; perhaps a pupil had been seen walking to school without wearing his cap, perhaps he had been wearing it but had failed to raise it to a member of staff who had passed him in the street; perhaps he had just been a nuisance.

Not surprisingly, there was a reasonable amount of singing at the school, because most of the Southwark Cathedral choristers numbered among the inmates. Later on, St. Olave's pupils were also recruited into the treble line for the choir at the Queen's Chapel of the Savoy, behind the more famous Savoy Hotel. We Southwark Cathedral choristers were most aggrieved when we discovered that they were getting more money than us for doing a lot less work. Indeed, they only sang one service weekly, on a Sunday morning, while we sang seven in the course of a week. Their organist was one of the few Old Olavians – as old boys of the school are called – to become a professional musician. He was Dr. William Cole, a friend of Ralph Vaughan Williams, who achieved eminence as Secretary to the Associated Board of the Royal Schools of Music and a member of the Professorial staff of the Royal Academy of Music. In truth, however, these were the days when music was just emerging from being a "Cinderella" subject in state education and although St. Olave's Grammar School still had one foot in the Public School/Headmasters' Conference camp, its other foot was now in the London County Council camp. At last, county council educational authorities were beginning to appoint peripatetic instrumental teachers and schools were being encouraged to take music more seriously.

My first Music Master at St. Olave's was Reginald Harris, a very dapper man with smooth, shiny black hair plastered back with a straighter than straight parting, always dressed in a blue pin-striped suit over which he wore his academic gown. An excellent musician, as well versed in French as he was in Music, he also played the organ superbly and was the Organist at the church of St. Simon Zelotes in Chelsea. When he was lured away to teach French at another school, he was succeeded by an eccentric, arty musician whose name, mercifully, I cannot remember. To the pupils he became known as Fly-Button Fred on account of his once commencing a lesson with his trouser fly buttons undone. When he realised his predicament he immediately sat down behind his desk and remained there until the end of the lesson (no handy zip in those days!) He didn't last long and then along came Gerald Wheeler. Being as superb a pianist as he was an organist and also holding the post of Third Organist at both St. Paul's Cathedral and Southwark Cathedral, he was too high-powered musically for us, with the result that his stay also was short, whereupon he went off to Canada, initially to be Organist at St. Matthew's Church, Ottawa. There, he was given a blank cheque to have the organ of his dreams built by Hill, Norman and Beard Ltd., before moving on to become Organist of Montreal Cathedral for thirty years.

Following Gerald Wheeler was a fascinating character by the name of Harold Last, eccentric but brilliant. At some time he had lectured in music at King's College, London, and on a recent compact disc made by the College Choir in 1990 is a very beautiful musical setting by him of "In the bleak midwinter". Why he came to teach at St. Olave's, I do not know. He had been ordained priest and school rumour had it that he had fallen in love with a nun, so maybe that had caused his change of direction to music. Be that as it may, he had a vital personality and he transformed music in the school. On special occasions the patronising School Song now rang out with impressive brass parts as the school sang, louder than ever, "Olaf to right the wrong, Olaf to bear along!" No wonder our rivals called us "Snotty Olivers"! Despite his strange habit of scratching his backside every so often, he had cast-iron discipline and a fearsome temper, so that no-one dared to cross him. He dragged us through a concert performance of Henry Purcell's "Dido and Aeneas". This was of great importance, because although there was a biennial performance of a William Shakespeare play, always a prestigious occasion, nothing musical like that had been done before. Sadly, Harold Last didn't stay at St. Olave's nearly long enough. He moved on to Felsted, a Public School in Essex, where he began as Director of Music but ended up as Chaplain. There, his main claim to fame appears to have been that during one term the Chapel Choir sang nothing but the music of Charles Wood.

Lastly, so far as I was concerned, came Desmond Swinburn, all the way from Richmond in Yorkshire. He took up where Harold Last had left off and soon the performance of great choral works like J. S. Bach's "St. John Passion" with soloists and an orchestra became a normality. For some reason, Dr. Carrington smiled kindly on Desmond Swinburn, so perhaps he was mellowing in his old age. He described his new Music Master as "arty", not in his usual caustic, disparaging, sneering tone, but in a kindly, fatherly way which was most unusual and quite out of character. He even turned an unusually blind eye to Desmond Swinburn not wearing a suit and academic gown, but rather appearing at school in a hacking jacket (albeit a very upmarket one), cavalry twill trousers and, a sign of moral decadence in the former opinion of Dr. Carrington, brown suede shoes. But, after all, Desmond Swinburn was arty, wasn't he! Not surprisingly, he stayed longer than all the other musicians before returning north to Yorkshire, whence he had come.

My relationship with other members of the school staff were rarely so congenial, but then I did not really distinguish myself academically at school. Could this have been because I was expected to do academic work, when really all I wanted to do was music? One problem was my father, who thought in both Latin and Greek and could not understand why I did not do the same. The floggings with the walking stick only happened when I could not do my Latin or Greek homework and I am sure that my father did this more in frustration than for any other reason. For my fifteenth birthday present he even gave me a hard-bound copy of the New Testament in Greek, expecting me to follow the Second Lesson at Cathedral

Evensongs from this. Wasn't I thrilled! My brother was no help, as he went and won a classics scholarship to Balliol College, Oxford, where he shone to such an extent that he was invited to read for a second degree, in Theology. Yet it does seem strange that Music should have been such a "Cinderella" subject at St. Olave's, only useful on show occasions like Prize Day, the Annual School Service in the Cathedral, at Christmas, at the annual School Music Competition and also at that one weekly morning assembly, because Dr. Carrington took great pains to smother the walls of his school with prints of great paintings so that we should become aware of such artistic creations. He even had an ancient painting restored to reveal the portrait of a grand Tudor lady – Queen Elizabeth I? Furthermore, he hired the noted artist Alan Sorrell to visit St. Olave's on a number of occasions to paint pictures of the school at work.

Few of the school staff ever tried to fathom out what made me tick. The first was Ken Matthews, a French teacher who was also my Form Master during the academic year 1952-3. In my first report he wrote two rather damning statements:

"He is rather babyish for his age," and *"I wish he were a little less timid."*

More was to come in the second report which included the following statement:

"It is to be regretted that he still enjoys the company of First Formers"

obviously failing to realise or understand that these First Formers were fellow choristers of Southwark Cathedral with whom I spent a lot of my spare time. Then he went on to write:

"He is a boy of excellent character who is obviously in need of a toughening-up course. I should be very glad to see him in the ATC or comparable organisation. He enters into everything he does with such enthusiasm that a year or two of preservice training might well develop the many qualities that he lacks at the moment."

At this my mother intervened. She pointed out to Mr. Matthews that, back in the autumn at the start of the academic year, I had taken the trouble to join the London Junior Orchestra. Every Friday evening now I went with my 'cello-playing sister Daphne to the Duke's Hall in the Royal Academy of Music, near to Regent's Park, to play great orchestral music. This was an unbelievably wonderful way for a thirteen-year-old enthusiast to learn about orchestral music from the inside. Conducting this enormous collection of people from all walks of life was the inspirational human dynamo Ernest Read, now seventy-three years young with twelve more to run.

Earlier in the century Read had been a pioneer in the youth orchestra movement, founding his London Junior Orchestra in 1926 and his London Senior Orchestra in 1931, as well as a choir during the war years and, after the war, organising holiday courses for young orchestral players out in the country. What a man!

He had a particular talent for communicating the enjoyment of music-making to the young and to amateurs and that was what made up the London Junior Orchestra. On Friday evenings I was in my seventh heaven and from dear old Ernie Read I learned or absorbed much about "bread and butter" classical music, along with many valuable tricks of the trade. One particular fad of his was getting us to play correctly the opening of Beethoven's famous Fifth Symphony: "♪♪♪|♪ ," he would shout, but "hm ♪♪♪|♪ ", the "hm" being a gigantic grunt for the first beat. Soon to join the orchestra as tuba player was the great and huge Gerard Hoffnung, cartoonist extraordinary, of German birth and Jewish parentage, who was one of many German Jews who took refuge in this country during the war. As he sat behind me, because I was in the back desk of the violas, I was guaranteed countless laughs at rehearsals. What fun!

Needless to say, my mother inveigled Mr. Matthews into coming to the first London Junior Orchestra concert in which I played at the Duke's Hall. We played a Gluck overture, Schubert's famous "Unfinished" Symphony and Gigout's "Grand Choeur dialogué" with the eminent organist Margaret Cobb as soloist. By the time the interval arrived I could tell that I had gone up in his estimation. After a second half of music by Roger Quilter, J. S. Bach, Joseph Jongen, Herbert Murrill and Bizet, ending with Elgar's "Pomp and Circumstance March no. 1", he had a completely different picture of me and what I did with my life. So in his third and final report for that academic year, he wrote of me:

> "He has worked hard, however, both in and out of school and is to be congrat-ulated on his award at the Royal Academy of Music. He is gradually maturing and I am quite satisfied with him."

What was this award at the Royal Academy of Music? Earlier that year I had won an exhibition to the Royal Academy of Music and therefore became a Junior Exhibitioner. This meant that in future, during term time, my Saturday mornings would be spent at the Royal Academy of Music from 9 a.m. to 1 p. m … There for my first study I had viola lessons with a lovely, minute lady called Pauline Jackson. Because piano was my second study, I had lessons with one of the adult third-year graduate students. This provided them with some teaching experience, but gave me a different teacher each year, which wasn't always a good idea as it meant that my lessons lacked continuity. Moreover, as one term passed to another and I began to increase in confidence, so I began to realise that these students with their inex-perience of teaching were ripe for fooling. One young Yorkshire lass endured me playing my piece in any key but the one stipulated by the composer and while she became more and more exasperated, I accepted it all as part of the day's entertain-ment.

However, unintentionally I may have helped a Jamaican student fail her Graduate of the Royal Schools of Music (G.R.S.M.) examination. I liked her very much, so I didn't fool around in her lessons. Sadly, one Saturday morning when we were working on a modern piano piece, full of good intentions, her examiner came into the room to eavesdrop on the lesson. Neither my student teacher nor I had noticed that the piano part was written out not on treble and bass clefs but on two treble clefs. Unfortunately, however, the examiner had noticed and pointed this out to the student. She and I had assumed that the strange musical noises were the result of the music being a product of the twentieth century. Partly as a result of this she returned to Jamaica without her G.R.S. M., which was tragic. At the Royal Academy of Music I also had lessons in Aural Training, Harmony and Musical history. Eventually, I even did my G.C.E. "O" level Music examination there rather than at St. Olave's Grammar School, not that the school authorities seemed particularly bothered. Highlight of the day was the orchestral rehearsal from 12 noon until 1 o'clock taken by the inimitable Rita Sharpe. She was one of God's loveliest creations, a charming lady who never aged, who never lost her temper, who never spoke ill of anyone and who never wore a skirt, choosing rather to wear slacks or, when conducting a concert, a glorious long dress which we used to call affectionately her golden dressing-gown. Rehearsals were always fun, never a chore and through her I learned to love Edward Elgar's two "Wand of Youth" suites in particular, and also Vaughan Williams's folk song arrangements. This was a perfect ending to a morning in which I had learned so much and met so many young people from all parts of London who had the same interests as me.

My other chance to meet people of a like mind also came that year, 1953, when I joined the London Schools Symphony Orchestra. This was the remarkable creation of Dr. Leslie Russell, the visionary and energetic Music Organiser for the London County Council's Education Authority. The orchestra was just two years old and so great was the desire to belong to it that, when I joined, there were around one hundred and twenty players, with every string department overflowing and each wind department filled twice over. The quality of some of these young musicians was breath-taking: violinist Alan Peters who went on to become an important orchestral "fixer"; another violinist, Mary Remnant, who later specialised in mediaeval music and published a book about mediaeval musical instruments; Derek Solomans, a future professional orchestral leader; Diana Cummings, a member of the Cummings family that produced some notable musicians; Ian White, a fellow Southwark Cathedral Chorister who at the age of seventeen found himself walking across Westminster Bridge with invitations in his pocket to play his viola in two major London orchestras and a few years later played the second viola d'amore on the famous recording of J. S. Bach's "St. John Passion" made by the choir of King's College, Cambridge, directed by David Willcocks; Peter Vel, who also attended St. Olave's Grammar School, where he was persuaded by my mother to exchange the violin for a 'cello and so eventually became a leading performer on that instrument and the viola da gamba; the ebullient Atarah Ben-Tovim who became a flautist in the Liverpool Philharmonic Orchestra until she took the television world by storm with her programme "Atarah's Band-Box" and so changed the face of classical music for countless young children; Sarah Francis the oboist who, with her mother, the eminent harpsichordist Millicent Silver, and her father eventually became the renowned London Flute Trio; the clarinettist Alan Hacker who has since become an expert in the performance of contemporary music; Michael Ogonovsky, for many years a horn player in the Liverpool Philharmonic Orchestra; and the percussion player Tristan Fry.

The music the orchestra played then was exciting too, not arrangements of classical music but the real thing. Full-blown symphonies by Brahms (no. 4), Sibelius (no. 2), Schubert (no. 8) and Dvorak (nos. 8 and 9 "From the New World"); concertos by Haydn (trumpet), Mozart (clarinet), Edward Elgar ('cello) and John Ireland (piano); together with such fascinating musical morsels as "Over the hills and far away" (Delius), the Hary Janos Suite (Kodaly), "The Banks of Green Willow" (Butterworth), English Dances (Malcolm Arnold), music from "The Firebird" (Stravinsky) and Ravel's "Mother Goose" Suite and "Pavane", to mention a few of the goodies that the orchestra performed. The most fascinating concert came about a few years after I joined the orchestra. Dr. Russell was always proud of the fact that he had been a pupil of the great Ralph Vaughan Williams. In 1958, therefore, the orchestra gave a concert in the Royal Festival Hall to celebrate the composer's 85th birthday, which had occurred on the previous October 12th. It opened with Vaughan Williams's Overture "The Wasps", then Sarah Francis played his oboe concerto and part one ended with his Eighth Symphony. One particular part of this symphony I could never play on my viola, but I noticed that a friend of mine seemed to have no problem in playing it. "How do you do it?" I asked. "Oh, I don't bother with the notes," he replied," I just run up and down the scale of C major!" The second half included the Grand Old Man's "Romance for Harmonica and Strings", his "Fantasia on Greensleeves" and also his arrangement of "The Old Hundredth Psalm Tune", whereupon he lumbered to his feet to acknowledge the tumultuous applause, although many of the orchestral players who could observe him during the concert were convinced that he had slept through most of it.

I loved every minute of these courses which took place three times a year: one week at Christmas, one week at Easter and two weeks in July. What an education, and free too! Soon after I joined there was a trip to Holland and the London Schools Symphony Orchestra enjoyed the privilege of giving a concert in the Concertgebouw, that marvellous hall in Amsterdam. A few years later, the orchestra also toured Norfolk and Suffolk and had to give a concert in the Market Hall at Bury St. Edmunds, not long after it had been hosed down and disinfected following a cattle market.

Yet for all the excitement of 1953, joining the London Junior Orchestra, joining the London Schools Symphony Orchestra and becoming a Junior Exhibitioner at the Royal Academy of Music, the highlight had to be singing in the choir at the Coronation of Queen Elizabeth II in Westminster Abbey on June 2nd. This fantastic choir was drawn from the choristers and lay clerks of the established Church of England Cathedrals in England along with a few colonial opera singers. Eight trebles, one alto, one tenor and one bass represented Southwark Cathedral and I had the good fortune to be one of those trebles. Every singer was required to be note-perfect before the first of the six rehearsals that were to be held in St. Margaret's Church, Westminster, next door to the Abbey. Each of these rehearsals lasted for one and a half hours and as each singer arrived, he was given a stamp to stick on a special card as proof of attendance. As Big Ben alongside chimed six o'clock in the evening, the doors of St. Margaret's were closed and locked. Woe betide anyone who arrived after that, late, and was unable to get into the church, because they were not allowed to take any further part in the proceedings. This led to a minor diplomatic incident, as some of the colonial opera singers arrived late, found themselves locked out and were told that their services were no longer required. Diplomatic pressure ensured that these singers were reinstated, but a point had been made. No-one was late again!

The initial six rehearsals were followed by a longer rehearsal at St. Margaret's and then a dress rehearsal in the Abbey itself by which time excitement was reaching fever pitch. On the day itself, Thursday June 2nd, my mother woke me at around 6 a.m., whereupon (living so near to Westminster Abbey), I was able to walk over Westminster Bridge and across Parliament Square to the Abbey, clutching my big green pass which enabled the policemen to make a way for me through the crowds which lined the streets. Once inside Westminster Abbey, I robed and made my way up to my seat up in the gallery specially built behind the organ case on the north side above the choir stalls. There, and on a similar gallery built behind the organ case on the south side, the choir of four hundred voices waited, munching sandwiches brought along to keep hunger at bay and sampling the loos that had been specially installed for our comfort. On the gallery connecting the two organ cases was seated a full symphony orchestra, with Dr. William McKie, the Abbey Organist who was to direct the musical proceedings, standing to conduct. There were two Sub-Conductors, one on each gallery, to relay Dr. McKie's beat to the vast array of choristers.

While we waited we watched the distinguished guests arrive - the most colourful of all was the Queen of Tonga. We also listened to the organ music and later to music played by the orchestra. Very near to the appointed time, we saw something extraordinary. An army of ladies dressed in long white coats and pushing carpet cleaners came into the Abbey to make presentable the long carpet that stretched from the Great West Door to the High Altar. Then, suddenly, we were on our feet singing Sir C. Hubert Parry's masterpiece: "I was glad when they said unto me, let us go into the house of the Lord", with trumpets blazing and boys from Westminster School shouting at the tops of their voices: "Vivat Regina Elizabetha". It was truly wonderful and emotional. "Zadok the Priest", composed by the great George Frederick Handel for the coronation of King George II and sung at every coronation since then, was simply stunning. When the great service ended some two hours later and the choristers had partaken of the enormous buffet laid on for their benefit in the ancient cloisters, I just wanted to be alone. I wandered out into Dean's Yard and found standing there, unattended, the great gold State Coach. I ran my hand over the side of this piece of English - British - history but it was all too much for me. I slid out into the vast crowd and melted away in the direction of Buckingham Palace. What a day!

Yes, 1953 was a very special year. At school, however, the last three months brought a new form master in the guise of Mr. Roebuck, yet another who made little effort to discover much about me. So my last form report of the year and his first about me included the statement:

"From time to time he makes determined efforts to keep abreast of his form. They bear however an uncomfortable resemblance to the desperate struggles of a drowning man."

VII

Millions of people throughout the world experienced the Coronation Service, mostly on the radio but some on the more recently-created television. However, to sing to so large a congregation was exceptional because, for the most part, at Southwark Cathedral attendances at weekday sung services were minute. Far back in time, cathedral choirs sang twice daily for fifty-two weeks every year both Matins and Evensong, with the choice of time (in many cases 10 a.m. and 3 p.m.) dictated by the fact that daylight plus candlelight was the only way that the singers could illuminate their music. Yet as the twentieth century ran its course, so cathedral authorities found less and less money for the education of their young choristers and the salaries of their organists and lay clerks. This led to financial cuts, with the result that choral matins on weekdays died and became a service of the past. Nowadays, Choral Matins is usually heard only on Sunday mornings, as is the case at Southwark Cathedral. This is sad because it has resulted in the loss of one-third of the British Cathedral Music repertoire and this includes many fine settings of the *Te Deum* and *Benedictus* which are now in cold storage.

Fortunately, Evensong is still sung regularly during the week in many cathedrals in England along with a few in Wales, Scotland and Ireland. Indeed, on a peaceful weekday evening, singing Evensong with a congregation numbering one, two or three worshippers – sometimes even none – is of great importance to young choristers because not only does it mean that they can perpetuate a lot of good music but also they learn that adulation is not important. So often at a Welsh male choir concert when an item ends loudly, the audience breaks into frenzied applause before the singers have even finished, irrespective of the quality of the end product. At a gentle Evensong, on the other hand, a cathedral choir can sing an exquisite sixteenth-century unaccompanied motet which ends with the sound melting into the dimly-lit building – and the better the choir's tuning the longer the echo will take to fade into blissful silence. Jesus said: "Where two or three are gathered together, there am I in the midst" and that is exactly what the clergy were constantly telling us at Southwark Cathedral.

If we sang our Evensong in an empty cathedral with the eerie product of a London "pea soup" smog seeping through the door at the far end of the nave, there with us in the atmosphere of mysterious gloom would be a mighty cloud of witnesses, saints and martyrs from the past, a heavenly host. While that may sound cosy and far-fetched, we did not think so, because there was a very special ministry in that house of God. When we sang Evensong on a Monday, Tuesday, Thursday or Friday evening at 5.15 p.m. with the additional accompaniment of the never-ending rumble of trains from Cannon Street, Charing Cross and Waterloo Junction in the background, as train after train carried countless thousands of commuters from their work in central London to their homes in Eltham, Lewisham, Orpington, Rochester and other parts of London and Kent, we offered worship on behalf of these work-weary people. Nor did we forget the multitude of white-collar office workers from the City of London, charging across London Bridge, making for the station and these and other trains, as we prayed for them also. For that very reason it was important that the Cathedral should be lit up so that it could be seen to be a working powerhouse of prayer, available also at that time to anyone who needed it for private prayer.

The Cathedral authorities – the Provost and the Canons – were well aware of the important role which the Cathedral had to play in this working community, They even created the position of Canon Missioner, which was filled by the energetic, hot-headed, kindly and enormously effective Colin Cuttell. His job was to establish links between Southwark Cathedral and the busy industrial world around it. One afternoon when an electric passenger train accidentally ran into the back of another train and its driver sat in his cab with a lump of metal stuck in his back, dying, the railwaymen knew what to do. They sent for the Canon Missioner, who promptly sat with the driver, holding his hand, praying with him and comforting him until he left this earthly life. Indeed, there was a wonderful aura of divine love at that Cathedral and it was largely created by a caring band of such clergymen. Furthermore, they ministered to the young choristers so effectively that of my generation as many as four eventually became priests themselves, while two others devoted much of their lives to church music.

At the bottom of the clerical hierarchy were the Minor Canons, the Cathedral's equivalent of a curate. It was essential that a Minor Canon be able to sing because it was his job to intone Evensong. One Minor Canon at Southwark Cathedral, who shall remain nameless, professed to having a B. Mus. (London) degree, until a chance "musical" remark led the Organist to make enquiries at the relevant university only to discover that there was no record of this degree having been awarded. In no time at all, the Minor Canon moved on to a parish in Essex, taking with him the academic hood that his mother had made for him.

Some Minor Canons, however, really were high-fliers: suave Douglas Rhymes later returned to Southwark Cathedral as a Residentiary Canon; charming John Lang went on to the B.B.C. where he rose to become Director of Religious Broadcasting and then, finally, Dean of Lichfield; kindly George Boorne Timms moved on to become Vicar of the liturgically forward-looking church of St. Mary the Virgin, Primrose Hill in North London, then Vicar of St. Andrew's Holborn and a Prebendary of St. Paul's Cathedral and finally Archdeacon of Hackney and Editor of the English Hymnal and Chairman of the committee that produced the New English Hymnal; yet none could fly as high, figuratively speaking, as Father Christmas, by which name the choirboys knew the Revd. Minor Canon Alan Christmas.

Next in the pecking order came the Honorary Canons but, unlike the Minor Canons, these were only seen on special occasions. There were quite a few of them because an Honorary Canonry was not unlike a reward for long service which was handed out to clergy who for the most part were not unnecessarily clever, nor pushy, nor cunning enough to become Residentiary Canons, but who had done their work well without upsetting too many people. One of the colourful characters who made this grade, unintentionally I am sure, was Father Potter of Peckham, a parish priest who ministered ceaselessly to the poor in his parish and who was also a humble Franciscan. The Cathedral Choristers were fascinated by his appearance, as Franciscans were not a common sight in London. To them, clad in his brown habit held together by a white cord tied around his middle, he looked like a smaller version of Friar Tuck of Robin Hood fame, and he was always so jovial and happy. It was right that so good, humble and saintly a man should, in the end, have had a book written about his life and good works, as was the case with Fr. Potter.

After the Honorary Canons came the Residentiary Canons, four in number. Unlike their counterparts in such grand cathedrals as Lincoln, Norwich, Salisbury and Winchester, they did not live in lovely, spacious and historic houses, because where the Cathedral Close should have been now stood the Borough Market and Hay's Wharf. They lived in houses in various parts of South London, some of which were still attached to parishes. Among the Canons I remember when I first sang in the choir was Canon T. P. Stevens who, as a Minor Canon many years before had written a book about the Cathedral. To the young choirboys he looked ancient, as old as the Cathedral – but then he could have been as old as the nave, because that had been completed barely fifty years before, an imitation of the original. Canon Stevens was inseparable from his equally aged wife, but sadly he was beginning to suffer from lapses of memory, which occasionally caused him to curtail his sermons.

The only other canon I can remember from this time was, I believe, a certain Canon Evans, a fascinating old man with a grating voice and endless information about insects. Among the later Residentiary Canons in my day were three who achieved high office in the Church of England. Who could dislike Lawrence Brown, a very dear man? He was much loved by my mother, my brother and me, but not by my father because he had the misfortune to chair the very committee which had been set up to reorganise the diocese of Southwark after the War and therefore had shut his church and declared his parish redundant! This was the Canon Brown whom my father had ridiculed in the first verse of the poem that had graced the front page of the final parish magazine of Holy Trinity, Lambeth. Fortunately, the Canon took this with a good heart and went on to become firstly Suffragan Bishop of Warrington and then Bishop of Birmingham. Next was the saintly high-ish churchman John Hughes, who became Suffragan Bishop of Croydon and, I believe, had a lot to do with the armed forces. Finally there was the dynamic Canon Fenton Morley who produced religious programmes for the television, but ended up only as Dean of Salisbury because his Morley Report concerning the future of the clergy of the Church of England was apparently so drastic and far-seeing that it may have cost him promotion to a bishopric.

Of Archdeacons there were three, whose job it was to oversee the activities of the many clergy working in their Archdeaconries. Each one was entitled to a stall in the Cathedral alongside the Canons and Honorary Canons. Among them was Archdeacon Sands, Vicar of St. Anselm's, Kennington, near to Holy Trinity Church. He was a friend of my father and I was sent to him regularly at Christmas and Easter to make my confession, but I must admit that I was not very good at it and did not take the matter as seriously as I ought – especially as my penance so often consisted of no more than sitting down in the church and reading through some hymns! Yet he was a kindly man and his church was lovely, spacious, well-appointed and warm. What impressed me most, however, was the fact that a door in the north wall led straight into the Vicarage, thereby eliminating the cold walks in the winter from the vicarage to the church, as at Holy Trinity. I really enjoyed the walk from my Vicarage on my visits to him, down Kennington Road, past the Granada Cinema where I would gaze upon the still pictures from the latest films, and on to St. Anselm's. These walks gave me time to contemplate Christmas and Easter, the seasons that I loved so much, which were celebrated so fittingly at both Holy Trinity Church and at Southwark Cathedral.

In charge of these celebrations and all other activities at Southwark Cathedral, in addition to the Archdeacons, the Residentiary and Honorary Canons, the Minor Canons, the three Vergers, the Organist, Assistant Organist and the Choir, was not a Dean but a Provost. This unusual name was reserved in the Church of England for the cleric in charge of a cathedral to which was attached a parish church. It was not so in the disestablished Church in Wales, where a Dean is a Dean whether or not a parish is attached to the Cathedral, as at St. David's, Llandaff and Newport. All the Provosts of Southwark Cathedral that I remember went on to greater work. When I arrived in the choir, Cuthbert Bardsley had just been appointed Bishop of Croydon; later he became Bishop of Coventry, where he was enormously success-ful. Although he was a dynamic personality, I never forgave him after my first Christmas at Southwark: he made a present of half-a-crown, a most impressive coin worth much more then than its equivalent 12½p now, to each choirboy but some-how forgot me, perhaps because I was so new.

He was followed by a North Country man, Hugh Ashdown, from the Newcastle area. He had been interviewed by the Bishop of Southwark, so it was said, with a view to being appointed to a vacant Residentiary Canonry, but had so impressed the Bishop that he was invited to become Provost. A tall, bald, gaunt-looking man, highly intelligent and with an eye for things beautiful, worship at the Cathedral became special and very lovely under his leadership. No stone remained unturned in this endeavour, and after one service I was summoned into his presence and asked why I was so dirty and unkempt. A good wash was recommended! So com-manding a presence had he that everyone began to wonder when he too would be whisked away to become a Bishop. When, after ten years, he was appointed a Chaplain to the Queen, we thought that his career was over, but to our surprise and delight shortly afterwards he was appointed Bishop of Newcastle. Back North he went!

Lastly, in my time, was the controversial character George Reindorp, Vicar of St. Stephen's, Rochester Row, just behind the famous Army and Navy Stores in Victoria Street, who soon became known to the choristers as "Raindrop"! He had achieved notoriety earlier when on being offered a bishopric in Australia he declared rather publicly that, after much prayer, he was declining it. After all, we at Southwark Cathedral were used to doing things more quietly. George Reindorp had some influential friends including, it was rumoured, royalty. Promotion was not long in coming and it was to Southwark Cathedral that he came. He came like a rushing wind, sweeping all before him. He would drive up to the Cathedral in his smart car, which annoyed us choirboys as the Bishop, whom we loved dearly (even though he had shut my father's church) arrived in a battered vehicle of some antiquity. Every morning he would breeze into the clergy vestry for the early morning service and greet the assembled company with: "Hello, Girls", until one day he was stopped in his tracks when a junior Verger replied: "Hello, Aunty", and he never again repeated the performance. "Wednesdays at Southwark Cathedral" was his creation. This was a weekly programme of events designed to draw the public into Southwark Cathedral at lunchtime, and it did. The trouble was that he spoilt it all by gleefully counting the number of the assembled multitude and then climbing up into the pulpit to declare to all and sundry how many people were present and by how many that attendance figure was an increase on that of the previous week. He did not seem able to do things quietly and this went against the tradition at Southwark Cathedral. Worse still, he took a stop-watch to the great Sunday Choral Eucharist and eliminated some of the lovely ceremonial in order to reduce the time it all took. That was sad!

Yet there was a different George Reindorp, one who could be caring and prayerful, although unfortunately this was the side we choristers did not see. He took the marriage service for my brother Peter and his wife Gwen and I know that they all got on famously. Interestingly, promotion was not long in coming to George Reindorp, firstly as Bishop of Guildford where his outward-looking ministry must have suited the exciting early days of the new Cathedral, then as Bishop of Salisbury when he was ready for the quieter life of a country diocese. His legacy to Southwark Cathedral was "change", whether it was wanted or not; but there are ways of achieving this more peacefully and less controversially.

Certain matters, however, never appeared to change. One was the special service to commemorate the Founders and Benefactors "who had left in this house of God enduring memorials to their munificence and care for religion." So were remembered Bishop Peter de Roches, Cardinal Henry Beaufort and Bishop Richard Fox among the builders of this great church; George Gwilt, Arthur Blomfield, Robert Wallace and Thomas Rider among its architects; Charles Eamer Kempe the stained-glass artist and Frederick Wigan in the number of those who had adorned it; John Gower, John Merbecke, William Shakespeare, Thomas Guy and John Harvard "who had enriched our worship and common life by their art and music, by their provision for the sick and afflicted, and by their institutions for the increasing of sound learning"; finally the first Bishops Suffragan, Anthony Wilson Thorold and Huyshe Yeatman-Biggs, and also Edward Stuart Talbot, first Bishop of Southwark, who were remembered for their work in transforming the ancient church of St. Saviour and St. Mary Overie into the mother church of the Diocese of Southwark.

It was a splendid annual occasion, one which never failed to leave a sense of pride in the young choristers' hearts. This was history coming alive and we were part of it. After all, Shakespeare's Globe Theatre had been close at hand, as had the Tabard Inn, the starting point for the pilgrims who told their entertaining stories in Chaucer's "Canterbury Tales". Nearby was, and still is, the amazing half-timbered George Hotel, off the Borough High Street, not forgetting St. Thomas's Church next to Guy's Hospital. A primitive operating theatre was recently found in this church, high in the tower, actually prepared for an operation and then left locked up. Inside the Cathedral was to be found more history: the colourful memorial to the mediaeval poet John Gower, which we choirboys called "The Rude Memorial" because the first letter of each line of the Latin inscription spelt the word ARSE; the memorial on the west wall of the north transept to a quack doctor who made his living by selling dud pills; the floor at the entrance to the Clergy Vestry where the original level is preserved at the side, several feet lower; the stone that could be removed from the wall of the Harvard Chapel to reveal part of an even older wall (the connection between this chapel and John Harvard, the founder of Harvard University, ensured a steady stream of American visitors to the Cathedral); the roof boss at the west end of the nave which came from the ancient ceiling and is carved into the form of a face with a body hanging out of its mouth, reputed to be Jonah being swallowed by the whale – or is it Judas Iscariot being devoured by the devil?

Southwark Cathedral breathed history and at the Founders and Benefactors Service I received an annual reminder of this and I loved it. As the choir processed into the Cathedral it was not unusual for us and the large congregation to sing the great mediaeval hymn "Blessed City, Heavenly Salem" to the equally great mediaeval plainsong melody that is associated with it. I loved that, too. Indeed, whenever I sing it now my mind is transported back to those wonderful days at Southwark. Sometimes the choir sang Sir Edward Bairstow's magnificent anthem-setting of these words, the music of which is derived from this plainchant melody. At the words: "Many a blow and biting sculpture fashioned well those stones elect" how I revelled in the crashing organ chords as they depicted the heavenly architect hammering away at huge lumps of stone to create great works of art like the Cathedral itself! Always this sent shivers down my spine.

It was during the time when George Timms was a Minor Canon that I remember particularly one of these services. The choir had sung the usual 5.15 p.m. Evensong and as there was an hour or so to wait for the "Founders and Benefactors" service, four of us at a loose end went for a wander, past ancient St. Katherine's Dock, and down the narrow dusky lanes leading to the River Thames. When we reached Bankside, by the ancient "Anchor" public house alongside the railway bridge which took the trains across the river to Cannon Street Station, we noticed a door in the wall standing slightly ajar. Passing through this door and slamming it shut so that we would not be discovered, we found ourselves at the foot of a long staircase which we immediately climbed. Suddenly, at the top, we found ourselves next to the busy electric railway line that carried trains from Cannon Street Station to London Bridge Station. Realising that if we were discovered we would be in deep trouble, we ran back down the staircase only to discover that in slamming the door shut we had locked ourselves in, as the door had no inside handle.

Beginning to panic, as we had lost track of the time and were worrying about arriving back at the Cathedral in time for the service, we looked around us and found, part of the way up the stairs, a ledge. Crawling on all fours across this mucky ledge we discovered that the other end was open and from it we were able to drop down, one by one, into the street below. Dusting ourselves down as best we could, we ran quickly to the Cathedral. The Choir Vestry was locked, but after ringing the doorbell we gained admittance, to find the choir and clergy robed and lined up, ready to process into the service. Dirty and dishevelled, we were certainly not the flavour of the evening, as Minor Canon Timms scowled angrily at us and Provost Ashdown, aloof, looked equally furious. Hastily we robed, picked up our service sheets and moments later were processing into the Cathedral, down the crowded nave, looking angelic and singing at the tops of our voices that wonderful hymn, "Blessed City, Heavenly Salem". It had been a narrow escape.

That morale in the choir was good in those happy days must largely be put down to the care lavished on the young choristers by the clergy. A gentle spirituality shone through the Cathedral services and this was encouraged by the Minor Canons. Obviously all the choirboys were prepared for confirmation, but there was more. In my early years as a chorister at Southwark Cathedral the choir endured two sermons, one at the 11 a.m. Holy Eucharist, the other at the 3 p.m. Choral Evensong. In the morning when the time for the sermon arrived, the choir processed down to the nave and sat in the front two rows of chairs so that, hopefully, they could hear better the learned discourses. I remember one preacher declaiming earnestly: "We are all in the same boat", whereupon the boy next to me muttered rather audibly: "It must be a bloody big boat"!

At Evensong, however, in the days when there was a sermon at this service, the choirboys were withdrawn and taken to the vestry to be given good, sound instruction on the Christian faith by one of the Minor Canons. However, this came at the end of a long, tiring day and the problem was getting us to behave ourselves and listen! When Fr. Timms was a Minor Canon he went one stage further and made a valiant attempt to curb our Cockney capers by forming a choir committee, in the hope that we might become more disciplined. I was so miffed at not being elected to this committee that I deliberately misbehaved and was duly fined half-a-crown (12½p), which I never paid! Perhaps the most important single contribution to the development of this high morale was the time spent by the choristers on holiday together, usually three times a year. Christmas was a busy round of services and carol singing – singing in all the wards in Guy's Hospital alone was an exhausting experience. Afterwards the choristers would go to Caterham for a week to Woodlands, the diocesan retreat house. There would be no retreat for us, as instead we would run wild in the woods around which gave the house its name and were such a contrast to the urban jungle where we lived.

Similarly, after Easter, which was perhaps more busy than Christmas as Holy Week was stuffed full with additional services, the choir would set off after Evensong on Easter Day from London Bridge Station to East Grinstead and on to Chelwood Gate. This was always a wonderful week at a place called "The Isle of Thorns", organised by the Canon Missioner, Colin Cuttell. We slept on primitive iron beds under itchy blankets in a long, draughty wooden hut, we ate scrumptious meals prepared by Aunty Dot who was caretaker of the Cathedral Chapter House and we played table tennis – something we were never able to do back in London. Best of all was the nine-hole golf course if the weather was fine, or the indoor soccer pitch if the weather was foul. It was sheer bliss. Every day started the same way with a parade: prayers and breaking open a flag. Some mornings, due to the cunning of some senior choristers, when the flag broke open out fell the Assistant Organist's pyjamas! As each day progressed, if we wanted something different we would scour the thick hedgerows and undergrowth armed with forked sticks, preparing to be hunters searching for grass snakes and adders.

The third trip, which always came at the end of the summer term and was also organised by Canon Cuttell, was a fortnight's camp under canvas for the scout troop that he ran on Friday evenings in the Cathedral Chapter House, to keep together past and present choristers. How the cost of these camps was so little remained a mystery, but it was always assumed that the Canon - "Skip" or "Skipper" as he was called on these occasions - begged financial assistance from the industries to which he ministered. These camps took choristers to Petworth in Sussex, where I lost one of my front teeth while keeping wicket in a cricket match played on a bumpy pitch, and to Kingswear, all the way from Paddington Station on a Great Western steam-train, as well as other sites in Devon. Among the many highlights were the "wide games" that we played, ranging over the lovely deep green countryside. Many was the time when, while being pursued across a field, I leapt over a low stone wall only to land in a foul, messy, evil-smelling cow-pat with disastrous results. Life indeed was fun!

VIII

Another refuge for Southwark Cathedral choirboys was my father's vicarage. If there was a special service on a Saturday, rather than travel home afterwards to such outlying places as Eltham, Grove Park, Lewisham or Tattenham Corner, some of them would bed down at Holy Trinity Vicarage, making the ten-minute journey back to the Cathedral the next morning on the no. 44 bus from Lambeth Baths. The Baths used to stand somewhere near to the junction of Lambeth Road and Lambeth Bridge Road but were flattened during the War although the name remained in use for many more years. Sometimes there were weddings on Saturday afternoons at the Cathedral, usually with the Assistant Organist in charge. It was his custom to pass onto the Head Chorister a bag containing £3 in half-crown coins. This money would be shared out among the twelve choristers who had been booked for the wedding, each one receiving two coins which amounted to five shillings (25p). Just occasionally not all the boys arrived for the service, with the result that those present received a larger share of the cash. Not unnaturally, therefore, we used to hope that not everyone would arrive so that, like Oliver Twist, we could have more.

It was not always a service, however, that brought choristers to the Vicarage. Sometimes it was my birthday, or even just a sociable tea party. On one of the occasions, I received a much-needed lesson in humility. I was rather too fond of my prowess as a violinist and showed off once too often to the choristers present. When I had finished, one of them, who had not long been in the choir, picked up the violin and proceeded to play music that left me in the shade. Far from being furious at being upstaged, I immediately struck up a great friendship with this lad. Ian White was his name and he was one of the few choirboys not to attend St. Olave's Grammar School or Archbishop Temple's School, which is why he was still relatively unknown to most of the boys. He lived in Battersea where he attended a local secondary school. His father was an Organ Tuner working for the firm of Alfred Hunter (which now no longer exists), who sang in his spare time in Westminster Abbey Special Choir.

Ian was such a modest and gentle giant that he soon became a greatly-loved member of the choir. He entered wholeheartedly into the spirit of everything, right down to playing (very clumsily) in the weekly soccer match on the strip of concrete by the Cathedral steps on a Sunday afternoon after lunch. Unfortunately his sense of co-ordination left much to be desired. When he went to kick the ball his foot arrived long after the ball had gone, with the result that he kicked his opponent's foot instead. Afterwards, as he surveyed the physical damage that he had inflicted, his apology always was so earnest and genuine that it was impossible to be upset with him. Because of this deficiency he was one of the unfortunate choirboys who had to be carted off to Guy's hospital on the occasion when he kicked the wall instead of the ball, which had long moved away down the pitch while he was starting his kick! Like me, Ian joined the London Schools Symphony Orchestra and it was he who at the age of seventeen years walked across

Westminster Bridge silently deliberating over invitations to play his viola in two of London's major orchestras.

Another future musician among the choirboys who frequented Holy Trinity Vicarage from time to time was Richard Marlow. We had long been good friends and I had spent as much time at his Tattenham Corner home, 52 Epsom Lane North, which overlooked the race course, as he had spent in my home at the Vicarage. It was while on our journeys from Tattenham Corner Station to London Bridge on a Sunday morning that we had been able to witness the unique procedure at Chipstead Station when Dr. Cook joined the train, not forgetting the equally unique procedure at London Bridge Station when he left it. An extraordinary but true story tells of Richard and me going to stay with a clergyman friend in Northamptonshire. This clergyman had been a devotee of choral services at Southwark Cathedral but was now Vicar of three rural parishes in the diocese of Peterborough: Hemington, Luddington and Thurning. Each evening, while there, the three of us would chant Evensong together to plainsong in one of the churches. This was fine until the night when the psalms for the day, always sung antiphonally, found Richard and me singing: "All that are fat upon earth have eaten and worshipped," at which point we sank to our seats and dissolved into laughter as our clergyman friend was exceedingly rotund. Fortunately, he took this in good heart!

While there, he took us to Evensong at Peterborough Cathedral which was being sung by the trebles only - eight boys on each side of the choir, Decani and Cantoris. Imagine our mirth as we watched a boy collapse during the singing of the psalms. He was so fat - the nearest to Billy Bunter I had ever seen - that it took four boys to carry him out; one for each arm and one for each leg. The Organist, Dr. Hopkins, was far from amused! The extraordinary part of this story is that my mother had arranged to take Richard and me to Cambridge to hand us over to this clergyman. When we arrived there, she took us first to have tea with her Uncle Stan in his rooms at Trinity College, where he was still Organist. Richard had never met him before and at that time had no idea what the future held in store for him. Strangely, only a few years later, having been Organ Scholar at Selwyn College, Cambridge and then a lecturer at Southampton University, he was invited to succeed Raymond Leppard as Organist of this same Trinity College, Cambridge, and so moved into those very rooms in succession but one to my great-uncle. What a coincidence!

My mother had quaint ways of influencing lives and of marking out special occasions. Every summer, for example, she bottled peach halves. The bottles were tall affairs with a rubber-lined screw top to keep the contents fresh. All family birthdays were marked with peaches and cream and the juice was always especially tasty. Christmas was never anything but a magical occasion, starting with Midnight Mass in an incense-filled Holy Trinity Church with so much high church ritual as to take one's mind off the fact that half of the building was being held up by scaffolding. Early next morning there would be stockings stuffed full of small goodies to open, then after the morning services there was a glorious turkey dinner to enjoy in the kitchen, leaving the remainder of the day to be enjoyed in the Blue Room. Here, in comfortable armchairs in front of an open coal fire, we would open presents, listen to the Queen's Speech on the wireless, play 78 rpm records on a gramophone, play party games or doze. Tea always included rich, fruity Christmas cake with thick white icing, while supper found us tucking into gorgeous turkey sandwiches. Best of all, to add to the magic of the day, I was always allowed on this one day of the year to sleep in front of the dying embers of the fire in my sleeping bag. That was a very special treat.

Waking next morning in a cold Blue Room with only a dead fire for warmth could have been an anti-climax, were it not for the fact that my mother had plans also to bring Boxing Day to life. It would begin with her giving my brother, sister and me a new annual. "Rupert" was for many years my favourite. She would also add one more Richmal Crompton "Just William" book to our family collection, which we would all enjoy reading over the coming year. In the afternoon she would take my sister and me to Baron's Court by underground train to visit her old violin teacher, Miss Sarah Fennings. This was always something of an adventure. The ancient wizened lady appeared to be half as old as time, seeming to belong to a bygone age, and lived in part of a Victorian villa. She would give us a slice of Christmas cake on a bone china plate and a glass of port. Although we enjoyed the rich cake, we didn't enjoy the port as at that time none of the Gedges ever drank alcohol. For the next twenty minutes or so, therefore, we would watch for an opportunity to dispose of the port in one of the many plant pots that decorated the room whenever she was not looking in our direction or was somewhere else in the house.

Sometime during the twelve days of Christmas, my mother would send me to a pantomime in a West End theatre. As I had been brought up on ancient Greek and Roman myths and legends, not forgetting Aesop's Fables and English history from the book "Our Island Story", I loved watching such stories as "Where the rainbow ends", "Babes in the Wood", "Jack and the Beanstalk" and "Peter Pan" come to life on the stage. What I didn't like were the added slapstick comedy interludes that destroyed the natural flow of the story but seemed to amuse most of the audience, who were obviously in need of such diversions. Once or twice a "Just William" play might be on for me to see and these I loved, because I used to identify myself with the untidy, scruffy William and his carefree way of life. As for William's barn-hide-out, when created in the theatre this was a perfect place of refuge, with its staircase rising from the centre of the stage to a landing which opened into hidden rooms on either side, both with straw-covered floors. Bliss!

Interestingly, there was never the same fuss about the New Year. Only Christmas seemed to matter and both Holy Trinity Church, while it was there, and Southwark Cathedral housed magical crib scenes to provide me with a vivid visual reminder of the Christmas story. So while Christmas for me began with my wandering down Kennington Road to St. Anselm's Church to make my confession and then going to Midnight Mass at my father's Holy Trinity Church, it always ended with the traditional service of Nine Lessons and Carols at Southwark Cathedral. This, quite rightly, took place with great ceremony on the liturgically-correct Sunday afternoon that followed Christmas Day. Here the nine lessons would be read in accordance with the cathedral pattern of hierarchy, starting with a humble choirboy, then a Lay Clerk (choirman), moving on to the Organist and so on until the final three lessons were read by a Residentiary Canon, the Provost and finally the Bishop, who always read the opening verses of St. John's Gospel, for which the entire congregation and choir stood. While it was normal for the Head Chorister to be chosen to read, the junior choristers all jostled for another privilege. By tradition, two of the smallest choirboys robed in albs and escorted all the readers to the lectern and then back to their seats once they had read. Naturally, this was considered a great honour and when I was selected for this job one year, I thought I was the "cat's whiskers"!

The next special family occasion was my birthday on March 12th, which was usually marked by a party. On one famous occasion a few of the Cathedral choirboys slept on the floor of my playroom, which was on the ground floor of the Vicarage next to my father's study. Not surprisingly, no matter what the time was when we switched out the light, there was a lot of banter and chatter until, tired, we fell asleep. At around four o'clock in the morning, I was wakened by the feeling that a stranger was in the room. I looked up and, to this day, I am sure that a figure dressed in a monk's habit stood looking down at me, except that where his face should have been there was a bright light. I was mesmerized and terrified and woke up the other boys, whereupon the apparition turned to my left and walked out through the wall. I immediately got up and switched on the light: on it remained until it was time to get up. While I am convinced that I saw something and none of the others disagreed, over the months that followed they gradually became somewhat sceptical about the incident.

In searching for an explanation, the most obvious was that I had seen through the closed curtains the light of a train waiting to enter Waterloo Station and my imagination had done the rest. Had that been the case, however, then the figure would never have reached the wall because the window ended before then. For me, there was a possible explanation. The proximity of mediaeval Lambeth Palace, the London residence of the Archbishop of Canterbury, meant that during the Middle Ages monks must have travelled in plenty around this part of London. Secondly, the narrow lane which provided access to the Vicarage from the more substantial Carlisle Lane was once part of a right of way from Carlisle House to the Stangate Ferry across the River Thames, which originally belonged to the Bishop of Rochester and then to the Bishop of Carlisle. Thirdly, the area around the Vicarage had formerly been known as Lambeth Marsh. During the Middle Ages, with all roads no more than dirt tracks around property, any water-filled ditch became a major hazard and Lambeth Marsh was full of them. Was my ghost, therefore, a monk who had strayed from one of these narrow paths into Lambeth Marsh and so come to an untimely and watery end?

The taming of Lambeth Marsh really began with the building of Westminster Bridge, which opened in 1750 and rendered obsolete the historic Stangate ferry. Not surprisingly, the ferry operators had not given up without a fight. Fearing for their livelihoods they had continually sabotaged the work by cutting loose the stone barges and ramming the piers with them. However, once opened, the bridge heralded major changes in London's transport system which began the urban explosion that followed. First came the building of an approach road across the marshy fields of Lambeth Marsh which, unfortunately, for many years became the haunt of highwaymen who used to vandalise the lights to aid their foul endeavours. More bridges followed, at Blackfriars in 1769 and at Waterloo in 1817, which led to the creation of more and more roads along which were built countless houses until by 1820 the ploughed fields had gone and Lambeth Marsh had become a truly urban area. In 1839 Holy Trinity Church was opened and, if a picture hanging in the Vicarage kitchen is to be believed, the area around had become gracious and prosperous.

Sadly, such serenity was rudely obliterated in 1848 when the London and South Western Railway Company brought its railway line on a viaduct, high above Holy Trinity Church, to its new London terminus at Waterloo Station. The initial six tracks and four platforms grew and grew until by the time I was a young lad collecting engine numbers over one hundred years later, there were twenty-one platforms accommodating almost two thousand trains daily. Although the railway brought great benefits to London and to Britain, it spelt the end for Lambeth Marsh as the area lost its desirable residential qualities. With the steam trains came air that was full of sulphurous stench and solid black smuts, as well I remember since my mother brought up my brother, sister and me to keep our own rooms clean!

One curiosity came with the railway. During the nineteenth century the population of Lambeth Marsh had risen to thirty thousand people, with the result that burying the dead had become a serious problem. To overcome this, the London Necropolis Railway came into being in 1870, to provide a private railway line to the Necropolis Cemetery at Brookwood, near Woking. I can remember enough Greek to realise that the word "Necropolis" means "City of the Dead" and I was fascinated by the sight of the small special station that could be glimpsed high up on the left, close to the main railway line, when walking down Hercules Road towards Lambeth North Underground Station. Apparently the procedure followed was this: when the funeral cortege arrived at the special station, the coffin was lifted to the platform while the mourners used the rest rooms that were provided. Although the more wealthy people could hire an entire train for their own personal use, it was more normal for the regular service to be used by as many as fifty funeral parties a day from all social classes, the bereaved returning to Waterloo at the end of the ceremony. The Necropolis station that I saw was in a sorry state of repair and it was obvious that it had been out of use for a long time. Presumably its trade had been taken over by the motor vehicle which, when it came into being, could provide a more convenient service.

Mention of Lambeth North Underground Station serves to remind me of how this railway station, deep in the bowels of the ground, did double duty during the Second World War as a much-needed air-raid shelter. If my memory serves me correctly, wooden bunk beds were installed on the two platforms to provide a little comfort, as most air-raids occurred at night-time.

A stone's throw from the Underground Station, up Westminster Bridge Road towards the main railway line, is Lower Marsh, better known as The Cut. Here was, and still is, the most amazing street market, so near to Carlisle Lane and Holy Trinity Vicarage. There were shops on both sides of the road, including one where fish and chips in pieces of old newspaper could be purchased for sixpence (2½p), another selling newspapers and magazines situated next to the café where my sister worked to augment her meagre pocket money, not forgetting the clothes shop opposite that belonged to Monty Modlyn, a colourful local character who achieved notoriety by broadcasting a radio show called "Cockney Capers". This was only the top end of The Cut. By the time the bottom was reached at Waterloo Road, opposite the Old Vic Theatre, a multitude of little shops had been passed including a Woolworth's, which still bore the legendary sign stating that many items could be purchased for as little as 3d (threepence, 1½p) or 6d (sixpence, 2½p).

However, the glory of The Cut was the multitude of stalls selling absolutely everything. These were like mobile shops, because at the end of the day they could be wheeled away to a store which was situated in one of the many dark tunnels beneath the railway viaducts, secured by huge wooden gates. Fruit and Vegetable stalls abounded, book stalls, clothing stalls, stalls containing accessories for carpentry or electrical work. I was always mesmerised by the jellied eels stall, with countless of these creatures wriggling around awaiting their eventual end. Yet for me the most fascinating stall was one that appeared on Saturdays when the market was always crowded, the province of an American Wide Boy who auctioned the most amazing assortment of goods at amazingly low prices. "Come on ladies, " I remember him declaiming to the assembled multitude gathered around his stall one day, as he held up a see-through nylon nightie, "buy one of these and get your old man into bed earlier." Quip followed quip as he sold off cheap tea sets, cutlery, gardening tools, perfume, you name it he'd got it! It was like the 33 r. p.m. gramophone records that I used to purchase from a stall some years later when I was a student. I would ask no questions and be told no lies: some of the records had the word DELETED stamped on the sleeve, some were bankrupt stock, some were fire stock, some it seems may have fallen off the back of a lorry. Who knows?

What I do know is that at this time I spent many a happy hour at nearby Waterloo Station on the end of platform eleven, collecting engine numbers. By the time steam locomotives had given way to diesels, I had "spotted" all the named engines on the Southern Railway/Region. Most of these brought geography and history alive for me. The King Arthur class, for example, were locomotives named after the legendary characters that appeared in my much-read books about that great monarch whose famous Round Table was reputed to be in Winchester Castle. Even the name of his miraculous sword "Excalibur" adorned one of these many locomotives that regularly hauled the trains that left at fifty-four minutes past the hour bound for either Basingstoke or Salisbury, stopping at all stations on the way. Then there were the more powerful Lord Nelson locomotives that perpetuated the names of some of the great British naval leaders from past history. It seemed appropriate that these handsome locomotives should head express trains that left at half-past the hour bound for the port of Southampton before going on to the seaside resorts of Bournemouth and Weymouth. Even more powerful were the West Country class locomotives, named after towns and villages in what to me then was distant Devon, such as Bideford, Exmouth, Honiton and Ilfracombe, not forgetting their bigger cousins, the "Merchant Navy" class, the most powerful of all, named after various steamship companies. These Bulleid Pacifics, strikingly original and unique in design, took the express trains on the hour from Waterloo down through the suburbs of south-west London to Hampshire and beyond into Somerset and then deepest Devon. Most prestigious of all these trains was the "Devon Belle", a fantastic creation, glamorous, nothing but Pullman cars ending with a sleek observation car of great beauty. Quite magnificent and opulent, just like a four-star hotel-restaurant on wheels, each table lit by a tiny individual light and served by a white-coated waiter. I would dream about travelling on that train. Even though these great mechanical monsters used to belch foul-smelling smoke all over Lambeth Marsh and make the most horrendous noise as they slowly gathered speed, hauling their heavy load of passengers, I loved them. Within a minute or two of starting their journey, they would be thundering past the great red wooden cross that hung on the East wall of Holy Trinity Church to remind the passengers that God was there.

The passing of the steam locomotives with coal-dust stained drivers and firemen, who were my heroes, was a sad day for me, yet I suppose it was progress. With the diesels came drivers dressed in shirts and ties just like anybody else, and firemen with nothing much to do although the union officials insisted that they were still vital to the smooth running of the trains. There were also other delights to be found at Waterloo Station. To start with, there were crowds. I have always been (and still am) fascinated by watching people and there were plenty to watch at Waterloo Station, thousands upon thousands of young and old, thin and fat, rich and poor, black and white and all others that are to be found walking in this world; such a variety of clothing too.

Of course, this was a time of full employment when no-one could be found to do the menial tasks on the London Transport Underground Railways. So desperate was the need for platform staff and ticket collectors that everything possible was done, in a somewhat patronising way, to entice immigrants from India, Pakistan, the West Indies and other colonial countries to the motherland to do these jobs. Naturally, large numbers of them arrived at Waterloo Station on the Boat Trains from Southampton to begin colonising large areas of South London. What they made of the hustle and bustle of Waterloo Station I cannot imagine: the rasping noise of the loudspeakers giving advice about trains; the pigeons dive-bombing from on high, depositing mess everywhere; the motorised trolleys careering around dragging wagons laden with mailbags and luggage behind them; the taxis, cars, buses and coaches collecting and depositing passengers; the moving stairways conveying people to and from the underground trains; not forgetting the Southern Railway's own underground railway known as "The Drain", with its small electric trains travelling deep beneath the River Thames, connecting Waterloo to The Bank in the City of London. The station was truly enormous. Even the public toilets were palatial, complete with a barber's shop and marble wash-basins!

Yet one place of relaxation existed on London's busiest railway terminus and that was the News Theatre next to Platform One. I used to take refuge there from time to time to watch cartoon films of Mickey Mouse, Popeye the Sailor Man, Laurel and Hardy and other such characters. I also found the Pathé Movietone Newsreel films interesting, as these were still the days before popular television saturated screens with news programmes. Another attraction of the News Theatre was the opportunity to enjoy a quiet anonymous smoke during the hour-long show. One afternoon this almost led to my undoing, had I not been just a little streetwise. While seated in the warm darkness to watch the films, I had taken my packet of cigarettes from my pocket and put one to my mouth prior to lighting it, whereupon a lighted match was produced by the man sitting next to me on my right, I lit my cigarette and murmured my thanks, at which he put his left hand on my knee! At this I decided that a hasty exit was the best course of action. Imagine my alarm, therefore, when as I stood up to leave he stood up to follow me. I got out of the News Theatre as quickly as I could, pursued by the person, but fortunately was able to lose myself in the crowds milling around before I could come to any harm.

There were three ways out of Waterloo Station. The first was the road on the other side of the News Theatre which led down to Lower Marsh (The Cut), then across Westminster Bridge Road to Carlisle Lane and so to Holy Trinity Vicarage. In reverse this was the only route by which taxis could drive up into the station. The second way out was down a broad but dimly lit flight of stairs that led eventually to Waterloo Road where, some years later, the Great Train Robber Buster Edwards sold flowers. The third way out was opposite platforms 17-21 from where the Windsor electric trains departed. Next to this, many years later, the International Station was added for Channel Tunnel trains. Here was another broad flight of stairs, only much more grand, descending through a stone, gilded Victory Arch above which were fixed medallions bearing the names of the 1914-18 theatres of war. At the bottom of these steps was a continuation of the road that had brought the taxis into the station, only now it took them out into York Road under the watchful gaze of an enormous red lion, a statue standing proudly on a stone plinth.

On the opposite side of York Road was the site of the 1951 Festival of Britain. Designed to emulate the Great Exhibition of 1851, it was unfortunately only a pale shadow of this. All that remains now is the Royal Festival Hall, a magnificent venue for concerts with a superb acoustic and fine, but controversial, pipe organ. I visited the Exhibition along with the rest of my family. Even our mongrel dog, Dumbo, somehow gained admission. A little way further up York Road, towards Waterloo Bridge on the right, stood the church of St. John the Evangelist, Waterloo Road, which was one of the first churches built to commemorate the battle of Waterloo. Opened in 1824, among its first Organists was the youthful Samuel Sebastian Wesley, grandson of Charles Wesley, the famous hymn-writer. Now it was designated "The Festival Church" and, as it was in the diocese of Southwark, the first service broadcast from there was sung by the choir of Southwark Cathedral. A coach was hired to ensure that as soon as this service was ended the choir could be whisked off to the Cathedral, which was little more than a mile away, so as to sing the normal Sunday services there.

That, however, was not my only dealing with St. John's, Waterloo Road. My mother's old violin teacher, Miss Fennings, also taught a certain Garth Gainsford. As he wanted a chance to try out Beethoven's "Kreutzer Sonata" in preparation for a B.B.C. audition, he arranged a concert in the church at which he would play the Sonata and I would contribute some vocal items to help fill up the programme. Lots of leaflets were distributed by my proud mother which described me as:

Master David Gedge
Boy Treble from Coronation Choir who will
sing among other songs Gounod's Ave Maria.

On reflection, this was highly embarrassing! So this concert went ahead on the evening of Friday, January 29th 1954, when I was nearing my fifteenth birthday and still happily singing with a strong treble voice. Meanwhile, Southwark Cathedral had a new Organist and Choirmaster.

IX

As Dr Cook had died in harness inevitably there had to be an interregnum while the process of selecting a new Organist and Choirmaster wound into gear. During this time the Assistant Organist took over running the choir. Ernest Herbert Warrell was his real name, but to his friends and colleagues he was known as John, perhaps because he was not overfond of his names, and who could blame him for that! Anyway, to us choirboys in those more formal times, he was known quite simply and correctly as Mr. Warrell, although unofficially we called him Bert. Born in 1915, he had become an Articled Pupil of Dr. Cook shortly before the Second World War, and Assistant Organist shortly after it. An Articled Pupil was someone who was taught by the Cathedral Organist without payment, but in exchange worked for him and in so doing learned his trade. This age-old and well-tried system of training Organists was dying out at this time and being replaced by the appointment of salaried Assistant Organists.

A mystery surrounded Mr. Warrell's war service. There were lots of rumours, but nothing definite. It seems that he may have been involved in some sort of secret undercover work, but that was all we choirboys could ever find out. A fine organist, he was equally proficient with the choir and on reflection I sometimes wonder if he, too, had been considered as a replacement for Dr. Cook. Certainly his organisation and control of the music at Dr. Cook's funeral had drawn admiration from the many musicians who helped to pack Southwark Cathedral for an occasion which, while sorrowful, was also one of gratitude for a life which had been so fulfilling.

However, other forces were at work concerning the appointment of Dr. Cook's successor. When the name of the new Organist was announced, it came as something of a surprise. Dr. Sidney Scholfield Campbell was well equipped musically for this position, but why was he relinquishing a similar job at Ely Cathedral, one of the most magical ecclesiastical buildings in Europe (where there was also a well-established choir school), to come to lowly Southwark Cathedral, which relied on local South Londoners for its treble line? Was the key figure in this appointment Dr. Gerald Knight, Director of the Royal School of Church Music, because Dr. Campbell also became Director of Studies at the College of St. Nicolas? This was at Addington Palace near to Croydon, the headquarters of the R.S.C.M., easily accessible to Southwark by car or train.

Dr. Campbell was a controversial character, never other than kind to me, but woe betide anyone who crossed him. His temper could be frightening. To my knowledge, only one person ever got the better of an exchange with him. This was an alto, a rather dapper individual with an eye for the ladies, who used to sing on Sundays and special occasions, Mr. Wilkinson by name. He had rather a fine voice and a suave manner to go with it. If I remember rightly, he claimed that he had sung in Durham Cathedral Choir, although he never claimed to have been a Lay Clerk there, which is a subtle difference. Anyway, when Dr. Campbell took up his work in September 1953, Mr. Wilkinson was nowhere to be seen until the final

Sunday of the month when, not long after the afternoon practice had begun, he waltzed into the choirstalls, took up his normal place and started to sing. When there was a break in the music, Dr. Campbell turned towards him and asked, "Who are you?" which brought the reply, "Mr. Wilkinson". "Where have you come from?" was the next question, to which he responded, "From the street." Dr. Campbell was nonplussed and soon gave up the unequal struggle so as to resume his practice. However, Mr. Wilkinson did not feature in Dr. Campbell's future plans for much longer.

One of the bass lay clerks, Harry Coles, was also rather unfortunate in his dealings with Dr. Campbell. Being the only one of Dr. Cook's boys ever to be kept on in the choir on a regular basis, he held dear his former master's memory and did not take kindly to the usurper and all his changes. Having that most dubious of gifts, perfect pitch, it was easy for Dr. Campbell to get back at him. The services of Matins and Evensong both opened with Versicles which were sung without organ accompaniment and invariably Dr. Campbell would have them sung in a key that differed from the one in the printed copy. Then, while Harry went through the awkward process of transposing the music in his mind, Dr. Campbell could be seen in the organ loft chuckling away to himself at Harry's discomfort.

It became evident that Dr. Campbell was either loved or loathed. Nevertheless, he had an exceedingly interesting past. To start with, he began his working life not as a musician but as either a bank clerk or as a local council employee, depending on the story believed. His detractors would claim that one of his jobs had been emptying the slot machines on the doors of public toilets, while his admirers would point to the tale that, through attending night school, he had acquired a Doctorate of Music from Durham University, which, if true, was an amazing feat. His flirtation with a musical career had begun early and in a humble way when, at the age of eighteen, he had become Organist and Choirmaster at St. Margaret's Church, Leytonstone. Two years later he moved to a similar position at Chigwell Parish Church before becoming Organist at West Ham Parish Church in 1931. After six years he transferred his allegiance to St. Peter's Church, Croydon, where he remained for a further six years.

In 1943, now a Bachelor of Music and Fellow of the Royal College of Organists, he took up his final parish church appointment at St. Peter's Collegiate Church, Wolverhampton. Here, in a church noted for its music, he must have attracted attention because within four years, in 1947 he was appointed Sub-warden of the College of St. Nicolas, attached to the Royal School of Church Music. Of his appointment in 1949 to be Organist and Master of the Choristers at Ely Cathedral in succession to Marmaduke Conway, Dr. Campbell himself suggested that he had got on so well with the Dean and Chapter while running a Royal School of Church Music choir course that they looked no further when appointing a new Organist. Significantly, he and his aged predecessor became good friends. It is quite possible that he didn't really want to leave Ely for Southwark because, when the time came for him to move, apparently he sat down in his favourite café and talked the lady owner into letting him take away with him a lovely print of Ely Cathedral that was hanging on a wall there.

Being a self-made man who had reached the top of his chosen profession by sheer determination and hard work, Dr. Campbell did not suffer fools gladly. He could also be very cunning. While driving down the Ilford High Road in his beloved Wolseley car one evening after Evensong at Southwark Cathedral, he was stopped by a policeman for speeding. Quick as a flash, he wound down his window and with that disarming smile which was a favourite weapon of his, he said, "Dr. Campbell; I'm hurrying to a case." At this the police officer stood aside and motioned him on his way. Yet Dr. Campbell had not uttered an untrue word, because his mother really was ill, which was the reason for his visit, while he himself was a doctor, albeit a doctor of music!

It was not long before sparks began to fly at Southwark Cathedral. A new Minor Canon began Evensong one day by uttering a prayer that none of us had heard before. Immediately the organ loft door flew open and Dr. Campbell poked out his head to utter loudly, "**That's** not in the Prayer Book," emphasizing his point by slamming shut the door. Dear high-churchman Canon Hughes one day had the misfortune to find himself the only clergyman present at Choral Evensong and so had to intone the Responses and Collects (the prayers for the day). He concluded the First Collect in a way that none of the choir had heard before and the resulting William Smith "Amen" was an indescribable cacophony of right and wrong notes. Dr. Campbell was furious, his artistic pride dented. He stormed down from the organ loft, marched round to the choir stalls and up to the Canon as he sang the Second Collect, put his face to his and barked: "Don't you do that again, my man!" The Canon didn't, as the next two collects ended conventionally with the "amens" sung as they should have been. There was never a dull moment.

By tradition in cathedrals, the entire Psalter was read or sung through every month, with psalms at Matins and Evensong every day. At Choral Evensong, they were sung to chants, of which there are thousands. Dr. Campbell's organ accompaniments were inspirational, transforming what could be a monotonous exercise (especially on the fifteenth evening of the month, when there were seventy-eight verses to sing) into something special. If he was in a particularly good mood, the organ loft doors would be opened, which was always the prelude to something exciting happening. Then, suddenly, to the delight of the choristers, he could be seen waving both hands in the air, grinning from ear to ear, sticking out his false teeth, yet still the accompaniment continued - which he played on the pedals with his feet; quite a feat as all four parts were there.

More fun was to be had on High Days and Holy Days when, with great pomp and ceremony, the clergy and choir processed around the Cathedral singing one of those great processional hymns that abound in the English Hymnal. Starting from the choir stalls the first piece of fun occurred if the crucifer unwittingly caught his processional cross in the magnificent brass candelabra that hung from the tower, and set it swinging. However, the main entertainment was to come. After we processed up the north choir aisle, past the organ loft and through the retro-choir, we began making our way down the south choir aisle with the main body of organ pipes on our left and a good view of Dr. Campbell at the console on our right. He invariably had the organ loft doors open so that he could see exactly where we were. Suddenly he would press down the Full Organ pedal which lit up what we called "The Blackpool Illuminations" and hit full organ just as we passed the site of the organ pipes. Our eardrums would be shattered and as usual Dr. Campbell would be grinning from ear to ear, enjoying our discomfort. He did this once too often one Christmas when, after the first hymn had been sung and the Crib was being blessed, as he was finding the second hymn he dropped his book on the keys of the great organ with disastrous effect, much to our delight; just recompense, we thought, for his having deafened us once again.

While this sort of showmanship and the humour with which it was delivered delighted the younger, more impressionable members of the choir, it merely antagonised their older colleagues; not that Dr. Campbell seemed to mind. One of his first actions when he arrived at Southwark Cathedral was to surround himself with young students from Addington Palace, home of the Royal School of Church Music, along with others from London music colleges. Devotees of the traditional cathedral choir arrangement of sixteen boys and six lay clerks, (eight boys, one alto, one tenor and one bass on each side of the choir, Decani and Cantoris), were much discomfited by the addition of these extra singers on Sundays. Truth to tell, five of the six lay clerks were very aged, as were their voices. One of the altos was known to the boys as "Mr. Hooter". The other alto was in such poor health that there was no guarantee he would still be alive at the end of the service. One tenor had the remnants of a magnificent voice, but the other was well past his "sell-by date". One bass was so lackadaisical in his approach that, as the previous regime came to an end, he used to annoy everyone by not even taking the trouble to sing his master's music correctly which was, we thought, an insult to Dr. Cook. Now on a Sunday there could be as many as twenty-four choirmen including nine first-class altos and basses that included Frank Keyte of the BBC Singers and his son Christopher, a future Choral Scholar of King's College, Cambridge and an international soloist in the making. They made a magnificent sound and led Dr. Campbell to introduce such goodies as "Let us lift up our heart unto God", a twenty-minute masterpiece by the nineteenth-century revolutionary cathedral organist Samuel Sebastian Wesley, and Orlando Gibbons' great anthem "O clap your hands together, all ye people".

However, there could be tantrums. On one famous Sunday, while we were assembling in the choir stalls for the afternoon practice before evensong, Mr. Wallace, the kindly, saintly Head Verger, was moving chairs in the nave. As the chairs were grouped together in fours or fives, he could not help but make a noise. Dr. Campbell said, suddenly, "Mr. Wallace, at two o'clock I have a choir practice and you will stop moving the chairs," to which Mr. Wallace replied: "The Provost has asked me to move the chairs." When the appointed hour of two o'clock chimed on the Cathedral clock, Dr. Campbell turned to Mr. Wallace and said sharply: "Wallace, stop moving those chairs!" Mr. Wallace quietly repeated: "The Provost has asked me to move the chairs". At this Dr. Campbell turned around and said to the assembled choristers: "Choir, dismiss!" Naturally, we boys needed no second bidding and vanished. Five of us walked down to Bankside and then crossed Southwark Bridge to visit St. Paul's Cathedral, but suddenly had a fit of conscience and made our way quickly back to Southwark Cathedral. There we found eighteen of the choirmen standing around in the garden outside the Cathedral not really knowing what to do. Five minutes before evensong was due to begin, at three o'clock, we made our way sheepishly into the vestry to get robed for the service. As the Cathedral clock chimed three, the choir processed down the nave, five trebles and eighteen lay clerks. Stanford in C was on the menu that afternoon, so we boys gave it all we'd got, as much of the music was loud. After the service Dr. Campbell expressed his delight at our efforts. However, this proved to be a turning point. Certain people were not happy about what had happened, especially with regard to Mr. Wallace who was a dear man, much-loved and respected, for so many years a faithful verger. He did not deserve such treatment.

Not long afterwards, Mr. Warrell moved on. This was not really his scene, although he was far too tactful to say so. In any case, he had recently been appointed Organist and a Lecturer at King's College, London, where he developed a rather fine choir of undergraduates. In addition to this appointment he now became Organist and Choirmaster at the church of St. Mary the Virgin, Primrose Hill, in north-west London, where the Vicar was the former Minor Canon of Southwark Cathedral, George Timms.

At the Cathedral matters went from bad to worse. Dr. Campbell was brilliant at extemporising on the T. C. Lewis organ, the resulting music often being French in flavour. His extemporisations at the Sunday morning Holy Eucharist, when the choristers and lay clerks processed from the choirstalls to the front of the nave, for the sermon were eagerly awaited. These had none of the gentle reticence of Dr. Cook's musical offerings, but were powerful musical statements which could leave the congregation standing for up to three minutes before the preacher could preface his offering with a prayer, whereupon everyone could sit down. There was, however, a non-musical counter-subject to this music which was provided by the Verger, Mr. Wallace. He had the task of switching off many of the lights in the Cathedral. This he accomplished with the aid of three heavy, noisy switches that, with three loud "clunks", controlled three large fuse boxes. Unfortunately, these boxes were sited next to the organ loft where Dr. Campbell was deeply involved in making music, separated from it only by a thin wooden partition.

In due course, Dr. Campbell became irritated by this unwelcome intrusion into his music and decided to do something about it. One Sunday morning, before the service began, he piled on top of this partition a number of heavy music books. When the appointed time arrived, the choir processed down to the nave while Dr. Campbell extemporised in his usual brilliant fashion. As the music built up in a great crescendo, the first of the loud "clunks" was clearly heard and out went some of the lights. On went the masterly crescendo, but as the second loud "clunk" extinguished another block of lights there was an even louder crash, followed by a sharp cry of anguish as the great pile of books descended onto the head of the unfortunate Mr. Wallace. Then, as the organ music rose to a triumphant conclusion, the remaining lights were switched off gently, one by one, using the small silent switches. The servers now took it upon themselves to join in the fray. They had to pass the organ console when they walked up the north choir aisle to tidy up the High Altar after the service, so they now began to make as much noise as they could, clonking their feet on the stone floor and talking loudly while Dr. Campbell played the final organ voluntary. In retaliation he would now hurl books in their direction over the top of the wooden partition that separated him from them, much to their unconcealed delight.

Yet, despite all the eccentricities displayed by Dr. Campbell, he had many winning ways, especially when dealing with professional musicians and people he admired and respected. When he arrived at Southwark Cathedral, he did not take over the Cathedral Special Choir. Indeed, it was Dr. Cook's good friend Harold Darke, celebrated Organist of St. Michael's Cornhill in the City of London, who conducted the annual Passiontide performance of J. S Bach's "St. Matthew Passion". The distinguished soloists included the famous soprano Isobel Baillie, the contralto Nancy Thomas, the tenor Eric Greene, of Ibbs and Tillett agents fame, who sang the important part of the Evangelist, the bass Norman Lumsden, who sang the part of Jesus, another bass, William Parsons, who sang the lesser parts of Pontius Pilate, Judas Iscariot and the high Priest, plus a tenor long associated with Southwark Cathedral, Alfred Safhill, who sang the tenor arias. The harpsichord continuo part was played by the renowned C. Thornton Lofthouse, while at the organ was Dr. Campbell himself. Most interesting was the pensioning off of the aged Cathedral Special Orchestra, replaced for the first time by Denys Darlow's professional Alexandra Orchestra.

Dr. Campbell used this orchestra himself for the first time later that year, directing a performance of Gabriel Fauré's "Requiem". On starting the rehearsal, he said to the leader of the orchestra, Emanuel Hurwitz: "What do you want me to do?", to which the distinguished violinist replied: "Give a down beat and we will do the rest." So, putting on his benign, disarming smile, Dr. Campbell gave a down beat saying to the orchestral players, "All right, off you go," and from that moment on they proverbially "ate out of his hands".

Dr. Campbell's concert programmes were always adventurous. Earlier that year, on Ascension Day 1954, the Cathedral Choir had sung a special Evensong which included William Byrd's Evening Service for five voices, "Ascendit Deus" by Peter Philips, "In Manus Tuas, Domine" by Thomas Tallis and the great "O Clap your Hands Together" by Orlando Gibbons. There followed an organ voluntary by John Blow, which prefaced a performance of Blow's magnificent motet "Salvator Mundi", which Dr. Campbell always maintained was the nearest an English composer came to the music of J. S. Bach. The concert ended with two anthems by John Blow's pupil, Henry Purcell: the lovely full anthem "Remember not Lord our offences", and the fine verse anthem "O sing unto the Lord". Such a programme was very far-seeing for its day, taking one stage further Dr. Cook's pioneering work on behalf of Tudor Church Music by extending it to include music of the next important period in English Church Music, the Restoration of King Charles II which produced John Blow and Henry Purcell. Finally, perhaps by way of a tribute to Dr. Cook, we sang his fine chant to Psalm 24.

However, it was a concert on Guy Fawkes' Day, November 5th 1955, that completely bowled me over. This began with Giovanni Gabrieli's "Sonata pian'e forte", which was new to me. I had heard nothing like it before. More novelties followed, including Henry Purcell's verse anthem "My song shall be of the loving kindness of the Lord" and J. S. Bach's amazing Cantata no. 53, "Schlage doch, gewunschte Stunde", a mourning aria scored for countertenor, strings, continuo and campanella, the notes of this bell signifying the hour of death. For its time, it was an amazing opening half to a concert that ended with a performance of Mozart's "Requiem".

Sad, therefore, to report that still the lunacies continued in the Cathedral. Back on Maundy Thursday, April 7th 1955, the Office for the Royal Maundy had been sung in Southwark Cathedral, which was, I believe, the first time this service had taken place outside Westminster Abbey. By then my treble voice had changed and I now sang alto in the Cathedral Choir, but that day was surplus to requirements because, as this was a royal occasion, the Cathedral Choir was joined by the Choir of Her Majesty's Chapel Royal. Dr. Campbell also was supposed to share his Organist duties with the Organist of the Chapel Royal, Harry Gabb, but apparently for some time before the ceremony began he locked himself in the organ loft and played one G. F. Handel Organ Concerto after another to his heart's content! Even so, this service was a great success.

Others were less enjoyable. One day at Evensong Dr. Campbell conducted a simple, unaccompanied Tudor anthem and the performance was a disaster. He was so furious that when it ended he tore his copy into little pieces and let them drop to the floor before he stormed back, scowling to the organ loft. Not long afterwards, at another Evensong, when he conducted a similar simple unaccompanied Tudor anthem, the performance went well. He was so delighted that when the last chord had melted away into that lovely Southwark Cathedral acoustic, he beamed at the choir, sticking out his false teeth as he did so, jangled his loose change in his trouser pocket, took out a sixpenny piece and gave it to the Head Chorister before returning to the organ loft, thereby allowing the final prayers to be read.

By now, musical performances were either brilliant or awful. There was no happy medium. The trouble appeared to lie in his dealings with the choirboys. Dr. Cook had been at Southwark Cathedral long enough to develop a foolproof system of admitting boys into the choir at an early age, usually eight years old. He spent up to three years letting his assistant teach them to sight-read, then, because of his old-fashioned methods of voice training, he benefited from their singing a confident treble for at least five years. When Dr. Campbell had arrived at Southwark Cathedral he had been bowled over by the ability of the choirboys to read at sight any music that he put in front of them. Unfortunately, however, he had let the old ways die out and put nothing in their place, with the result that as Dr. Cook's boys were pensioned off one by one, so problems escalated because they were replaced by boys mostly devoid of any musical training. So while the repertoire naturally declined, Dr. Campbell's frustration with the state of affairs increased. Careful study of Cathedral Service Sheets of this era are very illuminating. By the summer of 1954, not only had the boys' voices evensongs on Mondays and Fridays vanished, but there was also considerable repetition of musical settings of the Evening Canticles at full choir Evensongs on Tuesdays and Thursdays. By the autumn of 1955, matters had gone from bad to worse. On Tuesday evenings, Evensong was sung by the Lay Clerks without the choirboys, who now sang at divine service only on Sundays and Thursday evenings.

This was sad, because Dr. Campbell had built up a wonderful morale among the Lay Clerks, particularly the younger ones. Not only did he take great interest in their musical development, but he encouraged them all to socialise by joining them in the Cathedral Café after Evensong. This café was situated in an archway beneath the railway viaduct, opening into the Borough High Street. It was owned by a family of Italians, which included in their number a daughter bearing close resemblance to the famous Italian film star Gina Lollobrigida, particularly in the generosity of her bosoms. Here we whiled away many a happy hour drinking tea or coffee and eating cream cakes. One evening was enlivened by the sight of London evening newspapers bearing the large headline: "Dr Campbell: Bishop of London". This referred obviously not to our Dr. Campbell, but to a certain Dr. Montgomery Campbell who had been translated from the Bishopric of Guildford to that of London.

One Saturday afternoon on which there was a special service in the Cathedral, matters were made all the more lively in a most unexpected way. A few of the younger lay clerks had been enjoying a snack before choir practice. On leaving the Cathedral Café, which we affectionately called "Smokey Joe's", we walked down the alleyway towards the Borough Market beneath the railway viaduct, only to be confronted by an extraordinary spectacle. There before us on the paving stones lay a scruffy-looking man, face upwards, with his trousers down displaying his testimonials! Presumably he had come out of a nearby hostelry very much the worse for wear and in trying to relieve himself in the darkness of the archway had toppled over and gone to sleep. Rather than pass him by, we made sure that he had not hurt himself and then made our way to the Cathedral. After the service curiosity got the better of us and we returned only to find that he had vanished. However, the incident did bring to life for us the words of the Psalmist: "They stagger to and fro like a drunken man."

Dr. Campbell was not at Southwark Cathedral for much longer, but the end came in a most unexpected way. We in the choir had fully expected him to be dismissed, so it is easy to imagine our amazement and pleasure for him when we heard that he had been appointed Organist and Master of the Choristers at Canterbury Cathedral. He might have wreaked havoc at Southwark Cathedral, but at Canterbury Cathedral there was a Residentiary Canon who had worked with him at Ely and understood his worth. How Dr. Campbell loved the term "Master of the Choristers", "*Magister Choristarum*". So many young, egotistic choirmasters like to award themselves this title, but Dr. Campbell was adamant that only Organists working where there was a choir school, as at Canterbury and Ely, were entitled to call themselves "Master of the Choristers", whereas those who worked where there was no Choir School, as at Brecon and Southwark, were plain and simply "Choirmaster".

Other words of wisdom uttered at practices or in our many discourses at "Smokey Joe's" included advice about publishing musical compositions. It appeared that when his first anthem was published he waived a fee in favour of accepting royalties, only to find that the music did not sell. For his next effort he accepted a fee, only to find that this time the music sold all over the world and he lost out on a lot of money. (I have often wondered if this was his arrangement of the carol "Praise to God in the Highest".) He also recommended that we purchase a copy of a book he had written about the "ins and outs" of running a church choir – as if he realised that we wouldn't learn this by attending his choir practices at

Southwark Cathedral! Two of the most entertaining but useless pieces of information which he imparted to us at his practices were the names he gave to accidental, horrible-sounding chords that defied musical analysis: these he called either "Pregnant Ninths" or "Chinese Nineteenths"!

His final weeks at Southwark Cathedral were unbelievable. As the end approached he played more and more outlandish pranks. Perhaps the most startling was his accompanying chaste plainsong psalms on colourful solo reed stops. However, his solo organ playing was about to be missed very much. Who can forget his stunning rendition of the Franz Liszt "Prelude and Fugue on the name of BACH" after Evensong one Sunday afternoon in the Cathedral made prematurely dark by thunder and lightning in a storm raging outside? With his magnificent playing of this eerie and dramatic music and the raging storm outside, the trains for once did not stand a chance!

Dr. Campbell was as happy as the proverbial sandboy at Canterbury, where he was Organist and Master of the Choristers for five years. So happy, in fact, that when the invitation arrived for him to move to St. George's Chapel, Windsor, he was loathe to accept it. Yet accept it he did, out of courtesy to Her Majesty the Queen, but his apprehension was justified. At Windsor he found that many of the Choirmen still held freehold of office and therefore could not be pensioned off. Three of the four tenors, for example, were more than seventy years old and their voices, formerly good, now left much to be desired. Sadly, once again, Dr. Campbell found himself in the midst of controversy. While he worked wonders with the choirboys there was little he could do with the choirmen and, as at Southwark Cathedral, frustrations crept into his work. Sometimes, seated at the organ during divine service, he would give vent to his wrath by lobbing a hymn book over the organ screen down to the floor beneath. Nor did his reluctance to let the royal children play their favourite nursery rhymes on the organ help his popularity. At the start of each term it eventually became his custom to disappear to Ely to stay with his old pupil Arthur Wills and his wife in the Organist's House at the Cathedral where he had been so happy, unable to face the return to work. After thirteen years existing at Windsor Castle, it was rumoured that moves were afoot to oust him, but his unexpected death at the age of only sixty-four relieved him of this indignity. It was a sad end to a brilliant and lovable man.

X

I suppose by this time my father was technically unemployed, although I would go further and suggest that he was unemployable. Now that Holy Trinity Church had been razed to the ground, he was adamant that he would not accept another living. Yet how were we to exist on his pension? While he did take the occasional church service to help clergymen friends, for which presumably he would receive a small fee, Wendy at the same time began to do a little more violin teaching, sometimes flirting with the idea of working for a diploma to support this. Paul, having a lot of spare time on his hands, dabbled with amateur dramatics. For some time already he had been playing bridge regularly in Rotherhithe with friends who dated back to his working days there. Now he involved himself in a play there, which in some ways was controversial. It concerned eyes, and the possibility of transplanting whole eyes or parts of them, a topic which at that time was new and provoked a lot of discussion. I believe that the title of the play was "Eye Will", because this pointed to the possibility of willing your eyes to help people with visual problems.

The play was produced by an extrovert Polish gentleman who was an out-of-work actor answering to the name of Stanislaus. He had achieved notoriety in the popular press on February 14th when, dressed in Elizabethan costume and carrying a large envelope, he had arrived at the gates of Buckingham Palace shouting, "Ho! A Valentine for the Queen" only to be rebuffed by a smiling policeman who said "Send it by post". Stanislaus was an experienced actor and he worked his cast hard and well, and the end product was a play which carried an important message that made a considerable impact. For Paul, however, it became a trial of nerves because not only was his part important, but it had so many words for him to learn that he began to doubt his ability to cope. However, cope he did, but never again did he personally attempt anything on this scale, realising that perhaps he was just too old. My mother suffered a similar experience when she had played the slow movement of Felix Mendelssohn's Violin Concerto at a local concert and had many problems playing in the upper reaches of her violin. Never again did she mention diplomas.

One way my father added to his income was by hiring out some of the twenty-two rooms in the Vicarage, although he never charged much in the way of rent and looked on this as more of a service. The five rooms on the top floor were let to Sid and Tony who worked in some Public Baths nearby. They were kind, considerate and quiet, except on the rare occasions when they had a violent quarrel and Tony would beat up Sid! Even so, they lived happily together for many years and in so doing contributed a little money towards my father's income.

It was at this time that Paul discovered the Talyllyn Railway in North Wales. Only now was this narrow gauge railway being restored. My father was a useful addition to the volunteer workforce that was struggling to make this enterprise work out. Sometimes Wendy and I joined him, camping in tents close by Rhydyronen Station - or was it Brynglas? All I can remember is that at night I was kept awake by the sound of rushing water until I got used to it. My father revelled in it, with his experience on the River Thames. In the daytime while Paul and I worked on the track, Wendy cycled around the lovely countryside of Meirionnydd. One afternoon after the scheduled train had gone past towards Abergynolwyn, the gang we were working in set about changing a rail. Having removed the defective rail, suddenly we heard the shrill whistle of another train approaching. We had not been told about this extra train, so hastily we stopped it and put the new rail in place before it could continue its journey. Sometimes I worked as a relief guard on a passenger train, which also involved selling tickets at the intermediate stations and selling refreshments at Abergynolwyn Station.

One year I prefaced my summer visit by attending an Ernest Read orchestral course at Sherborne School. This was tremendous fun: orchestral playing in the morning, tennis and other sports in the afternoon, more orchestral playing in the evening and dancing after supper. Every night I danced with the same lovely blonde girl, but we were both too shy to swap addresses! In the dormitory after "lights out" there were recitations from Chaucer's Canterbury Tales, usually the naughty bits from the "Miller's Tale" in the original mediaeval English! After this marvellous week I travelled by train all the way from Sherborne to Towyn, which in itself was an adventure. Somewhere along the way I travelled the entire length of the Somerset and Dorset Railway, across into South Wales and continuing up into Mid Wales along lines that Dr. Beeching was soon to cast into oblivion. Imagine my surprise when looking out of the window at Builth Road Station to see above me a higher-level station which took the line from Swansea Victoria to Shrewsbury, high over our line. My train had come from Talyllyn Junction near Brecon to Three Cocks in Breconshire, through Builth Wells to Builth Road (lower level) and now went to Rhayader, Llanidloes and on to Moat Lane Junction where I changed and boarded a Cambrian Coast Line train. This took me through Machynlleth, Dovey Junction, Aberdovey and so to Towyn after an amazing journey which had lasted the entire day.

Towyn was a small sleepy seaside town about which I remember nothing except that in the ancient Parish Church, a ledge on the north side of the nave was the home of a lonely 'cello, a momento, perhaps, of the days when some churches had instrumental bands to lead the singing. One Summer I took my friend Richard Marlow to Towyn for company and we camped close to the beach, which was a big mistake. A violent gale sent in massive waves from the Irish Sea which broke onto the houses on the front and sent spray cascading over the roof tops and down to everything beneath. It also blew away our tent!

As usual, the summer of 1955 was going to find me in Towyn again, working on the Talyllyn railway. First, however, I had had something important to do, namely take my 'O' level exams. I had never doubted that in two years' time, at the age of eighteen, after my time at St. Olave's School, I should be going to the Royal Academy of Music. What I did doubt was my ability to achieve the academic qualifications needed to take the graduate course: one 'A' level pass and five 'O' level passes. So, early that summer I sat my 'O' level examinations but passed only one, inevitably Music. When the summer term ended I went to enjoy my beloved London Schools Symphony Orchestra course for a couple of weeks and then went to while away some more time on the Talyllyn Railway up in North Wales.

One day, unexpectedly, I received an urgent message to return home to London; apparently my mother had met with an accident while riding on her bicycle. When I got back to London I was taken to see her in hospital in Reading. Unfortunately, no-one had prepared me for what I was about to see. The hospital ward was crowded with beds that were filled with patients, but Wendy's bed was the only one surrounded with screens. I was taken through an opening in the screen and gazed down on a hideous figure. My initial reaction was to go back out again, but I forced myself to stay put and look more carefully. Wendy's mouth was completely sunken and no teeth were to be seen, which is how I learned that she used false teeth. All that I recognised were her hands, which she took great care of, with beautifully manicured nails. That was it. Two days later she died, without ever regaining consciousness. My father took the funeral service in a nearby church in the company of only Peter, Daphne and me. From there we went to a Crematorium, where the unfortunate undertaker had forgotten to cancel the canned music. Nevertheless, my father gave vent to his wrath and ensured silence before we all made our final farewells to Wendy. In Paul's own words, this is what happened:

"Wendy Gedge set off for her camping holiday on August 12th, riding a new cycle after many years with a heavier one. This new cycle was her own choice as a silver wedding present and had a back-pedalling brake, to which she was not yet fully accustomed. Going down a moderately-graded hill between Pangbourne and Streatley, she somehow got into a wobble and fell on her head in the road. A witness saw this. She was quickly taken to Battle Hospital, Reading, where for three and a half days she put up a vigorous struggle, though unconscious. One of her family was present or on call all the time and Paul was by her bed when she died at 1.25 a.m. on August 16th without regaining consciousness. She had such serious injuries to the skull that, if she had lived, she might have found herself a permanent invalid, a state of affairs which we all know would be detestable to Wendy. The police and all the people at the hospital were kind and helpful beyond description.

Paul was camping on the river, David filming, Peter about to go off to the Army and Daphne Elizabeth to Sweden with a choir. Wendy had always hated fuss. So we arranged a private Requiem and cremation at Reading and interred her ashes on August 20th in the grave of her own child Daphne Margaret in a quiet country churchyard at Warblington, near Portsmouth."

Paul added one more short paragraph:

"Please forgive this rather impersonal letter. It would be difficult to write individually to everybody who knew and appreciated Wendy. And please do not feel bound to reply. We shall not be at home together for some weeks."

A few days later he wrote to Wendy's mother the following extraordinary letter:

"Dear Mrs. Middleton,
We do not go in for gazing at corpses and it never occurred to me that you would want to do so. Her own children did not want to do so and the only people

who saw her after death were myself (I had to identify the body for the coroner's court) and the medical and police people.

You would not have enjoyed it; her injuries did not make her look at all nice or like herself.

Wendy had trained her children to be independent and they will get on without her, though of course we would all rather have her with us. But one must not be greedy. I am profoundly grateful for the privilege of having had her delicious company for 25 years and feel that I cannot grumble now that she has gone on to a life which she richly deserves.

Yours sincerely,
PAUL GEDGE."

Adding at the end: *"My love to Janet".*

I have never tried to fathom the reasons for the strange relationship between the Gedges and the Middletons. Only after my father's death some years later did this begin to be put right. It was sad.

The local newspaper report filled in a few more details:

"Mrs. Gwendoline Gedge, aged 47, of Holy Trinity Vicarage, Carlisle Place, London, S. E. 1, was cycling to join her husband, the Rev. Arthur Gedge, at Suttons Pool, Sutton Courtenay where he was in camp with a party of seven London boys when she fell from her cycle, receiving fatal injuries.

The Rev. Gedge told the Reading deputy coroner (Mr. A. E. Sheppard) at the inquest yesterday (Thursday) that his wife left home on August 12th to cycle to Paddington, where she would catch a train to Reading and cycle from there to join him. His wife, he said, had been on cycling tours all over the country.

Mr William George Antell, of Streatley Hills Guest House, said that at 2.30 p.m. on August 12th he was in a van outside the Guest House, and had just moved off when he saw a lady cyclist approaching him from the Pangbourne direction. "When the woman was about 25 yards away from me the cycle seemed to wobble and she appeared to lose control of it. She fell off and the cycle landed partially on top of her."

Mr William Henry Robinson, of Henley, said "Mrs Gedge leant forward, apparently to adjust something. She seemed to lose control."

Dr. Oliver Todd said death was due to a fracture of the base of the skull.

The coroner said he would have to make a formal adjournment of the inquest for two or three days, as it was a road accident and they would have to call a jury."

The irony of it all was quite simple: the only extravagant gesture that Paul ever made in his entire married life was in purchasing (adapting words of the Psalmist) "the instrument of Wendy's death." This thought was to bug him for the remaining years of his life. The final poignant twist in the sorry tale is that afterwards, when Wendy's purse was opened it was found to contain just one sixpenny piece.

I was fortunate to have the perfect foil to this tragedy, as I really was involved in filming, as Paul's letter stated. This was one of those events in my life which I would never have wanted to miss. Only the English can make films like "It's Great to be Young" and I was part of it. It told the story of a popular Music Master in an old-fashioned Grammar School, who ran a first-class symphony orchestra despite opposition from a new Headmaster. When the Headmaster eventually did have his way and curtailed the activities of the orchestra, the players and their sympathisers organised a protest which ended with the musicians undertaking a sit-in in the school gymnasium at the start of the summer holiday. Naturally, there were several amusing side issues, but all ended happily and the whole story was a bundle of fun. This was not really surprising, however, when the part of the Music Master, Mr. Dingle, was acted by none other than (Sir) John Mills, while the part of the Head Master, Mr. Frome, was played by Cecil Parker. Among the lesser actors involved were Bryan Forbes, who was cast as a flashy musical instrument salesman working for a firm called, rather aptly, Mellotone, and a young lad barely in his teens, who regularly stole the show in this film and later achieved notoriety on the television, Richard O'Sullivan.

Most of the filming was done in the Royal Masonic School at Bushey, near Watford, where ironically the Middleton family was living at this time. The scenes that involved the school orchestra and the gymnasium, however, were shot at Elstree Studios, Hertfordshire, on the outskirts of London. How I came to be involved began when the London Schools Symphony Orchestra, on one of its courses, recorded the sound track of all the music which was to be played by the school orchestra in the film. This included some of Bizet's "L'Arlesienne", a Polka by Johann Strauss and a sparkling Scherzo specially composed by John Addison, which was quite tricky to play. After this music had been recorded, some of the LSSO players were invited to volunteer to take part in the film as members of the school orchestra. I put up my hand and that was it!

We spent almost three weeks at Elstree Studios, having to arrive by 8 a.m. which was not always easy, but at least we were paid £2 a day each, which covered our train fare, meals, drinks and still left over some pocket money. I was amazed not only by the amount of time spent sitting around doing nothing while scenes were set up, but also by the number of times scenes were filmed. The scene showing food being stockpiled in the gymnasium at the time of the sit-in was done three times, always using the same food. By the last time, much of this had become quite revolting. Whenever the school orchestra played on the set, **we** played, always to our own recordings so that the movement of our bows matched the sound of the music. John Mills as the conductor made a very good job of synchronising his beat with that of our real conductor, Dr. Leslie Russell. On watching the film - and it is repeated on the television regularly - it wears its age well, showing what an English grammar school education was like in the 1950s, reminding us of the courtesy and discipline that went with it and also of the value placed on a good musical education. Yet the story line is good, in turn funny and exciting, delivered with a complete absence of violence and sex, any humour always being clean and pleasant. I am glad I was part of that.

It was not long after this that I saw on the notice board at the Royal Academy of Music while I was there one Saturday morning, an advertisement requesting an Organist to play the harmonium for Sunday morning services at St. Paul's Church,

Camden Square. Why a harmonium? Camden Square contained some pleasant Victorian houses, but its centrepiece, St. Paul's Church, was missing, destroyed during the war. Presumably it had been badly bombed, then demolished, because I learned later that the organ was in store. Indeed, I believe that part of it was put to good use when Noel Mander's illustrious firm of organ builders put an organ into the famous restored church of St. Lawrence Jewry in the City of London. Sunday morning services were therefore held in the large church hall, which had been converted into a church and this was why there was only a harmonium to play. Now that my voice had changed, I sang alto at Southwark Cathedral but was no longer paid. This job at St. Paul's, Camden Square was worth, if I remember rightly, £1 per week which was actually more than I received when I sang treble at the Cathedral. The experience of playing the services would also be of great value to me, because I was terrified of playing a keyboard instrument in public. This was strange, because I would play my violin or viola just anywhere!

Not surprisingly it was at least three months before I began to play even a hymn on that harmonium with any degree of confidence. From that confession, you will gather that I was given the job. As I was also required to accompany John Merbecke's music for the Holy Communion Service, I had many an uncomfortable Sunday morning before I began to get matters under control. The Vicar was a kindly, middle-aged man who fascinated me by possessing a bald head with a small bump on it and because he was not averse to wearing a coloured shirt and ordinary tie rather than a dog-collar; what I would call "disguise". He answered to the most appropriate name of Christopher Christian and the fact that he was addressed as "Father" demonstrates his high churchmanship. He was a good man who did much social work and helped people who were on probation. My year and a half there was important to me, as I just had to get on with playing the harmonium for the small congregation whether I liked it or not. Also, for my further entertainment at St. Paul's church hall, were six young ladies who made up the choir. They were lovely company and most supportive, but were also quite mad and led me a merry dance, particularly their leader, Doris, who was three years older than me. Yet before I moved on they managed to sing a fully choral Evensong, even if only with harmonium accompaniment, helped by an alto, tenor and bass from Southwark Cathedral whom I imported for the occasion, which rounded off a Spring Fair.

Back at Southwark Cathedral, Dr. Campbell had been more amused than upset that I should have deserted him on a Sunday morning now that I could no longer sing with the trebles. Knowing of my situation at home, he must have realised that I could do with the money. One day, when I arrived at the Cathedral for Evensong clutching my viola, football boots around my neck, he took me aside and said that I must play to him afterwards. Strange to relate – and because it was so strange, I remember the incident vividly, I played the Magnificat from S. S. Wesley in F on my viola while he filled in the missing parts on the piano. Afterwards he beamed at me kindly and confessed sorrowfully that he had not the time to help me as he would like, but by way of recompense he had asked one of his musical friends to take me "under his wing". So I met Chris Tanner, who was to play such an important part in the next stage of my life.

XI

Chris Tanner was befriended by Dr. Campbell during the war when they were both in the R.A.F., as was another of the Sunday afternoon singers in the Cathedral Choir, Aubrey Ellisdon. However, it was always a point of fun that, whereas Dr. Campbell and Chris Tanner had been plain and ordinary Aircraftsmen at that time, Aubrey Ellisdon had been an officer and a gentleman and therefore of much more importance. Interestingly, after the war both Aubrey and Chris became parish church organists in London. During the week Aubrey Ellisdon worked in a bank in Sloane Square but on Sunday mornings and evenings he played the organ at St. Luke's Chelsea. This church was famous for a number of reasons; because its first Organist was John Goss who later became Organist of St. Paul's Cathedral and who composed the melodies for "Praise my soul the king of heaven" and "See amid the winter's snow", because Charles Dickens was married there and also because the illustrious composer, John Ireland, was Organist there at the beginning of the last century. Aubrey Ellisdon had a daughter, Hilary, who played the 'cello and, like me, was a Junior Exhibitioner at the Royal Academy of Music which meant that we met up there on Saturday mornings. As I rather fancied her, I offered my services to Aubrey Ellisdon to sing in his choir on Sunday evenings so that I could engineer further meetings between us. There was an unexpected bonus to all this, because after Evensong I would have some supper with the Ellisdons in their flat in Lower Sloane Street, which was very cosy while it lasted. That was not long, sadly, because Hilary was far too sane and level-headed for the likes of me. In any case I soon became involved in the activities of Chris Tanner on a Sunday evening, although I remained good friends with Hilary.

Chris Tanner was Organist and Choirmaster of St. Stephen's, South Dulwich, in College Road, next to Sydenham Hill Southern Railway station. While this may have been a less glamorous church, nevertheless it was situated in a very lovely and interesting part of South-East London. Below it, Dulwich College was but a short distance down the road; above it, ancient woodlands abounded, along with Victorian villas which may have been built when the Crystal Palace, home of the Great Exhibition of 1851, was moved from Hyde Park to Sydenham. Here the young Arthur Sullivan, of Gilbert and Sullivan fame, conducted a clandestine love affair with Rachel Scott Russell of nearby Westwood Lodge, daughter of John Scott Russell who had been a major force first in the creation of this Great Exhibition, then in its removal to this leafy suburb of London. Here also the great French Impressionist painter Camille Pissarro took refuge with a married sister during the Franco-German War. His famous painting of Lower Norwood, London, in 1870, can be seen in the National Gallery; another painting shows the road to Sydenham. Lesser known, however, is his painting of this very St. Stephen's Church and its surrounding woodland which was published in the Times Newspaper on December 4th, 1984, in support of opposition to a plan to build a council estate of ninety-three houses here. Apparently this is the largest remaining area of ancient woodland in inner London, comprising twenty-three acres of oak, beech and hornbeam which it seems had been here largely undisturbed since the Ice Age. Beneath the photograph of the painting was published a photograph of the same scene today which showed it to be much the same now as it was in the 1870's, one hundred and ten years earlier.

Chris worked in the offices of Rowe and Maw, an eminent firm of solicitors in Surrey Street, off the Strand, near Aldwych. He called himself a Solicitor's Managing Clerk, always placing great emphasis on the word "Managing". He was highly valued by his boss, F. Graham Maw, who treated him more as a friend than an employee. Indeed, when Mr. and Mrs. Maw went on holiday, it was Chris who would look after their house for them, as it was not far from St. Stephen's Church. Graham also sang in the church choir and was always generous with the financial help that he gave both to the church and to the choir. Chris himself was a superb pianist as well as an excellent organist. He told me that the famous Gerald Moore, on hearing him play the piano accompaniments to a singer, had invited him to have some lessons, but, sadly, Chris had to earn a living and could not afford to take up so kind an offer. It was fun to watch Chris working at a piano with a singer or perhaps an instrumentalist. Inevitably he would have a cigarette in his mouth with the smoke drifting upwards between his eyes and the ash at the end getting longer and longer, sometimes dropping on the keys if he failed to get it to the ash-tray quickly enough. As an organist he was well-qualified, being both a Fellow of Trinity College, London (FTCL) and a Fellow of London College of Music (FLCM) which was no mean achievement, but he never tried the Royal College of Organists examinations because he was not good at academic paperwork. His *forte* was dealing with people and from him I learned ("absorbed" might be a better word) so much about getting the best from people.

With me, Chris was kindness itself. At Dr. Campbell's request he took me on as a pupil but then went further by making me his Assistant Organist, even sharing his salary with me and buying all my organ music. Coming at a time when my mother had just died and my father, bemused with recent events, really did not know what best to do for me, this was all very reassuring. So I had two incredibly happy years at St. Stephen's Church both socially and musically, even if the evangelical liturgy did leave much to be desired.

The first few months were enlivened by a very dear old clergyman. He was doing duty for the previous Vicar who had either departed this life or just departed, I know not which. On a Sunday evening he would come into the Choir Vestry immediately before Evensong and welcome Chris with the words: "Hello Governor, what's the anthem?", only as he had a speech defect, probably caused by ill-fitting false teeth, this inevitably became: "'Ello Guvna, wash the anthem?", the last three words all running into each other. Even better occurred in the service itself when he sang the responses, because he would reduce the choir to hysterics by singing: "O Lord, shave the Queen". No wonder he never tried to say: "Please sit down", always preferring to say: "Pleash be sheated". At a wedding in the church one Saturday afternoon he went into the service without his spectacles and couldn't read anything, least of all the names of the bride and groom which were printed on the service sheet. Fortunately he knew the service from memory so that all went well until the time came for him to declaim to the Bridegroom: "I take thee," then, in what he thought was a hushed whisper, he asked: "Washyaname?". Then, having been told the Bridegroom's name, he was able to continue. When next he came to address the Bride, exactly the same happened as he declaimed once more: "I take thee, *washyaname? …*" It was a priceless spectacle. When he preached on a Sunday evening I never could understand why an old lady sitting at the front of the nave removed her hearing-aid at the start of the sermon only to replace it in her ear later on. It didn't make sense. All was revealed, however, when it was explained to me that without her hearing-aid, the old lady could still vaguely hear parts of the sermon, whereas with her hearing-aid she could listen to the sound of television programmes being transmitted through the Crystal Palace T.V. mast that towered over the church from the top of Sydenham Hill. Any doubts that I may have entertained over this explanation were swept away when I recorded a concert at St. Stephen's on an old reel-to-reel tape recorder. On playing back the tape I heard no music, only the sound of T.V. broadcasts! Incidentally, so anxious was I to hear this recording that on the train journey from Sydenham Hill back to Victoria Station, I removed a light bulb in the compartment so as to plug in my tape recorder, only to extinguish all the lights on that side of the train. Hastily replacing the bulb, I sat down looking innocent, only to hear a commotion at the next station when the guard angrily reprimanded some unsavoury-looking characters in the next compartment, for interfering with the light fittings. Their protestations of innocence rang in my ears for some considerable time.

The church choir was a happy collection of individuals and from such a wide sphere of life. Apart from Chris's boss, solicitor F. Graham Maw, there was his boss's son Nigel, a future Cambridge University Choral Scholar, who was quite an accomplished musician and often gave us the benefit of his knowledge. Several of the others dabbled in music too. There was a bass named Graham Stewart, who conducted a chamber choir consisting mainly of civil servants with whom he worked in Central London and with whom he sang some quite daring music to an excellent standard. Most interesting was Michael Smythe, a head-strong tenor, who used to roar around on a massive motorbike at frightening speeds. He soon launched the Vista Record Company, a one-man band (himself), which revolutionised pipe organ recordings. Some of the sopranos were accomplished singers who used to learn songs with Chris and then perform them at local Music Competitions in South London or at charity concerts. They were so talented that Chris frequently had to walk the tightrope of discretion to alleviate any possible rivalries between them.

Another bass, a gentle soul named Paul Gibbons, also used to work somewhere in London and was always smartly dressed in collar, tie and suit, carrying a rolled umbrella and a briefcase. "God moves in a mysterious way", for he eventually became a devout, high-church Priest, beginning as Curate of St. Michael's Croydon and ending up as a much-loved Vicar of St. Michael's near to Maidstone, where he strenuously opposed the ordination of women priests, forged links with Orthodox churches in Russia, and was so highly regarded in the community that he was invited to become a J. P. and finally Chairman of the Bench. In his garden, he keeps a donkey who makes an annual appearance in his church at Christmas. One more bass was Humphrey Booth, always immaculately dressed, always immaculately spoken. A student at London University he had an eye for the ladies and made many a young soprano's heart flutter. He too was a useful singer as was his lovely sister Felicity, who had beautiful black hair hanging down to a great length. And there were more of them, a "happy band of pilgrims", many of whom would tread the path down to a smart pub nearby for a pint, a chat and a game of bar billiards after choir practice. As for me, I would board a number 3 bus outside the pub and be back home within twenty-five minutes. What could be more convenient?

Such a diverse collection of singers was held together by Chris. I only heard him once make a mistake with anyone, when in the middle of a choir practice he asked a soprano how her boyfriend was, not realising that the gentleman in question had just dumped her. She stormed out, embarrassed, and did not return for a fortnight or so. Meanwhile Chris would redeem the situation as only Chris could, by passing around copies of Stainer's "Crucifixion", for example, saying: "Find that 'Christ in abasement' bit", adding as an afterthought while puffing away at his cigarette: "What he was doing there, I do not know!" Surreptitious fun and games were to be had in the choir stalls during services too. When the collection bag went its rounds among the choristers during the sermon, some put in money and took out change. During these sermons, Chris was wont to sit with his back to the wall, put his feet on the organ stool, pull his surplice over his head and nod off to sleep. One day the preacher in the course of his sermon quoted a prayer and as he finished with the conventional " ... through Jesus Christ our Lord", Chris, from sheer force of habit, suddenly sat upright and blurted out a loud "Amen"!

On another occasion, the preacher began by congratulating the Organist on his choice of anthem because the words included the text of his sermon, whereupon some of the choristers rose to their feet also in order to congratulate Chris warmly. Such hilarity sometimes extended to other parts of the service. As the fine Hill organ behind the North Choir Stalls was in a bad way, notes often played themselves – what organists call "a cypher". When this happened in prayers, Chris could be seen pulling stops vigorously in and out in an attempt to eliminate the unwanted notes. However, what could not be seen was Chris's foot holding down a note on the pedal board to create this problem and so draw attention to the parlous state of the organ. There was another problem: while some notes stuck (cyphered), other notes did not play at all. So Chris delighted in playing over hymn tunes loudly in the key of D major, knowing that many of the notes would not sound, thereby rendering the music unrecognisable.

This led to concerts in aid of the organ fund. One in particular stands out for the quality of its music, showing the influence of Dr. Campbell and Southwark Cathedral, because although the main item was Gabriel Fauré's "Requiem", supporting this were four interesting verse anthems: "Out of the deep have I called unto thee, O Lord" by the sixteenth-century composer Thomas Morley, "Thy word is a lantern unto my feet" by seventeenth-century Henry Purcell, and two by the eighteenth-century Maurice Greene, "Lord, let me know my end" which was sung at Lord Nelson's funeral, and the little-known "Arise, shine O Zion, for thy light is come". A classy programme indeed for a London suburban parish church with a voluntary choir. Chris conducted, Frank Keyte from the Cathedral Choir was the bass soloist and Eric Fletcher, a future Organist of Llandaff Cathedral but at that time a Cambridge University Organ Scholar friend of Nigel Maw, played the organ.

I am glad that I was made part of this community at St. Stephen's, South Dulwich, for here was parochial worship with music playing just as important a part as it did at Southwark Cathedral, although at St. Stephen's there was more congregational input. At St. Stephen's, therefore, the choir's contribution was restricted to an anthem in the morning, be it Matins or Holy Communion, and an anthem at Evensong. On special occasions there might be more choral music, but in general the choristers were there to lead the congregation in singing psalms, canticles and hymns and were perfectly content to do so; concerts were the "icing on the cake". At the Cathedral, however, the choristers sang almost all of the service and the congregation worshipped through the choir's musical offerings. Of course, on Sundays there would be hymns for the congregation to join in. At choral communion the Creed always was sung by everyone to John Merbecke's immortal music, but it was worship in which the object of the music was to create a beauty of holiness and "bring all heaven before our eyes". However, I could only enter fully into this life at St. Stephen's by sacrificing my Friday night rehearsals with the London Junior Orchestra and my Sunday morning services at St. Paul's Church, Camden Square. Furthermore the time was drawing near when, in starting my 'A' level courses at school, I also had to start preparing for the audition at the Royal Academy of Music which would decide whether or not I could be taken on there for the full-time Graduate Course. What a strange time, therefore, to start a string orchestra with several of my friends to specialise in playing music of the Baroque era. So was born the Thomas Morley Chamber Orchestra and one of its first concerts was given, naturally, in St. Stephen's Church, South Dulwich.

Life was good and I was content, happy in my music at Southwark Cathedral, happy in my life at St. Stephen's, excited by my Thomas Morley Chamber Orchestra. Even my school report said: "The outlook is more hopeful"! Come summer, my happiness knew no bounds when Chris decreed that Richard Marlow and I should join him and his lady-friend Vivienne, one of the St. Stephen's choristers, on a holiday in Devon. So we set off one Friday evening, driving down the A3 as Richard and I goaded Chris to exceed the 38 mph which seemed to be the car's top speed. In the middle of the night we dozed in a lay-by, in the morning we drove into Sidmouth and I was as happy as a sandboy (although the beach at Sidmouth was covered with pebbles), because in place of a tent and a bicycle I was actually going to stay in a guest house and travel around in a car.

My heart went out to Viv because for the next week we all went on a mega church and organ crawl. Exeter Cathedral obviously was a "must" and while in the city we took the opportunity to watch Exeter City F. C. play. Nearby at Exmouth we found a superb mini nine-hole golf course which just about suited our level of play, but what really took our fancy was a big town church which boasted a lady organist who gave a short recital every week before evensong on Sunday. True enough she did just that and very good it was too, but what we weren't prepared for was the sight of a full church. Ottery St. Mary Church was magnificent, long famous for being a miniature replica of Exeter Cathedral; the only disappointment was the organ. Sometimes we sought out the local organist, but generally he or she seemed to be conspicuous by their absence. One of these displayed the most fascinating brass plate outside the front door of his house declaring himself to be a Professor of Organ, Pianoforte, Singing, Harmony, Counterpoint, you name it he was it, and all with just an L.R.A.M. to his name. Sidmouth itself was the most delightful town, with many gracious Regency buildings and attractive antique shops. One item of interest for me was the town cricket team playing a visiting team on each and every day during August on a magnificent pitch overlooking the sea. One of these teams turned out to be the Old Olavians - the old boys of St. Olave's Grammar School on a tour of South Devon. What a coincidence!

XII

When I returned to St. Olave's in September 1956 to start my final year, my mind was quite made up with regard to a future career. I was going to teach music in a country grammar school and be Organist and Choirmaster at the local parish church. That was my idea of bliss. First, however, I had to get the necessary qualifications. If I passed my audition to the Royal Academy of Music, I still had to pass one 'A' level and five 'O' level examinations before being accepted on the graduate course. At that time there was also one other route to graduate status, which was an FRCO plus five 'O' levels, but at that time the FRCO examination looked well out of reach. Little by little I was amassing my five 'O' levels and had managed to add to Music, (the only 'O' level that I passed at the first attempt), English Language, Latin and French, all of which I passed at the second attempt.

Naturally I was also studying for the customary three 'A' level examinations: Religious Instruction which, while I was interested, I found to be as dry as dust; History, which fascinated me, especially the unification of Italy and that led me to read avidly three massive books about Garibaldi, the great Italian general; Music, which was the obvious choice, which I loved and at which I excelled. Yet there were certain aspects of music at which I did not excel, notably harmony and counterpoint and the problem here was exacerbated by the fact that the only other 'A' level pupil, namely Richard Marlow, could do this work so effortlessly that we spent little time on it in class and I developed an inferiority complex about it. Indeed, Richard Marlow was an amazing pupil because at this time not only did he win an Organ Scholarship to Selwyn College, Cambridge, but he also passed the FRCO examination, winning the paper-work prize whilst doing so. It was difficult growing up alongside him because he was so good that, unintentionally, he made me aware of my own deficiencies.

That, presumably, was why my Thomas Morley Chamber Orchestra and all my viola playing were important to me. The previous April I had been entrusted with providing some musical items at a concert in the Chapter House of Southwark Cathedral organised by the Southwark Cathedral Old Choristers' Association. Richard Marlow, Leslie Goldstone (who was a friend of mine from the Royal Academy of Music Junior Department) and I had combined to play a Sonata in D major by Dietrich Buxtehude. Then I directed a band of string instruments in a performance of music by Charles Avison and William Boyce, but the *pièce de resistance* was a performance of Haydn's "Toy Symphony" by past and present Choristers and friends, also directed by me. Imagine my delight, therefore, when I was asked to bring my Thomas Morley Chamber Orchestra to play at the Eleventh Annual Reception and Supper of the Southwark Cathedral Guild of Stewards, at which the Guest of Honour was none other than the Archbishop of Canterbury, Geoffrey Fisher. This, on January 19th, 1957, was a wonderful way to start an auspicious year and what made it all the more special was the fact that the venue was the great hall of St. Olave's Grammar School, where I was not expected to do anything so illustrious.

Such an ego trip was but the prelude to my Royal Academy of Music audition which came a few weeks later, early in the spring. Ideally, I would have liked to have made organ playing my first study, but I had not really been playing the instrument for long enough to be sufficiently advanced. So I auditioned on the viola, although even here I was on thin ice because, despite all my orchestral playing, I had yet to take the Grade 8 examination, which was considered normal as an entry requirement. Those of my fellow Junior Exhibitioners at the Royal Academy of Music who had been auditioned had received their result on the very next day and none had been turned down. Imagine my horror, therefore, when on the day after my audition nothing relevant arrived in the post, nor on the next day. By the third day I was beginning to panic and started to consider applying to lesser musical institutions. On the fourth day, thankfully, I received the letter I had been anxiously awaiting, telling me that I had been successful. My relief knew no bounds.

All I had to do now was pass one more 'O' level examination along with at least one 'A' level. I was taking the Mathematics 'O' level examination for the fourth time, along with the 'O' level General Paper. Everyone in the senior school was prepared for this General Paper by the Headmaster, Dr. Carrington. He taught us the history of the U.S.A. and made us *précis* an article from a weekly magazine produced by the B.B.C. called "The Listener". The end product of this routine was that everyone produced decent handwriting (otherwise the weekly essay had to be done again), as well as learning enough to be entered for this General Paper. So my final school examinations came and went and the only tragedy was the lack of any questions about Garibaldi in the History 'A' level examination. On the plus side, however, the music history paper was riddled with questions about Baroque music. As a result of my work with the Thomas Morley Chamber Orchestra, I was in the fortunate position of being able to write copiously on this subject and, more importantly, could support my answer with examples from music that I really did know. The end result was a brace of 'O' levels – Mathematics at last, and the General Paper, plus a pass in 'A' level Music, even if I did do badly in the Harmony and Counterpoint paper. In the Religious Instruction 'A' level papers I received the dubious distinction of an 'O' level pass, while my History 'A' level papers were a glorious failure although to this day I have maintained a great interest in things historical. So I ended up with a total of one 'A' level and seven 'O' levels, but it can be argued that as I only needed one 'A' level and five 'O' levels, I had in fact overachieved by a total of two 'O' levels!

Meanwhile at Southwark Cathedral a new Organist and Choirmaster had been at work for the past year or so, a gentleman by the name of Harold Dexter. He had come to London from the Midlands. As a boy he had come under the influence of George Gray, the illustrious and long-serving organist of Leicester Cathedral where he had been a choirboy. After being Organ Scholar at Corpus Christi College, Cambridge, he served in the Navy for a time until the end of the war, whereupon he became Organist of Louth Parish Church, the stamping-ground of a number of high-flying organists including Michael Smith, later Organist of Llandaff Cathedral. I remember Harold Dexter telling me that this very English country town in deepest Lincolnshire was so old-fashioned that some of its more affluent inhabitants still left visiting cards when making social calls. From Louth he went to fashionable Leamington Spa to be organist at Holy Trinity, another church which produced some eminent Cathedral Organists at this time, notably Stanley Vann of Chelmsford and then Peterborough Cathedral, and Peter Hurford of St. Alban's, who established the great International Organ Festival there.

Harold Dexter was an exceedingly devout man, the only Cathedral Organist I have known to have a prayer desk in his Organ Loft and at Southwark Cathedral that made for cramped working conditions. Having sung at Leicester Cathedral, which relied on local boys for its choir and worked in parish churches, where the treble line also was found in the highways and byways around, he was just what was needed at Southwark Cathedral. No sooner had he arrived than he set about recruiting boys for the treble line and as soon as possible he re-instated the Evensongs sung by boys' voices on Monday and Friday evenings. Initially the Canticles were sung to plainsong and a short anthem was sung, but eventually the Magnificat and Nunc Dimittis also were sung to musical settings for trebles. At the same time the full choir continued to sing Evensongs on Tuesday and Thursday evenings along with the three services on Sundays. Furthermore, he encouraged choirs from parish churches in the diocese of Southwark to come along to sing Evensong in their Cathedral on Saturday afternoons, with the result that Chris Tanner's choir from St. Stephen's South Dulwich, sang on more than one occasion. So, within a couple of years, Evensong was sung on every weekday except Wednesday, which was quite a feat for a Cathedral that had no choir school, although, to be fair, this is what Dr. Cook had also done in the years between the two World Wars.

The fact that Wednesday was a "Plain Day", meaning that there was no Choral Evensong at Southwark Cathedral, was actually fortunate because at this time there was a sudden unexpected transformation of the London concert scene. It was now that Thurston Dart took London music-lovers by storm when he directed the Boyd Neel Orchestra from the harpsichord (this in itself was a revolutionary act) in a series of early evening concerts of Baroque and Early Classical music at the Royal Festival Hall at 5.55 p.m. on Wednesday evenings. Thurston Dart was a highly ebullient character who lectured in music at Cambridge University. Only two years before, he had published a short, fascinating, learned book entitled "The Interpretation of Music", which transformed performing practices of Baroque music. Indeed, I had purchased a copy and modelled my performances with the Thomas Morley Chamber Orchestra upon its contents. A writer in the Observer newspaper went so far as to declare that the book had to be "read by all who perform anything dating from before the nineteenth century." Now he produced the most marvellous series of concerts in which the *concerti grossi* and organ concertos of G. F. Handel and other similar works by J. S. Bach were performed properly. Then he went further and introduced surprise items, the composer and title of which were never revealed until after the performance. So the audience was unexpectedly regaled with organ concertos by John Stanley or Epistle Sonatas by W. A. Mozart, always played with great effect. Next, Thurston Dart renamed the Boyd Neel Orchestra, calling it the Philomusica of London, and equipped all its string players with Corelli bows, which lightened the sound considerably. Always he supplied his own highly erudite programme notes, thereby adding greatly to the understanding of these revolutionary proceedings.

Thurston Dart went one stage further; he began an annual concert featuring the concertos of J. S. Bach and Antonio Vivaldi for three and four harpsichords. At the time this was sensational and the sight, let alone the sound, of four harpsichords took one's breath away. On May 1st, 1956, at the Royal Festival Hall, Thurston Dart, George Malcolm, Denis Vaughan and, of all people, the Australian pianist Eileen Joyce, gathered together as harpsichordists to perform these striking concertos. Still more sensational, however, was the introduction of lutenist Julian Bream, whose performance with the orchestra of John Dowland's "*Lachrimae*" was a revelation. Even the conductor for that concert was a surprise, for there, directing a section of the Philharmonia Orchestra led by Manoug Parikian, was none other than the celebrated Boris Ord, eminent Organist of King's College, Cambridge. Sadly, in the following year, Boris Ord was not well and his place was taken by Raymond Leppard who was soon to take over my great-uncle Stan's position as Organist of Trinity College, Cambridge. Raymond Leppard's youthful, dashing appearance on the conductor's rostrum and the way in which he instilled such vitality into the music excited much curiosity and pointed the way towards his later success as an orchestral director.

This interest in musical scholarship had far-reaching effects. When Harold Dexter devised a musical extravaganza at Southwark Cathedral, he perpetuated Dr. Campbell's idea of adopting a liturgical plan for the event. Beginning with Evensong, he had the Responses sung to music by William Smith, a sixteenth-century Durham musician, a psalm was sung to mediaeval plainsong and the Office Hymn was sung in Latin – "*Christe qui lux es et dies*", using William Byrd's music which was modelled on the ancient plainsong melody. The Magnificat and Nunc Dimittis were sung to music from the Short Service by Orlando Gibbons and the anthem was his masterpiece, "O clap your hands together, all ye people". After this, Harold Dexter played on the organ a *Fantasia in C fa ut* by William Byrd and, as far as I could recollect, this was the first time any sixteenth-century organ music had been played at Southwark Cathedral in living memory. Furthermore, none of us had the remotest idea as to the meaning of "*C fa ut*".

Next came the Mass for three voices, sung by the lay clerks, which was also by William Byrd and still no music had been performed that was composed after 1625, the year that marked the end of Tudor Church Music. The programme was completed by Harold Dexter playing the Fugue in D minor which the great J. S. Bach had arranged for organ from his own Suite for Unaccompanied Violin in G minor, and the Cathedral Special Choir ended the evening by singing Gustav Holst's Two Psalms, both of which are modelled on ancient psalm tunes. While such a scholarly programme was but a prelude to some even better and more enterprising events, for the moment it merely complemented the reputation which Southwark Cathedral Choir already had for its championing of Tudor Church Music, a tradition that dated back to the early years of Dr. Cook's reign as Organist, but which was shared by no other Anglican Cathedral. When in July 1957 the International Congress of Organists brought countless organists to London from Australia, Barbados, Canada, Norway, South Africa and the U. S. A., not forgetting those from around Great Britain, many of them found their way to Southwark Cathedral to hear this music.

By this time there were some quite interesting Lay Clerks in Southwark

Cathedral, because Harold Dexter had continued Dr. Campbell's policy of encouraging students and other people who loved cathedral music to sing in the choir. Harold Dexter also was on the professorial staff at the Guildhall School of Music, with the result that some of its students found their way to the Cathedral. Among the more illustrious of these singers were Michael Blackley, later a Vicar Choral of St. Paul's Cathedral, along with Graham Sorrell, who moved on to Salisbury Cathedral and then to St. George's Chapel, Windsor, where he achieved notoriety by being the first Lay Clerk in living memory to resign when he too was appointed a Vicar Choral of St. Paul's. Another was Roger Cleverden, who moved on to be a Lay Vicar at Westminster Abbey, not forgetting the two Davids, David Hill, later a Lay Clerk at St. Alban's Cathedral, and David Huke, a brilliant jazz pianist, who later became a Lay Clerk at Hereford Cathedral. One that stayed for many years was Lewis Burden, an engineer who was endowed with a lovely tenor voice and drove a beautiful old Morris car. Eventually he transferred to Hampstead Parish Church, where a certain Martindale Sidwell ran what was generally considered to be the finest ecclesiastical choir in London.

The most interesting appointment made to an actual Lay Clerkship was that of James Perry, a counter-tenor with an amazingly large voice, who had been recommended to Harold Dexter by a fellow Professor at the Guildhall School of Music. James Perry worked by day in a warehouse where, it was rumoured, he was the foreman in charge of a large number of women packers. When first he appeared at the Cathedral and sang, there were some in the choir who, hearing his high voice and remembering the nature of his work, could not but be reminded of the eunuchs in charge of harems that appeared every so often in Old Testament lessons at Evensong. So little experience had James of Cathedral Music that I was deputed to sing alto next to him to guide him through the psalms that featured so prominently at Evensong but were so difficult for the uninitiated to sing. As he gained in experience so he increased in confidence, with the result that his voice blossomed accordingly. Soon his easy-going nature, his cheerful disposition and his magnificent voice made him an integral part of the Cathedral Choir.

Harold Dexter was not one to let such a voice go to waste. One Sunday afternoon the anthem at Evensong was Samuel Sebastian Wesley's lengthy "Let us lift up our heart unto God" which is rarely performed in its entirety. At its centre is a magnificent aria, "Thou O Lord God, art the thing that I long for", a *tour de force* for bass soloist. Unfortunately, Harold Dexter had noticed that in the copy, in small print, was the suggestion that this could also be sung by an alto voice. Not being one to shy away from controversy, he decreed that when next this particular anthem was sung, James Perry should sing the aria. So it came to pass that the Cathedral Choir was given the unique opportunity of hearing this wonderful music sung most passionately by an alto. Indeed, it is quite possible that never before nor never since has that aria been sung in this way. James's impassioned plea of "Thou art my God" towards the end, with his voice rising to its highest point, was full of an intensity that could only be described as magnificent but at the same time was almost obscene, simply because such a sound was completely unexpected. A great character, James Perry sang on for a few more years at the Cathedral, where he became the life and soul of the choir, until a career change took him with his wife to the South of England where they now happily run a hotel, visited from time to time by ex-Lay Clerks from Southwark Cathedral.

After Harold Dexter had been working at Southwark Cathedral for around fifteen months, he was asked by Dr. Gerald Knight, Director of the Royal School of Church Music, how he was finding the work. He replied that he had yet to find any flaws in the job. And so it was. Morale in the choir was back up in the clouds and Harold himself was happy. Furthermore he was also supported by his wife, Faith, who started appearing in the Choir vestry after Evensong on Sundays, making a welcome cup of tea for the choir. Sunday Evensongs always seemed to be happy occasions and sometimes we became so high-spirited that Harold would have to call us to order. One Sunday afternoon during Evensong while the choristers were on their knees as the Minor Canon was singing the statutory three Collects, the bass who was kneeling next to Chris Tanner leant across and whispered: "I can have children, the doctor said so." After singing the first "Amen", Chris replied, "I'm so glad," whereupon they sang the second "Amen". While the third and final Collect was being sung, the bass volunteered the information: "You see, Chris, I've only got one ball", whereupon they both sang the final, more intricate, "Amen". So it came to pass that on the Sunday before the wedding of this bass, the anthem at Evensong was William Harris's "O what their joy and their glory shall be", which includes the line: "Those sabbath-keepers have one and no more". On the Sunday after the wedding, the anthem at Evensong was H. K. Andrews's "The spacious firmament on high", which includes the line: "Move round the dark terrestrial ball". I have never been able to discover if this happened by accident or by design.

Such hilarity should not be allowed to disguise the fact that I had now reached a highly significant time in my life. Almost without my realising it, my days as a schoolboy were coming to an end and I was about to become a full-time student. In some ways also this time became a parting of various ways. My good friend Richard Marlow, who for the past two years while in the sixth-form at St. Olave's Grammar School had also been Organist at St. Anselm's, Kennington (Archdeacon Sand's church, where I used to go to make my confessions), was now off to Cambridge University to take up his Organ Scholarship at Selwyn College. In future years our paths were to cross far less as our lives went separate ways. Chris Tanner, meanwhile, had been losing interest at St. Stephen's, South Dulwich, because the new Vicar was not really enthused by the music at the Church. Sadly, after looking at various vacant Organist positions, he left St. Stephen's to become Organist of St. Margaret's, Lee. This church had an air of self-importance, perhaps because it was one of the most carpeted churches in South London and this added to the affluence that shrieked at you everywhere in the building. Furthermore, its Vicar was more than a mere Reverend, being an Honorary Canon of Southwark Cathedral. To add to these illusions of grandeur, any appointment made at the church had to be ratified by the Lord Chancellor's Office, even that of Organist – much to Chris's amusement.

The choir at St. Stephen's wanted me to succeed Chris as Organist and Choirmaster and I would have been happy to do so had I not already been sounded out for another appointment. The former Assistant Organist at Southwark Cathedral, E. H. Warrell, had been Organist at St. Mary the Virgin, Primrose Hill, for the past three years but, much as he loved the church, the fact that it was in N. W. London while his home was in S. E. London, at Eltham, eventually militated against his staying there because of the amount of travelling involved. So he recommended me for this job to the Vicar, the former Minor Canon of Southwark Cathedral, George Boorne Timms. I was amazed that the Vicar even entertained the idea of me being his Organist because he and I had disagreed so often at Southwark Cathedral, largely on account of my bloody-mindedness. However, he must have seen some good in me, because he offered me the job at a salary of £100 per annum which was to supplement my student grant of £270 per annum very nicely. There was one proviso: as plainsong (monastic music) featured prominently in the church services, I was to have lessons in plainsong accompaniment from Mr. Warrell who, after all, was recognised as an authority on the subject. So I was duly appointed Organist and Choirmaster of St. Mary the Virgin, Primrose Hill, London, N. W. 3 ... I was very pleased with myself. Desperate to create a good impression I purchased some smart clothes, including shirts with stiff collars, so that I would look important! A new life was beginning. However, before the parting of our ways, Richard, Chris, Viv and I had one more enjoyable holiday together in Sidmouth ...

XIII

The Royal Academy of Music is the oldest of Britain's music colleges, dating back to 1822, when King George IV numbered among its patrons. Found in Marylebone Road, close to Madame Tussaud's Waxworks, opposite St. Marylebone Church, alongside Regent's Park, the building I knew dated from 1912, but it came as something of a disappointment for what is supposed to be the premiere musical institution in Britain. Certainly it bore no resemblance to an Oxbridge college, nor even to the spacious and grandiose Addington Palace, then home to the Royal School of Church Music. Nor was its setting as striking as that of its arch-rival, the Royal College of Music, which nestles in the shadow of the Royal Albert Hall, standing, as it did then, opposite the extraordinarily ornate Royal College of Organists and having for neighbours the famous Science Museum and the magnificent Victorian Gothic building that houses the Natural History Museum.

If the exterior of the Royal Academy of Music was a disappointment, so too was the interior: dark, dreary and dingy. The toilets left much to be desired, as did the food in the canteen and the sound-proofing in the teaching-rooms. Most unbelievable of all was the existence of separate common rooms for male and female students. Indeed, the ladies "waiting room" was ruled by a Lady Superintendent. It was positively archaic. Nevertheless there were compensations, which chiefly revolved around the personnel of the Royal Academy of Music. There was the minute Dickensian figure of Alf, who looked after the gents toilet; the jovial canteen ladies who so happily dispensed the dubious food often accompanied by a saucy remark; the Porters in the Entrance Hall, including Fred and an Irishman with a gammy leg, named Paddy, who seemed to run the place with the utmost efficiency, rather like the humble Vergers did at Southwark Cathedral.

There was also a vast array of Professors and sub-professors and these included many characters in their own right. The interior walls of the building were fascinating, festooned with large black or brown boards on which were painted in gold or white lettering the names of past prize and scholarship-winning students, some of whom had become international celebrities and household names. Inevitably some had returned to their Alma Mater to teach their successors, often driven by an overwhelming loyalty to the institution where they had spent so much of their youth and from which they had derived so much benefit. This single-minded loyalty was vital because while the prestige of being a Professor at the Royal Academy of Music was enormous, the pay was not! Some Professors had been there long enough to recall the good old days when students had to pay their own fees. They declared how this made them more likely to work than the present-day students who were cushioned from financial hardship by having their fees paid for them by Local Authorities. As for the maintenance grants paid out to them, that was sheer luxury, the "icing on the cake", and it seemed to upset some of them terribly, causing them to rail mercilessly upon us, beseeching us to appreciate our privileged position. Just occasionally these aged Professors would recount how in **their** student days they used to go on an annual boating outing on the River Thames and how on special formal occasions the girls would wear long white dresses bearing a sash on which were pinned the medals that they had won at the annual examinations.

By the time I arrived at the Royal Academy of Music as a full-time student, medals had given way to certificates and outings were no more. Nor was there any accommodation in the building for the students who came to live in London, many feeling ill at ease away from their homes in the provinces for the first time. Perhaps it was this that inspired the recently-appointed Principal, Thomas Armstrong, to hold tea parties for new students to get them to mix socially. Dutifully I turned up at one of these gatherings in time to hear the Principal exchanging conversation about Exeter and Devon with a girl I had not seen before. When he had moved on, I said to the girl: "Are you from Devon?" to which she replied quite simply: "Yes". I asked her if she knew much about Sidmouth and when again she replied: "Yes", I continued disparagingly: "Do you know that Professor who is the Church Organist?" to which she replied enthusiastically: "That's my Daddy." Hastily I changed the subject.

Not long after this, an introductory session found a group of new students, which included me, closeted with John Gardner, who has recently composed an opera "The Moon and Sixpence". A rugged, good-looking man, he was considered the model of a modern musician because he daringly wore coloured linen shirts with striking ties, and he was treated with due deference. He decided to give us a quiz to discover the extent of our musical knowledge. Imagine his mirth when on playing a recording of Wagner's Overture to "The Mastersingers", someone, obviously anxious to impress, suggested that this was the Overture to "The Moon and Sixpence".

Some among my fellow students at this time have gone on to become musical giants. This happened to be a golden age for violinists, the best of whom were John Georgiadis, a future leader of the London Symphony Orchestra, and Kenneth Sillito who later led the English Chamber Orchestra. Other student of this era also reached positions of eminence in their chosen profession. The flautist Atarah Ben Tovim first joined the Royal Liverpool Philharmonic Orchestra. Later with her "Atarah's Band Box" and bubbly personality, she developed a new and revolutionary approach to music-making with children. The clarinettist Alan Hacker carved out a name for himself in the world of contemporary music; so did the soprano Jane Manning. The Welsh soprano Elizabeth Vaughan has achieved much in the world of opera. However, among the most interesting of these students was Steuart Bedford, brother of the composer David Bedford. While at the Royal Academy of Music he became Organist of a church in Tottenham where he devised a complicated gadget which was connected up to the organ keyboard from the choir stalls by a length of string and, when pulled, could supply him with a chord to enable the choir to start singing the next unaccompanied ditty. As fine a pianist as he was an organist, Steuart actually went on to accomplish much as an orchestral and operatic conductor, particularly in connection with the Aldeburgh Festival.

Three other organists of this generation deserve mention. Simon Preston went from the Royal Academy of Music to King's College, Cambridge, where he was Organ Scholar, which is always a stepping-stone to greatness. So he became in turn

Assistant Organist of Westminster Abbey, Organist of Christ Church Cathedral Oxford, then finally Organist of Westminster Abbey from which position he courageously retired at quite an early age, partly as a protest against the adoption of modern liturgies and partly so that he could devote more time to his blossoming career as an international organ recitalist. The second of these Organists was the unorthodox yet remarkable Barry Rose. He came to the Royal Academy of Music from an office and deliberately shunned all examinations that led to paper qualifications. For a while he sang in the choir at Hampstead Parish Church but left it when he was appointed Organist of St. Andrew's, Kingsbury, in North London, taking with him some of the singers who had grown tired of choirmaster Martindale Sidwell's autocratic ways.

At St. Andrew's Church, Barry Rose soon developed a fine choir of his own and, ever an opportunist, having discovered that Leslie Woodgate, conductor of the BBC Singers, lived nearby, he persuaded him to help with choral recitals and this led to broadcasts for his Jacobean Singers. Sensationally appointed Organist of the new Guildford Cathedral without a qualification to his name and with the Dean ignoring all advice, he soon created a remarkable musical tradition there which became the envy of many more historic establishments. That was not all. Some years later he became Master of the Choristers at St. Paul's Cathedral where he led the choir to new heights and brought its work to a far wider audience in recording more popular music, notably the theme music to a BBC TV spy thriller, "Tinker Taylor", when one of his choirboys sang a hauntingly beautiful Nunc Dimittis specially composed by Geoffrey Burgon. The wedding of the Prince and Princess of Wales thrust his name before a world-wide audience, but something went wrong. Shortly afterwards the Dean and Chapter of St. Paul's requested his resignation, a controversial action which was surrounded by mystery and much reported in newspapers. Nevertheless this did not prevent the authorities of King's School, Canterbury, from creating a job for him which he held for a few years until he was appointed Organist of St. Alban's Cathedral.

Meanwhile, in addition to all this, Barry Rose was responsible for religious musical services on BBC radio and for many years the incredibly high standard of the weekly Wednesday Choral Evensong programmes, along with the much-improved singing on the Daily Service programmes, was very much the result of his labours. The third notable Organist was completely different but, despite being a superb performer who was not afraid to improvise an item in a public recital, he eventually went into music administration. So the gentle and lovable David Robinson returned to the Royal Academy of Music to become, first, Director of its Performers' Course and, later, Director of its Graduate Course. Despite the numerous problems arising from such work, his winning ways won him many friends among the students and staff alike.

These three organists along with Steuart Bedford had one thing in common; all were pupils of that remarkable and inimitable teacher Caleb Henry Trevor. Born in Much Wenlock back in the year 1895, of ancient Shropshire stock, he was most aristocratic both in manner and demeanour. At Oxford University, he took a degree in Classics; in music, he was largely self-taught. Nevertheless he was Organist at the Oxford churches of St. Michael at the North Gate and St. Michael's Summertown.

Asked to play the organ accompaniment for John Stainer's "Crucifixion" he did so and received a crate of beer for payment. Asked to play the organ at Blenheim Palace, he was handed a cheque on the return journey and, on examining it, handed it back saying: "Put it in the children's box." A brief period in India as Organist of Calcutta Cathedral was brought to a close by the climate, which did not suit him. Back in England he was one of two candidates on the short-list for the position of Assistant Organist at Manchester Cathedral. At dinner with the Dean, he was far too outspoken and independent, while his rival behaved with due deference and received the required job.

However, he did succeed in being appointed Director of Music at Sherborne School and afterwards was Assistant Organist at Wells Cathedral. Judging by the number of antique prints featuring Wells that hung on the walls of his home in North London many years later, he must have become very attached to this remarkable Cathedral and its unique mediaeval close. Next he became Organist at the fashionable London church of St. Peter's, Eaton Square, from where in 1937 he moved to the Honourable Society of Lincoln's Inn in succession to Reginald Steggal. In that year also he accepted an invitation to join the professorial staff at the Royal Academy of Music. For the next twenty-seven years during term time, on Sundays and special occasions, he played the organ and directed the choir at the Chapel in Lincoln's Inn, while during the week he taught countless pupils to play the organ at the Royal Academy of Music until he retired from both positions in 1964.

As a teacher he was second to none. Often the strong discipline behind his teaching either made or broke his pupils, which was not necessarily bad, because too often recitals are given by organists who are incapable of playing all the notes correctly, a sin which would never be tolerated in a piano recital. I was fortunate to number among his pupils, as playing the organ was among my second studies, but this privilege probably came my way because Mrs. Trevor and my paternal grandmother had a mutual friend. At my first lesson I was full of good intentions and played to him some of J. S. Bach's great Prelude and Fugue in D major, but there were no compliments, only the words: "You need to fix yourself up with a good piano teacher." Then he went on to explain how the art of organ playing is dependent on a good piano technique and in that I was most deficient. I went away very despondent. However, C. H. (as the students called him) was right, as usual. During my years as a Junior Exhibitioner at the Royal Academy of Music, as the piano was my second study I had been taught by a student, a different one every year, with the result that my keyboard technique amounted to a conglomeration of several different ideas and left much to be desired.

Many of C. H.'s pupils were indignant that he was only allowed rarely to teach on the main organ at the Royal Academy of Music, the large, three-manual Hill, Norman & Beard instrument in the Duke's Hall. It seemed that other organ Professors like Douglas Hawkridge and Dr. Douglas Hopkins, had more than their fair share of teaching time on this organ. Yet, knowing the complexities in the mind of C. H., this may all have been part of a plot devised by the great man himself. He did most of his teaching at the Royal National Institute for the Blind nearby, where not only was the organ better, but in addition it was identical to the organ at the Royal College of Organists, which was most helpful when it came to preparing pupils for the ARCO and FRCO examinations.

Regularly, therefore, when I had a lesson with C. H., I travelled on a Bakerloo Line underground train from Lambeth North to Regent's Park. However, on leaving the station I turned not left, to walk to the Royal Academy, but right, to walk towards Great Portland Street and on to the Royal National Institute for the Blind. On reaching this institution, I climbed the many stairs to the organ loft where I would be confronted by the commanding figure of C. H., tall and well built, his immaculate attire culminating in a colourful bow-tie and a handkerchief in the top pocket of his jacket, his brown trilby hat resting upon the top of the balustrade that surrounded the gallery. As there was little room to manoeuvre in the organ loft, I was constantly reminded that if I knocked his hat from its perch I would have to go all the way down the stairs to retrieve it.

My lessons must have been a constant source of boredom to him. I had never excelled as a keyboard player and, try as hard as I could, I pleased him but rarely. The same mistakes crept in with such regularity that he would say: "I will never be out of a job because I say the same things each week" adding with a wry smile: "If everyone did what I said, I would be out of a job, because they would all play too well." As for mistakes, these he considered to be an insult to the composer. "Pay attention to detail," he would say, "Perverting the scriptures and unauthorised readings are not allowed." He decreed that no matter what music you played, always make it sound "as though it was the most wonderful piece ever written." One pupil was told: "Don't play as though you have rheumatism; play neatly and crisply." Another pupil was told: "Remember that **you** are an organist and might be able to stand the row you are making - others may not like it!" Some organs, because of their age and condition, could sound terrible. Nevertheless, C. H. would say: "Never make excuses about the organ: organists have to put up with such things." Continuing on the same theme, he once remarked: "If your organ is out of tune, play French music; their organs are always out of tune." Not being particularly fond of French music he offered the opinion: "Never play French music unless you have a swell-pedal: it helps to relieve the monotony," adding: "When playing French music obey the dynamics closely - use the registration they suggest, because although they were organists, which accounts for the poor music, they did know the various effects!"

Sometimes it seemed that C. H. held organists in contempt. So he said: "Play musically, and above all, rhythmically: never, on any account, like an organist. They are a law unto themselves." To one of his pupils he offered the advice: "Don't play like an Organist." Of himself, he once said: "I am not an organist, I am a musician!" Of J. S. Bach's three "Kyrie" organ preludes he said: "Wonderful music, real musicians' stuff - far too good for the organ. " Of works by the Scandinavian composer Jean Sibelius, he claimed: "Ah! Real music!" He admitted that bad music was "difficult stuff to play" and advised: "Always try to make a musical sound - if it is humanly possible." However on occasions the instruments themselves militated against this, whereupon he would declare: "English reeds are like second cousins to motor horns - bloody awful!" So he suggested: "Try not to offend anybody - choose registration which suits the piece concerned and do so with conviction," adding,

"If the music sounds dull, that is your fault."

C. H. worked hard to ensure that his pupils gave interesting performances. "Listen carefully," he would say, "and concentrate upon the balance and phrasing – the phrasing must be consistent, not merely convenient." As for practice, he advised: "Always analyse the difficulties and find out exactly why mistakes occur. Use fingering which suits the position of the hands, also, before a difficult passage, get your body in the proper position", words of wisdom which, while they may appear obvious, are often completely overlooked. So, too, his observation that "*Rallentandos* and *accelerandos* should be so organised that the listener does not realise immediately that anything unusual has been done." Something obvious, but often ignored, was: "Learn what the organ sounds like away from the console, then make up your mind how **you** wish to play – but always listen and respect other people's views." Another recommendation from C. H. was: "Add stops in rests, and where there is need for a change", but remember that "simple registrations are always the safest, and usually the best." An interesting piece of advice was: "if you wish a part to be clearer, add upwards – not downwards" in tonal pitch. Also valuable was his suggestion that, "when starting a soft piece, never have the [swell] box fully shut; shut it after you have begun and keep the listeners' attention by so doing." C. H.'s comments on the controversial subject of musical ornamentation made good sense: "The type of ornament to be used depends on the speed and context of the piece and," most importantly, "it should help, not hinder, the flow of the melodic line." Furthermore, while "the speed of the ornament should be equal to half the smallest note in the context, the ornament itself must be rhythmical, especially on long notes."

With less able pupils, C. H. insisted on detailed practice; one hand at a time, then both hands together. One day I played to him some music by the late seventeenth-century composer Dietrich Buxtehude, imitating a highly rhetorical performance by a German organist that I had heard and found stimulating. I had not gone far into the music when he stopped me and insisted that first I played the notes with the correct rhythm before I introduced any deviation, suggesting that unless I knew what the music sounded like with the correct note values, how could I introduce any sensible *rubato* effects? One of C. H.'s most interesting comments to a pupil was: "Amateurs practice to get things right – professionals practice to stop things going wrong."

Many a lesson was enlivened by such remarks as: "The organ was made by the devil, that is why it is the devil to play and why organists are such a wicked lot." More drily he said to a pupil who had won the Lady Wallis Budge Prize at the Royal Academy of Music for performance and extemporisation at the annual examinations: "Make sure they don't give you a budgerigar." Of another talented student, he said: "One of my best students used to play the Jongen Sonata, then he joined a bank: sensible chap."

C. H. Trevor himself was a recitalist of rare distinction. In 1935, he had played at the Brussels Exhibition. His recital in the church of St. Sepulchre, Holborn, during the International Congress of Organists in London in 1957 created a sensation, so much variety of sound did he succeed in extracting from the small Harrison & Harrison organ. His programme on this occasion admirably illustrated his catholic taste for music ranging from the 15th to the 20th centuries and ended with a work by Max Reger, whose organ music he had done so much to introduce into this country. Three years later such activities stopped. Always he had maintained that he would retire from giving organ recitals at the age of sixty-five years; when he reached this self-appointed dead-line, he said: "I have never made any mistakes and don't intend starting now." So he turned to editing organ music. For many years his pupils had endeavoured to find organ music that he did not know, an extraordinarily difficult challenge because at one time, so he claimed, his repertoire numbered as many as one thousand items. Few succeeded; indeed my own contribution to this game was to produce, proudly, a sonatina by a certain Valdemar Söderholm, only to be put back into my place when he said nonchalantly: "Ah yes, I play this! The composer and I used to correspond."

Thus for the final years of his life, C. H. produced a succession of books containing the most fascinating music, much of it unknown. His musical taste was interesting. To a pupil he said: "When I became Organist of Lincoln's Inn, I took one look at the music in the cupboard and then shut the lid." Now he set about supplying the average organist with a wealth of good, simple music to play. He cast his net widely and caught many a musical "winner", like the "Three Dances" by Frantisek Tuma, a Bohemian composer who was taught by "the father of Bohemian music", Bohuslav Czernohorsky, in Prague, whose music was in the repertoire of St. Stephen's Cathedral, Vienna, when the young Joseph Haydn was a choirboy there. As an arranger, he was the "Organist's Friend", avoiding the fault of filling the page with a multitude of notes, choosing rather to put only those that were essential. Thus when arranging the orchestral sinfonia to J. S. Bach's Cantata No. 106, "God's Time is Best", for inclusion in a collection of Funeral Music for the organ, he had the courage and common sense to merge the two overlapping solo flute parts into one, thereby clarifying the part without destroying the musical sense. Always in his publications C. H. suggested possible organ registrations, indicating the stops which gave the most suitable tonal colour for each piece. So much interest was aroused by his introduction to each volume of "The Progressive Organist" series that one eminent organist was moved to say: "C. H. Trevor has given away all his secrets."

There was one other Professor at the Royal Academy of Music who was especially good to me. This was John Albert Sowerbutts. Like me he had been a pupil at both St. Olave's Grammar School and at the Royal Academy of Music, but that was more than forty years before my time. His quiet voice and gentle nature glossed over the fact that during the First World War he had been awarded the Military Cross. He had taught for a few years at Winchester College before becoming Organist at Guildford Pro-Cathedral when he was also appointed to the staff at the Royal Academy of Music. He resigned from his cathedral work shortly after the Second World War ended, but continued teaching at the Royal Academy. Later, his additional appointment as Honorary Secretary to the Royal College of Organists showed the esteem in which he was held in the world of organists.

Sadly, by the time I became a pupil of his, he was looking far older than his sixty-five years. Many of his other pupils took advantage of his advanced years by not turning up to harmony lessons, although this worked to my advantage. Sometimes I arrived at 12.30pm for my weekly harmony lessons and two hours later was still there because the next pupils had not bothered to put in an appearance. At school I had detested harmony and counterpoint, but through the patience of J. Albert Sowerbutts I learned to love it. During my long lessons he often recounted fascinating stories about cathedral music and cathedral musicians. At around 1 p.m. he used to unpack his sandwiches and slowly work his way through them; afterwards he usually nodded off for a moment or two. On more than one occasion this happened while he was writing the notes of a ground bass for me to work, whereupon his pencil slid down the page of my manuscript book only to jerk up with a start as he resumed consciousness and my ground bass.

It was through the kindness of Mr. Sowerbutts that I was given the most interesting job of invigilating at the Royal College of Organists examinations, which also brought me some extra cash. So for one week in January and one week in July I would turn pages and assist candidates during their practical examinations at the College organ. Always the ARCO candidates far outnumbered those for the FRCO, but then these included such characters as an elderly gentleman from the provinces who continually entered for the examination although he had no hope of passing it. When asked why he did this, at considerable expense to himself, he explained coyly that it was the only way he could get away from his wife for a few days.

At that time the building was a curious mixture: exuberant decoration outside, dark and dingy inside. What a depressing experience it was to walk up the stairs all the way from the ground floor to the top where the examinations were held. Small wonder so many candidates felt demoralised in such miserable surroundings before they had played a note of music. The large room on the top floor contained the organ at one end and the examiners at the other end, seated at a table. Once upon a time, a curtain had hidden the candidates from the examiners and legend has it that on one occasion footsteps had been heard walking from the door to the organ, then back again without a note being played, as the candidate had lost his nerve! Some candidates did extraordinary things. One appeared with his J. S. Bach music written out in a minute hand on sheets of pocket-size manuscript paper. Another attempted to follow every dynamic marking on music by Max Reger, not realising that this is virtually impossible on a traditional British pipe organ. At one point, in desperation, he gave the swell pedal so hurried and mighty a shove that it bounced back and left him with exactly the opposite effect to what he had planned.

Frequently candidates, in their panic, started playing their piece before they were really ready, with the result that their hands were on the wrong keyboards. During one session a flustered candidate held his hand in the air and made three attempts to land on the correct keyboard. One elderly lady had to have her hands placed on the correct keyboards before she could begin playing. Another candidate, complete with bristling moustache, positively oozing *bonhomie*, proceeded to remove one item of clothing after each item that he played. First to be removed was his jacket, then his sweater, followed by not only his tie but by his collar also, leaving the examiners to wonder what might next be discarded! Far more candidates failed than passed and of those that passed, only two performances remain in my memory: David Lepine, a future Organist of Coventry Cathedral, for his brilliant sight-reading, and John Poole, a future conductor of the BBC Singers, for his imaginative and, at the time, novel registration of a J. S. Bach Chorale Fantasia. Yet this invigilating was most fascinating and the experience made me realise just how unique and important are the Royal College of Organists examinations. Furthermore it was fascinating watching some of the country's leading organists at work examining. I shall never forget the sight of Allan Wicks, who had succeeded Dr. Campbell as Organist of Canterbury Cathedral, stuffing his handkerchief in his mouth in an effort to hide his merriment at the antics of one of the candidates.

XIV

I did not find many of my remaining activities at the Royal Academy of Music particularly satisfying but maybe that was my own fault to a certain extent. I suppose, if I were honest, I had got in by dubious means. By applying for the GRSM (graduate) course with viola as my principal study, I was in a fairly strong position, the GRSM being a teaching course which involved students who were not primarily performers and viola players at that time were in such short supply. In any case I knew that at the earliest opportunity I was going to transfer my first study from viola to organ.

I was given as a pupil to Max Gilbert who led the viola section in the Philharmonia Orchestra until he began to suffer with arthritis. He was kindly and long-suffering over my half-hearted efforts to please him, until one day his patience snapped and he barked at me: "Which is it to be, viola or organ?" I said: "Organ" whereupon he said, "Find yourself another teacher". So I found myself having viola lessons with lovely Winifred Copperwheat, a tiny, gentle lady who played an enormous Richardson viola. We got on famously, largely because she understood where my interests lay, was sympathetic and therefore did not push me too hard for work. With the shortage of viola players somewhat acute, I was thrust straight into the First Orchestra. Clarence Raybould conducted. He was coming to the end of a long and distinguished career and was, I suppose, tired. As he had worked miracles with the National Youth Orchestra of Wales, my expectations were high. However, the first concert I can recall provided me with a frightening experience: I found myself sight-reading a Haydn Symphony, terrified of making a mistake, yet as far as I could remember I had not missed any rehearsals.

The next concert by the prestigious First Orchestra of the Royal Academy of Music really was an embarrassing disaster. The time had been changed from evening to afternoon and presumably Clarence Raybould assumed that everyone in the orchestra knew. The main work was the First Symphony by Jean Sibelius. As the orchestra had worked hard at this, all was going well until at the end of the first page, where the viola part has a number of bars' rest, as do all the other players. Clarence Raybould turned to bring in the two harp players who had an important solo part to play, but to his horror they were not there and the Symphony ground to a halt. Immediately the building was scoured for the two absentee harpists, but they were nowhere to be found. Obviously they knew nothing about the change of time. All Clarence Raybould could do was re-start the Symphony and play it through to the bitter end without the harp parts! What a come-down!!

The Academy Choir was a vastly different affair. This was the province of Frederick Jackson, one of the Piano Professors, who was also Chorus Master to the London Philharmonic Choir. He was not only a fine musician but also was the possessor of a magnetic personality, a born leader. His rehearsals were riveting affairs with compulsory attendance demanded from certain students and rightly so, for much was to be learned. He was particularly fond of making verbal assaults on first-study singers, who, as potential soloists, thought it beneath their dignity to sing in a mere chorus.

What a chorus! Under Freddy's direction it gave an electrifying performance of William Walton's "Belshazzar's Feast", with the Academy Orchestra providing a stunning accompaniment, playing as I had never heard it play before. I had moved down to the Second Orchestra by this time which, conducted by Maurice Miles, I found a much more sane and satisfying proposition. Equally amazing was the performance of Vaughan Williams's unjustly neglected "*Sancta Civitas*", a deeply moving work. Much less memorable was the rendering of J. S. Bach's "Mass in B minor", but only because the Principal decided that he, and he alone, was the person to conduct this great religious musical masterpiece.

Thomas Armstrong, a highly cultured man, was a Cathedral Organist by training. He had been Assistant Organist of Manchester Cathedral and afterwards Organist at the London church of St. Peter's, Eaton Square, before moving on to Exeter Cathedral as Organist and Master of the Choristers (hence his knowledge of Devon), ending this aspect of his career at Christchurch Cathedral, Oxford. At Oxford he also lectured in music and conducted the University Choral Society of which, for a short time, my brother had been Secretary during his student days there. The climax of his life's work came when he was appointed to succeed Sir Reginald Thatcher as Principal of the Royal Academy of Music and in due course, as now so often happened, he received the honour of a knighthood. That Sir Thomas was a deeply religious man there was no doubt, but unfortunately very few of the Academy students shared his beliefs. Thus when he climbed up onto the rostrum to take over the final rehearsals of the "Mass in B minor", then began to preach eloquently, even condescendingly, on the religious implications of the work, his words fell on many deaf ears, particularly on those of students already angered by his pulling rank over their esteemed conductor.

This highly-charged situation became even more tense one Wednesday afternoon when, during a rehearsal, Sir Thomas's chair moved closer and closer to the edge of the platform and a fall of several feet, yet no-one would tell him. Eventually one of the tenors leapt forward to point out to him just how close he was to disaster - a fate to which many seemed only too happy to condemn him. On the morning of the performance, at the conclusion of the final rehearsal in the impressive Duke's Hall, he fervently beseeched all the young musicians to dedicate their performance to Almighty God. Unfortunately, however, all he succeeded in doing was to demonstrate how important it is for God to have effective agents to undertake his work on earth. As the performance began, Sir Thomas raised his eyes heavenward and with a suitably inspired look gave such a down beat as to cause the choir and the organist to start the opening "*Kyrie*" with eight beats to a bar while the orchestra accompanied with four beats to a bar. For some moments he was blissfully unaware of the chaos that he had set in motion.

More disasters followed but these were, I suppose, inevitable. A few days earlier the leader of the orchestra had become ill, so Sir Thomas offered all the violin *obbligato* parts to another student. Naturally, this violinist seized the opportunity of personal glory that had arrived completely unexpectedly, but failed to give ample consideration to whether or not there was sufficient time to do justice to such intricate music. As a result, some of these arias were far from the idyllic experiences that J. S. Bach and the Principal had intended. How sad! Indeed, many hearts went out to Freddy Jackson as he sat in the audience listening to this charade and musing on what the performance might have been.

It was to Freddy that I owed one of the most fascinating experiences of my life. The London Philharmonic Orchestra was to perform Maurice Ravel's music to the ballet "Daphnis and Chloë" in a concert at the Royal Festival Hall and the Royal Academy of Music was asked to supply voices for the wordless chorus parts. I volunteered to make up the number of tenors required, strain though it was, but the fact that the performance was to be conducted by Sir Adrian Boult made all the effort worthwhile. The final rehearsals were pure magic. He directed and, true to form, proved to be a man of few words, having economic hand gestures that were given, oh so clearly, with a baton of great length! It was inspiring stuff! However, when the evening of the concert arrived, London was enveloped in a gigantic, thick, pea-souper of a smog, the like of which is never experienced nowadays. So thick was it that one side of a road was invisible to the other. Not surprisingly, but all the same very disappointingly, the Royal Festival Hall was barely half-full at the start of the concert. As it was, the start had been delayed because the timpani player had failed to put in an appearance. When finally he did arrive it was 8.20 p.m., but only later did the reason emerge. A Southern Region electric train had somehow become derailed and in so doing had subsequently struck a bridge which partially collapsed, only to derail another train. All this precipitated the dreadful Lewisham train disaster and the thick smog could only intensify the problems. On one of those trains had been travelling the poor timpani player, but fortunately for him he lived to tell the tale and to play in part of the concert!

As much as I enjoyed the weekly choir practices at the Royal Academy of Music, less inviting were the weekly History of Music lectures which were delivered in a small, dark hall buried in the bowels of the venerable building. Every session began in the same way: a register was passed around into which we inscribed our name. Eventually it dawned on us that if we also inscribed a few other names then those students could be spared this regular hour of boredom. Nor were keyboard harmony classes any better. Those that I attended were by a Professor who, although highly qualified, was exceedingly boring. As his students, including me, made feeble attempts to extemporise dances at the piano, he attempted to goad them on to greater heights by beseeching them to think of fairies or hobgoblins dancing in a ring! However, Hugh Marchant's aural training classes were a distinct improvement. He might not have been as well-qualified on paper as the Keyboard Harmony Professor, but he certainly knew how to do his job.

His pedigree was interesting. His father, Sir Stanley Marchant, had been Principal of the Royal Academy of Music and before that a highly esteemed Organist of St. Paul's Cathedral. Hugh Marchant himself, as a young man, had been Organist of Christ Church, Newgate Street, the church that stood within the shadow of St. Paul's until German bombs removed it. Now he was Organist of St. Mary's, Bryanston Square, a church situated in a pleasant Regency square behind Marylebone Library. He had an abiding passion for London Underground Trains. He was also very fond of a young lady organ student. However, he was a perfect gentleman and behaved with the utmost decorum: sadly, much as he may privately have entertained thoughts of marriage, he had so formidable a mother living in the South of England that the subject never rose to the surface.

Hugh Marchant was not alone in this dilemma. Others of the professorial staff also formed romantic attachments, only they were far less discreet. One highly-esteemed member of the establishment was seen on a platform in Baker Street Underground Station holding the hand of a blonde pupil. Another was seen walking around Regent's Park holding the hand of one of his students, but in his case this liaison did end in marriage. Most of them, however, just went about their work to the best of their ability, like the slim, dapper Dr. Arthur Pritchard, Organist of St. John's Wood Church, close to the Lord's Cricket Ground. Usually he wore a three-piece, blue, pin-striped suit, with a pocket watch in his waistcoat which he would consult from time to time, frequently punctuating his observations with a sniff through one nostril, almost reminiscent of (but not) a sneer. His gentle but precise remarks were coloured by his Gloucestershire brogue which betrayed his origin. Indeed, he was fond of explaining how, when a pupil of Sir Herbert Brewer, Organist of Gloucester Cathedral, he had never been allowed to practice upon the Cathedral Organ on any but the softest stop (*voix celeste*), yet even this he deemed a privilege. So he would lament the fact that the younger generation of Organists often made so much noise both in practice and performance. Inevitably, then, he would go on to remind his students that when **he** was a student he had to pay his own way as financial grants had been non-existent.

Despite these grumbles it was impossible not to like Dr. Pritchard, just as I could not but admire chain-smoker Robert Edwards, to whom I had gone to have my lack of a piano-playing technique put right. He was a fine musician, so I learned much from him about the inside of music even if he did do little for my piano technique. Frequently he eased me off the piano stool and would then sit himself down to play the instrument and so illustrate the musical point that he was making. Eventually, I believe, the poor pay drove him from the Royal Academy of Music to a new life in Canada, where he was better able to support his wife and young children. No such problem for Leslie Regan, one of the Professors who seemed to have been there as long as the building itself. When he died, followed by his wife, a sum of money rumoured to be a quarter of a million pounds was willed to the Royal Academy of Music for the purchase of a building which could be used as a hostel for first-year students, thereby filling a need in providing somewhere where students could be together.

Always a weakness at the Royal Academy of Music had been its lack of community spirit, as the only place where the students could congregate was the canteen. It was interesting too to see how pupils from a like subject group usually seemed to gather together: the organists – particularly on a Tuesday morning when there was a choir-training class; the singers – when there were opera rehearsals; instrumental players – before and after orchestra rehearsals. Rarely, however, did these groups mix except in the famous soccer team! This was largely the creation of violinist John Farnon. He persuaded the R.A.M. Club to purchase soccer shirts, nice old-fashioned ones, long-sleeved, large-collared, having red and white quarters. Home games were played on a pitch deep in the heart of Regent's Park, where a shower-free hut offered changing facilities. The only problem was George the Park Keeper, who had a nasty habit of cancelling games at the first sight of a heavy dew, let alone a little rain.

Away games were another matter. These found the team boarding an underground train at Baker Street Station at mid-day on a Saturday, bound for some far-flung field in the Home Counties, even Hertfordshire. So soccer matches were played at the luxurious sports complexes owned by such colleges as Imperial, University, King's or Goldsmith and the team would give its all against their sixth, fifth, fourth or even third XI. On the field John Farnon was joined by more violinists: John Greensmith, David Goodall, Edwin Dodd, Frank Doolan and occasionally Jim McLeod and Alan Traverse. Neil Dodd, brother of Edwin, Mike Dunn, Brian Creswell and Brian Martin, all keyboard players, also played. Double bass player Trevor Lowe and Tony Randall, the only blower, anchored the defence, while I played in goal.

The first few games were disastrous, until that magical day came when bass-baritone William McCue arrived at the Academy having just been on trial with the Scottish first-division team Motherwell, but had decided instead to become a singer! Naturally he was a magnificent asset and as centre-half he cemented our defence. Furthermore, he could take penalties. By the 1959-60 season, the team was the best in the London Universities sixth division. Only a poor start, along with a few violinists unable to find deputies for the occasional Saturday matinée, cost possible promotion. Unfortunately, by this time, three years was up for most of the players and this particular team broke up. For John Farnon himself, the crunch came when an important tie against Trinity College of Music in the London University Cup competition clashed with a job interview. So, while John got the job, the team lost 3-4. What has always amused me about this is that, although John was a dedicated socialist, he ended up by marrying the daughter of an admiral, an Academy 'cellist named Margaret Halsey, and spent his entire teaching career working in a famous Wiltshire public school.

Those in the team who were on the Graduate Course now had to prepare for their final examinations. Unfortunately, all had not gone according to plan with the re-organisation of this course. Indeed, it was a positive disaster. A few years before, when I had been a Junior Exhibitioner at the Royal Academy of Music, the Graduate Course had, I believe, been the sole responsibility of the formidable Miss Margaret Donington. I remember students singing her praises, telling how they came away from the Academy with a complete scheme of work covering class music lessons for the first five years in a secondary school, for which they were eternally grateful. Unfortunately, Miss Donington had retired, leaving the powers-to-be with the opportunity to modernise the course in their own way, using us as "Guinea Pigs". Not long before the final examinations it became obvious that all the required work was not going to be covered, whereupon the staff concerned suddenly began dropping hints as to possible questions. When the day of the final written examination arrived, students were ushered into the Duke's Hall and, to this day, I am amazed at what happened.

Students were seated on both sides of a succession of long trestle tables which had been set out close together so as to accommodate us all in the space available, making it a simple matter to assist anyone experiencing difficulties with the questions by turning around answer papers for them to read. It was a shambles. Under these circumstances it was difficult to fail anyone and if I remember rightly, only three people were unsuccessful. One of these was failed supposedly on account of illegible handwriting but, coincidentally, that student was returning anyway for another year having won an additional scholarship, which made it easy for the examination to be taken again and this time, not surprisingly, with a successful outcome.

While on the three-year journey to my final examinations I had acquired the LRAM diploma for organ teaching and had made my first attempt at passing the ARCO. Now, although the GRSM gave me graduate status, it did not give me a passport to teach in a state school although I could work in a private school if I so wished. In order to teach in a state school, a further year of study was necessary for what was called the Dip. Ed. (Diploma of Education) and to this end I enrolled in the Institute of Education attached to London University, which was situated in two Georgian terrace houses close to Euston Station, not far from the Royal Academy of Music. During my year there I would be required to do teaching practice in a Primary School, in a Secondary Modern School and finally in a Grammar School, one month in each, although as far as I was concerned the first two were a waste of time as I was determined to teach in a boys' grammar school!

Despite continuing to have organ lessons with C. H. Trevor at the Academy, I was not exactly looking forward to the next twelve months and vowed that I would keep going as much of my other musical activities as I could to relieve the possible boredom of studying Philosophy and Psychology of Education and whatever else the course entailed. As far as I was concerned, the only psychology of education I understood from my days at home and at school had been a walking stick across my backside from my father if I failed to do my Latin and Greek homework correctly, a smack across the back of my legs with an ebony hairbrush from my mother whenever I was rude and a caning at school if I did anything wrong, all of which seemed to produce the desired results, so why should it be different now? Naturally, in my simple reasoning I had been blinkered. I had failed to understand and absorb all that had been done for me at Southwark Cathedral by the clergy, by Dr. Campbell and Harold Dexter, not forgetting Chris Tanner at St. Stephen's, South Dulwich. That was, I suppose, an alternative psychology, one that was based on kindness and love, on give and take, but that would come later, when I was wiser and more tolerant.

XV

One last evil at the Royal Academy was attending the hour-long Choir-Training class on Tuesday mornings. Firstly, this was taken by Dr. Douglas Hopkins and, as Organist of Peterborough Cathedral and then Canterbury Cathedral, he had never been renowned for his work with either of his choirs. Secondly, there was always the possibility of such eminent students as Simon Preston and Barry Rose being present and as someone in the class had to take a rehearsal using the remaining students as a choir, there was never a rush to volunteer because of the constant fear of being made to look a fool. In any case, it was agreed by common consent that the most successful way of learning about choir-training was to have a church organist appointment. This many organ students did and in learning about training choirs by working on their own church choir, they also earned some extra pocket money. Thus Nicholas Jackson, a future Organist of St. David's Cathedral, had a job somewhere in Notting Hill; David Robinson undertook such work near to his home at Sanderstead before landing the Organist appointment at St. Marylebone, the church opposite the Royal Academy of Music for which John Stainer composed his "Crucifixion" - which made an annual performance on Good Friday obligatory; Robert Cruden, a doctor's son from Exeter who eventually became a lecturer at Southlands College, was Organist at Christ Church, Albany Street; Brian Preston - not to be confused with Simon - was Organist at St. Luke's, Ramsden Road, a church in Battersea where a former Minor Canon of Southwark Cathedral was Vicar; Barry Rose, of course, was Organist of St. Andrew's Church, Kingsbury in North London, while I, by now, had taken up my position of Organist at the church of St. Mary the Virgin, Primrose Hill, half-an-hour's walk through Regent's Park from the Royal Academy.

At that time I had no idea of the importance of St. Mary the Virgin, Primrose Hill, in the history of the Church of England. This was all due to a celebrated Vicar, Percy Dearmer, who had been appointed Vicar in 1900. He had inherited a twenty-seven year-old red-brick church, built in the French Gothic style with a stone-vaulted apse. Within a few years Percy Dearmer had transformed the interior with the aid of whitewash and in so doing had initiated a fashion for all-white interiors which soon spread through the country. As time went on, so he did more. He lowered the G. F Bodley triptych reredos above the High Altar, he had coloured shields made to adorn the pulpit and choir stalls and a rood was also incorporated. When he had finished, he left a church which at that time was unique in Britain, yet all he had done was to put into practice much of what he had advocated in his famous "Parsons' Handbook", published shortly before his appointment to St. Mary the Virgin, Primrose Hill. Here for the first time, the Book of Common Prayer was carried out to the letter and with an elaborate ceremonial that was neither illegal nor contrary to episcopal legislation, despite the suspicion with which it was viewed by the religious hierarchy.

Percy Dearmer had called in the best craftsmen of the day to create appropriate ornaments and fittings to beautify his church: even the hymn-board was something special. However, he went further and insisted on there being good music at divine service. The Mass was frequently sung to plainsong. Furthermore, none of the more popular and sentimental Victorian hymn-tunes were ever sung. To this end he had set about producing a new hymn book which was to contain nothing but the best in both music and words. He even had the wisdom to invite Ralph Vaughan Williams to be the Musical Editor and the future great composer determined that the book be not only a compendium of all the tunes of worth already in use but in addition, "be a thesaurus of the finest hymn tunes in the world". So had been born the epoch-making English Hymnal which had set new standards in such books and later became known as the "Rolls Royce of Hymnals". As a further result, Vaughan Williams had come to compose great tunes for the hymns "Come down, O love divine" and "For all the saints". He had also adapted old folk songs to such hymns as "He who would valiant be" and had discovered the haunting melody which became the basis of his "Fantasia on a theme of Tallis".

So involved had this work become that Vaughan Williams invited the brothers Martin and Geoffrey Shaw to help him and in due course, first one, then the other, had become Organist at St. Mary the Virgin, Primrose Hill. Thus it can come as no surprise to find that the folk tune which Geoffrey Shaw had adapted to the hymn "For the beauty of the earth" is called "England's Lane", for this stretch of road is barely two hundred yards north of the church. Furthermore Martin Shaw composed his "Folk Mass" for services at St. Mary's and within a short time this setting of the Holy Communion was being sung in all corners of the British Isles. Another musician of note who was caught up in the creation of the English Hymnal and subsequently became Organist of St. Mary's was J. H. Arnold, who provided many of the chaste accompaniments to the plainsong that abounds in this book.

I had been associated with this hymn book for as long as I cared to remember. My father had used it at Holy Trinity, Lambeth, and it had also been used at Southwark Cathedral. Now I was about to follow the book to its birthplace. When I arrived at the church to play the organ for my first service I was immaculately turned out in a black suit with waistcoat, wearing a white shirt with stiff collar. I did not have to wait long to make a fool of myself. As I set out to play verse two of the communion hymn I became aware that no-one was singing and suddenly realised that there was no verse two. Embarrassed as I was, Fr. Timms, the Vicar, was exceedingly patient and persevered with me as I grew into both the church and the job. The services were stunning, so well-ordered, but unobtrusively so. The church itself was indeed colourful, but it was also spotlessly clean and kept so by Bob Fake, the verger with a pronounced Yorkshire accent.

The area that formed the parish impressed me very much too. Much of it was owned by Eton College and this was echoed by such street names as Eton Crescent, Oppidans Mews and King Henry's Road. On one side of the church was Elsworthy Road and almost next door lived Eric Robinson, brother of Stanford Robinson, both of whom were notable musicians. At no. 4, not long before, had lived Sir Henry Wood, founder of the Henry Wood Promenade Concerts. This eminent conductor and his wife had entertained here such notable musicians as Camille Saint-Saëns and Jean Sibelius, not forgetting the German Max Reger, who, during luncheon, had consumed four whiskies and twenty bottles of beer. When

Frederick Delius had stayed here for the month of September 1918, he had been unable to bear the ticking of any clocks, so, one by one, every clock in the house had been left to unwind into silence. On the other side of the church was King Henry's Road itself, along which at a respectable distance from one another stood a succession of spacious Victorian villas, many of which had been converted into flats. Along this leafy, tree-lined road lived Ernest Read, conductor of the London Junior and Senior Orchestras who, with his wife, organised some of the orchestra courses that I had greatly enjoyed during my summer holidays. So too lived dear Rita Sharpe, who had conducted the Junior Exhibitioners' orchestra at the Royal Academy of Music that I had enjoyed playing in on Saturday mornings.

Not far away could be found Hugh Marchant, the underground-train-loving Professor at the Royal Academy of Music, and John Poole, soon to become Director of the BBC Singers. At one end of King Henry's Road was Swiss Cottage and the main road to St. John's Wood and Baker Street, at the other end was Chalk Farm and the main road to Camden Town and Euston. Across the East End of St. Mary's went Primrose Hill Road. One end of this led to England's Lane and then on to Hampstead Town Hall, the other end skirted Primrose Hill and ended near to Regent's Park Road and St. Mark's, a very resonant church, and also the famous London Zoo. Primrose Hill itself was magical. Small wonder that, on Midsummer's Day at dawn London's "druids" were in the habit of gathering together at the top for a special ceremony. Often I made a point of going to the top, but only to enjoy the amazing panoramic view of London, as from here can be seen not only St. Paul's Cathedral but also, on a clear day, the Crystal Palace television mast, beneath which stood St. Stephen's Church, South Dulwich. The Vicarage, No. 7, Elsworthy Road, backed onto Primrose Hill, so that when Fr. Timms had a garden party, he would open his garden gate and let his guests spill out on to the lovely grassy slopes.

My priority at St. Mary's was to build up a choir of boys and men and I set about this task with great enthusiasm. I held regular practices, visited the homes of choristers, and in time the Choir Vestry became a hive of musical activity. The clergy could not have been more supportive. In addition to Fr. Timms, there was a young curate, Fr. Peter Thackray. By chance, Fr. Peter had served a previous curacy at the church of St. Mary the Less, Lambeth, a parish which almost bordered my father's parish of Holy Trinity. Strange to relate, Fr. Peter had even brought over from there a Housekeeper for Fr. Timms, Mrs. Keown, whose husband was an ambulance driver. As all three of them knew my father well, as did Fr. Timms, it was not long before the parish team became a happy family. By the time the first Christmas had arrived, the choir was well and truly moving forward, with a dozen or so boys and a few men. Midnight Mass was a magnificent spectacle, with the church lit by countless candles. For this service, some elaborate plainsong had been learned and, while putting the final polish to the music shortly before the service was due to begin, two former choirmen arrived and deigned to offer their assistance. At that time there was considerable controversy over how plainsong should be sung, particularly over whether or not notes should be of a variable duration. My ideas about this had been influenced very much by what Dr. Campbell had done at Southwark Cathedral and he had favoured notes of equal duration. Evidently this did not please the two visitors, who at this last minute took it upon themselves to tell me how we should be singing the plainsong and when I ignored their advice and went my own sweet way, they stormed out, joined the congregation and sang it their way from there!

Unfortunately, the influence of Dr. Campbell was not restricted to music alone. Any choirboy misbehaving in a service might find a small hymn book thrown at him; a hymn sung badly might find me giving vent to my frustration by slamming the large organ stops in and out rather noisily; an anthem sung badly might find me tearing my copy into little pieces in full view of the choir. I had not yet learned to discriminate between the good and bad points of my mentor, yet still Fr. Timms was patient. One Sunday evening, his patience snapped. Certain anthems have nicknames: William Crotch's "How dear are thy counsels unto me" is known as "The Lawyer's Anthem", while John Hilton's "Lord, for thy tender mercy's sake" is known as the "Tart Anthem", because the line "that we may walk with a perfect heart" is often sung incorrectly as "that we may walk with a perfec-tart." On this particular Sunday, the anthem was to be "Let thy merciful ears, O Lord", then thought to be by Thomas Weelkes, now known to be by John Mudd. The choirboy responsible for writing out the service sheets had produced two proper copies, one each for the Vicar and the Visiting Preacher, but had saved himself time on the remaining copies for the choir by designating the anthem as "Luggoles". Unfortunately one of these copies found its way to the Visiting Preacher's stall and Fr. Timms was not amused.

The choirboys themselves were an interesting assortment. There was Maurice Duffield, one of the parish heartthrobs and his younger brother Ivan, who also was a "hit" with the girls. Their father, Mick, sang bass and looked far older than his forty-odd years: indeed, unbeknown to us all, he had not long to live. Quiet and shy David Weaver also numbered among the trebles and eventually became a Head Chorister; his father, Bob, was eventually persuaded to sing bass. Another choirboy was James Jelley, who turned up again in my life unexpectedly working for the examinations department of the Associated Board of the Royal Schools of Music, before even more unexpectedly becoming a clergyman and serving as a parish priest in a difficult part of the diocese of Southwark, where his vicarage regularly received the unwelcome attention of local criminals. His friend Jamie Milford, quiet and reliable, who lived in the same block of flats also worked his way through the ranks of the choir to become a Head Chorister. He, too, turned up again many years later working in a voluntary capacity for the Friends of Cathedral Music. Another loyal and dependable boy in the choir was Steven Lake, whose father drove trains out of Euston Station, past the huge engine sheds at Chalk Farm, through the tunnel beneath Primrose Hill Road and out to the countryside.

Another choirboy had a father who drove underground trains. From him I learned just how disastrous it is for a driver when someone chooses to end their life in front of his train. Such discussion arose because, on my way home from Swiss Cottage to Lambeth North late one night, the Bakerloo line train on which I was travelling, stopped in a tunnel between Regent's Park and Oxford Circus stations. Some minutes after the guard had run through from one end of the train to the other, it limped slowly into Oxford Circus Station where all the passengers were requested to leave. Idling away time, curious also, I wandered the length of the platform towards a cluster of people. There to my horror, I saw a corpse covered over and laid out on the platform. Some yobs laughed and asked heartlessly, "Where's 'is 'ead?" Obvious to all were the wheel marks cut into the body, but there was no blood. This puzzled me, until it was explained later that the person must have been electrocuted first before being hit by the train, because the blood had congealed. According to my choirboy's underground train-driving father, such a disaster has a traumatic effect on the unfortunate driver. Thereafter, for whatever time is necessary to recover from such an ordeal, the driver slows down before every station a few seconds earlier than usual, fearful lest history repeat itself, with the result that, by the time he arrives at the end of the journey, his train is a few minutes late and the entire tight schedule is disrupted. If the driver has more than one such journey on his daily shift, the problem can only be compounded and in the busy rush-hour period, this becomes especially inconvenient.

Other choirboys who stand out in my memory include a tubby dark-haired boy with a Greek name, who tried so hard, but accomplished so little, and a highly musical boy, whose doting mother had gone through a marriage ceremony with a Welshman only to find that he was married already. Two of the most interesting were the brothers Nigel and Noel, highly talented sons of Eric Rogers who had composed the incidental music to the famous film "*Genevieve*" and also had actually played the trumpet solo attributed on the screen to the famous actress Kay Kendall. Eric was a well-built, jovial character who used to drink at the local pub, "The Eton", with his glamorous second wife. The boys, however, lived nearer Finchley Road with their mother, his first wife, an attractive, intelligent lady from Swansea. It appears that this was a sad case of a first marriage where the wife had worked hard to keep the family while the husband struggled to make a name for himself in his chosen showbiz career. When the goal was reached the marriage fell apart as the wife could not cope with the new experiences which inevitably accompanied the bright lights of success.

Of all the boys in the choir, the two most entertaining were Nicholas and Tony Taylor; never did they cease to delight! Regularly in the garden at their home in Fellows Road, they tied to a tree their sister Peggy Anne; then, dressed as Red Indians, they would prance around the tree waving mock tomahawks and uttering blood-curdling cries. When their unorthodox behaviour sank below a certain level, their father was wont to bestow on them a hefty wallop to enable peace to be restored for a while. One Friday evening they departed from choir practice in St. Mary's Church through the Choir Vestry at 8.30 p.m. as was their custom. An hour later, the choirmen also departed from the church, their thoughts focussed on the Eton Hotel, a pint of beer and a game of bar billiards. However, when they came to walk through the Choir Vestry they found it under water, because Nicholas Taylor on his way home earlier had turned on the tap in the toilet sink and then had stuffed a tennis ball up the drainpipe outside.

From now onwards Midnight Mass on Christmas Eve was enlivened by the first breakfast of Christmas that followed at the Taylor house. No longer did I return to Holy Trinity Vicarage. Instead, after the food and fun I returned to the Choir Vestry at St. Mary's to sleep in front of the gas fire. Nevertheless, these meals were famous occasions with lovely food and drink, the children behaving outlandishly, overcome by excitement, with Peggy their long-suffering mother doing her best to keep them all (and her husband Harry) under control. At around this time one year she brought forth yet another child, her fourth, Susie, a reinforcement for Peggy Anne, who became the first of my appallingly-kept godchildren and a second sister for the two boys. Some of the more respectable members of the congregation were quick to express their horror at Peggy adding to her family at this late stage in her life, but then Harry and Peggy Taylor were a remarkable couple. They had met during the Second World War when Harry, amazingly, had been involved in the disastrous Arnhem parachute droppings, yet had lived to tell the tale. After the war, he and Peggy married and then opened a hotel on a hill leading out of the lovely North Devon seaside town of Lynmouth. When an extraordinary flood destroyed Lynmouth they received no compensation because their hotel had been untouched, yet no account was taken of the lack of any tourist trade while the town was rebuilt.

With their livelihood lost, they sold up and went into advertising in London with considerable success, until an unexpected newspaper dispute destroyed this enterprise. By now Harry and Peggy with their young family were living in Fellows Road and attending services at St. Mary the Virgin, Primrose Hill. Soon, through the influence of Fr. Timms, Harry began to work for the Church, taking on the mammoth task of revitalising Christian Stewardship in the enormous Diocese of London. His simple faith led him to adopt a basic approach to this task. For example, while he was not against prayer and contemplation (and how could he be, worshipping in such a deeply spiritual church as St. Mary's?) he did firmly believe in people getting off their backsides and slogging around their parish galvanising others into action. He argued that if people expected the Church to provide facilities for baptism, marriage and burial, they should help to maintain and keep alive this institution. In any case, there was always a chance that so direct an approach might jolt some part-time Christians into the realisation that the Church was alive and well, infinitely worthy of their loyalty and support for more than just these basic needs. Not surprisingly, Harry met with fantastic success. Financial giving throughout the Diocese of London rose by leaps and bounds, with the result that the Church both here and overseas benefited considerably. One outcome of a Christian Stewardship Campaign at St. Mary's was that my Organist's salary was raised from £100 to £150 *per annum*. Successful as that campaign may have been, less successful was a Parish Mission organized by a visiting cleric of note who failed to make allowances for the eclectic nature of the congregation. Disaster was averted only by the tactful, surreptitious activities of the ever-watchful Fr. Timms.

One Sunday morning, history was made at St. Mary the Virgin, Primrose Hill. Instead of young parishioners being taken to another church in the area for confirmation as was so often the custom, this was to be done in St. Mary's itself – on the television! Not only was this to be the first time that such a service was televised, but furthermore, this was to be the one and only visit to the church by the Bishop of London, Dr. Montgomery Campbell. This in itself made the event special, because as Bishop of Guildford this aged and witty prelate had become a legendary figure around whom developed countless legends. One Sunday on entering a West Country church while on holiday, the local Vicar was reputed to have rushed up to him saying, "My Lord, many years ago I took a vow always to preach *extempore* sermons." After the service it was said that the Bishop went to the Vicar and said: "I absolve thee of thy vow." When translated to the Diocese of London in succession to the great Dr. Wand, he proved to be the ideal choice because, although his advanced years suggested a stop-gap appointment, his commanding presence and forceful, grating voice demanded attention. Yet he could be charm itself. On his arrival at St. Paul's Cathedral for his enthronement he knocked loudly on the Great West Door with his crozier, as was the custom, to demand admittance, but nothing happened: the massive doors remained firmly shut. With a twinkle in his eye, he turned to his Chaplain and said gently, "Have I come to the right place?" So he came to St. Mary the Virgin, Primrose Hill, to preside and preach at the Confirmation Service. The only small blot on the occasion was that a rival television company also chose this day to televise a confirmation service. Yet what did it matter? The church looked lovely on the screen, the ceremonial was beautiful, the choir acquitted itself well, the Bishop was pleased, the congregation was happy and countless viewers expressed their satisfaction. All in all it was a great and special occasion, eminently memorable.

Indeed, as time passed by, so much became eminently memorable, particularly the observance of Lent and Holy Week, culminating in the Easter festivities. Obviously Lent began on Ash Wednesday and this was always marked by the cross on the High Altar being veiled and the doors of the great ornamental triptych-reredos above it being closed. Throughout this penitential season, Compline was sung by the choirmen on Wednesday evenings in the lovely South Aisle Chapel. By now Harry Taylor had joined the tenors and Robert Thackray, Fr. Peter's brother, was among the altos. One or two treble voices had also changed, so that these lads also numbered with the choirmen. Another recent recruit turned out to have a personal freshness problem, so that the copious use of incense on Sundays now assumed an importance that had nothing to do with any religious observance but was essential to the well-being of the choir! One Wednesday evening a new bass made his debut at one of these devotional services. Having heard about this strange character in the choir who needed to bath more often, he was naturally curious as to who this might be. That evening six choirmen processed into the chapel for Compline and after a cunning manoeuvre, four ended up sitting on one side while two ended up sitting together on the other, one of whom was the new singer. After the service he reported that his curiosity was well and truly satisfied.

Holy Week itself started on Palm Sunday, when High Mass began with a procession around the church with everyone singing the hymn "All Glory, Laud and Honour": this was to represent the triumphal entry of Jesus into Jerusalem. It was on occasions like this that the William Hill organ of 1872 came into its own, its bright tones adding lustre to the occasion. At the entry to the Chancel a note of drama was added to the proceedings when a veil was ceremonially stripped from the figure of Christ which hung high up on the rood. As the week moved on towards Easter, so at the daily services were read the various stories of the Passion of Our Lord as told in the gospels. On Maundy Thursday evening a Festal Eucharist commemorated the Last Supper. The joyous nature of this contrasted greatly with the stark solemnity of the stripping of the altars that followed in preparation for the next day, the organ silent, the choir singing four large sections of doleful plainsong.

The climax of Good Friday was the liturgical Three Hours' Service lasting from 12 noon until 3 p.m., the hour when Jesus died. This service began gently with the saying of Matins followed by a hymn and the first sermon. The choir then processed in to sing the Litany and Ante-Communion, during which the choirmen intoned the story of the Passion as told in the Gospel according to St. John. One choirman would narrate the story, a bass would sing the words of Jesus, a tenor would sing the words of Pontius Pilate, the Roman Governor, while the remaining choirmen represented the High Priests, the Jews or the Roman Soldiers as they were needed. Afterwards the Reproaches were sung to the magical music of the Italian composer, G. P. da Palestrina, and while this happened the clergy and congregation venerated a crucifix that had been ceremonially unveiled. Another sermon led to a winding-down of the dramatic tension that had been created and Evensong brought the service to a gentle conclusion. After such an emotionally-charged experience it was lovely to go out from the church and melt away over Primrose Hill down to Regent's Park, contemplating all that had happened that day.

Yet despite such seriousness there were moments of light relief. During the final sermon, it became my custom to sit on the steps that linked the organ console to the choir vestry to eat my sandwiches. I argued that, having worked since long before this marathon of a service (there being a children's service earlier), I needed sustenance. Sometimes, however, my conscience pricked me and I thought of Peter who, in a weak moment, denied any knowledge of Jesus. This also reminded me of a former Bishop of Salisbury who, when riding in state in his coach and four, heard a bystander shout, "Very pretty, when your Master only rode an ass" - an obvious reference to Palm Sunday. Then I would take comfort in the fact that when one of my esteemed predecessors, Martin Shaw, had been asked to take part in a vigil of prayer one Maundy Thursday evening, he had requested to be allowed to play the organ instead as he was not very good at praying!

In the hours between Good Friday afternoon and Holy Saturday evening, time hung in abeyance. There was an air of expectancy. As night fell on the eve of Easter, so people were drawn to St. Mary the Virgin, Primrose Hill, for the Easter Vigil, a dramatic service which started in darkness and ended in a blaze of light when the huge Paschal Candle had been lit and Fr. Timms, small and dumpy, with his head inclined slightly to one side, had sung the ancient plainsong *Exultet* in his own inimitable way. High Mass on the morning of Easter Day, "the Queen of Seasons", opened in the only way it could, with a great procession during which the hymn "Hail Thee, Festival Day" was roared to the strikingly original tune by Ralph Vaughan Williams. Banners were carried aloft, the clergy were arrayed in colourful robes, the cross on the High Altar had been unveiled and the doors of the triptych-reredos opened. Clouds of incense hung in the air and the Mass was sung to ornate plainsong. It was glorious! Yet times were changing. Not long afterwards the church was visited by thieves. They stole the new cross and candlesticks that had recently been dedicated to the memory of three past organists, Martin Shaw, Geoffrey Shaw and J. H. Arnold. Worse was to follow. One day a tramp wiped clean what the psalmist called "his hinder part" on the curtain hanging across the passage leading from the church to the choir room. Attitudes were changing; soon the church would have to be locked during much of the day. How sad!

XVI

The Choir Vestry at St. Mary the Virgin, Primrose Hill, was soon doing double duty as a venue not only for church choir practices but also for rehearsals of the Thomas Morley Chamber Orchestra. Furthermore, the church itself, with its generous acoustic and three-second echo, made a superb concert hall. More and more, on Wednesday evenings, the orchestra met there to rehearse its latest finds in Baroque music. Violinists tried out concertos by the Italians Antonio Vivaldi and Giuseppe Tartini and also by the "Father of Swedish Music" Johann Helmich Roman; Ian White delighted everyone with the viola concerto by G. Ph. Telemann; Sally Le Sage sang solo cantatas by Dietrich Buxtehude. Meanwhile, the orchestra had acquired a new leader, Elizabeth Copperwheat, niece of Winifred Copperwheat my future viola teacher. Diz, as she was called, was like an auntie to all the players and a very sobering influence, so lovely and gracious in her ways that we were all very fond of her. Coming from a very closely-knit family that lived in Pinner with a bank manager at its head, a lovely supportive mother, a delightful younger sister, I do not know why she threw in her lot with us. Like most of the other players in the orchestra, Diz was a student at the Royal Academy of Music, but she took her responsibilities seriously. It was she who ensured that everyone was punctual for concerts and properly turned out, that music was in order and that we behaved ourselves, for we were a mad lot and quite irresponsible.

One Wednesday evening Ian turned up at rehearsal riding a smart, new motor scooter. As the players stood outside the Choir Vestry admiring it, someone said: "Hey, Ian, have you got a licence for this?" to which he replied innocently: "Why? Do I need one?" One Saturday found the orchestra rehearsing at Southwark Cathedral Chapter House for a concert that evening. The orchestra had attracted the attention of Montague Cleeve, who was Chairman of the Viola D'Amore Society, and he was playing two Vivaldi concertos. Despite all his pioneering work on this instrument, he did not play it particularly well, which was rather unfortunate because, after the rehearsal, dear innocent Ian put on a cherubic smile and asked if he could try out his viola d'amore and proceeded to play part of one of these concertos perfectly, never having played the five-stringed instrument before. It was most embarrassing. Three months later Ian turned up at a Wednesday evening rehearsal clutching a viola d'amore that he had made from soap boxes. Soon we were performing Vivaldi viola d'amore concertos with great regularity. Not very many years later, when a recording was made of the Choir of King's College Cambridge singing J. S. Bach's "St. John Passion" in an English version prepared by Peter Pears and directed by David Willcocks, the number two viola d'amore soloist was Ian White. Ian White was not the only illustrious member of the Thomas Morley Chamber Orchestra, because sometimes among the violinists was Philip Langridge, whom I had befriended before my Academy days. He had entered the Royal Academy of Music as a violinist and only started singing lessons with Bruce Boyce towards the end of his time there, beginning as a bass, but ending up as an internationally-famous tenor.

Another interesting personality in the orchestra was Mark Knight. He and I had first met when he moved with his family from Kidderminster to London and he became a pupil at St. Olave's Grammar School. From there he went to the Guildhall School of Music to study violin playing with Yfrah Neaman, who was a very special teacher. Mark was passionate about matters of tuning and encouraged me to think more carefully about this. One day he was in ecstasy over some recordings of Schubert chamber music, which he claimed were impeccably tuned; and they were, amazingly so, played by some Czechoslovakians. So he outlined his theories: intervals of a major third and a major seventh sharpened, intervals of a minor third and a minor seventh correspondingly flattened. The key to it all was that performers needed to listen more critically. However, if you follow this advice, the sound of a major chord has added brightness, while a minor chord gains in depth. Naturally this is fine for a singer or a string player, who can make minor adjustments to the tuning, but for a pianist no alteration is possible because the distance between notes on a piano is permanently fixed and it is a compromise to make every note equidistant from the next. One result of all this is that a singer or a violinist accompanied by a piano is not the most ideal combination, whereas a string quartet can sound magical because of this extra careful tuning.

It was interesting, therefore, to hear about two concerts on consecutive days at the Royal Festival Hall given by Russian Orchestras. The first was a magnificent musical extravaganza given by a large symphony orchestra; the second was given by a small chamber orchestra which, by dint of well-nigh perfect tuning, created a volume which resonated around the building and sounded little different in quantity. It was about this time that a parishioner of St. Mary the Virgin, Primrose Hill, gave me a pile of old 78 r. p.m. records of Cathedral Music. There I found an amazing recording of S. S. Wesley's anthem "Cast me not away from thy presence", sung by Boris Ord's choir of King's College, Cambridge. The tuning was so impeccable that the resonance almost hurt my ears, particularly at the words "that the bones which thou has broken may rejoice", where the diction also was well-nigh perfect and added considerably to the effect.

These new ideas I was now able to try out with my Thomas Morley Chamber Orchestra, of which Mark was now a member. As most of the music played was in the clean-sounding Baroque idiom, the exercise became particularly rewarding. The orchestra gave concerts here, there and everywhere in various London churches: in Dorking Parish Church, where the Organist was Desmond Swinburn, the last music master to teach me at St. Olave's Grammar School and, best of all, at the amazing mediaeval church in Thaxted, where the whitewashed interior pointed to the fact that one of the most influential Vicars there had once been a curate at St. Mary the Virgin, Primrose Hill. Small wonder this great church reeked of incense! The orchestra also was much in demand to accompany oratorio performances for groups ranging from choral societies at Morley College and at Holy Trinity Church, Brompton, to the Civil Service choir run by my chorister friend from St. Stephen's South Dulwich, Graham Stewart. Most fascinating was working with the London Transport Choral Society which used to sing at Southwark Cathedral, where the orchestra now also worked with the Special Choir. In this way the players got to know the Passions of J. S. Bach, the oratorios of Joseph Haydn

("The Seasons" being particularly difficult to play), and also G. F. Handel's "Messiah". As for the orchestral repertoire, we played the violin concertos of J. S. Bach and his Flute Suite in B minor, copious concertos by Antonio Vivaldi including those for flute, piccolo and mandolin, not forgetting one for two trumpets, organ concertos by G. F. Handel and John Stanley, concerti grossi by Charles Avison, symphonies by William Boyce and so much more. It was all a wonderful journey of discovery, as at that time little of this music was known to most people.

For the great choral works I often had to find additional wind-instrument players and so I became a "fixer". I would not wish such a job on anyone and I learned the hard way just how unreliable some people can be. Many was the time that players failed to arrive at concerts, leaving me in a cold sweat at the prospect of having to face another irate conductor to explain why he had an incomplete orchestra.

The loyalty of the main body of players was never in doubt, but their tolerance could be tested at times. This happened regularly at Southwark Cathedral, for what seems now to be a comic reason. My friend Harold Dexter had been courageous enough to employ the Thomas Morley Chamber Orchestra on a regular basis to accompany his Southwark Cathedral Special Choir when it was going through yet another financial crisis. However, he had an unfortunate habit of unconsciously spraying saliva when he became worked-up or excited in speech. Richard Marlow, for example, while playing the cathedral organ during a lesson had to watch as one such unsavoury missile struck the top of a page and rolled slowly down all the way to the bottom! So my string players became increasingly reluctant to sit in the front desks of their sections because they knew that they would be on the receiving end of an unexpected shower every so often; nor was this greatly conducive to concentration. Yet working with Harold Dexter had its compensations, because he was very imaginative in his choice of repertoire. At that time, performances of Claudio Monteverdi's "Vespers" were few and far between, yet he masterminded one at Southwark Cathedral and, as modern performing editions had not long been available, here again was history in the making. Neither the singers nor the orchestral players were prepared for the intricate rhythms which abound in this great work but, because the orchestra was not professional (and Musicians' Union fees did not apply) many full rehearsals were possible, which was most beneficial.

More history was in the making when Harold Dexter put on a performance of Handel's "Messiah". Not for him Ebenezer Prout's age-old, well-trodden version as used by choirs throughout the country, not that of the great W. A. Mozart with its additional wind parts. Rather, he had acquired vocal scores of the new, epoch-making edition by Harold Watkins Shaw, which swept away the many ancient customs and traditions that surrounded the old edition of this unique work. First, however, there was a problem. When Harold Dexter tried to hire the orchestral parts, he was given a polite refusal by the publisher, Novello and Co. Ltd., and was told that he could not have them until after the official first performance. His fury knew no bounds. The publisher had advertised the availability of these parts: why, then, could he not have them, particularly after he had taught this controversial version to his choir? Eventually he had his way and actually directed a performance of the Watkins Shaw edition of Handel's "Messiah" in Southwark Cathedral before the official "first" performance.

So the Thomas Morley Chamber Orchestra was part of this auspicious event and I remember still the trepidation that was felt by many of the performers who were making history. "Messiah" was a sacred relic which you tampered with at your peril, yet here was a cathedral full of people presumably expecting a traditional performance. However, there were shocks for them in plenty: some of the choruses bowled along merrily at unexpectedly fast speeds and a harpsichord jangled away merrily in the background; trumpets and drums were heard only in a few choruses; woodwind instruments were restricted to oboes and bassoons; male altos added strength and clarity to the contralto line; occasionally a counter-tenor replaced the contralto soloist; the Pastoral Symphony was transformed from a dirge into a sprightly country dance; most daring, I suppose, was the ornamentation in the repeat of the aria "I know that my redeemer liveth". While all this is now normal, at that time it was tantamount to stepping into unknown territory, as if the cobwebs of two hundred years had been swept away unceremoniously from a masterpiece. Gone for ever were the additions made by Ebenezer Prout. Even the Mozart edition had to be viewed in a new light, with questions asked as to why he had made such drastic alterations to the orchestration.

Performances of the J. S. Bach Passions continued to be a regular feature of the Special Choir programmes and gave the Thomas Morley players the much valued opportunity to become acquainted with such glorious music and to come to terms with its difficulties. Naturally, this was of enormous value to those who were aiming to become professional orchestral players. At the same time, it was also of benefit to those in the orchestra who were to become teachers in provincial communities, where they might be of help to a local orchestra.

If 1959 was the two-hundredth anniversary of the death of George Frederick Handel and an excuse for celebratory events, so too was it the three-hundredth anniversary of the birth of Henry Purcell and Harold Dexter was not going to let that event go by without doing something special. He devised a programme that consisted entirely of music by this illustrious English composer, including the verse anthem "O sing unto the Lord" and the fascinating "*Te Deum*". Again, for many in the orchestra these also were uncharted waters and yet the music was of great historical importance. Unfortunately Harold Dexter was taken ill a few days before the concert. I fully expected the Assistant Organist, Denys Darlow, to take over. He was a conductor of considerable standing in his own right and had masterminded the Tilford Bach Festival, which at that time enjoyed much renown for the quality of its music. Indeed, not long before, I had been amazed that he had allowed me to play my viola in his professional orchestra in a performance of J. S. Bach's "Mass in B minor" at his Festival, something which I had deemed a privilege.

It is easy to imagine my horror, therefore, when Harold Dexter summoned me to his house to ask me to take over this concert. Initially I was not happy about it but he insisted, saying that as I knew both the singers and orchestral players so well I was better fitted to do the job. Denys Darlow could not have been kinder or more supportive and all went well. I remember little about this concert other than the amount of time spent in setting out the chairs for the choir and orchestra, despite the extraordinary *Te Deum*, so unlike C. V. Stanford in B flat or C, yet so obviously a model for Handel's more celebrated Dettingen Te Deum which appeared some fifty years later.

Unbeknown to me, in the audience at that concert was a young Welsh music student, from the Royal Academy of Music who was also a pupil of C. H. Trevor and who was later to play a big part in my life. She was a considerably better organist that me, having at the end of her first year won the prize awarded to the student who gave the best performance in the annual examinations and in her second year winning an organ scholarship. She made her mark on me a few weeks after the concert when I saw her storm down the main staircase in the Royal Academy of Music in a temper, after an organ lesson during which the student awaiting the next lesson had made some derogatory "tut tut" noises behind her back while she was playing. C. H. Trevor had tried to console her by pointing out that this student was not good enough even to begin learning the piece she had been playing, but still she was in a fury as she descended the stairs. I was fascinated. I decided to find out more about her and to that end enlisted the help of some fellow students. One Saturday afternoon during the summer term, after the football season had ended, a number of us found ourselves at Felsted (of all places!), a public school in Essex, maybe because one of my old St. Olave's Grammar School music masters, Harold Last, was there and I had used him as an excuse. I engineered other reasons for the two of us to meet up as often as I could, so that I slowly worked my way into her confidence.

When the summer term ended, however, she returned to her home in Kidwelly (mid-way between Llanelli and Carmarthen), while I remained in London. An eight-week holiday is a long time, so eventually I wrote to suggest a meeting one day in Bath and she agreed readily. As my train drew into Bath I could see her on the platform, but when we met up she looked a little sheepish. She went on to explain that in preparation for the trip she had visited the local hairdresser in Kidwelly who had pruned the back of her hair rather drastically and given her what in South London would have been called a "tupenny 'aul-off".

Before the end of the holiday, I made my first visit to Kidwelly. This is a small town of great antiquity with a charter dating back to around 1115, a fascinating ruined mediaeval castle which deserves to be better known and a beautiful church, also mediaeval, which boasts the tallest spire in Wales. The townsfolk are very proud of their heritage and the local boast is that anything produced in Kidwelly is twice as good or twice as big as anywhere else in the neighbourhood. At that time, the main street was a nightmare, because it was not only busy with traffic from Llanelli and Carmarthen, but it was also the main shopping thoroughfare. There were shops of all descriptions on both sides of the road: a bakery, a butcher, two chemists, a shoe shop owned by the conductor of the local choir, a newsagent, an Italian café, a hardware store and two general stores (not forgetting the statutory fish-and-chip shop), the local council office, two pubs and the Working Men's Club. Another road leading off this main road towards the railway station led to a hair-dresser and to the Post Office, where people kept up to date with the latest local gossip. There were even two part-time banks which were manned by peripatetic bank clerks to serve the town's financial needs. Unfortunately the road could only just accommodate traffic in two directions, and the smooth flow of traffic was not assisted by the number of cars parked on one side of the road by the steady stream of shoppers. At certain times of the day pedestrians diced with death as they stepped in to the road to find a way round chatting shoppers who were blocking up the narrow pavements.

At the far end of the street was an ancient stone bridge which carried the road over the River Gwendraeth that flowed between the castle and the church, through the centre of the town and out towards the sea. Being tidal, the river was full of water for part of the day, while for the other part of the day mud banks reigned supreme. Many years before, when the Great Western Railway had built a new bridge to carry the railway line over the river, an offer had been made to the town council to dam the river so that it would always be full of water, but this was refused. Next to this bridge was the English Methodist Chapel. Afterwards, a small car park bordered on to Bridgend House and its large garden, which was where Hazel (for that was my beloved's name) lived with her English mother, Mabel, and Welsh father, John Davies, as well as her aged grandfather Thomas Davies, who originated from Narberth, a lovely, benign old gentleman who said little but was always contentedly observing.

Four generations of Hazel's father's family had been born in Bridgend House, although he had only owned it since 1937, when he had purchased it for £250. Her mother had come to Kidwelly from Oving in Buckinghamshire early in the 1930s. She and her sister Dorothy had worked at the big house, Broome Hill, the home of Sir Alfred Stephens, the local magnate who had made his money out of bricks. Aunty Dorothy was still in Kidwelly living with her husband, Ivor Anthony, at the Llanelli end of that main road, around half a mile away, up Pinged Hill. Bridgend House itself was at least two hundred years old, if not older, and Hazel's father was proud of all that he had done to modernize it, mostly by himself but sometimes with the help of his cousin Olland. With so little spare cash, he had to learn by experience what he didn't know. His workmanship was impeccable - so highly thought of that the local council even let him connect up his own drains to the main town system. However, when he installed the first flush toilets ever seen in the house, grandfather Thomas Davies still insisted on using the privy at the bottom of the garden! In this huge garden were fresh vegetables galore and, for me, pride of place went to the magnificent runner-beans. I grew to love eating platefuls of these covered with butter. The entire garden was enclosed by two high hedges which were hard work to cut, but so beautiful to behold when done.

Hazel's father was quite a character. In his youth he had been full of fun. After watching cowboy films at the town's only cinema, he and his friends were not averse to going down to the river bank to try out what they had seen on the screen. So they would have a go at rustling cows, catching them by the horns to throw them to the ground, until one day a cow's head stuck for a while at a rather odd angle and they ran away to avoid trouble. He had been a staunch churchman all his life and was a good Anglican. His own grandfather had been verger of St. Mary's church when the Church in Wales was disestablished early in the 1920s and had to deal with the troubles caused by the Non-Conformists, who would invade the churchyard during Sunday evensong, claiming that the church now also belonged to them. His father, Thomas Davies, had climbed the tower to ring the bells carillon fashion for many many years, but had not attended a service for more than thirty years because of a dispute with the then Vicar, even though there had been two more Vicars since then.

He remembered vividly the famous Greenwood murder which had put Kidwelly into the national newspapers when a local solicitor was accused of murdering his wife by administering arsenic to her. His grandfather had been one of the first on the scene and had later helped exhume the body from its grave in the churchyard. It took the skill of the famous lawyer, Marshall Hall, and the dubious evidence of a maid to get the accused off the hook, but he did not stay long in Kidwelly. His house is now a chapel: Capel Sul. Hazel's father would take me to the "Boot and Shoe" opposite Bridgend House where, over a few pints of Felinfoel Ale from Llanelli, I listened while he and his cronies recounted stories of old Kidwelly; as they became more and more worked up, so they would drift off into Welsh, returning to English only when they remembered that they had a foreigner in their midst.

It was a different world.

XVII

That my year at the Institute of Education was something of a disaster was largely my own fault. Not only did I dislike the course but I also disliked the premises which housed the Music Department. Externally, the Georgian terraced houses in Woburn Square which provided this home looked lovely. Internally, however, the rooms were heavily sound-proofed using hard boards that were covered with tiny holes which appeared as spots in front of my eyes. These centrally-heated rooms, filled with students, created such a hot, heavy and soporific atmosphere that I slept through most of the lectures, not that philosophy of education and educational psychology interested me greatly. Of the lecturers, one weird intellectual gentleman declared that he was writing a book about Tudor Music and explained how he gained inspiration from dressing in Elizabethan costume. I remember thinking that he himself might benefit from a dose of psycho-analysis.

Another lecturer chain-smoked incessantly, partly (so legend had it) because she had been crossed in love by a famous viola player. However, she was a compelling teacher and from her I learned useful tips about arranging violin music for beginners by implementing the technique of finger-patterns: using the identical distance between the four left-hand fingers on all four strings when writing out the notes - a simple but effective idea. My own tutor irritated me enormously because she (quite rightly) expected me to concentrate on the course work. Unfortunately for her, I had other ideas and certainly did not want my work at St. Mary the Virgin, Primrose Hill, interfered with, nor what I did with the Thomas Morley Chamber Orchestra. Yet, on reflection, she was a marvellous lady, an unsullied spinster, a rare species. This came home forcibly not only to me but also to the other members of her tutorial group on the famous occasion when she was giving us some ideas for class singing repertoire. Passing around copies of a song, she told us that the composer was Gerald "Coshaw", adding suddenly: "Why he calls himself that, I do not know." Puzzled by her remark, we all looked hard at our copies and saw immediately that the name at the top of the first page was, in fact, Gerald Cockshott. Suddenly a sea of faces was wreathed in smiles and many of them disappeared behind these copies, sniggering hopelessly in silence. Yet often I feel shame and embarrassment when I recall this incident because there was so much kindness, goodness and innocence in dear old Doris Gould.

What I really did enjoy that year was my three sessions of teaching practice. The first of these was in a primary school not far from the Royal Academy of Music. Here, the latest fads were all the rage: self-expression and free-discipline, exactly the opposite to life at St. Olave's Grammar School. Presumably the combining of the two top classes into one large class was to enable another member of staff to devote much of his time to producing third-rate musicals with no finesse at all. Sadly, this had resulted in only one pupil passing the 11+ examination in the previous year and had left the girls and boys subjected to poor music. In addition to this, it transpired that the bachelor headmaster and his divorced senior mistress often worked together until quite late in the evening, closeted in the privacy of his office,

My second dose of teaching practice could not have been more convenient as it was undertaken in Archbishop Temple's Secondary Modern School, which was situated in Lambeth Road, next to Archbishop's Park and close to Holy Trinity Vicarage. This was where the Southwark Cathedral choirboys who had failed the 11+ examination were sent to school. The Music Master was the latest Cathedral Assistant Organist, John Flower. Good as he was, I was unable to take advantage of his expertise because on the day I arrived he was taken ill with piles and I was left to undertake his entire timetable of teaching. What a nightmare - made all the worse one day when, during the lunch-time break, an ex-pupil walked into the school armed with a knife, intent on forcibly sorting out a squabble with a boy who was still attending the school! Needless to say, in the classroom the boys quickly brought me under control.

One of the first-floor rooms in which I "taught" was level with the main line into Waterloo Station. Whenever a steam train passed by, the entire class stood up, made a note of the engine number and then sat down again! This room contained gas heaters which hung high up on the walls and which were switched on or off by pulling one of two chains which hung on either side. The boys used to release gas into the room while watching me cross the playground on my way to the lesson, switching off the fire just before I arrived. Because the weather was not cold the fires were never ignited during my time at the school. However, on these occasions when the boys were fooling around, one of them would start sniffing, then ask innocently if I thought that gas was escaping into the room. Naturally, with the smell of gas hanging in the air, I was forced to agree, whereupon the boy would suggest that perhaps he should pull a chain to turn off the offending gas. What else could I do but agree again. So the room would start to fill up again with gas, amidst considerable coughing and spluttering, as gas would be turned on and off with great regularity while we all struggled to find the offending gas jet which, of course, did not exist. I was in a complete mess!

My third and final teaching practice was in John Ruskin boys' grammar school in Croydon and it restored my faith in teaching as part of my future career. Some of these boys sang in the choir of Croydon Parish Church while some others sang in the choir at Addington Palace, then the home of the Royal School of Church Music: both of which were noted for their music. Furthermore, on the staff was the father of the concert pianist Valerie Tryon. The Music Master, a charming, diminutive man whose name I cannot remember was kindness itself. We got on so well together that he kindly gave me a free hand with his classes and I had a lovely time. Interestingly he told me that when he first set out on his teaching career it took him two years to get his first job and, strangely, this was at Archbishop Temple's School!

As my year at the Institute of Education drew to a close, my spirits began to rise. All that remained for me to do was a five thousand word thesis on a topic of my own choice which, I believe, had something to do with boys' voices. I remember my brother looking this over and not being particularly enamoured, but it seems that the examiners were even less impressed because my work was referred back, which was a polite way of saying that it was not good enough. However, I was not particularly bothered as I was returning to the Royal Academy of Music for one final year and had ample opportunity to repeat the work, only this time taking more trouble over it. I had much to look forward to. During the past year, against the wishes of dear Doris Gould, I had taken the ARCO examination and passed it – that was my second attempt. Now, my next aim was the FRCO and with it an Inter B. Mus … Unexpectedly, good news appeared on the horizon. Until then I had followed the idea that the longer I studied the longer I avoided doing National Service, although secretly I had hoped to be rejected for health reasons: the double mastoids in my ears. Anyway, I no longer had to worry because suddenly, during the next six months, National Service was abolished and I was free, free to pursue my musical ambitions.

Hazel, meanwhile, had been awarded a John Williams (Kidwelly) Scholarship for postgraduate studies, financed with money by a certain John Williams of Kidwelly who had made good in the U. S. A. and, in gratitude, had endowed scholarships for young people from around his home town. This gave her a sixth year at the Royal Academy of Music during which time she also worked as Assistant Organist at Holy Trinity, Brompton, a job which she had acquired some time before. In those days, Holy Trinity, Brompton was something of a society church with a semi-professional choir, a high-profile congregation and an ambitious Organist and Choirmaster by the name of Robert Munns. Here was worship which was completely different to what went on at St. Mary the Virgin, Primrose Hill, but nevertheless was perfectly legitimate in its own way, an excellent example of how the dear old Church of England could cater for all sorts and conditions of men. On a Sunday morning there would be what I called irreverently "Solemn High Matins", with elaborate musical settings of the canticles and an equally elaborate anthem, all sung on behalf of a congregation comprising men of consequence accompanied by their ladies dripping with pearls, purring with delight at the music and passing comment on the sermon. One Sunday, Hazel was required to play for the choir in performances of both Edward Bairstow's "Blessed City, Heavenly Salem" and Basil Harwood's "O How Glorious is the Kingdom", which at that time were considered to be the two organ accompaniments best to be avoided at all costs. Special services could be interesting. At one Memorial Service, Princess Margaret and Earl Mountbatten numbered among the congregation; at one wedding the Bridegroom fainted and had to be revived in order to be got through the ceremony!

Hazel still had lessons with C. H. Trevor, although with this scholarship, the world was her oyster and she could have studied with whoever she wished, in any part of the world. Visits home to Kidwelly were now much more rare because her church work required her to be in London at the weekend. One morning after a lightning visit to her mother and father, Hazel took the 5.30 a.m. train from Kidwelly to Paddington, from where she made her way immediately to the Royal Academy of Music for her weekly organ lesson. As she approached the organ, C. H. was busily engaged in giving a lesson. Even so, he sniffed loudly a few times and then turned towards her and asked abruptly: "Do you smoke?" Hazel was rather irritated by this question and replied spiritedly: "Good gracious, no, but I couldn't get into a non-smoking compartment!" To this, C. H. retorted humorously: "Good God, woman, have you been cockling again?", whereupon, as if to redeem the situation, he turned to the pupil he was teaching, Nicholas Jackson, a future Organist of St. David's Cathedral and said: "Just look at her, she looks as fresh as a daisy!" The reference to cockling showed how C. H. had guessed rightly that Hazel had travelled up from Kidwelly that morning, because the sandy beaches at Ferryside four miles on from Kidwelly were noted for cockles.

Indeed there was an elderly lady, Mrs. Rees, who had been born and bred in Llansaint, a small village up a hill midway between Kidwelly and Ferryside, who used regularly to go cockling nearby. She would put the products of her expeditions into four sacks and then hang these over two donkeys named Twom and Jac and walk them into Kidwelly to sell. All the money raised in this way was put towards a memorial in Llansaint Church to her brother, J. C. Jones, a missionary priest who had ended his days not long before as a much-loved Bishop of Bangor.

By now Hazel had moved into a flat at the top of No. 29, Upper Montague Street, not far from Marylebone Library and near to the Royal Academy of Music, roughly equidistant from Holy Trinity Brompton and St. Mary the Virgin, Primrose Hill. By chance, her landlady was a certain Mrs. Thomas who hailed from Pumpsaint in Wales, not very many miles from Kidwelly. I used to call in for a coffee with Mark Knight after Thomas Morley Chamber Orchestra rehearsals at St. Mary the Virgin, Primrose Hill, on Wednesday evenings. Invariably, Mark would stop on our way at a garage near Baker Street and I would hide my face in embarrassment as he would try to purchase one pint of petrol for his motor scooter, as his financial resources did not run to the price of a gallon. Then, after we had spent some time drinking coffee and socialising in Hazel's flat, we would set off for South London, push-starting his motor-scooter. I would push and he would eventually start the engine after several attempts. When finally we met with success, we would ride away into the night roaring with laughter, leaving behind an embarrassed Hazel pleading with us to make less noise, as it was usually close to midnight!

At this time, Mark used to play seventeenth and eighteenth-century violin sonatas, with Hazel playing the accompaniments on a lovely, small Dolmetsch harpsichord that she had recently acquired. He had also become very involved in studying the Alexander technique, a method for relaxing the muscles which he took very seriously. One morning he arrived to rehearse with Hazel and having put down his violin case he made three attempts to open it. Suddenly he said: "It's no good", whereupon he picked up the case and left without another word. It seems that his muscles were not relaxing properly that day ...!

However, the time for such endless fun and games was coming to a close as Hazel and I were planning to get married and I had to find a job. I don't know why, but I had never envisaged staying in London. Indeed, for many years, I had harboured in my mind an idyllic picture of being an Organist in a country town church and Music Master in the local Grammar School. Nor had I ever doubted that God would organise this for me. At Holy Trinity Vicarage my brother had some books about the great mediaeval churches that litter the countryside of England and from these I had developed a liking for Selby Abbey in the West Riding of Yorkshire. Quite by chance, two sisters in the choir of St. Stephen's, South Dulwich, Jo and Grizel Fenton had a sister, Alison, who lived in Selby. From her I learned that the Abbey Organist, Walter Hartley, was about to retire. This was hardly surprising, as he was eighty-four years old and had been Organist for forty years. All I had to do was wait for the job to be advertised in the Church Times, then apply and try my luck.

As weeks slipped by and nothing appeared, in desperation I wrote reluctantly for details of organist positions at East Dereham in Norfolk and at Blandford Forum in Dorset. At last, however, there appeared the advertisement that I had been waiting for, announcing the vacant position of Organist and Choirmaster at Selby Abbey. I sent in my application and eventually was summoned to Selby for an interview, during which I was to play the organ to the legendary Dr. Francis Jackson, Organist of York Minster. The day was bitterly cold and, to make matters worse, Walter Hartley had locked into his music cupboard the plug of the fire close by the organ. Fortunately he had not indulged in his other trick of taking home to Leeds the relevant fuse in order to prevent anyone else from playing the organ. I played on the large four-manual Hill organ the "Prelude, Fugue and Chaconne" by the seventeenth-century composer Dietrich Buxtehude.

Afterwards Francis Jackson showed why he is so greatly loved and revered. In his most endearing and disarming way, he explained to me that he had long wanted to know how to play that piece of music and now he knew exactly what to do. I was charmed! An interview with the Vicar followed and not long afterwards I was offered the job at an annual salary of £250, which was £100 more than I was earning at St. Mary the Virgin, Primrose Hill. To this would be added three guineas (£3-3s-0d:£3.15) for every wedding at which I played the organ and two guineas (£2-2s-0d=£2.10) for every funeral. A teaching job was needed to supplement my stipend and soon the Vicar had me appointed to the staff at Selby Abbey School, an old-fashioned educational establishment catering for pupils of both primary and secondary modern ages up to fourteen years.

Next, Hazel and I had to find somewhere to live. Needing a day or so to explore the town to look for somewhere suitable, the Vicar offered us beds for the night. We travelled on the night train from King's Cross station which deposited us in Selby Station in the early hours of the morning, just as the Abbey clock was chiming three o'clock. We crept into the vicarage close by, through the back door, to find on the kitchen table a bottle of whisky along with the message "Help Yourselves!" Obviously the Vicar was a character, of which fact I became more certain when I spied him a little later, running naked from his bedroom to an extraordinary bathroom which had an enormous bath that stood all alone in the middle of the room. His pedigree was interesting, He had been Chaplain to a former Archbishop of York, Cyril Garbutt. Whilst on a visit to the U.S.A. with the Archbishop, he had met Bess, daughter of the Bishop of Boston and before much time had elapsed, he had married her. She, too, was a fascinating character, with very forthright views. Deciding to pursue a career of her own, she applied for a lectureship in Psychology at Hull University. When interviewed, she was asked how she could undertake this work when she was already a Vicar's wife, meaning "an unpaid helper to a Vicar"! She retorted: "I am not a Vicar's wife, I am married to a Vicar!" and promptly got the job.

John and Bess Kent complemented each other perfectly and as a result, Selby

Vicarage was full of life and fun, as we were soon to discover. Another character was Alison, the sister of Jo and Grizel Fenton of St. Stephen's, South Dulwich. She was married to a local builder, Peter Poskitt, whom she had met when they were both studying at Cambridge University. These two found us somewhere to live: the first and second floor flat of a large Edwardian house, 23 Doncaster Road, situated at the bottom of their garden. Needing to furnish this large flat, Hazel and I now began to scour the back streets of Marylebone and Camden Town seeking cheap items of antique furniture to add to the many old prints that we had collected.

Meanwhile, I had work to do as I prepared for my Inter B. Mus. examination at Durham University and as I attempted the FRCO examination for the first time: it was a well-known fact that few organists passed this at the first attempt. My father offered to drive me to Durham and the thought of saving the train fare unfortunately got the better of me, which was a mistake because his driving was legendary. Many years before he had let his driving licence lapse, then, when he had realised how useful a dormobile could be for transporting youngsters around, he applied for another. Failing the first test he could accept, but failing the second left him in a fury – after all, he had only driven through one set of red traffic lights. So he wrote to demand his third driving test from the Chief Examiner, tore up his provisional licence and "L" plates and calmly proceeded to drive around London without them, even enlisting the help of a policeman in pushing his dormobile to the nearest garage when he ran out of petrol. After his passing at the third attempt, my sister remembers walking by the battered dormobile standing at a parking metre near to Holy Trinity Vicarage and seeing two policemen taking down the details of offending vehicles. She overheard one say to the other as they gazed at his vehicle: "Better give this one a bit longer; it's Gedgie's."

He drove me to Durham via Selby and as we approached the town from the south, I saw for the first time all three hundred feet of the magnificent Abbey, stretching from West to East. For a moment, it took my breath away. Further on, north of York, as he drove at great speed with the setting sun glaring in his eyes, the road suddenly became exceedingly bumpy. Unbeknown to him he had left the main road, which actually had a 90 degree bend to the right, and instead was hurtling up a gravel track full of potholes. At Durham, in the University Music School, I attempted the papers. All went reasonably well until I started to wrestle with some harmony and counterpoint exercises and the Cathedral bell was tolled for a full quarter-of-an-hour to announce Evensong. The bell sounded also a death-knell for my Inter B. Mus. attempt as my concentration vanished. Never again did I bother to try, despite the encouraging report that I received from the dynamic Professor Arthur Hutchings, who had made Durham University famous for its music. On the journey home, my father lived up to his reputation yet again, As we approached Lichfield, he pulled out to overtake the car in front only to find a car bearing down on him coming from the opposite direction. He reached safety just in time.

On reaching home, I prepared myself for the FRCO examination. I had spent the entire academic year working at nothing but the examination pieces and the keyboard tests that went with them. How I must have tried C. H.'s patience. I even had an extra lesson on his pedal piano at his home, 72 Talbot Road in Highgate. As I walked up the garden path to his front door I couldn't believe my ears: through an open window, I heard him playing a Czerny exercise. Sometime before he had told me that he kept his keyboard technique in good order by playing Czerny exercises for two hours daily. Naturally I didn't believe him, yet here he was playing a Czerny exercise – or was he pulling my leg? On the day of the examination I had another extra lesson, this time on the organ at the Royal National Institute for the Blind. As I left, C. H. wished me well and said: "Don't worry, you can always take it again."

Because I was a candidate, Hazel had taken over my invigilating duties at the Royal College of Organists, which meant that as I entered the examination room I was assured of at least one sympathetic friend. However, when the time came for my ordeal to begin, I found that I had one more sympathetic friend in that room as there, numbered among the three examiners, was none other than Dr. Sidney Scholfield Campbell. From that moment until the end of the examination my mind was a complete blank. A few days before this, I had done the paperwork examination which had begun with some aural tests and, being a hot day, I had heard these twice: once when they were played to the candidates seated on the first floor, of whom I was one, and moments later when they were played to the candidates seated on the second floor and I heard them again through an open window! Perhaps this was a good omen, because when I received my results I found that not only had I miraculously passed at the first attempt, but that I had won the Turpin Prize for gaining the second highest marks in the performing tests. All that upset me was that the Entry Fee had been seven guineas (£7-7s-0d=£7.35), while the prize was only five guineas (£5-5s-0d=£5.25)!

Now I was free to concentrate on the wedding. First, however, there were two unexpected matters to deal with. The first concerned dear Christopher Tanner, who had recently suffered a stroke which had partially paralysed him down one side but from which he had made a remarkable recovery. One day he asked Hazel and me to call on him, which we did. He told us that he had left us his lovely black Bechstein grand piano in his will, but as he would never again play it to his own personal satisfaction, he wanted us to accept it as a wedding present. The second concerned Harry and Peggy Taylor. They owned a magnificent six-stone hulk of a Boxer dog named Gunner and had mated him with the adorable Juno, the lovely Boxer bitch belonging to Fr. Peter, the curate of St. Mary the Virgin, Primrose Hill. Harry and Peggy wanted us to accept the pick-of-the-litter as a wedding present and so beloved Hannibal came into our lives. Initially this tiny scrap of a pup, who eventually grew into a six-stone monster of a boxer dog, shared Hazel's flat. Every morning she would creep downstairs from the top floor of no. 29 Upper Montagu Street and walk with him to Regent's Park to do what was required of him. Quickly Hannibal found a place deep down not only in our hearts but also in the hearts of Hazel's parents, particularly that of her father who inevitably after the death of his last dog, Chum, had vowed never to have another dog. Hannibal to him became like a child and a strong bond of affection grew up between them.

The week before our wedding Hazel and I devoted to a singing holiday with the choir of St. Mary the Virgin, Primrose Hill, at St. Davids Cathedral in deepest Pembrokeshire. This was the second visit that the choir had made to this, the smallest city in Britain, with its priceless jewel of a cathedral and therefore everyone knew what fun to expect. To wake up in the early light of day in a long wooden hut alongside the ruin of the great mediaeval Bishop's palace was always a thrill. Nearby was a sparkling swiftly flowing stream, through which, every so often, cars drove, splashing loudly and setting up great ripples of water. Regularly mornings of practice gave way to afternoons of sunbathing and swimming at nearby Whitesands Bay with its long expanse of yellow sand. Such bliss! Later, at teatime, everyone walked back up a hill, across some green fields and down the other side into the vast hollow where the great mediaeval Cathedral had been built, out of sight of the marauding pirates that abounded in those far-off dark times. After a short practice, the choir sang Evensong in those matchless stalls beneath the tower, beyond the great stone screen on which stood the organ. So close together were the choir stalls that the boys on one side could almost shake the hands of the boys on the other. One strange tradition at St. David's Cathedral allots one of the beautifully-carved oak stalls to the reigning monarch, which meant that theoretically at this time Queen Elizabeth II numbered among the Cathedral chapter.

Some enterprising choirboys found their way to the top of the tower. Nicholas Taylor took his baby sister, Susie, with him and then held her over the balustrade shouting to his mother down below as he did so. How she did not have apoplexy on the spot I do not know but certainly, in later life, Susie never displayed any ill-effects from this further escapade of her naughtiest brother. Hazel left on the Thursday to prepare for our wedding on the following Saturday, August 18th 1962. The choristers followed on the Saturday morning as they were singing at the service in the lovely old mediaeval Priory Church of St. Mary, Kidwelly. At the last possible moment before the bus left St. Davids for the fifty-five mile journey to Kidwelly, Nicholas and Tony Taylor switched the "Ladies" and "Gentlemen" signs on the Cathedral loos situated close to the hut, thereby wreaking a little more havoc.

I didn't travel on the bus: instead, I went with Harry and Peggy Taylor in a car. As there was no particular rush we made a short detour to Laugharne so that I could show them Dylan Thomas's grave in the churchyard. Meanwhile, unbeknown to me, my father had created havoc at Bridgend House by arriving with a dormobile full of youngsters from Pimlico where he was helping at St. Gabriel's Church – "on their way to Loch Ness to see the monster," he had explained. These young ones commandeered the bathroom to put on their best party clothes, leaving Hazel in a cold sweat, desperate to be on time at the church. Yet the service started punctually at 1 p.m., but not before the Organist, Grace Jones, had played in our honour an organ piece edited by C. H. Trevor. She had chosen the beautiful Sinfonia "God's time is best", not realising that it came from a funeral cantata! Hazel had one little bridesmaid, Susan Munns, daughter of Robert Munns, the Organist at Holy Trinity Brompton, along with a Matron of Honour, my sister Daphne. The Nuptial Mass was shared between the local Vicar, Douglas Walters, Fr. Timms and my father and all went happily, with the combined choirs of St. Mary's Kidwelly and St. Mary's Primrose Hill leading the singing. Photographs were taken outside the church in the minimum of time, whereupon there was a general exodus in the direction of the Ashburnham Hotel at nearby Pembrey where the reception was to be held. This was a happy affair, yet so skilfully managed that by not long after half-past four, Hazel and I were waving off the choristers of St. Mary the Virgin, Primrose Hill, as their train pulled out from Llanelli Station bound for Paddington.

As for our honeymoon we could not go into England as the choir had used the most convenient train, nor did we want to go back into Pembrokeshire, so Harry and Peggy drove us to Carmarthen Station to catch the 6.10 p.m. that took almost three hours to reach Aberystwyth. Next morning at breakfast in our hotel, two elderly ladies looked us up and down most suspiciously and then muttered something to each other. We decided to go to Towyn so that I could renew my acquaintance with the Talyllyn Railway and introduce it to Hazel. While there we met the sister of another of Hazel's London landladies. She was full of the fact that at Towyn Church that morning, a strange man had appeared with ten children whom she presumed were all his because they had all called him "Father"!

On Monday morning at breakfast in our hotel, the two elderly ladies looked us up and down again most suspiciously, as if we had been enjoying a naughty week-end together and one of them asked: "There was a wedding last Saturday in Kidwelly; was it yours?"!

Holy Trinity Church.

My Mother.

My Father.

Throwing stones at the chimney which was all that remained of the Fields Soap Factory alongside the approach to Waterloo Station. David Gedge is second from the left.

The Cathedral and Collegiate Church of St Saviour and St Mary Overie, Southwark, showing some of the railway lines and the Borough Market that surround it.

The first London Performance of Benjamin Britten's 'St Nicholas'.
Benjamin Britten, Ernest Warrell (Assistant Organist of Southwark Cathedral), Peter Pears
with the four choristers: 'Dumbo' Webb, David Gibbs, David Gedge, Michael Riggs.

Ken Matthew's class at St Olave's Grammar School.
David Gedge, front row third from the right.

Parish Mass at St Mary the Virgin, Primrose Hill.

Hazel Davies and David Gedge with Toffee the Dog,
when students at the Royal Academy of Music.

Published by permission of the Ross Parry Agency/ Yorkshire Post.

Selby Abbey Choir.
Published by permission of the Ross Parry Agency/ Yorkshire Post.

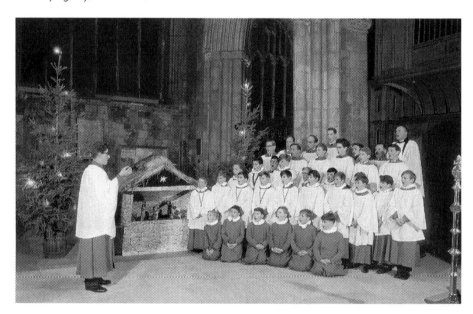

XVIII

Back at Bridgend House, Kidwelly, Hazel and I enjoyed a week when time stood still. We had no responsibilities and could spend many happy hours dreaming dreams, riding bicycles around leafy Carmarthenshire lanes and also walking the ever-growing Hannibal along the banks of the River Gwendraeth or on the remote sandy beach at nearby Ferryside. My Pitkin guide-book to Selby Abbey was never far from my side, as I was still overawed by the magnificence of the building and read about it constantly. Selby itself was of more than passing interest.

The town of Selby had long been notorious for its toll bridge. By some strange quirk of fate a bye-law protected its owners from paying income tax on the takings, nor could anyone build an alternative bridge across the River Ouse within five miles on either side. Always there was a waiting list of people wanting to work there. Local legend had it that when crossing the bridge in a car, if the driver received no ticket in exchange for his money then the proceeds had been diverted elsewhere. Certainly, it appeared that many people who had worked on the bridge had done very nicely, yet still the owners had amassed a huge annual tax-free profit. This was hardly surprising, however, because the bridge was situated on the main road from Leeds to Hull, which had a constant flow of traffic that turned into a veritable stream on Mondays - Market Day. Indeed on Bank Holiday Mondays the traffic became a nightmare. One enterprising Selebian chose such a day to walk the length of the car queue, collecting the toll in advance to save time for the drivers when they reached the bridge. Only when they actually arrived at the bridge did they discover that they had been duped as they had to pay a second time.

The land at Selby is amazingly flat, so much so that in 1947 when the River Ouse overflowed its banks it flooded the entire town. That was when insurance companies discovered that so many Selebians were in possession of German-made pianos! Yet despite the wide extent of the flooding, one place remained untouched by the water and that was the Abbey Church itself. It seems that it had been built on the one piece of land that was higher than all that lay around it. Apparently the founder, Benedict of Auxerre, had been directed by a vision of St. Germain as to where the Abbey was to be built. Upon sailing up the River Ouse he had recognised what is now Selby as the chosen place and his choice was confirmed by three swans alighting on the water, which he took to be a sign of the Holy Trinity. Subsequently the three swans were incorporated into the Abbey coat of arms. The ground was so marshy that oak saplings had to be sunk into it to provide a firm foundation for the great church, which was started in the year 1069. In 1690 the tower had fallen, taking with it the South Transept. In 1906 a fire, which had started in the organ chamber during the installation of a new organ, gutted the entire church. The restoration work that followed resulted in the Abbey Church being returned far nearer to its former glory than ever before. As the year 1960 drew nearer, Selebians began to wonder what more was in store for their beloved Abbey Church. Nor were they to be disappointed.

One morning in that fateful year of 1960, while the Vicar, John Kent, sat reading his daily paper, he noticed an article about Jacob Epstein. On perusing this, he discovered that the sculptor was offering his statue "*Ecce Homo*" – "Behold the Man" to any suitable church. He thought for a moment, reached over for his telephone and immediately contacted the great man and offered him a home for his statue in Selby Abbey. Jacob Epstein was delighted, as was John Kent. However, when news of this coup leaked out, the influential churchwarden, Donald Cochrane, was far from delighted; in principle he opposed much that was suggested by the Vicar. Unfortunately, by virtue of owning Cochrane's ship-building yard in Selby, he numbered among the wealthiest men in the town and wielded a considerable amount of influence. Without even seeing the statue other than in a photograph he launched a campaign to stop it coming to Selby Abbey. Tempers rose as a petition was circulated and signed by many people who knew little if anything about art.

Inevitably the matter came to the attention of the Chancellor of the Diocese of York, who gave the order for a Consistory Court to be held in the Abbey so that the matter could be discussed sensibly. Among the notable persons gathered to argue against the Vicar's proposal was Charles Moody. He had not long retired at the age of eighty years after having been Organist of Ripon Cathedral for fifty-two of those years. He was a renowned fighter. When the Dean and Chapter of Ripon Cathedral had forbidden his using musical settings for the Canticles at Sunday evensongs, he had retaliated by arranging for the choir to sing them to the same two monotonous chants week by week for all of two years. During that time he had enlisted the support of no less a musician than the great Ralph Vaughan Williams as he took his Dean and Chapter to court, ultimately to win his case and have his music restored to its rightful place on Sunday evenings. A man of volatile temperament, it was rumoured that there lived in Ripon a former choirboy, now fully grown-up, who was partly deaf in one ear as a result of being clouted by Dr. Moody during a choir practice. His considerable interest in Selby Abbey had resulted in his writing a book about it, but being of Victorian vintage it was perhaps inevitable that he should speak out against Jacob Epstein's statue coming there. Obviously set in his ways and unable to accept change, two years later he wrote to his daughter who was married to the conductor Alan Melville, to complain that a "young upstart" (me) had been appointed Organist of Selby Abbey, not knowing that his granddaughter Clarissa Melville sometimes played her flute in my Thomas Morley Chamber Orchestra. When he rose to speak at this Consistory Court and introduced himself as Dr. Charles Moody, CBE, FRCO, I wonder how many of the assembled company realised that his academic qualifications had been given him in an honorary capacity.

However, as the case wore on, it became obvious that there was no reason why Jacob Epstein's statue should not come to the Abbey. The Vicar had planned to have the statue placed at the east end of the south choir aisle, where it could be approached by walking the entire three-hundred feet length of the narrow south nave and choir aisles. What an impact it would make! But it was not to be, as the Chancellor decided against the statue coming to Selby Abbey for fear of the dissension this might cause in the parish. Jacob Epstein was furious and declared that no church should have his statue. The Vicar was sad. As for the Churchwarden, did he have a twinge of conscience about the unfortunate affair, because not long afterwards a cheque for £10,000 arrived: a donation towards the new heating system that was being planned for the Abbey? Undoubtedly the great church was the loser in this dispute. Had *"Ecce Homo"* been placed in Selby Abbey, it would have become as much a tourist attraction as has the famous Jacob Epstein figure "Christ in Majesty" which dominates Llandaff Cathedral.

On reflection it is easy to see why Dr Moody loved Selby Abbey so dearly. The nave alone is an amazing study of twelfth-century architecture, beginning with massive circular pillars in the east, like those at Durham Cathedral and ending with much lighter clusters of pillars in the west, like those in the crypt at York Minster or in the retro-choir at Chichester Cathedral. Apparently it had taken one hundred and twenty years to build this part of the Abbey Church. Several bizarre features fascinated me in other parts of the building, such as the two amazing stone figures seated high up astride the parapet above the organ where for centuries they had gazed down upon the worshippers. Near to them, set in the tower wall, can be seen two more figures: these look like monks sitting on privies, one hiding his face in embarrassment, the other brazenly full of glee! Then there are the many stone capitals in the north choir aisle, each one carved individually by Tom Strudwick, the Abbey stonemason, after the great fire. One of these is hollow and inside can be seen a carved head of King Edward VII; black marks made by lighted matches give away its whereabouts.

The High Altar has an impressive reredos carved by Peter Rendl of Oberammergau in the year 1909 and to the right of this is an ornately carved sedilia so obviously the work of "England's greatest architect" Henry Yevele, as it mirrors his Neville Screen at Durham Cathedral. Perhaps the Abbey's greatest glory is the enormous Jesse window at the east end of what was once the Monk's Choir, said to rival only the great east windows of Carlisle Cathedral and York Minster. The stained glass shows the family tree of Jesse: Mary and Jesus can be seen in the centre at the top, beneath them can be seen St. Michael weighing souls, representing the Last Judgement. All this was depicted in priceless mediaeval stained glass until a great hail storm in 1827 decimated much of it. Perhaps St. Michael was not pleased with the performance of the bass soloist and the trumpeter in "The trumpet shall sound and the dead shall be raised" when Handel's great oratorio "Messiah" was sung a few days before on September 15th, as part of a great Music Festival held in the Abbey Church. In a glass case on the wall of the south nave aisle can be seen a musical instrument called the Serpent, that was actually played in this performance, along with a copy of the programme naming its player. Close by, set into the floor, is a gravestone, a memorial of one of the souls weighed by St. Michael, which gives considerable amusement:

"Near to this stone lies Archer (John)
Late Saxton (I aver)
Who without Tears thirty-four years,
Did Carcases inter,
But death at Last for his works past,

Unto him thus did say,
Leave off thy Trade be not afraid,
But forthwith come away.
Without reply or asking why
The summons he obey'd,
In seventeen hundred and sixty-eight
Resign'd his life and spade."

Perhaps the author of this epitaph had been inspired by a similar work of art, dated 1706, which reads:

Here lies the body of poor Frank Raw
Parish clerk and gravestone cutter
And this is writ to let you know
What Frank for others used to do
Is now for Frank done by another."

Outside the Abbey, on the northern side of the churchyard is an unmarked memorial to death of a different sort, for here, during the years 1846-8, were buried the victims of the cholera plague. Above, on the north wall of the Monk's Choir, gargoyles jut out, shaped in the likeness of demons; upon them the sun never shines. On the south wall, facing the main road past the Vicarage, there are more gargoyles, but these are shaped in the likeness of angels and upon them the sun shone with some regularity!

With such a stunning building to look forward to, even larger than Southwark Cathedral, my euphoria knew no bounds. All the more strange, then, to relate what happened next, because God indeed does seem to move in mysterious ways. Towards the end of the month of August, Hazel and I set out from Kidwelly for Selby in a dormobile that we had hired to take all our luggage and wedding presents to our first home. On our way we stopped for "elevenses" at Brecon, a town that was unknown to us both. We got out from the dormobile at the bottom of Ship Street, walked up Market Street past the yard of Williams the Builder, crossed the River Honddu by the bridge in Castle Street, turned right into The Postern where we passed the old gaol and finally turned left to walk up Priory Hill alongside the wall that encircled the old Priory Church which since 1923 had been Brecon Cathedral.

I was completely unprepared for what happened next. As we walked through the door in the north porch into the Cathedral I was gobsmacked. It was the wide expanse of blank wall with a door in it which did that to me and I later learned that this had been part of a great golden rood screen which had been swept away when the Benedictine Priory had been dissolved in 1539. There was more: the amazing colour of the Cathedral stone walls and all the outbuildings, not forgetting the serenity of it all. The Cathedral was dedicated to St. John the Evangelist but there had been a time when as a Priory, it had been known as The Church of the Miraculous Rood. Well, the Rood had worked one more miracle. I was smitten and, even though by Selby Abbey standards it was a humble building, I knew that

I was coming back. From that moment onwards I have understood the story of Saul being struck by a great light and being converted to Christianity, the very faith which he had been persecuting but now began to preach, under the new name of Paul of Tarsus. Before I left the Cathedral I purchased a copy of the small but very informative guidebook, which I read often in the months that were to follow.

For now I had to concentrate on Selby Abbey as we resumed our long journey northwards and across the Pennines. By nightfall we were installed in no. 23, Doncaster Road, Selby, along with our bits of furniture that we had picked up in the back streets of London, various items from Holy Trinity Vicarage, a lovely big mahogany table from Kidwelly Vicarage, not forgetting Chris Tanner's Bechstein Grand Piano and our boxer dog Hannibal, now fast approaching his eventual weight of 6 ½ stones, a living reminder of the happy times at St. Mary the Virgin, Primrose Hill. On Sunday morning I made my debut at Selby Abbey. As I sat at the huge four-manual Hill organ, I was completely unprepared for what was to come. Unfortunately, the console was sited a considerable distance from not only the pipes of the organ but also from the choristers, thus not only was there a time lag between playing the notes and then hearing the sound, but it was also virtually impossible to see the singers.

As the service was Matins, I put down a chord for the *Venite* and immediately my ears were assailed by the most incredible sound. In a broad Yorkshire dialect, the choir launched vigorously into:

"*O coom let us sing to the Lard.*"

It was appalling. Worse was to follow in the *Te Deum* when, at the tops of their voices, the choristers sang:

"*The gloorious coompany of the Apostells.*"

"Martyrs" became "Mayters" and I felt as if I was enduring the most terrible nightmare. Afterwards I went to drown my sorrows with some of the choirmen, who had no sorrows to drown, they having sung Matins in the way to which they had become accustomed. Not being used to Yorkshire beer, I drank my customary three pints with the result that the walk home became a precarious affair. Fortunately being a Sunday lunch-time the streets were quiet, because as I staggered down Doncaster Road I periodically steadied myself at lamp-posts. At no. 23, Hazel had cooked our first Sunday lunch but I was in no fit state to eat it. I was bundled off to bed unceremoniously and Hannibal slunk alongside to keep me company! Needless to say, Evensong was no better.

The next day I presented myself at the Abbey school. I was given a small class of twenty-two youngsters which, I was assured, would give me a gentle introduction to teaching. Until this time, I had always been patronising about Primary School teachers, holding them in contempt; to me their work had needed scant brain power and had amounted to little more than child-minding. How wrong I had been! Within a very short time chaos reigned supreme in my classroom and, to make matters worse, all my mistakes were witnessed by the highly-effective teacher in the adjoining room, because all that separated us was a thin wooden partition with windows and a door. I felt such a fool. Every minute of the day these children demanded attention, especially the eight who were classified as E. S. N. – Educationally Sub-Normal. So quickly did I lose confidence in my ability to cope with the situation that I failed abysmally when I took over the Headmaster's music class with the fourteen-year-olds. The nightmare which had begun when I played the organ at Matins on my first Sunday now took on another dimension. However, whereas I had sufficient experience to cope with the problems concerning the Abbey Choir, at the Abbey School I was completely out of my depth.

In looking for a way out I realised quickly that I had to find teaching in either a grammar school or a secondary school. Fortunately I heard about a new secondary school being built at Howden, a small town ten miles away in the East Riding of Yorkshire. I contacted the County Music Organiser, Peter Fletcher, who was also Organist at Beverley Minster, and he appointed me Music Master at the school from the beginning of the New Year. I was overjoyed as was also the Headmaster of the Abbey School. Knowing that the end was in sight made my work there bearable, although the children still ran rings around me. Only once did I succeed in ending the day in control with all the boys and girls out of my room quietly and quickly soon after the final bell had rung. Yet, as I savoured success, something seemed wrong; it had all been too easy. When I entered the cloakroom I found the local eight-year-old Salvation Army Queen displaying her credentials to the boys, who were reduced to a silence of sheer fascination.

Unfortunately the job at Howden County Secondary School was not a full-time affair, there being work for only three days each week, and the question of money therefore reared its ugly head. However, when Hazel and I arrived at Selby we had made it our business to call on the town's leading piano teacher to make ourselves known and to ask advice on the possibility of acquiring some private pupils without upsetting her. After some discussion she had put us firmly in our place by explaining that while she charged five guineas (£5.25) for a term of ten thirty-minute lessons, we could not expect like remuneration since we were fresh from college and therefore inexperienced. Fortunately, Hazel had little difficulty in building up a private teaching practice as there proved to be no shortage of pupils at three guineas (£3.15) a term. She also taught piano pupils and junior class music at Read Grammar School in nearby Drax, a village soon to become famous because of the huge power station that was built there. This ancient, extraordinary educational institution accommodated those boys from Selby who had passed the 11-plus examination, along with a number of fee-paying boarders from further afield. The Selby boys were taken there and back daily in a fleet of five or six noisy buses!

The extra money to be had at the Abbey from playing the organ at weddings and funerals also turned out to be more lucrative than first thought possible, with an average of around fifty weddings annually and a smaller number of funerals. Most local couples were married in the Abbey – at least that is how it seemed, judging by the number of photographs I saw during my time in Selby in private homes and in local newspapers. The favourite place for this photograph to be taken was outside the great West Door. Unfortunately during the winter opening this enormous door caused the temperature inside the church to fall by five degrees Fahrenheit and therefore an extra charge of £5 (my weekly wage as Organist) was made. One couple, to avoid paying this extra money, left the Abbey by the South Transept door after their wedding service, but were later seen slinking round the outside of the building to the great Norman West Door, there to have the customary photographs taken. Sometimes on a Saturday there were two or three weddings in quick succession and I would take sandwiches to the organ console for sustenance. Just occasionally, choirboys were required to sing at these services, which procured for them some additional pocket money as they were paid five shillings each (25p) for their labours.

However, this turned out not to be the only perquisite of the Abbey choirboys. After Evensong on the Sunday of the first Harvest Festival I experienced at Selby, the boys made it quite clear that they were in a hurry to leave the choir vestry. When I did dismiss them, they made off hot foot not out into the churchyard but back into the church, pulling out bags from their pockets as they did so. Being curious, I followed them and, to my horror, found them helping themselves to the fruit that had been set out in various parts of the building. When I remonstrated with them they assured me that this was the normal procedure but, needless to say, it never happened again!

Such choir disciplinary problems really originated with my predecessor, Walter Hartley, but only because of his kind-heartedness towards young people. Truth to tell, had never really been interested in training the choir and when appointed Organist back in 1922 had handed over the boys' practices to Albert Cryer, one of the tenors. This had left him free in the week to help run the family paper-bag business in Leeds and then at the weekends he would travel over to Selby and play his beloved Abbey organ. There came a time when Albert Cryer wanted to retire and Walter Hartley was left to cope with the choirboys himself. Much as he enjoyed working with the youngsters he was getting old and losing his control over their behaviour. Thus on the quarterly pay-day the boys would line up in the choir vestry and as each one was paid so he would disappear through the door into the Abbey, come back out into the churchyard through the small south-west aisle door, re-enter the vestry so to join the queue again and be paid a second time, hopefully, until the money ran out!

A local doctor told me how, when making a call, he had noticed a small boy busily working at the sink."What are you doing, laddy?" he asked, to which the boy replied: "Making bread pellets for choir practice." So the boy had explained how on Friday evenings the choirboys rehearsed in the Abbey, beyond the choirstalls, one group sitting on chairs opposite the organ console where Walter Hartley sat, the other group sitting on chairs placed against the console completely hidden from his view. Then, while Walter Hartley played the organ to accompany the singing, some of the boys would be busily engaged in firing bread pellets at each other with the aid of bicycle pumps.

If the Abbey choirboys tended to be somewhat unorthodox in their behaviour, so also did the choirmen. One of the tenors had such a weak heart that he was only able to stand for half a service. His brother, who also sang in the choir, ran a pub and therefore could only sing on a Sunday morning, which he did sparingly; presumably in the evenings he was too busy pulling pints to attend Evensong or Choir practice. Then there was Claude who sang alto, for whom I would write tonic sol-fa symbols all over the music, yet still he sang the melody an octave lower. Furthermore, he stubbornly refused to say or to sing the Creed because it began with the words "I believe", which, he claimed, left an element of doubt, as it was not as positive a declaration as "I am sure". Such a theological argument was beyond my understanding.

Among the basses was a stout gentleman with a bushy moustache who, at some time, had worked in the R.A.F ... Legend had it that whenever the hymn "Ride on, ride on in majesty" was sung, he would lean over the choirstalls as if holding reins while riding a horse. Another bass who lived in Doncaster, kindly visited Evensong monthly when in Selby to visit his aged mother. The Verger also sang bass and had done so for years, either very loudly or very softly and there was no happy medium. An ex-Sergeant-Major, he was very set in his ways and found my ways difficult to accept. I heard him tell someone: "I've got more music in my arse than Gedge has got in all of 'im"! Pride of place went to the bass who was living with a lady who, he would explain proudly, had once been engaged to a clergyman. This was the infamous Jack, father of seven children, two of whom numbered among the choristers. If anyone called at his home he would, as a matter of course, shut the dog in the stair-cupboard; every six weeks, as a matter of course also, he would arrive at choir practice drunk. On one such occasion the choirmen and I tipped him out through the vestry door whereupon he staggered up the path-way and bumped into the Vicar."You're a bloody hypocrite, " he said with slurred speech, thumping the Vicar in his chest as he did so."You're bloody drunk," retorted the Vicar, before walking on round him, grinning from ear to ear.

There was another Jack in the bass section, Jack Latimer, who also achieved notoriety by attending every choir practice but no services. He was a painter and decorator by trade. When in desperation to achieve something positive I began to teach the choirmen to sing the well-known short sixteenth-century anthem "Lord, for thy tender mercy's sake", I tried very hard to get them to shape phrases musically. I need not have bothered. As I attempted to highlight a certain word with a subtle, gentle crescendo, I was told irritably by the painter: "If Farrant had wanted a crescendo, he'd have written one." When I gave the assembled company the benefit of my knowledge and explained firstly that the anthem had actually been composed by John Hilton and not by Richard Farrant as was stated on the copy and secondly that, in their day, composers did not add such dynamic indications to their music as these had yet to be invented, no-one seemed the least bit impressed. I gave up the unequal struggle, collected in the copies, returned them to the cupboard and shut the door firmly.

Clearly there was but one way forward and, screwing up my courage, I did something that I had never done before: I asked the choirmen to leave, and most of them obliged. Then, to my amazement, they were quickly replaced by new singers. So arrived Peter Warham, Headmaster of Barlby Primary School on the other side of the toll bridge; he with his two sons proved to be a tower of strength. Meanwhile, for many months since, before my arrival, two members of the congregation had organised a weekly club to keep together the choirboys; now one of these, Don Riches, was prevailed upon to learn to sing tenor. Slowly progress was made, but it was uphill work. As Christmas approached, Jack, the bass with seven children, asked to take some of the choirboys to The Blackamoor, a pub close to the Abbey, to sing carols on Christmas Eve before the midnight service. The Vicar and I along with the Churchwardens all said a firm "No!" but to no avail.

As Hazel and I approached the Abbey at around 10.45 p.m. to prepare for the service, to our horror we saw in the distance Jack with some choirboys clad in cassocks and surplices disappearing into The Blackamoor. Although they returned in time for the service, nevertheless, they had cast a cloud over the proceedings, as had the weather, which was bitterly cold. Locally it was claimed that the winds which were sweeping across the Plain of Selby that winter had come not only from the East Coast but even from Siberia, because apparently the land remains flat all the way to there. After all, the highest land around Selby is two miles to the west of the town at Brayton Barff, where a hill rises to all of 200 feet, which is barely higher than the Abbey's central tower, and that was the only hill for many miles.

That night, after Midnight Mass, Hazel and I walked slowly down Gowthorpe, then Doncaster Road, with the bitter cold biting through our clothes. Arriving at no. 23, in the early hours of Christmas morning, we sat down in our huge sitting room with its bare floor painted because we could not afford a carpet and huddled around a coal fire, each clutching a tiny glass of sherry. We felt thoroughly miserable and depressed.

XIX

Our first Christmas Day was saved by John and Bess Kent, who welcomed us into the Vicarage for a marvellous Christmas Dinner; not surprisingly the day sparkled. Meanwhile, in moments of depression, and there were many, I continued to be drawn to the guidebook on Brecon Cathedral which I read and re-read avidly. Imagine my confusion, therefore, when quite unexpectedly at this time there appeared an advertisement for an Organist at this very Cathedral. I knew that I shouldn't apply, having not been long at Selby Abbey, yet I did make an enquiry. Fortunately my dilemma was resolved for me by the Dean of Brecon who wrote back to say that unfortunately the job would not support a married man. Apparently the previous Cathedral Organist had also been Music Master at Brecon Boys' Grammar School but had played off one job against the other; he would use one job as an excuse for not doing extra work at the other. When he moved on, the authorities at the school made sure that anyone interested in the Cathedral appointment was not on their shortlist. As at Selby, the Organist's salary at Brecon Cathedral made other paid work essential if one was to have any hope of remaining solvent. So there was nothing left for me but to make the best of my present situation.

One night, feeling blue, Hazel and I shut ourselves in the Abbey and on full organ, which was so loud that it was clearly audible from the main road that skirted the Abbey grounds, we hammered out the songs "What shall we do with the drunken sailor?" and "Rule Britannia". Having given vent to our frustrations we locked up the organ, switched out the lights, whereupon in the total black darkness, the two curates leapt out from behind one of the massive Norman pillars to give us the fright of our lives. Attracted by the terrible noise they had let themselves silently into the Abbey to discover what was going on. When we had recovered our composure, they took us for a drink in the hope of reviving our flagging spirits.

However, Hazel and I did begin the New Year, 1963, positively. We started a Choral Society. Initially there were a dozen or so singers who rehearsed in our sitting room, but the number grew quickly as we worked towards a concert sometime during the month of March at St. Wilfred's, Brayton, the church situated nearby, down the other end of Doncaster Road. I knew well this lovely Norman Church because I used to walk Hannibal regularly down Doncaster Road to a field nearby, hopefully to exhaust him before returning home. He had grown into a fully-fledged Boxer dog of six-and-a-half stone and, with nine champions in his pedigree, was a magnificent specimen. If his teeth were sharp, so too was his brain. At No. 23 Doncaster Road, he had worked out how by standing on his hind legs and putting his front feet onto the top part of the door, he could pull down the handle and enter any room that he chose, there to create havoc. So he demolished an eiderdown that had been a wedding present, and a much treasured record of brass band suites by Ralph Vaughan Williams and Gustav Holst.

However, worse was to follow. One day Hazel returned to no. 23 after playing the organ at a funeral, to find Hannibal foaming at the mouth. Immediately she suspected that he had eaten something poisonous, yet the smell was too fragrant; on looking into the bathroom she discovered the tell-tale remnants of a bar of soap. On another day it was chocolate that he had found and this dribbled from his mouth and oozed from his nose, so much had he devoured. A dose of pepper produced the sneezes that improved his breathing but did not improve the state of the walls and floor around. A few days later, as I was returning from school I noticed all the windows wide open, despite it being a winter's day. Puzzled, I opened the front door and was immediately struck by the smell of gas hanging in the air. Once again Hannibal had been up to his tricks. Letting himself into the kitchen he had bitten through the rubber tubing leading to the pilot light on the gas cooker. On a never-to-be-forgotten occasion, Hazel entered no. 23 after playing the organ at another funeral and found the most incredible sight. Into the hallway Hannibal had dragged anything that was moveable: cushions, bed linen, clothing, even the coal hod and this had been tipped over, leaving a black mess everywhere. That was the proverbial straw that broke the camel's back! If Hazel was to play the organ for services in the Abbey while I was in school, then Hannibal had to go with her. So Hazel sitting at the Abbey Organ with Hannibal stretched out alongside on a carpet became a familiar sight. On hearing about it, the Editor of the Yorkshire Post sent along a photographer and reporter; soon after, there appeared a photograph of them both in that newspaper with the caption: *ABBEY DOG WELL ORGANISED - FOR HYMN, SLEEPING TIME.* An explanation followed.

Hannibal was happy with this arrangement and never put a paw wrong except on two occasions. Firstly, he took a liking to the great Norman pillar outside the choir vestry and whenever possible staked a claim to it by lifting a leg and doing what was necessary! Secondly, Hazel gave an organ recital before Evensong one Sunday and thought it best to leave Hannibal in the choir vestry while the choristers rehearsed with me. All went well until Hazel began her recital and Hannibal heard the sound of the organ in the distance. With me preoccupied and the door having accidentally been left slightly ajar, he slunk out and bounded down the south nave aisle. At the entrance to the choir stalls, apparently, he stood and momentarily assessed the situation, looking first to the left and then to the right. Suddenly he darted to the choir stalls on the south side and bounded along the back row, leaping over the legs of anyone sitting in his path. Arriving at the organ console he stood to his full height, putting his two front paws on the top and leaned over as if to say to his surprised mistress: "Here I am, why did you leave me behind?"

Apart from those two misdemeanours, Hannibal was the model of good behaviour, so much so that when the tall Bishop of Whitby, father of Jon Snow the broadcaster, leaned over the top of the console to thank Hazel for playing the organ at a special service, he got the surprise of his life to see this monster dog lying there. Regularly on a Sunday morning when Hazel played the organ so that I could direct the singing of the choir at Choral Communion, Hannibal settled down for an hour's sleep. However, intuitively he seemed to know when the final hymn was being sung because he would sit up, stretch, yawn and make his way to the curtain at the side where he waited until the service had ended because he knew that old

Mr. Thompson, a kindly widower, would then give him a biscuit!

So it was that Selby Abbey became part of Hannibal's empire as he happily strutted along on the end of a choker chain, behind or alongside Hazel, meeting and befriending all manner of people. It was the same at no. 23 Doncaster Road where Hannibal had by now become used to the constant coming and going of Hazel's piano pupils, not forgetting the ever-increasing number of people who turned up to sing with our Choral Society. Initially called "Selby Abbey Special Choir" (just like "Southwark Cathedral Special Choir"!), these singers gave their first concert on Saturday March 3rd, 1963, when they sang music by John IV of Portugal, Mozart, Palestrina and Christopher Tye and Hazel played organ music by Thomas Arne, J. S. Bach and Samuel Wesley, in St. Wilfred's Church, Brayton. This concert was repeated as part of a series of concerts during Lent and Holy Week in Selby Abbey, the second being given by the Leeds Cantata Singers who sang a Motet by J. S. Bach and Lennox Berkeley's "Missa Brevis" which was a little too modern for Selby tastes.

The third and final concert was the most interesting, being a performance of Joseph Haydn's fascinating "Seven Last Words of Jesus on the Cross" by a string quartet from the Guildhall School of Music, London. This brought to Selby our good friend Mark Knight, who played first violin and therefore led the proceedings. He was in sparkling form and had not changed at all. In a party after the concert, when suitably oiled by the liquid refreshment on hand, he launched into one of his expositions upon the virtues of socialism as preached by Bertrand Russell. With our humorous landlord, Peter Poskitt, present and also his genial wife, Alison, both highly-intelligent Cambridge University graduates, he was on a hiding to nothing. Thinking that he was not being taken seriously, Mark had worked himself up into such a frenzy that he stormed out of the house in a fury. Unfortunately, he was staying with Alison and Peter who to him must have been an embodiment of the very capitalism he despised, with their two houses and the family building concern which employed a large body of men. When finally he returned, suitably chastened and very embarrassed, it was late, so he chose to sleep on the sitting room floor at no. 23 Doncaster Road. It was a very quiet Mark who left for London on the next morning.

This music making marked an upturn in musical affairs at the Abbey, the only blot on the horizon being a final fracas with Jack the drink-loving bass, who threatened to put me into hospital even if he did time for it. However, that was the last we saw or heard of him. Spiritually matters were less encouraging and although when compared to St. James, the other Anglican church in the town, the Abbey may have seemed to veer towards middle-of-the-road churchmanship, to me it was a come-down from the High Church ceremonial that I had always been used to and loved.

This was brought home to me forcibly on my first Good Friday at Selby. On the television that morning was a liturgical service from none other than my beloved St. Mary the Virgin, Primrose Hill. Hazel and I went to the Poskitt home to watch this, as we could not afford a T.V. ... There on the screen was that lovely whitewashed yet colourful church, suitably decked out for Holy Week, with Fr. Timms officiating and all the familiar faces in the choir that we had waved good-bye to on the platform of Llanelli Station only seven months before, singing the lovely music that I had associated with this day for the past fifteen years. I was nearly in tears as all that was on offer that day at Selby Abbey was a "Hymn-Sandwich" as we irreverently called a formless service made up of hymns, readings, prayers and a sermon. It all seemed so unworthy a memorial to the man who had died an agonising death on a cross for the sake of Mankind, especially when so fantastic a church could lend itself easily to such magical, meaningful liturgical worship. Yet to put this all into perspective, I found it fascinating that Alison Poskitt who was watching the T.V. service with us remained quite unmoved by all the ceremonial, presumably because she was used to Selby Abbey ways.

Yet if we were disappointed with John Kent's churchmanship, we could not fault him over his enthusiasm and support for our work. Indeed, he explained how the improvements in the music left him feeling that he should raise the quality of his sermons. However, when he chose he could preach well, as he did when the string quartet had played Haydn's "Seven Last Words" and he had introduced each one by reciting the words of Jesus and speaking briefly about them before the music was played, as was the original intention of the great composer.

Meanwhile, Hazel and I had taken it upon ourselves to make ourselves known to the parents of the choirboys. We invited them to tea at no. 23 Doncaster Road and eventually invested in a washing-up machine before purchasing even a washing machine! When we tried visiting them in their own homes, at the first one we were kept talking on the doorstep for some time until, realising that we weren't going to go away, the father reluctantly invited us in. Obviously such tactics were new in Selby, yet they had the desired effect, for not only did the choir grow in numbers but so also did parental interest and involvement. The Special Choir also was growing, so much so that it adopted the name "Selby Choral Society" and moved to larger premises. New recruits included Thea Hinds from the nearby village of Burn, who was married to a farmer from Carmarthenshire and numbered among her friends the eminent soprano Honor Sheppard, an asset which was put to good use later when the choral society began to perform large-scale works requiring soloists. Another recruit was gracious Mollie Blake, Headmistress of Selby Girls' High School, eventually to become Headmistress of the prestigious Manchester High School for Girls. With Peter and Alison Poskitt and also John and Bess Kent, who were all founder members, we made a close little inner group that sometimes adjourned to the Vicarage after rehearsals. On these occasions, John would go next door to the Conservative Club and return with a jug full of beer which would keep our conversations going until the early hours of the following morning.

A second concert was planned and the Choral Society was hard at work preparing music by sixteenth-century composers along with "Three Hymns to the Virgin" by the young contemporary composer Peter Aston, who at that time worked at York University. By now, through *The Selby Times*, we had come to know Royston Ashby, a tall lad with a phenomenal technique on the violin and an equally phenomenal bass voice. He lived with his adopted parents not far from the Abbey, in Leeds Road, and attended the local Secondary School. He had an extraordinary hobby which was cleaning windows and to that end had even purchased his own ladders with money he had earned from financially exploiting his hobby. One day we saved him from disaster when we saw him about to climb up his ladders, having placed them against the enormous plate-glass window of a shop in Gowthorpe, Selby's main street. In a moment of absent-mindedness, it hadn't occurred to him that as he set about climbing his ladders his weight would have propelled them straight through the very glass windows he was intent on cleaning, with disastrous consequences to himself. This also would have had disastrous consequences to our concert because Royston was due to play some eighteenth-century violin sonatas accompanied by Hazel playing on her harpsichord.

Strangely, however, we were beginning to find other string players at this time. There was Raymond Pigott who led the West Riding String Quartet, and his wife Sheila who was also a violinist and whom I had known at the Royal Academy of Music; they lived at Wakefield. Another violinist was Stella Kemp-Welch who lived near York in a house called "Farthings", because some farthings (coins worth 1/4 d) had been embedded in concrete by the front door. Also from near York came viola player Austin Wright, a noted sculptor, while 'cellist David Mair taught at St. Peter's School, York. So on Saturday July 20th 1963 the Selby Choral Society gave its second concert in the Abbey, the first under its new name. During the previous week, preparatory concerts had been given in churches at the nearby villages of Drax and Thorganby: here Hazel found a small but lovely old organ to complement her programme-filling solos. In the Abbey the Choral Society sang its unaccompanied items, Royston and Hazel played their eighteenth-century sonatas and the proverbial "icing on the cake" was provided by Hazel playing G. F. Handel's Organ Concerto in F, op. 4 no. 4, accompanied by our little string orchestra. We felt we were getting somewhere at last!

In the autumn, on Saturday October 5th, Hazel and I launched the Selby Music Society in an attempt to bring more "live" music to the town. The opening recital was given by Stella Kemp-Welch in her capacity as a soprano and her songs and arias were accompanied by Hazel on the piano. Admission to non-members of the Society was priced at four shillings (20p). From the very beginning we gave the audience the chance to meet and talk with the soloists over tea and biscuits, and this went down well. So we utilised our musical friends and organised recitals by Clarissa Melville, the London flute-playing grand-daughter of Dr. Charles Moody, Raymond and Sheila Pigott and also Raymond's West Riding String Quartet, which, in playing music by Mozart, Ravel, Shostakovich and Webern caused a few eyebrows to be raised by Selby music-lovers who were unaccustomed to hearing twentieth-century music. However, eyebrows were raised even higher when we managed to persuade Dr. Francis Jackson, the esteemed Organist of York Minster, to give his first-ever piano recital, much to the delight of his wife Priscilla. His programme included the technically-demanding "Ballade No. 3" by Chopin and Ravel's "Le Tombeau de Couperin". So we went on to bring the internationally-known bass Owen Brannigan to Selby and his inimitable way of singing North Country Folk Songs delighted everyone. Archie Camden came too and the humour he conveyed through his bassoon playing was infectious. Soprano Jill Knott-Bower and Robert Spencer (baritone, lute and guitar) not only gave us a fascinating evening of music but showed us how a novel use of lighting can add a new dimension to concert presentation.

Most extraordinary was the programme given in the Abbey by the Derby Cathedral Choir and Brass Ensemble, which included some fascinating nineteenth-century Russian Orthodox Church Music. Although this concert was timed to start earlier than usual to enable the choristers to get back to Derby for adequate sleep in preparation for Sunday's services, Wallace Ross, the Organist and Choirmaster, experienced considerable difficulty in extracting his choirmen from the Londesborough Arms and his choirboys from the fish and chip shop, not that he tried very hard! By now, these activities were receiving financial support from the National Federation of Music Societies, but what was particularly gratifying was the interest shown by Selby Urban District Council and the increasing number of Society members.

At the same time, membership of the Choral Society was approaching forty, with twelve sopranos, nine contraltos, six tenors and ten basses. Towards the end of that year, 1963, on Saturday November 30th, after the usual preparatory concerts at nearby Barlby Church and lovely Snaith Priory Church, the Choral Society performed the first part of Handel's "Messiah" accompanied by an orchestra led by Sheila Pigott. This brought to Selby Abbey not only my sister Daphne as soprano soloist, but also the Watkins Shaw edition, which was still revolutionary. Admission to the performance cost just two shillings and sixpence (2s 6d=12 1/2p). Increased membership brought two new people into our lives, John Barnett and Bruce Robinson, who numbered among the basses. John came from a musical family and his sister, Jane, studied the piano at the Royal Academy of Music; in due course she too gave a piano recital for Brecon Music Society. John was an engineer working on the construction of the enormous Eggborough Power Station and being such a useful bass he was soon persuaded to sing in the Abbey Choir in addition to the Choral Society. Bruce was very different, much more of an extrovert, with a flair for big business and plenty of money behind him. As Manager of the Danepak factory in Selby, he had been given the challenge of producing half-a-million packets of bacon each week and, naturally, he attained his target. One day he showed Hazel and me around his empire and I remember some conveyor-belts churning out packet after packet of bacon to the accompaniment of loud canned music. Every so often, white-coated young ladies removed a few packets to check that the seals were air-tight. What happened to the rejects? We returned home with some!

However, this was not the only time that we sampled Danepak rejects. Sometimes now on a Wednesday night after the Choral Society rehearsal we adjourned not to the Vicarage but to the lavish Robinson household in Leeds Road. Such luxury I had only experienced in my dreams; certainly, it had not been attainable in my part of South London. We enjoyed more Danepak rejects in toasted sandwiches produced by Bruce's wife Pam, who numbered among the sopranos, while drinks flowed freely as we sang madrigals or just talked. If we saw in the dawn, Bruce provided a car to ensure that Hazel reached Read Grammar School, Drax on time.

So, as the year drew to a close, the future looked good, so different from twelve months before and because of this we were able to enjoy our Christmas Day at the Vicarage that much more. Indeed the next few months proved to be exciting as the

Abbey Choir planned its first-ever singing holiday, inevitably to St. Davids Cathedral. One of the choir's fund-raising ventures took it to the nearby magnificent former collegiate church of St. Mary in the village of Hemingbrough, where a concert was given. This church is noted for its tall, needle-like spire which is visible for miles around, but at that time it was also noted for its eccentric Vicar. This ancient gentleman always bicycled the three miles into Selby not along the main road from Hull but on the pedestrian footpath alongside and he was oblivious to anyone walking along. Such were his eccentricities that when one of the Abbey choirmen, Peter Warham, visited Hemingbrough Church with his wife, Dorothy, she was sent out by the Vicar because her head was uncovered; only when she had covered her head with a handkerchief was she allowed back in again.

As the Vicar showed them around the church, Peter commented on how the Victorian stained glass spoiled the otherwise magnificent interior, whereupon the Vicar flew into a rage: "What do you mean?" he shouted, "My generation won the Empire, all yours can do it is lose it!" Legend has it that when the famous firm of wood-carvers, Thompson of Kilburn in Yorkshire, did some work in his church and he found one of the men busily carving the mouse that is the firm's trademark, he flew into another rage and insisted that a cat be carved nearby. When the Abbey Choir gave its recital in the choir stalls, the Vicar appeared to sleep through it all. When it had finished, he jerked upright and barked out "Is that it?", then, leaping to his feet, he uttered a blessing and that was that!

The visit to St. David's Cathedral during the next summer was a resounding success, the only major problem being how to get there. In the end we opted to go by train from Selby to Leeds, from Leeds to Shrewsbury, from Shrewsbury down the lovely Central Wales line to Llandilo in Carmarthenshire, from where an Eynons bus from Trimsaran near to Kidwelly took us the remaining sixty-two miles to the smallest city in Britain. At St. David's the wooden hut by the ruined Bishop's Palace was no longer available, so we stayed in a primary school above the Cathedral. Singing the services was fun and so too was the social side of the visit. As always the Cathedral Organist, Peter Boorman, was most hospitable, regaling us with countless stories about cathedral musicians and cathedral clerics. While Hazel was in the organ loft on the Sunday evening, he showed her some music as the Canon-in-Residence preached."Don't worry," he said, "This sermon lasts twenty minutes. I've heard it three times before." And so it might have been, only unbeknown to Peter, the Canon omitted some of it with the result that when the final hymn was announced it was some considerable time before Hazel played the tune over on the organ.

It was on this trip that Peter Boorman delighted us with his stories about hymns."Do you know the Footballer's hymn?" he asked, and when we looked blank he continued: "One the earnest looking forward" which is to be found in the hymn "Through the night of doubt and sorrow". Then came the Car Driver's hymn: "Sunbeams scorching all the day", from the hymn "Forty Days and Forty Nights" – "Sunbeams" in those days being a flashy brand of car! This was followed by the "Midwife's Hymn": "Strong Deliverer", a line from the famous Welsh Hymn "Cwm Rhondda" – "Guide me, O thou great Jehovah". Then he went on to tell us how the Archbishop of Wales had rushed up to him one day announcing a new one: "The Nudist's Hymn": "More and more thyself display", which is to be found in "Christ whose glory fills the skies". To these we added our contribution, "The Prostitute's Hymn": "Thou didst note my working breast", from "King of Glory, King of Peace". Peter also mentioned "The Deaf Man's Psalm", Psalm 130, which contains the line: "Before the morning watch, I say, before the morning watch."

While in Pembrokeshire the Abbey Choir visited Kidwelly and gave a concert in St. Mary's Church. However, my abiding memory of this trip was the fabulous wide games played using the rich countryside around over a two-mile radius. The idea was to divide everyone into two teams, each with a flag, and the winning team had to be in possession of both flags by the end. To avoid fights, each person had a piece of wool tied around the left arm, and when this was broken that person was out of the action until he had returned to a central point to have another piece of wool tied on. During one such game, while being pursued, I ran down a narrow lane and leapt over a hedge to avoid being seen, only to land next to someone doing his gardening. Mumbling profuse apologies and being very embarrassed, I leapt back over the hedge into the lane and ran away as fast as I could.

When the choristers were back in Selby, they were all the better for their trip. Daily practices and services had worked wonders with their singing, while being together for nearly two weeks had moulded them into a happy and sociable group. Yet life would soon change for ever because Hazel was now, as the Authorised Version of the Bible graciously puts it, "with child" and the expected time of arrival was before the end of the year.

XX

For the previous five terms I had taught Music at the County Secondary School in nearby Howden and had enjoyed every minute of my time there. This small market town was full of dilapidated Georgian houses and shops. It also had an air of desolation about it: nothing appeared to happen there. It was dominated by the most tall Perpendicular crossing tower imaginable which belonged to the church of St. Peter, formerly collegiate but now always referred to as Howden Minster. The entire building originally had not been much smaller than Selby Abbey but now all that remained was the nave, which had become the Parish Church because the Chancel was in ruins. The glory of the Minster was its beautiful but roofless Chapter House and I had a useless longing to see this restored so as to take its place alongside other such Chapter Houses like that at Southwell Minster. Howden had its moments of glory, once being the site of the biggest horse fair in England, then shortly before the Second World War the birthplace of the famous R101.

Neville Shute worked on this airship as an engineer before he became known as a writer. In his autobiography, "Slide Rule", he wrote much of interest about Howden and its inhabitants, some of whose children and grandchildren I must have taught. In particular he claimed that some in-breeding was brought about by brothers and sisters rearing children, which I found unbelievable although he must have had some foundation for his claim. Yet there was a fascinating variety of youngsters in the school including many local products of variable ability, most of whom were fun to work with. However, the daily ritual of the Senior Mistress, a delightful spinster named Miss Ringrose, amazed me. Every morning she would meet a brother and a sister at a side-door before school officially began, wait while they removed their not-very-delectable clothes, give them a wash, then put clean clothes on them; at the end of the school day this process was reversed, whereupon the two children would set off happily for their walk home, back in their own clothes. The Headmaster had divided the schoolchildren into four houses, naming one after the famous Barnes Wallis, inventor of the Bouncing Bomb of "Dambuster" fame, who had also designed the R101. So the great man came to Howden County Secondary School to celebrate his distinction and great was the excitement of both staff and pupils alike. Unfortunately the day turned out to be an unqualified disaster. Barnes Wallis was a precise and exact person, but everything that could go wrong did, culminating in the overhead projector refusing to show his pictures. Yet the great man was long-suffering in adversity and at the end of his day had the grace to say how much he'd enjoyed himself.

At that time I could not drive a car, so on the days when I taught at Howden I had to be at Selby station at 7.30 a.m. to board the slow train to Hull which stopped at Howden. While Selby Station was in the centre of the town, unfortunately Howden Station was some distance outside it, so that the lengthy walk past the flat fields where I believe the R101 was built became a regular part of my routine. The return journey was slower. As there was no convenient train I travelled by a double-decker bus which passed through the centre of Howden, then through

Hemingbrough on its way to Selby. In the course of my time at Howden County Secondary School I had the time to read six complete Waverley novels by Sir Walter Scott while travelling to and from work! Yet happy as I was at that school, when the Head of Music position at Selby High School for Girls became vacant, I had to apply for it and my application was successful. This meant an end to my nomadic existence, as from now on all my work would be in Selby itself, within walking distance of 23 Doncaster Road. I was looking forward to working for Mollie Blake as she was such a lovely person who tried hard to cultivate a suitable environment for civilised learning, with good manners high on the agenda. Sadly she was not always given adequate support, nor did she convince all the parents of the folly of their daughters working in a shop on Saturdays and courting in the park on Sundays when there were "O" and "A" level examinations to be taken.

There were some interesting characters on the staff whom I had come to know during my time at Selby, indeed, two of them lodged at the Abbey Vicarage. Some were middle-aged, very respectable and genteel, so much so that when one of the local papers carried a headline to the effect that the High School staff had won on the Football Pools, these quaint ladies protested to the Editor that they did not gamble. All was revealed in the following week's paper when it was stated that the Caretaker and cleaners together had won some £4,000, which was a considerable amount of money in those days. The Caretaker himself was a formidable character whom I had befriended through using the school as the regular venue for the Selby Music Society concerts. We employed him but did most of the necessary work ourselves for which he received overtime pay, yet it was an arrangement which suited us both. He chose this time to get himself elected to the local council with the result that on prestigious Prize Day he refused to function as Caretaker but appeared in his official capacity as a local Councillor, sitting among the V. I. P. s, clad in a suit.

While I set about my first term of teaching at Selby High School, the Choral Society which now rehearsed in my music room made its final preparations for a performance of much of G. F. Handel's "Messiah". Some of the choruses were tried out at concerts in nearby Cawood Methodist Church and in Pollington-cum-Balne Church near to York. The actual performance was given in the Abbey on Saturday November 28th, with the Choral Society and Abbey choirboys joined by an orchestra again led by Sheila Pigott. The list of soloists was like a trip down "Memory Lane": soprano Sheila McShee who had been in the choir at Holy Trinity, Brompton, when Hazel had been Assistant Organist there, along with tenor Michael Blackley and bass Christopher Keyte, who had both been Lay Clerks at Southwark Cathedral during my time there – Michael went on to be a Vicar Choral at St. Paul's Cathedral and Christopher became a Choral Scholar at King's College, Cambridge. By using friends as soloists, it was possible to keep down costs and it also made for easier and happier working conditions because we all knew each other. Hazel played the organ while Michael Smith, Organist of St. Giles' Church, Pontefract, later of Llandaff Cathedral, played the harpsichord. For the first time newspaper critics were in attendance and comments were suitably favourable, although while "*The Yorkshire Post*" and "*Selby Times*" stated that a little more weight in the tenors and basses would have been welcome, "*The Selby Gazette and Herald*" stated that the choir was "well-balanced".

A fortnight later there was a Carol Concert at the Abbey and Hazel's first baby was also due. The Choral Society and Abbey Choir were in the nave along with the large audience, the organ was on either side of the choir stalls a little way off, but Hazel was at the console around one hundred feet further on, so a television screen was used to keep her in touch with the musical proceedings. As there was always the chance that the exertion of playing the organ, especially the pedalling part of the operation, might bring about a premature birth, Michael Smith was paid three guineas (£3-3s-0d=£3.15) to sit in the audience, ready to take over from Hazel should this happen! However, Hazel survived not only this concert but also the Christmas Services which she accompanied with her usual aplomb.

By this time her mother had moved into no. 23 Doncaster Road, on loan from her father, but still the baby showed no signs of arriving. All sorts of weird and wonderful things were given Hazel to drink, or were done to various parts of her anatomy in desperate attempts to start the baby on its journey. When it was three weeks overdue an X-ray photograph was taken which showed the baby lying in Hazel's womb, perfectly content. On the morning of January 18th, Hazel started to clean the house and suddenly the baby was on its way. Hazel always had a predilection for the number eight; after all, she had been born on the 8th, married on the 18th and now this...! The midwife moved in; she was bothered by the fact that the ambulance crew were waiting in the sitting room, playing with Hannibal, while the doctor was in the humble kitchen. I was present when the miracle of creation brought Harriet Rachel into this world. It was a wonderful moment which will always live with me. Being a month late, Harriet had a fine head of hair and when I proudly showed her to Hazel's mother within minutes of being born, all the new grandmother could say was: "Just like a Jap." Soon Hazel was tucked up in bed and, with the help of an injection, was sound asleep.

Two hours later, at around 11 p.m. there was a loud, ominous thud; when I rushed into the bedroom there was Hazel lying on the floor, haemorrhaging badly. A doctor was quickly summoned; he sent me down to the local hospital which, fortunately, was just a little way down Doncaster Road, there to collect some plasma so that a blood transfusion could be set in motion. At around 4 a.m. an ambulance team arrived to take Hazel and Harriet to the maternity hospital near to York. As they were carrying the two of them down the garden path on a stretcher, I noticed the next-door neighbour peeping through the curtains, determined not to miss anything despite the early morning hour. For all the unexpected problems I was glad that Harriet, like King Henry I, had seen her first light of day in Selby because it entitled her to be called a Selebian, a much-prized distinction granted only to people who had either been born in the town or lived there for forty years or more.

So began an auspicious year which was full of surprises. Among them was the Selby Festival that I instigated, comprising one week of artistic activity in the early summer. Looking back I cannot but be amazed at my cheek, but everything worked out. There was a committee which numbered twelve people of whom eight represented music and art and four were local councillors. Fortunately two Abbey choirmen who were council employees acted as Secretary and Treasurer: Alan Wilson and Jack Thompson. They worked tirelessly for the project.

Amazingly the Labour-controlled Selby Urban District Council had actually backed its interest with cash and had voted a penny rate for the Festival, to produce £1,300, which at that time was more than five times my annual salary as Organist at Selby Abbey. Indeed, to put this into perspective, Hazel and I had been contemplating buying a small house close to the Abbey for £3,900. I organised the musical side of the proceedings while Joe Doyle, Art Master at Read, Grammar School, Drax, organised the art section; I was Chairman and he was Vice-Chairman.

On June 12th 1965, the opening day of the Selby Festival got off to an unexpectedly good start with "Peterborough" writing in the *Daily Telegraph*:

> *"I recently mentioned musicians' complaints about the lukewarm attitude of local councils to events in their districts.*
>
> *One place with a happier situation is Selby, Yorks., where a week's festival of music, photography, films and art opens today under the patronage of Lord St. Oswald.*
>
> *Selby U. D. C. has offered a guarantee against loss of up to £1,300 because it is anxious to stimulate public interest and four councillors are on the festival committee.*
>
> *For an area with a population of only 20,000 this is pretty good."*

This augured well for the week and quite rightly so. One highlight of the festival was an exhibition of seven sculptures created by my viola-playing friend Austin Wright which were exhibited inside and outside the Abbey. This drew from *The Guardian* newspaper an enthusiastic article stating that:

"A town miles from a busy road can have disadvantages. Peace becomes a synonym for backwater. Selby ought to qualify, but in fact has often been far too vigorous for some tastes. It took the intervention of the Chancellor of the Diocese of York, for instance, to prevent Epstein's "Ecce Homo" from being installed in Selby Abbey ..."

The writer, M. G. McNay then proceeded to the work of Austin Wright. He suggested that "out of the context of art galleries" his work was "a revelation", showing him to be "a romantic who avoided the excesses and clichés alike of modern sculpture." He claimed that Austin Wright was to aluminium what Henry Moore was to stone, which was praise indeed. Furthermore he went on to write that although the work was modern, somehow it still related to the Norman and Mediaeval architecture of the Abbey. To him the three works standing outside on the lawn gleamed "in the light reflected from the Abbey walls", while those in the venerable building itself gained from being viewed in a dim light "against dark stone and stained glass." So he considered that Selby had been provided with a new experience, one that was almost, but not quite, too well stage-managed. Obviously the Festival had backed a winner - or had it? One of the exhibits outside was slightly damaged and no-one could decided if this was deliberate or accidental. Fortunately, however, the sculptures were fully insured. So much enthusiasm from such a highly-respected national newspaper came as a complete surprise and the committee wallowed in reflected glory.

The visual arts were also represented by an exhibition of Contemporary Painting and Design which was open throughout the week at the Museum Hall, showing the work of three Yorkshire artists: John Ridgewell, Marcia Tyler and Charles Wright. There were even four art films along with a film about Selby itself, all made by members of the local Cine Club. As for Selby Camera Club, its members produced a programme of colour slides covering the subjects of portraiture, architecture, pictorial history and natural history. Of especial interest was the evening designed by the Abbey Architect George Pace, who, in his own inimitable way with the help of specially-taken photographs, made his audience take a second look at Selby. He illustrated how, despite there being enough industry in Selby for its inhabitants to hold down one-and-a-half or even two jobs, the town still retained some of its rural charm. So a photograph of the Abbey taken from the side of the Vicarage garden where all looked coy and countrified was very different from a photograph taken a few yards on, nearer the Abbey, almost on the pavement outside the Vicarage, as this revealed some less attractive aspects of urban life.

As so often happens, musical activities consumed the lion's share of the money available for festival activities; only the opening service cost nothing. At this, music by C. Hubert Parry and Sidney Campbell, sung by the Abbey Choir, provided the sparkle that was missing from the address given by Professor Cleanth Brooks, Cultural Attaché at the U. S. A. Embassy in London.

The first concert, given later that evening as "the rays of the setting sun could be seen shining through the windows, dappling the soft lines of the stonework and window tracery with warm light" was given by the Sylvan Trio. This featured oboist Sarah Francis, who had played alongside me in the London Schools' Symphony Orchestra, her father, distinguished flautist John Francis, and her mother, an equally distinguished harpsichordist with the delightful name of Millicent Silver. In *"The Guardian"*, Anthony Hedges praised Selby for its "enterprising week of artistic activity", praised the Trio for its "nicely balanced programme" and praised the Abbey authorities for allowing the audience to express appreciation through applause.

The esteemed Music Critic of *"The Yorkshire Post"*, Ernest Bradbury, thought differently. He was outspoken in his condemnation of this applause, stating that "Selby Abbey is, after all, the house of God, not a secular Concert Hall." Nor did he approve of "the standard lamp with a deep red shade, at the head of the red carpet in the choir," which had been placed there to give warmth and additional colour to the proceedings, not to mention extra light to the performers. He claimed that this "gave the historic building a secular look." Yet he was full of praise for Sarah Francis's performance of Benjamin Britten's *Six Metamorphoses after Ovid* for unaccompanied oboe and ended with: "As Miss Francis began to play Britten's last movement, 'Arethusa', the nine o'clock chime of the Abbey bells began *"We love the place O God""*", which to him was "the sacred and the profane, in very truth." A third critic, who remained anonymous, mentioned neither applause nor the standard lamp but did single out the printed programme as "a thing of beauty and distinction." Indeed, these had been specially produced on the hand printing-press belonging to Peter Boorman, Organist of St. David's Cathedral, which he operated in the back room of his ancient house in the Close.

As it actually happened, the applause had been entirely spontaneous and unexpected. Now the Vicar and Churchwardens of Selby Abbey had until Friday to decide on whether or not this should be allowed to continue, for on that night there was to be an orchestral concert in the Abbey. While they were busily deliberating, a fine recital of music for three hands on one piano was given by Cyril Smith and Phyllis Sellick on the Tuesday night in the High School Hall, where there was no problem about applause. Indeed, so enthusiastically did the audience applaud these two delightful pianists that they played not one but two encores. Meanwhile, the Vicar was thinking long and hard about applause in the Abbey. Immediately before the Northern Sinfonia Orchestra began its concert on Friday evening, he announced that he saw no reason why applause should not be offered. Ernest Bradbury was horrified. In "*The Yorkshire Post*" he wrote: "Confusion in the Church of England (I write as a member) extends to small things as well as great." With the neighbouring York Minster always printing on programmes the warning: "It will be understood that no applause can be allowed in the Cathedral", where, he asked, did the bewildered laity stand? Then he revealed that during the concert interval, John Kent had told him: "I used to feel exactly as you do. I've now changed my mind."

As for the concert itself, Ernest Bradbury was full of praise for the orchestra, particularly for its performance of Bartok's "Divertimento for Strings", which was marred only by sounds of passing traffic – "a motor bicycle quite ruined the finale"! To him, "the building allowed wonderful sonority, especially to lower instruments, and the programme gave ample scope for delicacy and musical artistry of a high order." His report was most detailed not only about this great work but also about Mozart's "Divertimento in F, K. 213" and about Gordon Jacob's "Flute Concerto" in which the soloist was another of my Royal Academy of Music contemporaries, David Haslam. However, Haydn's "Symphony No. 85, "*La Reine*"" was dismissed in passing as "a fitting end to a well thought-out programme": by the time that was played, directed by the conductor Boris Brott complete with harpsichord continuo, Ernest Bradbury was actually in his car heading home for Ilkley! As he left the Abbey he had whispered to me that, as he had heard the orchestra play this particular symphony during the previous week, he hoped I would forgive him if he had an early night. And why not? The next evening found him back inside the Abbey for the final concert of the Festival.

This was the only local contribution to the musical side of the Festival and therefore it was gratifying to read that Ernest Bradbury considered the concert comparable to "any of the more professional items earlier in the week". Gustav Holst's "Two Psalms" he reckoned to be "the best thing of the evening, beautifully in tune with a restrained but musical quality, well-balanced like good chamber music and most acceptable in articulation." He enjoyed Peter Aston's three short but charming *Hymns* which, happily, were given twice. The performance of Mozart's "Coronation Mass" in which Selby Choral Society was accompanied by the orchestra that was led as usual by Sheila Pigott, he claimed, "bore worthy musical comparison" to what he had heard at the Hereford Cathedral Three Choirs Festival four years earlier. Applause was not mentioned, nor can I remember if there was any, but I must confess that my upbringing had taught me not to expect any and I have never been very good at acknowledging any.

Numbered among the soloists that evening was another Royal Academy of Music product, the bass Michael Rippon, who was a fine, if extrovert, singer. The equally-distinguished tenor was Ian Partridge who, as he walked along The Crescent towards the Corunna Café for a concluding party after the concert immaculately clad in a morning suit – an almost unknown sight in industrial Selby – distinguished himself by giving with great aplomb a very deliberate V sign to an uncouth youth who had commented loudly and rudely on his elegant appearance from the other side of the road.

Sometimes after such a frenzy of activity there is a lull. However, there was no chance of that happening because within three weeks the Royal Liverpool Philharmonic Orchestra was coming to Selby to give a concert in the Abbey. How this came about I cannot remember, but with a programme of the "Tallis Fantasia" by Vaughan Williams, Beethoven's Sixth Symphony and Elgar "Enigma Variations", the concert was bound to attract a vast audience. And so it did: around six hundred people had come to hear Handel's "Messiah", but on Wednesday July 7th 1965, more than one thousand people crammed into the nave and transepts to hear this magnificent concert. Such support resulted in the following letter appearing in the *Selby Times*:

> *"Sir – It was surprising but encouraging to see so many new faces in those zealously guarded reserved seats in Selby Abbey on Wednesday night at the very fine performance of the Liverpool Philharmonic Orchestra.*
>
> *I trust we can look forward to their sustained support (both physical and financial) in our varied musical programme for the forthcoming season.*
> *Yours Faithfully,*
> *REGULAR PATRON.*

. It was indeed a magical concert and Ernest Bradbury was in his seventh heaven."The music," he wrote in "*The Yorkshire Post*" "appeared even more splendid because of the superb acoustics of the building." He declared that he had never heard such a lovely and radiant performance of the symphony: indeed, so "clear and leisurely" was the second movement that it seemed as if the brook was endless. When it came to the thunderstorm in the fourth movement, he wrote: "the first thunder-clap, with its swish of rain, was so realistic that it caused a small boy in front of me to put up his collar"! Throughout the concert he claimed that the conductor, Charles Groves, "allowed the music (and the players) to unfold without extravagant emphasis or unwanted gesture, and the music itself had a timeless aura in keeping with the ancient stones of the Abbey itself."

Hazel and I went for a drink with Charles Groves, the Orchestral Manager and a few other people connected with the orchestra in the Londesborough Arms. For fun I told them that the Verger, George White, had recorded the concert in order to entertain visitors to the Abbey. There was a deathly hush, then pandemonium. What about additional fees to the musicians in accordance with Musicians' Union regulations? When I explained that I was having a joke at their expense, everyone relaxed again to enjoy the remainder of the evening. On the next morning, as I walked into the Abbey to make sure that all was tidy, strains of the previous night's concert wafted through the air as George indeed was entertaining visitors. I turned around and fled.

XXI

One newspaper report about the Royal Liverpool Philharmonic Orchestra concert had been written in less than glowing terms. This was the work of John Kenney of the *Selby Gazette and Herald*. To him, the first two movements of Beethoven's "Pastoral" Symphony had been "pedantic … tinned and uninspired." However, my own personal doubts about John Kenney's abilities to operate as a music critic appeared fully justified when I read that, in his opinion, the final variation of Elgar's "*Enigma Variations*" had lost a certain amount of lustre without the organ." He went on to expound on the subject of the organ:

"The Abbey has one recognised as the finest of its kind in the country. It was a few feet away from the orchestra, but as they played it remained silent, possibly through a lack of foresight."

The silly man - obviously he was not good at sniffing out news. Only three months earlier, in the "Diary of a Yorkshireman" published in "*The Yorkshire Post*", he would have read that on Easter Monday, April 19th 1965, the Selby Abbey choirboys had attempted to collect ten thousand pennies in an effort to encircle the Abbey to help pay for the overhaul and cleaning of the Abbey Organ. Indeed, in *The Selby Times* a few days later, he would have seen a photographs of me pushing to the bank a wheelbarrow full of pennies, accompanied by one of the Abbey Wardens, the Verger and Hannibal my Boxer dog.

While the main job might have been getting the grime off the organ mechanism, the most important work was moving the organ console closer to the actual pipes in order to eradicate the time-lag between pressing the keys and hearing the actual sounds thereby produced from the instrument. While I had become used to this, as had Hazel, visiting recitalists were continually finding this time lag a problem. The report went on to explain how, some years before, the great Fernando Germani, Organist at the Vatican, had made two 33 r. p.m. records for H. M. V. on the Abbey organ. On that occasion, H.M.V. had insisted that he record the famous Widor "Toccata" and the poor man had found his hands playing three notes ahead of the actual sound, which made this recording session something of a nightmare. More recently, during the year 1964, he had made two more 33 r.p.m. records for H.M.V. on the Abbey Organ and in the programme this time was the Bach-Vivaldi Concerto in A minor, which had been even more problematical to record. The trouble here had been the double-pedalling in the fast movements, because the pedal action was even slower than the manual action, which meant that the sound of the pedal notes arrived later at the console than the sound of the keyboard notes, thereby creating a second time-lag. Recording this concerto, not surprisingly, had shown that moving the console was a matter of some urgency, especially as on Wednesday September 1st, Choral Evensong was to be broadcast by the Abbey Choir on the Home Service of BBC Radio. It was a great achievement on the part of the Abbey Choir to be invited to broadcast one of these prestigious services and it was therefore essential that the choristers should be able to excel themselves and to this end, the work on the organ needed to be done. So on July 7th, while John Kenney had been bemoaning the absence of the Abbey Organ from the final "Enigma" Variation at the Liverpool Philharmonic Orchestra concert, the great instrument had been lying mute in pieces on the floor in the choir aisles, barely a few yards away from where he had been sitting.

The broadcast Choral Evensong passed off happily and resulted in my receiving three interesting letters: one came from Glyndwr Williams, a former Curate of St. Mary's Church, Kidwelly, who was much loved by Hazel's family and who went on to become a Residentiary Canon at Bangor Cathedral. He wrote in appreciation of the hymn, "I heard the voice of Jesus say 'Come unto me and rest'" that was sung to the tune known as "Kingsfold", the sort of folk melody that is claimed as English yet its ending points more to its being Irish. Sadly, today, in this age of "Happy-Clappy Hymns", fewer churchgoers are given the chance to appreciate the simple, timeless beauty of such uncomplicated music. The second letter came from George Heath-Gracie, a former Organist of Derby Cathedral, who enjoyed the psalms. So began a happy friendship with him and with his wife which lasted until their deaths in their nineties. The third letter was from the new Dean of Brecon Cathedral, the Very Revd Gwynno James, who had listened to the service on a transistor radio while sunbathing on the beach at Whitesands Bay near to St. Davids Cathedral.

Why did he write? What I didn't know, but he did, was that his Organist at Brecon Cathedral was on the move again. What both he and I knew was that both Organist jobs, at Selby Abbey and at Brecon Cathedral, were very similar as far as the work was concerned. Strange to relate, the fiery Deputy Head at Selby High School, a great character named Bronwen Lewis, had been born in Brecon where her father had been a Councillor. She was a true Breconian, to the extent that every Friday morning a copy of the *Brecon and Radnor Express* was delivered to her pigeon-hole in the Staff Room at the High School. Often I would peruse with disbelief this amazingly old-fashioned newspaper, which still carried advertisements on its front page just like the ancient copies of *The Times*. Not long after this, while idling away a few moments in the Staff Room, I read in the *Brecon and Radnor Express* that the Organist of Brecon Cathedral, M. Bryan Hesford, was indeed moving on to King's Lynn. Soon afterwards the job was advertised in the *Church Times* and my life was in turmoil again.

Meanwhile, however, there had been three organ recitals in celebration of the work done to the Abbey organ. Obviously the first one had to be given by dear old Francis Jackson, Organist of York Minster, but sadly he fell ill and his place was taken at very short notice by Hazel's old boss Robert Munns, Organist of Holy Trinity, Brompton. The second recital brought to Selby Dr. Sidney Campbell, who by now was Organist of St. George's Chapel, Windsor Castle. He had incorporated this recital with a visit to Scarborough, where he was busily engaged in one of his sidelines, demonstrating Hammond Electronic Organs! He started off his visit to Selby and the Abbey by meeting the organ tuner and showing him those parts of the organ which he hadn't tuned properly. This was but a prelude to a magnificent recital. While playing the popular J. S. Bach "Toccata and Fugue in D minor", he began by playing very correctly in a pseudo-Baroque style until suddenly, towards the end, he muttered "To hell with this!", pressed various pistons which brought into play all the heavy, loud reed stops and then played the last line an octave too high and ended on a resounding major (instead of minor) chord, saying to me, grinning from ear to ear as he did so, "That'll make them curse." Later he ended with the extrovert "Final in B flat" by César Franck which he played with great aplomb, making the Abbey ring with lots of noise, but noise that was both brilliant and musical; it was the equivalent of a gigantic firework display. The third and final recital brought to Selby Abbey Dr. Campbell's successor at Southwark Cathedral, Harold Dexter, and with a little more normality the series drew to a close. It had resulted in much memorable music being played, along with another trip down Memory Lane for Hazel and me.

Everything was going so well now: the Choral Society had around fifty members; the Music Society had more than one hundred and forty members; the Festival had been such a success that there were thoughts of more; the broadcast Evensong had brought about the long-awaited resignation from the Abbey Choir of George the Verger – the last remnant of the old choir, he was mortified at having made a mistake in a Gloria during the Canticles very publicly on the radio; even school was going well; furthermore I had just posted a letter requesting that the Royal Maundy Service come to Selby Abbey sometime in the future. So I agonised as to whether or not I applied for the Organist job at Brecon Cathedral. Perhaps what pushed me over the top was my desire to make Cathedral Music – after all, I had been actively involved in such music-making for two-thirds of my short life. At Selby Abbey there was a building, an organ and a choir ideal for the performance of Cathedral Music, yet because the Abbey was a Parish Church, the canticles at Evensong (the *Magnificat* and *Nunc Dimittis*) had to be sung congregationally to simple chants and, furthermore, if the anthem sung by the choir lasted more than three minutes certain members of the congregation would grumble. Where Brecon scored was that the Organist at the Cathedral was also Organist at the Parish Church; similarly the Dean of the Cathedral was also Vicar of the Parish Church and this dual identity made possible Cathedral Music in the Cathedral and Parish Church Music in the Church. So I sent in my application and was short-listed, then summoned to an interview.

Early in November I set off from Selby in the evening and travelled by train to Leeds, then from Leeds to Crewe, finally from Crewe to Abergavenny, arriving there at around 8 a.m. As Brecon no longer had any railways I walked down the road from the railway station to the town bus station. On the way a passer-by advised me to cross the road and walk on the pavement on the other side, which dutifully I did. It had been raining heavily during the night and soon I gave thanks for the voluntary advice as I watched a lorry pound up the hill and shower the other pavement with rainwater from the gutter! At the Bus Station I boarded the Brecon bus and, while waiting for it to set off, watched a multitude of carefree youngsters, beautifully turned-out, full of laughter, with sing-song voices, making their way to school. The atmosphere was completely different, but then this was a market town in an agricultural community while Selby, with its BOCM oil and cake mill, its Rostrons Paper Mill, its Beer Bottling plant, its ship-building works and its bacon-packing factory, was an industrial town that stood on an important railway crossroad, where trains from Liverpool to Hull met trains from London to York and Edinburgh. A little later as my bus wound its way to Brecon through Crickhowell, Llangynidr, Talybont-on-Usk and Llanfrynach, I felt as if I was entering a strange, remote, green and beautiful land.

Arriving at Brecon by St. Mary's Parish Church, which many tourists mistake for the Cathedral, I found my way to Bronwen Lewis's mother's house nearby, where I cleaned myself up and had some breakfast. Afterwards I made my way up Priory Hill to the Cathedral and, on reaching it, wandered around and then sat down on a chair at the back of the nave, behind the font, lost in my thoughts. It was very quiet and I was miles away when suddenly a kindly voice enquired: "Are you alright?" That was my introduction to dear Edgar Hawkes, the verger, and from that moment onwards the day passed quickly. I played the organ to Harry Gabb, Organist of the Chapel Royal and Assistant Organist of St. Paul's Cathedral, who had formerly been Organist of Llandaff Cathedral. I took a choir practice with a motley collection of boys who made a dreadful noise but appeared to enjoy themselves. I had an interview with the Dean, the Precentor (Canon Harry Williams, Vicar of St. Mary's Swansea), the Headmaster of Christ College (John Sharp), Harry Gabb and the Chapter Clerk (Colonel Pryce). Later the Dean invited me to stay for tea as I had such a long journey ahead of me and during the course of this he offered me the job which I accepted without hesitation. When the appointment was subsequently announced in the *Church Times* it was pointed out that I would be the youngest Cathedral Organist in the country. Shortly afterwards, I received a kindly postcard from my old harmony teacher, J. Albert Sowerbutts, in which he congratulated me but then added: "Don't think you are going to a real cathedral"!

One end of this appointment which needed tidying up was the part-time teaching at Builth Wells Bilateral School and to this end, an interview was arranged with the Headmaster, although the Dean was convinced that this would be a formality. And so it was. I returned to Brecon whereupon I was driven with the Dean to Builth Wells Vicarage to meet the Headmaster, the indomitable J. Ewart Davies. He was a great character, very outspoken, Welsh-speaking and a Non-Conformist. He was quite convinced that instead of being Cathedral Organist at Brecon I should be teaching at his school and Organist of Horeb Chapel in Builth, where he was a Deacon! What delighted him most was to learn that my wife was a Kidwelly girl and Welsh-speaking (which she was, vaguely), and it was probably that detail which clinched my appointment at his school. So my living was made up in a variety of ways which made the work viable for a married man, which it wasn't back in 1963. As Organist of Brecon Cathedral I would receive £450 p.a.; as Organist of St. Mary's Church, Brecon, I received a further £100 p.a.; I was guaranteed £50 p. a. in fees for extra services like weddings and funerals; I would be paid another £250 p.a. for teaching piano pupils at Christ College, a Public School in Brecon; to all this would be added the statutory pay for two days of teaching in a state school – Builth Wells High School, around £300, making a total of £1150, plus a rate-free and rent-free flat.

After my first visit I had enthused about this flat to Hazel, mentioning a lovely, historic house with long corridors along which we could put bookcases for our many books, but my enthusiasm had got the better of me. Hazel accompanied me on this second trip to Brecon, anxious to view this accommodation for herself to see what it was really like, but was less enthusiastic. There were long corridors all right, but there were also staircases – in fact there were stairs everywhere. One staircase led from the scullery in the bowels of the building up to the kitchen, three steps led down into a bathroom, two led into a glorious sitting room, none into the main bedroom but a flight of oak stairs led up to the second bedroom. That was not all, however, for at the top of that staircase there was a second door that led into a passage which in turn led to a hall where a "gothic" arched front door opened onto a flight of stone steps which led down to land level! Incidentally, that hallway contained a coin-box telephone, installed because my predecessor had run up a big bill on his private telephone in the flat but had then gone off to Norfolk, leaving the Dean and Chapter to clear the account. Naturally, they had no intention of that happening again.

The Dean and his saintly wife were perfect hosts as we stayed in the Deanery, where our bedroom looked down the Postern and gave a bird's-eye view of Brecon roof-tops, which are such a feature of the town. They were also very encouraging, not that I needed encouragement as I was raring to start my new job. Hazel, however, had mixed feelings about the move; in particular she worried lest people would think that she was dragging me back to Wales, her homeland, when in actual fact she was very happy in Selby, where she had a circle of good friends with whom she would have been perfectly happy to stay. Indeed, once back again in Selby, the Vicar and the Poskitts worked hard to make me change my mind and stay. The Vicar offered me more money at the Abbey while the Poskitts offered us the flat rent-free, but to no avail as my mind was made up. Peter and Alison, with their wicked sense of humour, went further and suggested letting me go off to Brecon and leaving Hazel behind to take my place as Abbey Organist, especially as they had produced their most recent child, Bridget, as a playmate for our Harriet. Joking apart, a successor had to be found and I was anxious for John Kent to get on with this, so as to avoid an interregnum; having established so much music-making in Selby I wanted to see it continue. Now that the Abbey Organist position could be advertised with Head of Music at Selby High School, there was every possibility of a number of good applicants. Also, we were aided by the Royal School of Church Music authorities who directed applicants to the Selby job, while they had discouraged applicants to the Brecon job; why, I do not know! Making appointments always is a lottery and in this case the lot fell upon Mervyn Byers, an Australian, who had been Organist and Choirmaster of St. Andrew's Cathedral, Sydney, for a number of years and was a very experienced church musician.

So as my time at Selby was drawing to a close, nevertheless my father, unwittingly, had provided us with some final entertainment. Earlier in the year, on my birthday, he had given me his old dormobile – presumably the one that he had used to drive his parish children to our wedding in Kidwelly. Now Hazel and I had to learn to drive it, which would be especially useful in Brecon where there were now no trains and public transport was not very helpful. Obviously we had been spoilt for public transport in Selby, with regular trains to London, the north, Leeds,

Hull and across the Pennines to Lancashire and also frequent buses to York and the outlying districts of Selby. Indeed, our favourite pastime on a Saturday afternoon had been to sit on a bus from Selby to York, wander round the shops in the Shambles, visit Banks Music Shop, have tea in Terry's and finish up at Choral Evensong in the Minster. On our first visit to Banks Music Shop, the legendary Miss Banks walked up to me saying: "You must be a Gedge", but I never did discover what distinguishing feature I had that likened me to the York branch of the Gedge family which she obviously knew. So forceful a personality was she that, one day, when she repeatedly shouted up the shop staircase: "Send down the Scheidt", in the end a waste paper basket appeared, full of rubbish! As for Terry's Tea Shop, that not only had the most tasty toasted tea-cakes but also the most superlative shiny mahogany woodwork on the walls and tables.

The Minster on a winter's evening was full of atmosphere and, while Evensong was a variable feast with regard to the music, it was always prayerful and had some sort of magic about it which defied description. One particular Saturday, Dr. Jackson invited me into the Organ loft for Evensong. When I arrived he suggested that I play the final organ voluntary, but when I explained that I was not a good organist, he put on his cherubic smile and replied, "I know, but do play!" One evening when we had Harriet with us, we called at no. 1, Minster Court, to visit the Jacksons and to our delight Francis danced around the room carrying Harriet in his arms. Earlier, while shopping, we had seen a paper-back book: "Harriet and the Cherry Pie" and bought it; now we got Francis to sign it in memory of a special visit.

Hazel came to know a lot more of York while having driving lessons there and, at the second attempt, passed the dreaded driving test, which meant that we were mobile at last. At this time, as the year was drawing to a close, I taught the Choral Society to sing J. S. Bach's Cantata 140, "Sleepers, Wake!". It was hard work as the singers had never tackled Bach's music before and found the great opening chorale fantasia as difficult to learn as the *Selby Times* Music Critic found it difficult to understand. He clearly could not see that this was "one of Bach's greatest achievements" and felt that the singing at the concert lacked "a sense of purpose", obviously not realising that the great hymn tune (chorale) was being unfolded leisurely, one line at a time, with no thought being given to a build-up of musical tension.

The excellent team of vocal soloists included Honor Sheppard, Christopher Keyte and the very special tenor Wilfred Brown, who had so bowled me over when I heard him sing while I was playing my viola in a performance of "Messiah" for Peter Fletcher at Beverley Minster that I just had to get him to Selby Abbey. Furthermore, he was kind enough to sing for whatever Selby Choral Society could afford to pay. Early in the next year, 1966, another tenor, who was soon to become famous, sang in Selby, not at the Abbey but at the High School to members of the Music Society. He was Philip Langridge, whom I had first encountered shortly before he was accepted as a violinist at the Royal Academy of Music, when he used to play in my Thomas Morley Chamber Orchestra. One day he had fixed himself up with singing lessons at the Academy and his teacher, Bruce Boyce, soon converted him from a bass to a tenor with such fantastic results that eventually he became a world-class singer.

In the new year, March turned out to be a busy month. On my twenty-seventh birthday, March 12th 1966, the Abbey Choir gave a recital in the Abbey singing a wide range of music by Thomas Attwood, John Blow, Johann Eccard, Jacob Handl, Herbert Howells, John Ireland and S. S. Wesley. The choristers had come a long way in my three-and-a-half years with them and now numbered twenty trebles; three altos who were all ex-trebles; five tenors including Don Riches who still ran the club and with his wife Betty had become family friends sometimes baby-sitting Harriet, Alan Wilson who had been Festival Secretary and who with his wife Kath also were good friends, and Peter Poskitt, our kindly landlord whose wife Alison was Harriet's god-mother; and six basses, including our violinist friend Royston Ashby, Jack Thompson the poetry-writing Festival Treasurer, and Peter Warham, the primary school headmaster whose two sons Richard and Timothy were such excellent head boys.

Three days later, Hazel gave a "live" organ recital on the Abbey Organ for BBC Radio Home Service North, playing the chorale prelude "O Sacred Head" by Johann Kuhnau and Max Reger's *Toccata and Fugue* op. 59. Not long afterwards, on Saturday March 26th, I directed my final concert with the Choral Society, which included more unknown music in three fascinating Latin motets by Johann Eberlin, a contemporary of the Mozarts at Salzburg, and the Fauré "Requiem". The Requiem had been performed once before, two years earlier, when the singers found the music very different from "Messiah" and the Latin words far from easy. Even so, after that performance one of the Society's greatest supporters had whispered to me: "Do you know, I enjoyed the music even more than "Messiah", but don't tell anyone"! Although the Choral Society had been criticised for its policy of singing little-known music and music with Latin words, nevertheless it had gone from strength to strength and provided many people with an enjoyable and worthwhile pastime.

A few days later, on Palm Sunday, Hazel and I took part in our last services at the Abbey. No longer was Don Reasbeck there in the choir to lean over the stalls and pretend to ride a horse while singing the hymn "Ride on, ride on in majesty". Indeed, all was decency and good order in the choir, while the singing was so different from that first Sunday I had experienced back at the beginning of September 1962. The next day found us on the road for Brecon with Harriet and Hannibal in our dormobile, Hazel driving and me map-reading as motorways were few and far-between at that time. Our Selby adventure was over. As we crossed the Pennines, snow was piled high on either side of the road; it was bitterly cold and the dormobile had no heater. A long way on as we crossed from Herefordshire into Radnorshire, from England into Wales, cottages suddenly smothered their local features with anonymous pebble-dash. In the distance the snow-capped Brecon Beacons beckoned us into a new world. When finally we entered Brecon and drove up Priory Hill into the Cathedral Close, numb with cold, very tired, we found a welcome supper of lamb chops awaiting us in the Deanery, prepared by Mary, the Dean's wife.

XXII

To call Brecon Cathedral one of Wales's best-kept secrets is an understatement, as even some Breconians are ignorant of its existence. Hazel's cousin, Stuart Anthony, who lives in Cardiff, came to visit us not long after we had moved. He asked a local person the way to the Cathedral only to be told: "I've lived in Brecon all my life but I didn't know there was a Cathedral here." Yet while the Cathedral is a truly magical building, the tragedy at that time was that visitors saw only a fraction of what there is to be seen, because around the Cathedral Close are to be found a jumble of buildings: the tithe barn, the Almonry, the vestries, the Deanery and the Clergy House, but all these were kept from their prying eyes.

The entire complex was enclosed by a long stone wall and entry to the Close itself was through two tall archways, one of which had great double wooden gates. Cars entering the Close did so through the lower, more narrow gate, sometimes misjudging the width and as a result scraping one side of the car, as I did once when I was in a hurry! Cars leaving the Close this way had to run the gauntlet of traffic coming up or going down Priory Hill and it is amazing that there was never a serious accident. One kind member of the congregation even donated a special mirror which was fixed to the wall opposite to make it possible to view the opposition travelling along the road, but this was stolen within twenty-four hours. All the buildings in the Close were of great antiquity except the garage, which was merely Victorian! The Cathedral dates back to 1093, not quite as old as Selby Abbey, but little remains of the original building. Its glory is the wonderfully gracious twelfth-century chancel with its elegant triple lancet windows on the north and south sides flanking its great five-light east window, in front of which stands what has been called "the last great mediaeval reredos". This fine creation, with its elaborate "Perpendicular" carving in bluish Bath stone was the work of the Cathedral architect William Douglas Caröe and was installed in 1937 as a memorial to the first Bishop of Swansea and Brecon. The beautiful French-style chancel vault was added by Sir George Gilbert Scott during the 1861-2 restoration and is considered by some to be his most daring work of reconstruction. Sadly money ran out before the tower could be vaulted, even though the springers are there.

Most visited is the Regimental Chapel on the north side, which commemorates the achievements of the men belonging to the 24th Regiment, which became part of the South Wales Borderers, then the Royal Regiment of Wales. The film "Zulu" has captured so many people's imaginations that if they choose to search this Chapel not only will they find the very wreath of immortelles which Queen Victoria placed on the 24th Regiment's colours when the surviving soldiers returned to this country, but they will also find memorial brasses to Lieutenant (later Major) Gonville Bromhead V. C. and Private (later Sergeant) Hook V. C., who did so much to secure the famous defence of Rorke's Drift, when their small detachment of little over one hundred soldiers held at bay more than four thousand Zulu warriors. On the south side is the St. Lawrence Chapel, which looks as if it has been there for centuries but in fact was re-created from a ruin as recently as

1930. Miraculously, this restoration work was done by local builders and it has resulted in a beautiful, gentle Early English chapel with a lovely stone floor and a fine English-style mediaeval stone vault along with a small carved timber reredos above the altar. This altar is complete with riddle-posts on which then hung dark-blue curtains, all so restrained and combining to make a perfect understatement, complemented by the addition of a few simple chairs; so obviously the brainchild of that master-craftsman, W. D. Caröe.

Beneath the tower is the bishop's throne and alongside are the choir, clergy and canons' stalls, carved in oak with elaborate bench ends, designed by Sir George Gilbert Scott in 1872, not particularly comfortable to sit in and useless to sing in not only because there are no music rests but also because one side of the choir cannot hear the other side, let alone the singers hear clearly the other singers on their own side. Yet these stalls are visually perfect to the eye of the beholder and they in turn are surveyed by a face carved in stone high up on the pillar above the bishop's throne. Why can one side of the choir not hear the other side? The answer has to be because there are no backs to the stalls to reflect the sound back to the singers, nor is there a vault, which means that the music just disappears into the cavernous space above, beneath the tower. However, there is a plus side and that is the lovely feeling of space as the north and south transepts are not cut off from the tower area at the crossing.

To the west of these stalls is that area of mystery, two expanses of blank wall, each one containing a door that opens into thin air! Stone steps inside the wall reach down to ground level to give access to the side aisles when the space inside the wall is not used for storage. This, of course, is the site of the Golden Rood which was swept away at the dissolution of the Priory in 1539. By all accounts it was a massive structure, an enormous hanging crucifix with figures of the "beloved disciple", St. John the Evangelist, on one side and of the Blessed Virgin Mary, Jesus's mother, on the other. That there were doors at both ends of the Rood Loft signifies its importance, as this enabled pilgrims to enter by one door, cross the rood screen, kiss the feet of Our Lord hanging on the Cross, pray, then leave by the other door. Apparently most rood lofts had only one door by which pilgrims could enter and leave, presumably because they were visited by fewer pilgrims and there was no danger of congestion. Legend has it that miracles were wrought at this rood, with the result that the Priory Church of St. John the Evangelist, Brecon, also became known as "The Church of the Miraculous Rood". Certainly, the aura of this "Miraculous Rood" had cast its spell upon me some three-and-a-half years before.

Further down the nave, on the north side, was the historic Corvizor's Chapel, a relic of the middle ages, when town guilds often had their own chapels in their Parish Church. This, however, was now used as a Guild Chapel by the Cordwainers (leather workers and shoemakers) and they still made an annual pilgrimage to the Cathedral every summer, coming from all over England and Wales to march in procession behind their banner from the Guildhall in the centre of the town, along the Struet, up Priory Hill, to the Cathedral for their own re-union service. Indeed, not many years before, the Guild had employed Thompsons of Kilburn, Yorkshire, to carve a small wooden screen for the west end of their chapel to complement the sixteenth-century screen which graced the south side of the chapel adjoining the nave, thereby completing the enclosure of the chapel. Thompsons' trade mark, the mouse, can be seen low down on the right side of the entrance. Nearby, at the back of the nave, the west end, is a stone font of great antiquity; arguments rage as to its actual age. The gash in its side is attributed to Oliver Cromwell's Roundheads, but then there was an aged oak tree in the churchyard which one Breconian assured me was where King Charles I hid to avoid being captured by them, so who knows? Above the font hangs a magnificent eighteenth-century brass candelabra which is lit on special occasions. On the north side at this point is the main entrance to the Cathedral, two enormous, thick oak doors with magnificent iron hinges that spread out over most of the wooden area like the wings of a gigantic butterfly. Opposite, on the south side, is a smaller door, which then was next to an aged wooden vestment chest, and this leads firstly to the vestries and secondly to the secret gardens that few visitors ever saw. I grew to feel sad about this. I began to think that we who worked at the Cathedral and were privileged to live in this "fairyland", really were only custodians of these fascinating houses and grounds; why could we not sacrifice just a little privacy and share this with visitors, so that they could go home having experienced all that Brecon Cathedral has to offer? (Happily this is something that has since been put right.)

Passing through that small door in the south-west corner of the Cathedral certainly did take people into another world. How could vestries be interesting? Well, these ones certainly were. First of all, though, is the possibility that the entire range of vestries formed part of the original cloister. The Clergy Vestry itself gives every sign of having been converted from a stable, there being appropriate metal rings for tying horses and dogs, hanging down from thick wooden posts. As for the Dean's Vestry, photographic evidence points to this at one time being a Coach House; it has a magnificent open fire-place too. Mount the staircase by that small door and you really are transported into another world.

The first time I climbed these stairs I could not think why they seemed familiar; then I remembered. I cast my mind back to my childhood at Holy Trinity Vicarage, to the Christmas holidays, to my outings to the theatre, to the "Just William" plays that I sometimes saw and always enjoyed. In my imagination I could see on the stage a staircase rising to a landing off which, at either end, was a door. This was Just William's barn, his "hidey hole"; I had always coveted such a refuge and now here it was. Turn left at the top of the stairs, walk through the door and a most amazing sight meets your eyes: a large room straddled by three massive old oak beams with heavy timber framing reaching up into the ceiling. It seems that before the wooden staircase was added, this room might well have stretched across into the small room on the right of the landing, thereby making one single enormous room. Was this a dormitory for guests to the Priory, because a small squint looks out into the nave to where the rood would have hung? Interestingly, back in the nave, to the left of the small door on the south side, the stonework in the wall has so obviously been interfered with at some time; could this have been the site of a stone staircase leading from the Priory Church up into the guest room?

So much guesswork goes on when looking around Brecon Cathedral, but there is one certainty, that the architect, William Douglas Caröe, had done wonderful restoration work here in the vestries. Many of the oak doors are his, as are the elegant iron latches and also several handsome cupboards in the vestries are to his design, all inserted with typically casual understatement. While the downstairs rooms were used by the clergy, the two upper rooms were the domain of the choir, trebles to the left, lay clerks (alto, tenor and bass choirmen) to the right. Most of the choir practices took place in the large room where stood a mess of pianos in various states of health; a reasonable upright, a dismal upright and a wretched small Broadwood grand. The Lay Clerks' room was like the Black Hole of Calcutta, as the only window was so high up that there was little light; at the far end a door opened into a minute room with just enough space for a window and a primitive loo.

Downstairs, on the two outer walls, two doors opened into the Close: one led to the ruinous but roofed mediaeval tithe barn, to the main gate with the great double wooden doors and to the Almonry, which the second Cathedral Organist had refused to live in "because", he said, "he couldn't get his grand piano into it." If I had been offered it, Hazel would have got our grand piano in by any means possible; the other gate led to the garth where stood the Prior's House, which now housed the Deanery and Clergy House. The Vestries themselves merged into a small Tower and the Canonry, possibly also constructed from the original cloister. Sadly the remainder of the cloister and other buildings, including possibly a Chapter House, were demolished towards the end of the eighteenth century. Had they survived another hundred years, they would still most likely have been there now. The trouble was, that, at the dissolution of the Priory when the church ceased to be monastic and became the Parish Church of Brecon, all the buildings that remained passed into the hands of King Henry VIII's friends and associates: whatever they had no use for they presumably demolished and put the colourful pinkish-grey local stone to other use.

However, what remained was second only to Heaven itself. I used to walk around the grounds with Hazel and Hannibal, pushing Harriet in her pram, in a state of unbelief wondering how with my love of cathedrals I had never discovered this gem before. We could walk through the Close from the back yard of the Clergy House past the Canonry, along the path between the Tithe Barn and Almonry, through the main gate then through the Lych Gate, along the tree-lined path in the churchyard alongside the Cathedral into the grassy ground at the east end of the chancel, which looked as though in past times it had done duty as a tennis court, past a magnificent cedar tree of immense size and back to the Clergy House. The paths were immaculate and at the side of many were impeccably-kept hedges, all maintained by a lovely character called Ossie. It was his job to cut the hedges, mow the vast expanses of lawns and attend to the paths. He also maintained the flower beds, did odd jobs and kept the grounds tidy. His wages were small but he enjoyed life, followed the hunt on foot and was content living in a little terraced house close by, with his dear wife Aunty Griffiths.

Not many doors away in another terraced house (this one opposite the Lych Gate) lived Mr. Hawkes the Verger. The choir called him "Hawkeye" and used to mimic his habit of dropping yet adding "H" to words. So he would say, when describing a liturgical movement: "When Hi proceeds to the 'Igh Haltar . . . " and the choristers would smile to themselves. He used to be an engine driver, and therefore he was a stickler for punctuality and was himself completely reliable. He was fussed over by his kindly wife and, although she would talk to us about her "Edgar", she and he were both so olde worlde that we would never address them other than as Mr. and Mrs. Hawkes, whereas Ossie (short for Oswald) was always Ossie and never Mr. Griffiths.

Two Minor Canons was the sum total of the junior clerical staff, "Minor Canon" being an upmarket name for a curate attached to a cathedral. At that time it was customary for a Minor Canon at Brecon Cathedral to stay for seven years before receiving preferment – that usually meant taking a living, which is the ecclesiastical term for becoming the Vicar of a parish. The Senior Minor Canon when we arrived was David Evans, a Welshman whose father had been Headmaster of a Prep School outside Aberystwyth, who had a decidedly English accent and was an Oxford University graduate with so great a love of Cathedral Music that he sang divine service to perfection. Known to the choir as "Snurge" because of his impeccable accent and impeccable behaviour, he was nevertheless a good priest, always kind and caring. He had a conscience too and later, when Chaplain to students at Swansea University, he took their side in an internal dispute which made him unpopular with the authorities. So he moved to England, worked with "The Samaritans" and eventually succeeded Chad Varah as their Director. He ended up as the Vicar of a group of parishes in Northamptonshire and an Honorary Canon of Peterborough Cathedral.

The Junior Minor Canon was Peter George Russell Sims, a larger than life character from Swansea who arrived at Brecon just after we did and who lived in the other half of the Clergy House. When he arrived in the town centre for the first time on the bus from Swansea, he decided to start as he meant to go on, walked straight into The Wellington Hotel, sat down at the bar and ordered a pint of beer. Peter enjoyed his beer and after particularly heavy drinking sessions would stagger into the Clergy House late at night after closing time, hurl himself onto his bed with a loud guffaw of laughter, then throw one shoe into the air, which would land with a loud thud on the oak floor. Hazel and I, lying in bed not many yards away in our bedroom, often had to wait in suspense for some considerable time before the second shoe hit the ground with another loud thud. Next morning there would be a panic as a not-very-well Peter ran naked through the hall to his bathroom for his quick pick-me-up ablutions in a desperate attempt to be at the Cathedral punctually for the regulation 7.30 a.m. services of Matins and Holy Communion which all the resident clerical staff had to attend.

There was a famous occasion one Saint's Day when Peter was due not at the Cathedral but at the Parish Church to take an early morning service. Awakened by his alarm clock, he roared with laughter, hurled it onto the floor, then went back to sleep again. When finally he arose, it was with a heavy heart and an equally heavy head as he pondered over what he had done. Needless to say, he was equal to the situation. Guessing correctly which person would have been heading the queue of worshippers at St. Mary's Church, he hurried round to that person's house, apologised profusely, made a list of the other people who had turned up for the service, quickly visited them all and the Dean was none the wiser! Peter was the possessor of a superb bass voice which, I suppose, need not be thought surprising as his uncle, Ivor Sims, was renowned as the conductor of the Morriston Orpheus

Choir. He took an active interest in the Cathedral Choir, however, not because of his God-given voice, but because the regular Thursday-evening Lay Clerks' practice enabled him not only to avoid a weekly meeting of one of the parish organisations, but in addition gave him an excuse to join the choirmen on their regular weekly visit to The George Hotel, where they unwound after their musical exertions.

Such was the power of Peter's voice that one afternoon as Hazel stood at the bus stop in the town centre, she suddenly became aware of what initially she thought was someone singing in a public house. Slowly it dawned on her that it wasn't; it was Peter Sims, inside St. Mary's Church, leading the hymn singing at a Mothers' Union service! It was after one such service in the town church that the Dean invited Peter to join him in a drink at the Wellington Hotel. Peter, with a vision of a pint of beer in his mind, readily agreed. They entered the Wellington Hotel together, whereupon the Dean motioned to Peter to sit down at a table while he went to the bar to purchase the drinks. When he returned, he was clutching two glasses of sherry, which they proceeded to sip in total silence.

Dean Gwynno James might have been a most erudite man but he was not given to small talk. He was, however, one of the few clergymen in the Church in Wales who really understood what Cathedral Music was about and he loved it dearly. Worship through beauty of language, through beauty of music, through beauty of ceremonial, through beauty of holiness all meant much to him, but it had to be without pomposity or show. He had an uncanny eye for beauty. Within two years of his arrival at Brecon Cathedral he had created a tranquil expanse of lawn on the north side of the Cathedral by destroying a mess of old gravestones, iron railings and a maze-like collection of narrow paths, fulfilling all the necessary legal obligations along the way: strangely, the only objection had come from a family with very ordinary gravestones sited at the worst possible place, close to the main north door.

That he had chosen Harry Gabb, Organist of the Chapel Royal, to be the musical advisor when I was appointed Organist and Choirmaster was no accident of fate. Harry Gabb had been appointed Organist of Llandaff Cathedral back in 1937, but when the Second World War came along there was soon no Cathedral to work in as much of it had been destroyed in bombing. Services had of necessity been transferred to a nearby Parish Hall where a large two-manual harmonium-like contraption had done duty as Cathedral Organ. With no sign of the Cathedral being rebuilt in the immediate future, Harry Gabb had begun to look around for work elsewhere and was duly appointed Assistant Organist at St. Paul's Cathedral in 1946, by which time Gwynno James had become a Minor Canon at Llandaff Cathedral. Soon afterwards, Harry Gabb was asked to play the organ at a service in St. Paul's Cathedral before he had actually worked out his notice at Llandaff Cathedral, with the result that the Dean, as he was entitled to, had refused him leave. However, the Dean's sight was poor, which had made it possible for Gwynno James, who was himself no mean organist, to impersonate Harry Gabb at the "organ" for the service in "Llandaff Cathedral" while Harry Gabb himself went off to London to play the organ for the service at St. Paul's Cathedral and the Dean had been none the wiser, as he was at one end of his temporary "cathedral" while his Minor Canon had been at the other end, playing the harmonium-like contraption. Gwynno James had been a great friend of the Welsh composer William Mathias and had provided him with the libretto for his oratorio "St. Teilo". When appointed Dean of Brecon Cathedral, Gwynno James had asked William Mathias to compose an anthem for his installation service; this resulted in his producing the popular "Make a joyful noise unto the Lord, all ye lands", which was duly published by Oxford University Press.

Making Gwynno James Dean of Brecon had been an inspired appointment by the Bishop of Swansea and Brecon, the Right Reverend John James Absalom Thomas – who, with such a collection of names, could become anything other than a bishop? He was a gentle, quietly spoken but determined man, who loved music as much as Gwynno James but appeared to have wider interests. He it was who later introduced Hazel and me to the Preludes and Fugues for piano by Dmitri Shostakovich on the lovely Blüthner grand that he played in his sitting room at Ely Tower, the residence of successive Bishops of Swansea and Brecon, which was situated on the site of all that remained of Brecon Castle next to the Castle of Brecon Hotel. Before becoming Bishop, he had been Vicar of Swansea and had overseen the rebuilding of St. Mary's Church in the town centre after it had been destroyed in the heavy bombing that had been inflicted on Swansea during the Second World War. He greatly enjoyed choral services at the Cathedral and attended them as often as he could. If the choir sang any music that he did not know, he would mount the stairs to the choir-room, collect a copy and then take it home to play on his piano.

His wife, Betty, was a wonderful lady who complemented his work to perfection. Small, with a heavily-lined but attractive face, she was a bundle of fun, most hospitable and full of boundless energy. Having two brothers who had achieved eminence in the world of education, one as Headmaster of Harrow School, the other as Headmaster of Christ College, Brecon, it was obvious that she had an interesting pedigree. And so it was: a striking portrait of a clerical gentleman hanging in the dining room at Ely Tower pointed to the fact that her father had been Dean of Bangor Cathedral. It had been during this time that the Cathedral Organist, Dr. Leslie Paul, had won on the football pools and Betty Thomas laughingly recalled how her father had rushed to his house to beg him to keep quiet about his win, as many church and chapel people at that time still frowned upon gambling. Earlier, her father had been Vicar of a country parish in North Wales and she never forgot how he would take her with him as he rode around the parish in a horse and trap, collecting the tithes that made up part of his income; nor did she forget how some of the non-conformist farmers had set dogs on them in an effort to avoid paying their dues. Small wonder she was exceedingly luke-warm about Church Unity.

Disestablishment and disendowment of the Anglican Church in Wales in 1920 may have put an end to such antics, but it certainly did not bring about the cessation of hostilities between Non-Conformists and Anglicans. The Prime Minister, Lloyd George, was no help. On the day when the Bishop of St. Asaph was enthroned as the first Archbishop of Wales, Lloyd George had presented himself at the Communion Rail during the eight o'clock early morning Communion Service, completely disregarding the rubric of the Book of Common Prayer which states that only persons who are confirmed shall make their communion. On the day, this unfortunate incident at St. Asaph Cathedral was hushed up so as not to spoil the occasion. However, the question remains: was this really a friendly gesture on the part of a leading Non-Conformist or was it a calculated insult? Interestingly, Hazel's father recounted to me one day how, after disestablishment, Non-Conformists used to assemble in Kidwelly churchyard during Evensong on Sundays after their own services, intent on causing a disturbance, claiming that the ancient church was now as much their property as it was the Anglicans'!

One happy outcome of disestablishment was the division of the diocese of St. David's, which had contained the counties of Pembrokeshire, Cardigan, Carmarthenshire, Breconshire, Radnorshire and part of Glamorgan; an enormous area. Out of this, after much territorial argument, was carved the diocese of Swansea and Brecon, with the Priory Church of St. John the Evangelist, Brecon, as its Cathedral. First Bishop of this new diocese, which came into being in the year 1923, was the remarkable Edward Latham Bevan. His father had been Vicar of Hay-on-Wye for more than fifty years and Archdeacon of Brecon, during which time he had lived in Hay Castle. Both he and his son, "Teddy Bevan" are mentioned in the diaries of Francis Kilvert, the famous curate of nearby Clyro Church. "Teddy Bevan" was for many years Vicar of Brecon and in the year 1916 had been consecrated Suffragan Bishop of Swansea, which enabled him to undertake many of the menial episcopal tasks in the diocese of St. David's, so that its Bishop, John Owen, could devote more of his energies to the struggles in Parliament over disestablishment.

Seven years later, Bishop Bevan's election to the see of Swansea and Brecon was far from a foregone conclusion, simply because he was not Welsh-speaking. The new election process gave six votes to representatives of each of the other five dioceses in Wales (Bangor, Llandaff, Monmouth, St. Asaph and St. David's), twelve votes to the diocese to which the elected bishop was going, namely Swansea and Brecon, and one vote to each of the five bishops. Of the total forty-seven votes, the successful candidate required thirty-two votes, which was around two-thirds of the total. This was the Church in Wales answer to the system of appointments by the Crown which was the custom in the Church of England. The problem of not being Welsh-speaking was unfortunate, because Bishop Bevan was the obvious choice, being much loved in Brecon and in the new diocese, as well as being the chosen candidate of the Bishop of St. David's. On the day of the election, voting continued until late in the afternoon and the deadlock was apparently broken only when the North Walian voters had to leave in order to catch the last train home. As they constituted the majority of the Welsh-speaking vote, success was now assured and Edward Latham Bevan was elected the first Bishop of Swansea and Brecon.

It was fortunate that the lot had fallen upon Latham Bevan because he was not only a man of vision but was also a man of wealth and therefore able to create what he knew was right for his Cathedral. During his episcopate of eleven years, he initiated a number of major projects which left Brecon with a Cathedral that was both unique and of great beauty. Firstly, with his own money and with money belonging to his friend, Wilfred de Winton, the Chapter Clerk, all the ancient priory buildings that had been in private hands since the dissolution of the Priory were bought back for the Cathedral and restored to ecclesiastical use. Then the tiny, ruined, St. Lawrence Chapel was beautifully restored and brought back into use. Finally, an organ chamber was built above the Sacristy, facing into the Chancel, to house the William Hill organ which had formerly stood on the ground beneath. This released valuable floor-space between the chancel and the "new" chapel. One more project occupied his thoughts in his final years. At the time of his election, the chancel was filled with choir stalls while the area beneath the central tower was stuffed up with benches for the congregation. So he had the choir stalls restored correctly to the monastic choir at the crossing and restricted the congregation's benches and chairs to the nave, thereby leaving an empty but spacious and dignified chancel which emphasised its great beauty. When the reredos was added as his memorial a few years later and its great High Altar became the main focal point of the nave, choir and chancel, his work in his beloved Cathedral was complete.

XXIII

Hazel's father never could understand why I wanted to come to Brecon; according to him, neither the town nor the Cathedral had ever been noted for its music. However, in 1923, did Bishop Bevan have big ideas for the future of the Cathedral and its music? In that year he brought to Brecon Cathedral from Hereford, Humphrey Carden as Cathedral Organist; he had been an articled pupil of the Cathedral Organist, Dr. G. R. Sinclair (his dog, Dan, is immortalised in the eleventh of Edward Elgar's "Enigma Variations") and his successor, Percy Hull. Hereford, but thirty-six miles away, had always been a great centre of music on account of the famous Three Choirs' Festival, Britain's oldest Musical Festival. As an articled pupil of the Cathedral Organist, Humphrey Carden would have been closely involved in these activities. Interestingly, in the room above the north porch of Brecon Cathedral can be found the ten magnificent volumes of Tudor Church Music which Oxford University Press had published in that very same year, 1923. Were these purchased with an eye to the future?

Humphrey Carden's wife was a violinist who had trained at the Royal Academy of Music. She had married him in 1923 when she was twenty-one years old and lived on in Brecon for seventy-five years, not dying until 1998. When I arrived in Brecon, she became a wonderful source of information. For example, she adamantly maintained that one of her husband's predecessors, Rees Thomas Heins, who was Organist of the Priory Church from 1879 until 1918, had been badly treated by the people of Brecon during the First World War on account of his German origin, despite having lived in Brecon for more that thirty-five years. Incidentally, he had run a music shop in the town, opposite the old Post Office, close to St. Mary's Church, and had been part of the Heins and Allen connection which boasted shops also in Abergavenny, Hereford and Ross-on-Wye: even now, Heins pianos can be found in the neighbourhood. The last of these shops, at 23 Frogmore Street, Abergavenny, managed by Mr. and Mrs. Geoff Allen, only closed its doors for the last time quite recently. Rees Thomas Heins' successor, Ernest William Baker, had an interesting pedigree. He had trained at New College School, Oxford and at Norwich Cathedral, before proceeding to a succession of organist positions, firstly at Hingham Parish Church, Norfolk, then at Halton Parish Church; afterwards he became Organist at Evelyn, Countess of Craven's private chapel in Ashdown Park, Shrivenham, before moving onto St. Michael's Church, Bishop Stortford in Hertfordshire, then to Padstow Parish Church in Devon before coming to Brecon. Any ambitions he may have had about remaining at the Priory Church to become the first Cathedral Organist must have been dashed when he began to receive poison-pen letters from another organist with similar ambitions and he vanished from the scene in time for Humphrey Carden to arrive. The new Organist also received some of these letters but, being of sterner stuff, ignored them and proceeded to remain at the cathedral for thirty-three years, until 1956.

Coming from Hereford Cathedral, where there is a large four-manual organ, he must have found the three-manual Hill organ small by comparison. Furthermore, having been built back in 1886, its action was now badly in need of attention. Nevertheless, Humphrey Carden had set about establishing a tradition of cathedral music for, after all, what marked out a cathedral from a parish church was its daily round of services: Morning Prayer (Matins) and Evening Prayer (Evensong), which at that time in many English cathedrals like those at Hereford, Gloucester and Worcester had been sung daily by a professional choir of boys and gentlemen. Unfortunately, however, this particular tradition of choral worship was not really understood in Wales. Henry Walford Davies surely must have realised this when in August of the previous year, 1922, he had brought seven of his Temple Church choirboys from London on a "missionary tour of Welsh Churches", during the course of which they had sung at the Priory Church. Legend has it that when in the year 1897 Hugh Allen had arrived at St. Asaph Cathedral at the tender age of twenty-eight years to take up the position of Organist, he had been so appalled by what he had found there that he immediately enquired the time of the next train back to Cambridge. As it was, his stay at St. Asaph lasted only a few months before he secured a similar appointment at Ely Cathedral, but not before he had brought about such improvements to the Cathedral Choir that the Dean and Chapter wrote to him officially to thank him for his work.

Humphrey Carden obviously had experienced this great tradition at Hereford Cathedral. Later on, he and his wife had sent their two sons to be educated at St. Michael's College, Tenbury, in Worcestershire, a famous choir school which some fifty years later had the distinction of being the last place in England where daily services were sung both in the morning and evening. There had been four old foundation cathedrals in Wales, each having what passed for a choir school, but by this time the only school to survive was to be found at Llandaff Cathedral and in any case, none of these cathedrals had ever really been renowned for its musical prowess. A strong reason for this state of affairs was presumably the lack of financial resources, a problem exacerbated by disestablishment and disendowment in 1920, when there had been an appeal to raise the million pounds needed to restore the financial position of the Church in Wales to what it had been previously but, sadly, barely two-thirds of this had been collected. Humphrey Carden, from the very outset, had set about establishing a tradition of daily Choral Evensongs, but sung by boys' voices only with the canticles performed to nothing but Anglican chants, which must have been a thankless task.

Eileen Carden had recalled how undernourished the choirboys had appeared to be, yet always they had been very loyal in their attendance, encouraged, apparently, by the Headmaster of the local church primary school who, it seems, had been a Choral Scholar at King's College, Cambridge, and now sang in the Cathedral Choir. However, with no money available to pay Lay Clerks, it appears that the choirmen had only sung at Sunday services and at occasional special weekday services. One member of the musical establishment at Brecon Cathedral at this time later achieved eminence in the Cathedral Music world, namely Colin Ross. He had been born in Brecon and educated in Christ College, eventually becoming an Articled Pupil of Humphrey Carden before moving on to Hereford Cathedral to become first an Articled Pupil of the Organist, Percy Hull and then Assistant Organist. After being a répetiteur at Sadlers Wells Opera House, he became Organist and Choirmaster at St. Paul's Cathedral, Melbourne, later returning to England where eventually he was Organist of St. Nicholas Cathedral at Newcastle-upon-Tyne.

During these times there had been a number of historic services. On Easter Sunday, April 20th 1924 a new East Window for the Regimental Chapel had been unveiled and dedicated and the Colour Pole of the 2nd Battalion (24th) Regiment laid up. Next had been a service to mark the laying of the Corner Stone of the Chapel of St. Lawrence, which was about to be rebuilt from ruins. On this occasion, after singing the Evening Canticles to Anglican chants, the Cathedral Choir sang as an anthem Thomas Attwood Walmisley's "From all that dwell below the skies, let the creator's praise arise". On Friday October 27th 1927 had been the amazing "Solemn Thanksgiving to Almighty God for His mercy and goodness vouchsafed in the recovery and restoration of the Buildings and Grounds surrounding the Cathedral". The Archbishop of Wales and the five Welsh Bishops, along with a multitude of clergy and people, had assembled to give thanks to Almighty God for "that He had restored to this Cathedral Church the ancient buildings and Hallowed ground which men took from it some 400 years ago". Appropriately the choir had sung "How lovely is thy dwelling place, O Lord of Hosts" by Johannes Brahms. After the *Te Deum* had been chanted by the assembled multitude, this unique occasion had ended with the entire congregation processing out of the Cathedral and through the restored grounds singing the hymn "Now thank we all our God". On Whit Tuesday, June 10th 1930, the restored chapel of St. Lawrence had been dedicated "for the use of the Men and lads of the Diocese", as the Church of England Men's Society always had been very dear to the heart of Bishop Bevan; indeed, during the First World War he had worked ceaselessly for the welfare of the men of Brecknock who had been involved in the fighting. Again the Brahms anthem was sung.

By now the new organ chamber above the chancel was nearing completion and on Wednesday July 8th 1931 the organ, newly re-built there, was also dedicated. The anthem was John Goss's "Wilderness" and during the service Humphrey Carden had contributed to the proceedings the *"Andante cantabile"* from C. M. Widor's fourth Organ Symphony, along with "Two Trumpet Tunes and an Air" that Henry Ley had arranged from music by Henry Purcell, which must have shown off the new tromba stop to perfection; then as a concluding voluntary he had played S. S. Wesley's "Choral Song". How delighted Humphrey Carden must have been with his new organ loft, high above the choir stalls, approached by a staircase partly cut into the wall of the sacristy, so reminiscent of what he had left behind at Hereford Cathedral. However, he was unprepared for what had happened next. Mrs. Carden told me that one day he had entered the Cathedral only to find that the choir stalls had been moved from the chancel into the area beneath the tower. She mentioned that this had come as a complete surprise to him and that he had never been consulted over the matter; nor, I suppose, should he have expected to have been, as Bishop Bevan was notorious for having his own way. Furthermore, with no money available to pay a Dean, he himself was both Bishop and Dean, which had given him complete control of his diocese and its cathedral. To be fair to the Bishop, this had been an inspired re-arrangement of furniture as it had resulted in a spacious chancel and sanctuary along with a restoration of the ancient monastic choir. On the practical side, however, it had left the choristers on one side of the choir (Decani) unable to hear properly the choristers on the other side (Cantoris) now that there was no wall behind the singers to act as a sounding board and the organist was out of touch with both, hearing more of the organ than the choir.

However, with the organ now in good order, Humphrey Carden soon had set about organising recitals. The first had been given on Wednesday July 22nd 1931 by the renowned Birmingham City Organist, George Cunningham. He had started his programme with J. S. Bach's famous Toccata and Fugue in D Minor and continued it with the Chorale No. 3 in A minor by César Franck, Franz Liszt's dramatic "*Ad Nos*" Introduction and Finale and a strange "*Maestoso* A. D. 1620" by the American composer Edward Macdowell. Mrs. Carden had contributed some violin solos including J. S. Bach's "Jesu, joy of man's desiring" and the audience had sung the hymn "Ye holy angels bright". On the following Tuesday, Dr. Percy Hull, Organist of Hereford Cathedral, had come to play the organ, bringing with him Mr. Alfred Brook, a bass soloist from his choir, who supplied some vocal items to the evening's entertainment. Among the organ music that had been played was Rheinberger's Sonata in E flat minor and a "*Marche Triomphale*" by Sigfrid Karg-Elert; this time the congregation had sung the hymn "Hail to the Lord's Anointed". Over the years other recitals had been given in the Cathedral, but by the time Harry Goss-Custard, the Organist of Liverpool Cathedral, had played on Sunday June 25th 1944, no longer were other artists supplying supporting items; furthermore, the congregation contributed not a hymn but rather the National Anthem, presumably because of the Second World War. There was also a retiring silver collection for the Red Cross.

Humphrey Carden had not confined his musical activities to the Cathedral alone, as for some years he had conducted the Breconshire Orchestral Society which was led by his wife. At the annual concert, which was given in The Guild Hall, Brecon, on May 16th 1933, there were six First Violins, six Second Violins (among whom was a member of the Heins family, along with Albert Tilley the Cathedral verger), four Violas, three 'Cellos and a Double Bass, with Colin Ross at the piano, presumably supplying missing wind parts. They played C. Hubert Parry's "English Suite", Elgar's "Serenade" and some "Elegaic Melodies" by Edvard Grieg. There had also been some songs and the Brahms Trio in C minor had been played by the Dorian Trio. A year later the programme included a Mozart "Serenade", Elgar's "Wand of Youth Suite No. 1" and Gustav Holst's "St. Paul's Suite". Subsequent concerts found the orchestra playing Grieg's "Holberg Suite", a Charles Avison *Concerto Grosso*, a *Suite* by Arnold Foster and J. S Bach's "Suite No. 3 in D" – did Colin Ross supply the missing trumpet parts on the piano? The Dorian Trio completed one concert by playing Robert Schumann's Trio in D minor.

By the year 1937, the orchestra had increased in size to twenty-four players and boasted three distinguished Presidents, namely Lord Glanusk, the Bishop of Swansea and Brecon and Sir Adrian Boult. Other officials included Canon Donaldson and Canon Roberts from the Cathedral. In that year's programme were Mozart's "*Eine Kleine Nachtmusik*", Henry Purcell's "Chaconne in G minor" and the "Chiddington Suite" by Thomas Dunhill, while among the songs was one composed by Colin Ross himself.

Perhaps the Second World War had put paid to such activities, because the next orchestral concerts to attract attention in Brecon were those given in the Cathedral by the BBC Welsh Orchestra. With six first violins, four second violins, two violas, two 'cellos and one double bass, plus double woodwind, two horns, two trumpets, three trombones, one percussion player and a harp, led by Philip Whiteway and conducted by Rae Jenkins, this orchestra had come into being in 1935 when it had evolved from an *ad hoc* assembly of players known as the Cardiff Studio Orchestra. The first concert took place on Friday June 15th 1951, when it started "at 7.0 p.m. prompt", presumably because the first part had been broadcast "in the Welsh Home Service". So the first part had started with J. S. Bach's Brandenburg Concerto No. 3, whereupon the soprano Jennifer Vyvyan had sung Max Bruch's "Ave Maria" with the orchestra and the broadcast part of the proceedings had ended with Geraint Jones playing the Organ Concerto No. 14 in A by G. F. Handel. How only two violas and two 'cellos had been able to give an adequate performance of the Brandenburg Concerto with its parts for three violins, three violas, three 'cellos and a double bass was a riddle solved by a statement on the programme which read: "The orchestra is augmented by nine players"! Presumably these extra players also had made easier the performance of Beethoven's first symphony, which ended the evening's entertainment. Such concerts had ensured a steady stream of internationally-known soloists to Brecon Cathedral. Thus in the concert on Thursday September 18th 1952, the contralto Constance Shacklock added Elgar's lovely "Angel's Farewell" from "The Dream of Gerontius" to a programme that included Mozart's Symphony No. 29 and Beethoven's Symphony No. 8. A year later, Alfredo Campoli delighted Brecon concertgoers with violin concertos by Bach and Mendelssohn.

It was at this time also that an annual choral festival had been instituted for choirs in the Archdeaconry of Brecon. These had been organised by Hubert Hughes, a Minor Canon at the Cathedral who was the possessor of a sufficiently accomplished tenor voice as to undertake solo work in the vicinity. Interestingly, the musical side of these proceedings was directed not by Humphrey Carden by virtue of his being Cathedral Organist, who had chosen instead to preside at the cathedral organ as accompanist, but by George Bradley, Organist of St. Mary's Church, Builth Wells. George Bradley might have been an ironmonger by profession, owning a shop in Builth's busy High Street, but he had nevertheless been well versed in Cathedral music, having sent two of his three sons to be choristers at Worcester Cathedral. He had also conducted an enterprising choral society in Builth Wells, which had been sufficiently enlightened as to include Gustav Holst's "Two Psalms" in one of its programmes which had been sung with orchestral accompaniment.

Obviously George Bradley had been more than a passing acquaintance of Humphrey Carden as he had sent his daughter Ann to him for piano lessons; regularly she had made the train journey from Builth Wells Station to Brecon Station (changing trains at Talyllyn junction), then walked the short distance to the Carden household at no. 2 Alexandra Road, where her lesson would take place. Now her father and Humphrey Carden had joined forces to provide opportunities for local church choirs to get together to sing interesting church music and, in so doing, perhaps raise their own standards of performance and widen their choice in music. So the responses were sung either to the Ferial setting or to music by Thomas Tallis and usually two psalms were sung to chants, as were (still) the Magnificat and Nunc Dimittis. However, John Hilton's "Lord, for thy tender mercy's sake" and Tallis's "If ye love me" appeared, sung from scholarly editions, as did T. A. Walmisley's "From all that dwell below the skies" and Beethoven's "The heavens declare the creator's glory". There were copious hymns but mostly with good strong tunes, some of Welsh origin and a few with Welsh words, even though not much Welsh was spoken in the Archdeaconry.

Humphrey Carden always made an important feature of Christmas. Sometime during the week leading up to the festival there would be an evening of carols and other Christmas music in the Cathedral, but the Nine Lessons with Carols service was never allowed to happen until the Sunday that followed Christmas Day which, of course, was liturgically correct. He had spread his net far and wide and over the years had sung carols by a multitude of composers: Joseph Barnby, J. C. Bridge. A. H. Brown, Harold Darke, Walford Davies, Johann Ebeling, John Goss, Arthur Sullivan, Charles Steggall, R. R. Terry and Vaughan Williams, not forgetting Colin Ross's own setting of "It came upon a midnight clear", which had received its first perform- ance in 1933, and a setting of "Let Christians all with joyful mirth" by Molly Hull – was this the wife of Percy Hull, Organist of Hereford Cathedral? A great favourite of Humphrey Carden had obviously been R. L. Pearsall's magnificent arrangement of the great German carol "In dulci jubilo", for this was sung with great regularity. Another favourite had been Walford Davies's setting of "O little town of Bethlehem" with its introductory recitative, "There were shepherds abiding in the fields", which sets the scene so beautifully; that had been introduced in 1926.

A year later various items from J. S. Bach's Christmas Oratorio (parts one and two) were sung, but as year succeeded year, so arrangements of folk carols began to be heard. "The Holly and the Ivy", arranged by Cecil Sharpe and "The First Noel", in 1930; "Unto us a boy is born" and the "Lute Book Lullaby", both arranged by Geoffrey Shaw, in 1932; soon came Martin Shaw's arrangements of "Rocking" and "I saw three ships", then R. Vaughan William's lovely "O little town of Bethlehem" and Charles Wood's arrangement of "Ding dong merrily on high". The carol singing before Christmas Day always included instrumental items and Mrs. Carden played solos by Thomas Arne, J. S. Bach, Beethoven, Frank Bridge, Paradis Duskin, George Dyson, G. F. Handel, Henry Lawes, John Ireland, Gustav Merkel, Josef Rheinberger and a composer with the unlikely name of Efrem Zimbalist! Occasionally solos were sung. So in 1945 there had been Eric Thiman's "Madonna and Child" and also Max Reger's "Virgin's Cradle Song", while in 1954 there was Hugo Wolf's "Blessed Virgin's Heavenly Child". Early on, the Dorian Trio had been involved and in 1931 had played Franz Schubert's Trio in B flat op. 99 and Beethoven's "Archduke" Trio in B flat, op. 97. Naturally after the organ had been rebuilt there were organ solos: music by J. S. Bach, W. T. Best, Harold Darke and Alexandre Guilmant, plus a "Noel" by Balfour Gardiner and a "Fantasia on an old carol tune" by Colin Ross. Always there was a collection, initially to help purchase a piano for choir practices, then to help pay off the debt on the re-building of the organ; afterwards it was put towards the choir music fund and finally it was donated to the Musicians' Benevolent Fund.

The actual service of Nine Lessons and Carols had a liturgical beginning: a Processional Hymn followed by the Lesser Litany, Lord's Prayer and Opening responses. Afterwards had come the nine lessons interspersed with carols. The lessons were read by a variety of people in an ascending order of importance, beginning with a choirboy, then a choirman, afterwards Humphrey Carden himself, a Server, a Warden, the Chapter Clerk, ending with a Canon in Residence, the Dean and finally the Bishop. Three carol services were memorable for a variety of reasons: that of 1941 had ended not with the Blessing but with the singing of the National Anthem; that of 1947 had been the first time the English Hymnal had been used, replacing the Ancient and Modern Hymnal; that of 1953 included an "Imperial March" by Edward Elgar played on the organ, which perhaps had something to do with the Coronation of Queen Elizabeth II that had occurred earlier in the year.

Humphrey Carden's time as Cathedral Organist had been running out; he had experienced increasing difficulty climbing the steps up to the organ loft. One month before his seventieth birthday in May 1956, he had retired; on the following Christmas Day a presentation was made to him in appreciation of his long and devoted service to the Cathedral. Sadly, however, Humphrey Carden had little retirement, dying on September 21st 1957. Meanwhile, he had been succeeded as Cathedral Organist by Gwerfyl Davies, who had started work on Whit Sunday 1956. Born in Dowlais and educated at Merthyr Tydfil County Grammar School, Gwerfyl Davies subsequently had read music at University College, Cardiff, before serving in the R.A.F. during the Second World War. Afterwards he had become Music Master at Alderman Newton's Boys School in Leicester, but eventually did what so many of the Welsh do when they find themselves working in foreign lands: he made his way back home, to Merthyr, where he had become Music Master at Cyfarthfa Castle Grammar School and Organist at St. John's Church, Dowlais. On being appointed Organist and Choirmaster at Brecon Cathedral he had managed to secure also the position of Music Master at Brecon Boys' Grammar School, which really was vital because the Dean and Chapter had not been able to afford to pay him a living wage. Back in 1926, Humphrey Carden had been paid £120 per annum, which was around one-third of a clergyman's stipend; he had augmented his income by undertaking private teaching, giving organ and piano lessons. However, a delightful and very beautiful portrait of Mrs. Carden painted while she was a young girl pointed to a different lifestyle, as did the weekends she used to spend at Hay Castle playing Chamber Music.

So Gwerfyl Davies had undertaken a heavy workload, full-time teaching and the Cathedral work, yet it did not prevent him from initiating a series of organ recitals on Sundays after Evensong. He had also brought about a special Choral Evensong, under the auspices of the Royal School of Church Music, on the feast of St. Luke the Evangelist, Saturday October 18th 1958, when the Cathedral Choir had been joined by the choirs of Christ College Brecon, and St. Mary's and St. David's Churches in Brecon. For the first time the evening canticles had been sung to a musical setting, that of C. Hylton Stewart in C. Three anthems had also been sung:

"Hide not Thou Thy face" by Richard Farrant, "Through the day Thy love has spared us", to music by Thomas Morley and "In Thee is gladness" to Henry Ley's arrangement of a melody by an Italian composer named Gastoldi. However, by Humphrey Carden's standards, Gwerfyl Davies's stay proved to be short-lived as towards the end of 1962 he returned to Leicester on being appointed Music Adviser to the City Education Committee and Organist at St. Peter's Church, Highfields. Hence the advertisement for the position of Organist and Choirmaster at Brecon Cathedral early in January 1963 that I had answered during my early months as Organist of Selby Abbey.

In reply to my letter, the Dean had written to say that the job would not support a married man. The trouble had been the unfortunate breakdown of the relationship between the Boys' Grammar School and the Cathedral, which had left the Dean and Chapter unable to provide their Organist with a living wage despite the improved financial position of the Cathedral which in 1939 had made possible the appointment of a Dean who was not also the Bishop. So the Dean at this time had been the popular William Jones, who belonged to a well-connected Brecon family and had previously served the Anglican Church in Australia. His dilemma over the appointment of an Organist had been solved for him in a quite unexpected way. One day, Bryan Hesford, Organist of Wymondham Abbey in Norfolk, who had applied for the job but had tired of waiting for a decision, travelled to Brecon and presented himself at the Deanery, where he had proceeded to talk himself into the vacant position of Organist and Choirmaster at Brecon Cathedral.

There had been one curious coincidence about this appointment. Before becoming Organist of Wymondham Abbey, Bryan Hesford had been Assistant Organist of Newcastle Cathedral during Colin Ross's time as Organist there. On reflection, there was also one slightly disquieting fact; that Bryan Hesford had not stayed in any job for longer than three years. Two years as Organist at Glossop Parish Church had been followed by one year as Organist of Northenden Parish Church, then, after one more year as Organist of St. Philip's Church, Gorton, Manchester, he had been Organist at Prescot Parish Church for three years after which came one year as Assistant Organist at Newcastle Cathedral which had been followed by three years as Organist at Wymondham Abbey and Music Master at Wymondham Boys' School. Yet his pedigree as an Organist had been excellent as, apart from studying with William Hardwick at St. Anne's Manchester and with Caleb Jarvis in Liverpool, he had also had lessons with such distinguished organists as Marcel Dupré and Jean Langlais in France, Max Drischner in Germany.

His pedigree as a choirmaster, however, had been unproven, but at least he began at Brecon Cathedral full of good intentions and had set about teaching the choir real Cathedral Music. The Dean's wife, Rachel, had been an official with the B.B.C. and in due course a Wednesday afternoon Third Programme Choral Evensong followed. The Cathedral Choir had now begun to sing settings of the Magnificat and Nunc Dimittis and an attempt had been made to sing the occasional weekday Evensong. When Dean Jones had retired, Gwynno James arrived in his place and had brought with him an anthem "Make a joyful noise unto the Lord" composed specially for his Installation Service by his friend William Mathias. Unfortunately, Bryan Hesford had not been consulted and when the music arrived it caused the choristers a few headaches in preparation. Even so, at the Installation Service the choir had acquitted itself well and the proceedings had been further enhanced by Bryan Hesford improvising on the organ while the choir and clergy processed to their places, using a song melody from a popular show "Hello Dolly". What was not lost on many people present was the similarity of the words "Dolly" and "Gwynno".

Sadly, the writing was soon on the wall for Bryan Hesford as he had begun to arrive late at choir practices only to find that the Dean himself had got the proceedings under way. The Dean had been motivated by a desire to get good Cathedral Music at Brecon, but, not surprisingly, relations between him and Bryan Hesford began to deteriorate. When the Organist position at the Priory Church of St. Margaret's, King's Lynn, had become available, Bryan Hesford applied and was appointed and was soon on his way back to his beloved Norfolk. He had been at Brecon Cathedral for just three years. He remained at King's Lynn for just one year, then moved to Lancaster Priory for a year, after which he went to St. Barnabas, Tunbridge Wells for two years, then to Melton Mowbray Parish Church where he had lasted five years before going to Norway and finally to the Collegiate Church of St. Nicholas, Galway, in Ireland. Widely travelled as an organ recitalist, he was also Editor of "The Musical Opinion" and its sister magazine "The Organ" for some years. In addition, he had been an examiner for London's Trinity College of Music, eventually becoming Chief Examiner. He had also produced many interesting collections of organ music for the publishing company Fentone, as well as publishing a few of his own compositions.

Perhaps the most useful contribution to Cathedral Music in Brecon Cathedral that was made by Bryan Hesford was his tying to the Organist position a part-time music teaching job at nearby Builth Wells County Secondary School. Now the Dean and Chapter could offer a living wage to their Organist and that paved the way for my arrival at Brecon Cathedral.

XXIV

The first week in Brecon was eventful. My last services in Selby Abbey had been on Palm Sunday and, not surprisingly, these were moving occasions. Then on Monday we made the journey to Brecon. During the week we set up our new home in the Clergy House and I found the electric wall-plug in the sitting room that I had been told, unofficially, was wired into the Deanery circuit. On Good Friday morning was my first service in the Cathedral. Beginning with the litany sung in procession, the choristers responded to each petition using Thomas Tallis's four-part harmony as they ambled around the Cathedral. I vowed silently to use the unison plainsong version next year, as I disliked singing in harmony while processing because the congregation never hears all the harmony properly, just whatever voice happens to be passing by at that moment. Later the choir sang Dr. C. F. Waters' "Reproaches" and I decided that these would be consigned to the dustbin, as the music did not bear comparison to that of Palestrina.

Afterwards the Bishop and the Dean expressed their pleasure at what had been achieved in just a few practices; I, on the other hand, was demoralised. The only light relief that day came courtesy of a performance of Handel's "Messiah" at "The Plough" - that is what was stated on the poster, and listed among the soloists was my violinist friend from the Royal Academy of Music, Philip Langridge (tenor). First, however, where was "The Plough"? This I assumed to be a public house but no, it wasn't! It was indeed a chapel built on the site of a former pub named "The Plough", which had a rather fine Victorian interior. On Good Friday evening, Hazel and I took our seats in a crowded Plough Chapel, high up on a gallery. The aged choir was assembled on two levels around the organ, at which presided an equally aged D. T. Davies FRCO from Merthyr Tydfil, while standing in the pulpit below was the conductor, the even more aged Mr. Gravell from Llangadog, a village on the other side of Llandovery. We couldn't believe our eyes as the octogenarian conductor raised his arms to conduct the Organist as he launched into the slow introduction to the Overture with great solemnity. Then, with the performance set in motion, he sat down while the organist rattled off the fugue with the tracker action of the organ rattling away in sympathy. After this had been played, Philip Langridge rose to his feet, thrust out his chest and exclaimed dramatically, like the Old Testament prophet he was representing, in sonorous tones: "Comfort Ye, My People". So the performance gathered momentum and when the choir sang its florid runs in such choruses as "For unto us a child is born" and "His yoke is easy" it sounded as if the notes had been learned by tonic sol-fa, which indeed was the case. After the triumphant conclusion and tumultuous applause, we found Philip and took him home to the Clergy House for coffee. "Why did you do that?" we asked indignantly, "You know, stick your chest out and belt 'Comfort Ye'?" "Oh!", he replied disarmingly cheerfully, "they like that 'round here".

So we moved on through Holy Saturday to Easter Day. What the service was in the morning I cannot remember but I suspect that it was Matins because, if I remember rightly, the main service in the Cathedral at that time on major festivals like Christmas, Easter and Whitsunday was Choral Matins, usually attended by some of the local well-to-do families. I used to loathe wading through the Te Deum to a succession of chants and longed for the day when the choir would be able to sing this to a musical setting like C. V. Stanford in B flat. The Responses also were still sung to the parochial Ferial setting. Indeed, the end result at that time was a parochial Matins plus an anthem, which was hardly the fare for a Cathedral. Yet if the service had been Holy Eucharist it would have been little better, sung to a very ordinary setting: William Harris in F and nothing more.

Indeed the entire repertoire of the Cathedral Choir was exceedingly limited. There were only three anthems regularly sung: "From the rising of the sun" by Frederick Ouseley, "O come ye servants of the Lord" by Christopher Tye and something for two voices by William Harris. At Evensong on that Easter Day the choir sang a fourth anthem, the Dutch carol "This joyful Eastertide", and I have painful memories of the trebles straining desperately to reach the top note in the chorus after each of the three verses. It was a far cry from what I had become used to in Selby Abbey and before that in St. Mary the Virgin, Primrose Hill, but this was to be the third and, I vowed, last time that I would have to build up a choir from scratch. At that same Evensong the choir sang one of the four settings of the Evening Canticles that were sung in rotation, and not particularly well: Hylton Stewart in C, Hylton Stewart in C - unison setting, Tertius Noble in B minor and a plainsong setting with fauxbourdons by Thomas Morley.

Over the ensuing weeks there were three special occasions which helped make the job so endearing as each involved a service of some sort. Brecon then had the distinction of being an Assize Town, with a week-long Assize Court being held in the Shire Hall four times a year, or to put it quaintly, quarterly. The Judge's Lodgings were in a magnificent red-brick Georgian town house in The Struet, a street at the bottom of Priory Hill, and the house was opened up only for these occasions as here the judge resided during his stay in Brecon. Only once did Hazel and I ever get inside this gracious residence and that was when a judge invited us both to dinner one evening. He had studied at New College, Oxford, where he had grown to love Cathedral Music by attending Divine Service in the lovely chapel there and now he wanted to talk about it. Always before the Assizes could begin there was a service in the Cathedral, a sort of shortened Matins and, strangely, the Judges guarded this tradition jealously.

So a procession was drawn up outside the Judge's lodgings comprising at least the High Sheriff clad in his distinctive, historic, velvet costume, the Lord Lieutenant and also the town Mayor and his entourage and then all would process down The Struet, turn left at the Bull's Head, cross the ancient stone bridge above the River Honddu that gave the town its Welsh name, Aberhonddu, then walk up Priory Hill, turn right to pass through the Cathedral Lych Gate and down the path leading to the Cathedral. Once inside, a motley collection of boys with me at the organ would render the opening Responses, the *Venite* and a Psalm. At some point there would be a reading from the King James Bible, some prayers concerning justice would be read and that would be that. The main problem then would be getting the choirboys to return to school! Usually in the Brecon Assize Court, there was little for the judge to do, as Brecknock was a law-abiding county, so he was able to treat himself to some welcome relaxation. As a result, a few years later when the infamous Dr. Beeching, who had already deprived Brecon of its railways, set about re-organising the judicial system in the country he deprived Brecon of its Assize Court and the Court Room was reduced to a museum-piece.

The second of these special occasions was the unique service that took place annually during the summer as part of the Annual Pilgrimage to Brecon of the Guild of Cordwainers. In the Middle Ages, Brecon Cathedral had two Guild Chapels, one at the East End of the North Nave Aisle, which was for the Tailors and the Corvizors (shoemakers), the other at the East End of the South Nave Aisle, which was for the Weavers and Tuckers; the Skinners had no chapel and apparently held their meetings under a thornbush in the churchyard. In more modern times these guilds and their chapels fell into disuse. Indeed, the chapel in the South Nave Aisle was swept away to provide a processional way through to the South Transept, the Choir and the Chancel.

However, in 1935, a certain Miss Ruth Tomlison M.B.E. who was Secretary of the British Boot and Shoe Manufacturer Federation, became the first woman Master of the "Brecon Cordwainers" and she had grander ideas. Calling together all the Past Masters of the Guild, she persuaded them to develop it on national lines and as a result, in 1936 the "Brecon Cordwainers" became the "Guild of Cordwainers". Their chapel was restored to their use and members of the Guild decided to hold an annual pilgrimage to Brecon so that those who appreciated the opportunity "to commune together upon the inspiration to be derived from the ideals of the ancient guilds" could "forget for a short period the more mundane affairs of the present day", and "could dedicate themselves to fuller service to their craft, fellow-craftsmen, and to the community". So the day always started with Holy Communion in the Cordwainers' Chapel at 8 a. m ... At 10.30 a.m. Members and Visitors assembled in the Guild Hall in the town centre to receive the Mayor of Brecon and other Civic Representatives, along with the Master of the Guild, who was escorted by the Master-elect, Past Masters and Members of the Court of the Guild.

Afterwards a welcome was given by the Mayor, followed by a Response from the Master. At this point in the proceedings the new Master of the Guild was installed, whereupon he delivered an Oration to the trade before declaring the Guild meeting closed. There was now a procession from the Guild Hall along High Street Superior, then High Street Inferior and The Struet, up Priory Hill to the Cathedral for the Service. Finally the Procession re-formed and proceeded to the Castle of Brecon Hotel for a luncheon at which there were Toasts to the Queen, the Guild, Brecon and the Guests. The object of all this is best summed up in the words of the Master of the Guild for that year 1966–67, J. E. Payne J. P., A. B. S. I.: "To return to the Cordwainers' Chapel in Brecon Cathedral is an outward and visible sign of the dedication of those of us who believe that material wealth is not the answer to our spiritual needs". In the list of Past Masters I was fascinated by the name of Josiah Thomas because his only qualification was a musical one, L.R.A.M., while against his name was the sign "†" which indicated quaintly that he had been "Called to Higher Service"!

The third special occasion was the Festival of the Friends of Brecon Cathedral, when many people who held the Cathedral dear travelled to Brecon from far and near to spend some time together in that lovely building. In one sense this too was an annual pilgrimage. The Festival began with a Choral Evensong complete with a printed service sheet, then there followed an Annual General Meeting also in the Cathedral, after which all finally descended on the glorious Deanery for a sumptuous tea and to this the choristers were also invited. Usually up to two hundred or more of the nine hundred and fifty Friends attended and the Friends Committee went to great lengths to ensure that the Cathedral and its surroundings looked their best. The lawns were cut, the hedges trimmed, the paths cleaned and the Cathedral and the Deanery beautifully decorated. Furthermore, the tea was always something special. It really was a magical occasion, usually graced by glorious summer weather.

Many people went to enormous lengths to add to the natural loveliness of the Cathedral and to make it a welcoming and happy place. The Friends contributed endless sums of money to help pay for much needed work in the building and, above all, to help support the Cathedral's music. Without this support my annual salary would have been far less. Indeed, even with this continual injection of cash I eventually became the lowest-paid Cathedral Organist in England and Wales, a distinction I was to hold for many years. Worse still, Hazel, who over the years took on more and more work as Assistant Organist remained unpaid, but then, when the Dean had appointed me Organist he had remarked gleefully: "two for the price of one".

Among the various individuals who went to extraordinary lengths to make their own contributions to the smooth running of the Cathedral was dear old Mrs. Carden, who made the most wonderful floral arrangements. Of all the many ladies involved in this activity, she alone appeared to understand the gentle understatement of the Cathedral itself and how to complement the natural colours of the local Brecknock stone without overpowering it. These arrangements were as quiet as she was and they were pure magic. She never appeared to sleep and many a night she would appear at the Cathedral at some ungodly hour, dragging after her some enormous branch of a dead tree or bits of hedgerow which she would proceed to turn into the basis of something unexpectedly beautiful.

Another silent lady worker who spent the majority of her time in and around the Cathedral was Vera Williams, known to some people for some reason as "Blob". She lived with her two cousins in the Almonry, alongside the Cathedral, but while they never darkened its door she was rarely out of it. She pottered around all day cleaning brass and silver, dusting and helping to keep the place generally tidy. The choirboys called her "Poshie" because she was so gracious and well-spoken; even when one of them abused a hedge in any way, her delicate indignation was always most proper. One day she told me about the dying oak tree in the grounds by the railings at the North-East corner of the Cathedral, the one with the ridiculous King Charles connection, and how she had planted part of it alongside; many years later when it had grown into a strong, young oak tree, it became known as "Poshie's Memorial". The day that "Poshie" and her cousins moved away from the Almonry turned out to be a sad day for the Cathedral as for the first time local youngsters began to raid the collecting boxes in the now little-supervised building.

Oswald Griffiths, known as "Ossie", was another lovely, quiet, good-natured character, dedicated to maintaining the beauty of the Cathedral. The grounds were his domain, smothered in glorious hedges which he kept immaculately cut, just as he maintained to perfection the paths that ran alongside them and cut the grass on the many lawns around. It was a never-ending job in the summer and he too was poorly-paid, but he loved the open air life and was happy, living with his dear wife, whom we grew to call "Aunty Griffiths", in the end house in a terrace almost opposite the Lych Gate. A countryman through and through, he was never happier than when he was following the local hunt, either on foot or in his little blue A35 Morris car. He became like a grandfather to my family and while to the choirboys he became the enemy as he tried to combat their indiscretions to his beloved hedges, to us he became a very dear friend. In his love and hate relationship with the choirboys he was joined by "Hawkeye" the Verger, Edgar Hawkes, who nevertheless added considerable solemnity to any service by his dignified bearing in processions when leading the clergy, carrying his silver wand of office, which the choristers nicknamed his "poker".

His moment of glory came around once a year at Christmas when he constructed the Crib at the West End of the Cathedral around the font. This was a magnificent creation, originally the brainchild of his predecessor, Albert Tilley. Large expanses of thick, old, brown, sanded paper did duty for mountains and hills and to these Mrs. Carden added bits of trees and hedgerows to soften the effect and to add a touch of realism. At the centre stood a large, wooden stable with a sloping straw roof which contained a concealed light that illuminated a wooden crib for the baby Jesus, with a large figure of Joseph standing at one end and an equally large figure of the Blessed Virgin Mary kneeling at the other end. Nearby two shepherds, one playing bagpipes, both standing around a small, glowing log fire, tended their sheep: it was all very cosy and lovely. The "*pièce de resistance*" was the three wise men bearing gifts, travelling with their camels afar off on these mountains. Day by day they were moved nearer and nearer to the stable, arriving there on January 6th, the Feast of the Epiphany, when they monopolised the area in front of the manger and relegated the shepherds and their sheep to a secondary place in the display. A stretch of rich carpet now added a touch of opulence to the lowly stable as the wise men presented their gifts of gold, frankincense and myrrh. It was all so beautiful and, above all, so right in the gentle, darkened, peaceful old Cathedral. People both young and old travelled miles throughout the seasons of Christmas and Epiphany to view this and it was justly famous in the locality.

Bishop J. J. A. Thomas had the measure of this when he blessed the crib before Choral Evensong on the afternoon of Christmas Eve. Gathering around him the many children who had come along with their parents, he would draw them gently around the crib and tell them about it, pointing out various important features, whereupon choir, congregation and children sang first "Away in a manger", then "Rocking" ("Little Jesus sweetly sleep") whereupon the ceremony ended with the Cathedral choir launching happily into "Ding dong merrily on high". Afterwards, while the choir processed down the nave to their stalls, the youngsters departed from the Cathedral into the gathering dusk in the churchyard, laughing and chattering with their parents. It was all very lovely, very simple and so special.

So began our first Christmas in Brecon, one that had already promised to be special. First of all BBC (Wales) had booked the Cathedral for a recording of R. Vaughan Williams's unique Christmas cantata "Hodie". In this, various scenes are linked by short recitatives and my boys were invited to sing them. I jumped at this because it gave me the chance to have extra practices on a Saturday morning safe in the knowledge that I could bribe the boys with extra cash! The actual performance, conducted by John Carewe, with the BBC Welsh Orchestra, a combination of three choirs from around Cardiff, along with Jennifer Vyvyan (soprano), Kenneth Bowen (tenor) and John Noble (bass) was broadcast on the Home Service on the evening of Friday December 23rd and on BBC TV on Christmas Day at lunchtime. Not having a television of our own, we went to the home of one of the choirboys to watch the performance and I remember my excitement at hearing the battery of heavy brass instruments play the music announcing the arrival of the three Kings and my relief at hearing the Brecon boys acquit themselves satisfactorily. That was not all. While working for that, dear Mary James, the Dean's wife, also had the choir working for a Nativity Play which was put on at the beginning of December. Although the choir contributed six carols, the highlight for me was Minor Canon Peter Sims's impersonation of a shepherd – so obviously one from Herefordshire.

To me, Christmas Day began with Midnight Mass and here in Brecon it was no different, although this was always at St. Mary's Church in the centre of town and as I was also the Parish Church Organist I had to be there with my choir. Back at the Cathedral a quaint tradition found me with the Lay Clerks singing the early morning Communion Service at 8 a.m. to the timeless music of John Merbecke. The main service of the day still was what I called irreverently "Solemn High Matins", as I longed for it to be a glorious Choral Communion, like it had been at Southwark Cathedral and at St. Mary the Virgin, Primrose Hill. Later that day another quaint tradition found those of the Lay Clerks who were still conscious back in the Cathedral at 5.15 p.m. singing a plainsong Evensong in candlelight. The interior of the Cathedral lit in this way, just as it might have been five hundred years earlier, was a truly wonderful sight. As the choir and the clergy lined up in the vestry before processing into Evensong, Peter Sims, the Junior Minor Canon, nudged me and muttered: "Hey Dave, look at this." As he flashed open his cassock I saw that beneath his shirt he was wearing only his pants. "I ate so much dinner," he explained, "that I could not do up my trousers!" With so full a quota of clergy present from the two Minor Canons right up to the Bishop, all Peter had to do was announce the anthem: "The Carol of the Nuns of Chester." However, so well had Peter been fed and watered that he fell asleep in his stall almost as soon as he sat down in it. When the time for the anthem arrived, the choirman sitting next to Peter nudged him and muttered "Anthem", whereupon Peter leapt to his feet and blurted out: "The choir will now sing the carol of the sons of the nuns of Chester", then sat back down and immediately fell asleep again, not realising what he had said.

As Christmas Day was a Sunday, the service of Nine Lessons and Carols by tradition did not take place until the following Sunday afternoon, January 1st. That Hazel and I could enter the new year, 1967, so happy and confident of future success, was largely due to the Dean, Gwynno James. From the very beginning in

Brecon he had given us encouragement and taken an interest to the extent that when I held full practices in the Cathedral he was often to be seen there, sitting at the back of the nave enjoying the musical noises, having a gentle smile on his face. He was not just a good Dean who understood fully the tradition of Cathedral worship, he was also a good parish priest. So concerned was he about his flock at St. Mary's Church that he organised a Parish Mission which had taken place in November. He asked Hazel and me to do all that we could to get the Parish Church Choir and the Cathedral Choir to work together and to that end we started the Cathedral Singers, a choral society which included singers from both choirs. We also organised a small concert at St. Mary's Church in which the choir of St. Mary's, the Cathedral Choir and the Cathedral Singers all joined together. It was not easy to bring this about because not everyone wanted it to work, but at least the Dean gave it his blessing. At Christmas he gave me a Book Token in which he wrote "For doing twice as much as even I dared hope for".

By now he and I were good friends, just as our two families got on well together. One night I turned round our dormobile and in so doing backed it into Mary James's father's car; unfortunately it was so dark and his car was coloured so grey and was parked up against a dark hedge that I just did not see it. I was very troubled because money was tight and I did not know how I was going to pay to repair the damage. Mary was marvellous; she blamed her father for leaving his car in such a stupid place and would not hear of my contributing anything. That was typical of her kindness. Often I would sit with the Dean in his study on a Saturday morning talking about the choir, about Cathedral Music, about the future. Only recently he had told me how at the next Chapter meeting he was going to push through a motion allocating £500 per annum (more than my annual salary as Cathedral Organist) for the choirboys, in order to put them on contracts, binding them to attend all practices and services. We both realised that the main obstacle to running a successful treble line was that if boys did not want to sing on a Sunday, they would do just that, and we wanted a hold over them.

Imagine my distress, therefore, when the Dean was rushed into hospital for tests and afterwards, as January progressed, he was confined to his bed in the Deanery. It was bitterly cold and snow lay on the ground. Fortunately, however, the Cathedral heating system was connected to the Clergy House and Deanery; indeed, the pipes crossing beneath the garth were not lagged, with the result that the snow melted in a straight line from the boiler house to the Clergy House. Towards the end of the month I saw the Dean being driven away in a car, looking pale and drawn, but he managed a wan smile. I never saw him again. He was operated on for cancer in St Luke's Hospital and returned not to the Deanery but to Brecon War Memorial Hospital. The end came mercifully quickly and one night, Bishop J. J. A. Thomas gave him Holy Communion, administered the Last Rites and sat with him while he died. Afterwards the Bishop went to the Cathedral and despite the early morning hour, he knocked on the door of the Verger's house and persuaded Mr. Hawkes to come with him to pray.

The Dean's funeral was wonderful in its austerity. A pall of a deep red hue was draped over his coffin which was raised high and surrounded by six enormous wooden candlesticks holding tall impressive candles of the correct liturgical colour, just as he would have wished. The solemn procession at the opening of the service numbered in its ranks the Dean and Canons of Llandaff Cathedral and the Canons of Brecon Cathedral, along with a multitude of other clergymen which no man could number, so greatly was his memory revered. A vast congregation also had assembled, all of whom held Gwynno in high regard, believing that had he lived he would undoubtedly have become a bishop, even possibly Archbishop of Wales. The Cathedral Choir hurriedly had learned Henry Purcell's lovely funeral anthem "Thou knowest, Lord, the secrets of our hearts", safe in the knowledge that Gwynno would have approved. A few days later, when all was over, his widow, Mary, gave me a letter:

> *"For what it is worth, I enjoyed the music too ... May I give you 2/6 (12½p) a head for the Cathedral boys to be given out at the next Choir practice?*
> *I am sure the Dean enjoyed it. It was all so cheerful.*
> *Please thank Hazel for taking so much trouble – I wish we had been early enough to hear St. Teilo."*

She also called me over to the Deanery to give me first choice of all his music books and asked me what she should do with his Bechstein Grand Piano, which is how the Cathedral came into possession of a suitable piano for its concerts. Sadly, however, Gwynno's dream for the choir died with him as never again did I hear any mention of extra money for choirboys' contracts.

XXV

Despite this being a sad time there was, however, one advantage, that I was spared an argument with Gwynno which would have been our first dispute. He had been determined to have the Cathedral Choir sing Malcolm Williamson's "Procession of Palms" on Palm Sunday. I was equally determined that it should not, as I disliked the music. Now Hazel and I waited to see whom the Bishop would appoint as the new Dean. When this was announced, we were not alone in our surprise. As far as we knew, William Ungoed Jacob, Archdeacon of Carmarthen and Vicar of St. Peter's Church, Carmarthen, had little or no knowledge of or sympathy for Cathedral worship. Why, therefore was he being appointed? What we did not know, because we had not been long in Wales, was that he had worked tirelessly for Church Unity, a cause very dear to the Bishop's heart if not quite so dear to his wife Betty. What we did know was that the new Dean had a violent temper. One afternoon, while on holiday in Kidwelly after Christmas a year or two previously, we had walked into St. Peter's Church when shopping in Carmarthen only to find ourselves witnessing a blazing row between him and his organist, F. Vernon Curtis, an accomplished musician, over something to do with music for a carol service. So we awaited the new arrival with apprehension and pondered the future

Meanwhile, we had gathered a group of music lovers like ourselves, called them "The Cathedral Singers" and given a concert in nearby, historic Maesberllan Chapel. The father of one of the sopranos, Glenys Phillips, was a Deacon there. We had sung some sixteenth-century motets and Lennox Berkeley's "Missa Brevis". I should have known better, as the solo artist supplied by the Chapel, a tenor of local fame, sang "Bless this House", "Jerusalem" and other similar ditties. It soon became obvious that Brecon and district was not ready for our music. So we turned to Handel's "Messiah" and organised a performance of some of this with a small string band, using the Watkins Shaw edition and Baroque performing practices which we had grown up with in London but were still unheard of in this part of the world. The soloists included a local teacher with a lovely voice but an unfortunate name, Penny Croke, and a young contralto, Pauline Foulkes, whose father taught in the local boys grammar school. To these were added our friends Lewis Burden, tenor, from London and Royston Ashby, bass, from Selby. All went well and as the performance did not raise too many eyebrows, we were happy.

On the next evening, a Sunday, Royston and I visited the Old Ford Inn at nearby Llanhamlach for a drink. Some time after "Last Orders" had been called, Royston went up to the bar to order more drinks and, while doing so, struck up conversation with a stranger, not realising that this was kindly Inspector Gliddon of the local Police Force. Royston need not have worried. There was a famous occasion when Inspector Gliddon had been sitting in the corner of the bar at Brecon's "George Hotel" enjoying a quiet drink and chat with Mrs. Jones, the landlady, well after closing time, when two young, zealous police officers had walked in. On pushing open the door they had, unbeknown to themselves, hidden the Inspector from view. Just as they had begun to reprimand the customers who were drinking after hours, including some members of the Cathedral Choir, the Inspector pushed back the door, saying quietly: "All right Constables, I will take care of this." They had departed looking somewhat deflated.

Full of reforming zeal at this time, I had also gathered together "choirs" or collections of singers from churches in the neighbourhood of Brecon to teach them to sing John Merbecke's ancient music to the Communion Service. I had been brought up singing this at my father's church, at Southwark Cathedral and at St. Mary the Virgin, Primrose Hill, always to J. H. Arnold's plainsong-like version of this age-old setting, sung in free rhythm. So this is what I peddled, despite the fact that scholars were beginning to claim that John Merbecke had, in fact, intended a measured rhythm for his music, while down in Kidwelly Church John Stainer's slow and wearisome four-part setting was still being sung. These gatherings were of great value because through them it was possible to standardise congregational singing of the Eucharist throughout much of the Archdeaconry of Brecon.

While the Bishop gave his enthusiastic support to these ventures, he also drew me into the organisation of his Diocesan Clergy Choir. This, as far as I am aware, was unique: a choir run by the Bishop which was made up solely of clergy from the diocese who were happy to lead the singing at the Ordination Services which were held twice yearly on Saturday mornings in the Cathedral. Saturday was chosen to make it easy for as many clergy as possible to be present to welcome the new ordinands into the fold. With a choir of clergymen leading the singing of the Holy Eucharist to John Merbecke's ancient music, the plainsong litany, the "*Veni Creator*" and other liturgical hymns from the English Hymnal, the entire occasion took on a monastic flavour which was quite special. Particularly lovely was the way in which Bishop Thomas and his wife welcomed all the clergy choristers to tea inside their home at Ely Tower after the Friday afternoon rehearsal. Furthermore, they welcomed all the ordinands to breakfast on the Saturday morning. That year also, 1967, on St. John the Evangelist's day, December 27th, the name-day of the Cathedral, the Bishop saw to it that the Clergy Choir sang Evensong under my direction at the Cathedral, even though it was but two days after Christmas Day. Afterwards everyone had a special tea at Ely Tower to end a very special occasion.

By then Hazel and I had begun to know our new Dean. Highly-intelligent and an exceedingly fine preacher, he was also initially very ambitious, his eyes set upon the bishopric of St. David's, which would be vacant in the not-too-distant future. One of his biggest problems was wearing glasses that resembled plate-glass windows in miniature, with the result that he rarely recognised anyone in the street. This was unfortunate for a clergyman, who was expected to acknowledge almost everyone he met in the highways and byways, preferably by name! His wife, Ivy Matilda, obviously had once been a lovely looking lady but, sadly, had suffered from Bells Palsy, so that one side of her face was now paralysed. If only she had smiled more often she would have looked wonderful, but she chose instead to look forbidding and always behave formally. She and her husband were devoted to each other and it was wonderful to see them together.

Ivy Matilda's fame as a singer had reached us long before she herself had. Peter Boorman, the friendly Organist of St. David's Cathedral, had told us how when her husband came into residence for his month at the Cathedral each year, he would have to ask the Dean to ask the Archdeacon to ask his wife, Ivy Matilda, to sit at the back of the nave during choral services because her singing distracted the choir, particularly in the psalms. Fortunately, when she came to live in the Deanery at Brecon, she took it upon herself to attend only the morning services, be it Matins or Holy Eucharist. It did not take long, however, to find out that Peter Boorman had not exaggerated. Added entertainment was provided every Sunday morning now by the Bishop's wife, Betty, who could not bear the sound of Ivy Matilda's singing. She would arrive at the Cathedral on a Sunday morning as late as she could, stand scowling at the back of the nave surveying the backs of the heads of the congregation until her eyes came to rest on Ivy Matilda, whereupon she would sit as far away from her as was possible, to avoid having her ears pierced free of charge!

By now the service of Holy Eucharist sung in the lovely atmosphere of Brecon Cathedral was beginning to have an extraordinary aura of sanctity about it, with the choir singing the Kyrie, Sanctus, Benedictus and Agnus Dei, the congregation joining in with John Merbecke's Gloria and Creed along with the best liturgical hymns from the English Hymnal, and the Dean or Bishop preaching the most erudite sermons. Tragically, the arrival of Ivy Matilda brought about the destruction of the portion of psalm that was chanted between the Epistle and Gospel. For a while I was at a loss as to what I should do, because I had never been very good at confrontations. Suddenly, one day, I hit on the ideal solution: substituting plainsong sung by the Lay Clerks for Anglican chant sung by everyone. On the next Sunday the Lay Clerks did just that and Ivy Matilda was rendered silent. After the service, when the Dean had said the Vestry Prayer and the choir had started climbing the stairs to the Choir Room, I saw Ivy Matilda walk purposely through the door from the Cathedral, go up to the Dean and whisper in his ear. A few moments later the Dean began to climb the stairs to the Choir Room, then thought better of it and retreated back down. However, not long afterwards he plucked up courage and started back up the stairs: this time he reached the landing at the top, where I was standing. "Mr. Gedge," he said, "You changed the chant for the Psalm." I replied with a monosyllabic "Yes" and back he went down the stairs, his mission accomplished. Never again did the choir sing Anglican Chant at the Holy Eucharist, choosing instead to sing a gentle plainsong, always sitting. This was contrary to the instructions printed in the Church in Wales Prayer Book, but standing for the gospel gave prominence where prominence was due, by accident. Furthermore, somehow a plainsong psalm seemed to complement the John Merbecke Gloria and Creed, to add still more dignity to the proceedings.

Earlier that year my father, who was having trouble with his hips, made a flying visit to Brecon bringing with him, as usual, a dormobile full of youngsters from a parish in London's Pimlico where he was helping out. Needing to find somewhere where he could put up his tents and they could all camp for the night, I took him two miles down the road that passes the Cathedral to Glanhonddu, a lovely eighteenth-century house standing in its own grounds, owned by a highly-intelligent yet eccentric and hospitable couple named Johnny and Viv Dickinson. Viv made a great fuss of my father, and showed him where he and his entourage could camp. We left him pitching his tents and returned to the house for drinks, having begged him to join us when he had finished. When he had not reappeared an hour or so later, we searched him out only to find that he had gone, along with the youngsters, overwhelmed by such hospitality, to which he had now become unaccustomed. Next morning as usual, while travelling on the 7.30 a.m. bus from Brecon to Newtown which deposited me at Builth Wells in time to teach at the Bilateral (as it was then called) School, on the stretch of the A470 road between Llyswen and Erwood I saw in a field a collection of tents. On looking harder I saw the figure of my father holding onto a tent pole, pulling up his trousers with some difficulty owing to his hip problem. It proved to be the last time that I was to see him in Wales and outside of a hospital.

It was about this time that I received disconcerting news of Chris Tanner. Since moving to Brecon we had seen less and less of him, which was hardly surprising, as with no railway at Brecon and only a small fraction of the M4 in existence the journey to and from London seemed like a major expedition. For a few months lately we had heard nothing from him, which indeed was ominous, but when the news he had been keeping from us eventually did reach us, that he had terminal cancer, we were shattered. Typical of Chris, he worked as long as possible in Graham Maw's office and, latterly, had been heavily sedated to combat the pain. Later we learned the sad tale of how on his way home to Beckenham he would sit on a seat at the crowded platform of the Temple Underground Railway Station and, when the train arrived to take him to Victoria Station, would stand unsteadily on his feet and try to get to the automatic doors of a carriage before they shut, sometimes only to fall over in his helplessness. Worse, however, was that anyone who had rushed to his aid would be motioned away brusquely by a porter saying: "Don't bother about him, he's often drunk like this." How cruel life sometimes can be!

His funeral took place on a lovely summer's day at the church of St. Stephen's, South Dulwich, and a large gathering of his friends from the Church Choir and from Southwark Cathedral Choir came to sing the service. Even though Harold Dexter, the Organist of Southwark Cathedral, was there, it was I who had been asked to direct the musical proceedings and, while I felt humble and privileged, he was both gracious and supportive. That morning, the anthem by Samuel Sebastian Wesley could not have been more appropriate: "Thou wilt keep him in perfect peace, whose mind is stayed on thee." It was sung so beautifully and so meaningfully by that gathering of people whose lives had been affected in some way or another by dear Chris. I myself, however, could not but feel remorse that, unconsciously, I had begun to grow away from him simply because I had become so immersed in my work in Brecon and had never considered how his silence just might have been indicative of the insurmountable problems which he wanted to hide from Hazel and me.

Recently I had extended the John Merbecke Holy Eucharist sessions to the Archdeaconry of Gower, which is centred on the city of Swansea, and enthusiasm had been enormous. All this had become possible only because at the third attempt I had passed the Driving Test and was therefore able to undertake the enormous amount of necessary motoring. To go to St. Mary's, the mother church of Swansea, and back home in an evening involved a journey of around eighty miles. Now, the logical extension to all this was a Diocesan Choral Festival and to this end I organised a number of area rehearsals. The first was at Pontardawe, on the outskirts of Swansea, where the Vicar was the redoubtable and much-loved T. R. Walters James, one of the Cathedral Canons, a kindly man who rarely spoke ill of anyone. Small wonder that his church was a happy one, even though in the course of his sermons "one third of the time he talked to his congregation, the second third he talked to God, the third third God knows who he was talking to." There I met Ivor and Dotty, who later played a big part in Hazel's and my life, also Len and Edwina, Shirl(ey) and June, all of whom sang in the Church Choir, not forgetting Howard Madge, the Organist and Choirmaster. There was also Lyn, a larger than life character who had been ordained late in life and was an unpaid Curate with one strange ambition, to be Precentor of Gibraltar Cathedral! He had taken his place in the folklore of St. Peter's Church, Pontardawe, because of two incidents. Both of these had been witnessed by my new friends and were recounted with great glee by Dotty. Apparently Evensong on a Sunday at St. Peter's had always begun with a processional hymn and one Sunday the choir had set off at a faster pace than usual, leaving lumbering Lyn some way behind. When he looked up from his hymn book and saw the choir disappearing into the distance, he took a longer stride, caught his foot in his cassock and surplice and fell flat on his face in the nave. The second incident occurred when he was conducting a funeral service at St. Peter's. Having completed the first part of the service inside the church, he led the coffin bearers and mourners out into the churchyard reading Comfortable Words from his Prayer Book as he did so. So engrossed was he in this that he did not look to see where he was going and walked straight into the grave!

The Church, with its tall needle-like spire, was impressive both inside and outside and dominated the village. It was known as "The Cathedral of the (Swansea) Valley" and its floors were smothered with lovely Victorian tiles. However, we did not rehearse there for the Choral Festival, but rather in an old school nearby that served as the Church Hall. The first rehearsal was attended by choristers from parishes around and a good time was had by all, which ended with tea and biscuits. Afterwards some of the singers decamped to the Ivy Bush Hotel, on the other side of the road, for a drink of something stronger. On my way over I became engrossed in a conversation with the Canon outside the hall, when suddenly, by the light of a fire seen through the first-floor window of the house next door to the hotel, I saw a lady strip off all her clothing until she was stark naked. I was mesmerised and found extreme difficulty in keeping the conversation going! When finally the Canon finished talking and I reached the Ivy Bush, I recounted to Ivor what I had seen and asked him what on earth went on next door. "Oh!" he replied laughingly, "That's the local Shangri La!"

Meanwhile Hazel had been growing larger and larger with our second child and on the afternoon of my twenty-ninth birthday, March 12th 1968, she realised that delivery of my birthday present was imminent. Early that afternoon, therefore, she left Harriet with Granny Coppock, who lived in Priory Lodge opposite the Cathedral Close, and while looking for Ossie she met the wife of that month's Residentiary Canon, Essie Brunsden. "My dear," asked the inquisitive lady kindly, on looking her up and down, "When's the baby due?" to which Hazel blurted out, "Now!" Ossie drove her up to Brecon War Memorial Hospital and I went to visit her on my way home from school, but could not stay as I had to take the Cathedral Singers rehearsal. By 8.10 p.m. Nicholas Paul Gedge had come into this world and assisting was Dr. Aitken, who numbered among the basses in the Cathedral Singers. When he arrived at the rehearsal and announced to the assembled company the birth of my son, I, in fun, reprimanded him for arriving late!

Two days later my father died in St. Thomas's Hospital. He had always wanted to die within the sound of Big Ben and his wish had been granted. He had been well-known in that hospital because it was next-door to his old parish. Furthermore, over the years his Vicarage had provided refuge for countless medical students at exceedingly small rents. His health had deteriorated rapidly since that visit to Brecon. Firstly, his hips had worn out. In those early days of hip replacement operations, a long stay in hospital would have been necessary and as he never spent more than two days in bed for any illness, he had not wanted to start now. Secondly, he was having trouble with his "waterworks". Truth to tell, with Wendy and his parish gone and his children busy in employment, he had lost all interest in life and ceased to look after himself. The hospital staff had sorted out his problems to the best of their ability, so he really should have been sent home. However, home was a large, cold, dirty, semi-derelict Vicarage, hardly the place for someone not in the best of health. So he had been allowed to stay in hospital and with the sound of Big Ben ringing in his ears his health suddenly began to fail.

Over a period of two to three weeks he slipped in and out of consciousness. Sometimes his friend Fr. Rhys was with him and in lucid moments they would pray together. Occasionally my brother, Peter, who now lived many miles away in Lancaster, or my sister, Daphne, who lived in Battersea, or even more rarely I had visited, but we had all been wrapped up in our own new worlds. After all, he and Wendy had trained us to be independent, to lead useful lives of our own in our local communities and we were doing just that. The end was gentle and, to my sorrow, none of us was with him. It was a tragic end to a life that had started out full of promise but had been snuffed out by officialdom, lack of interest and understanding, yet, as his obituary in the Church Times stated, his enthusiasm had remained to the end so that he had been able to give many young people from deprived backgrounds "the time of their lives", and that had been important to him.

His funeral took place a few days later in the church of St. John's, Waterloo Road, where Fr. Rhys was Vicar. Some of these youngsters made the journey to be present. I played the organ and it pleased me to think that when this church was built in the 1820s, the first Organist had been my idol, Samuel Sebastian Wesley. During the course of that day I had met up with Peter and Daphne to share out all that remained in Holy Trinity Vicarage. I was given the task of taking away my father's dormobile, eventually to sell it. So I stuffed it full of the treasures that I had selected: an ancient oak chest, an equally old oak gate-leg table, a huge, wonderful brass fender (which I swear is of Regency origin), two family portraits, one of which I had sliced with a bayonet when a lot younger, and a painting of some dogs that appealed to me.

At around five o'clock in the evening, I filled the dormobile with petrol and set off. No sooner had I reached the main road than the gear lever came away in my hand, leaving me with a short metal stump with which to operate the gears. I made for Hyde Park Corner so as to reach the A40 road, but it was a Friday evening and the weekend traffic was terrible, so taking the coward's way out I turned left. I never did turn right and try cutting across London, but when the moment came and the traffic had thinned out considerably I was then on my way to Oxford. By the time I reached that city of spires, so much beloved by my father, I was desperate for a loo. Finding a narrow lane in a quiet part of Oxford, I did what was necessary, then leapt back in the van to continue driving. So slow and endless was the journey that not until midnight did I find myself leaving Abergavenny. Crickhowell came next then, as I approached Bwlch, the dormobile shuddered to a halt, the petrol used up. I had to stop a passing car to get a lift into Brecon, whereupon I drove our little car down to the Police Station and a kindly policeman siphoned off some petrol for me. Despite the early hour of the morning I drove out to the dormobile, put the petrol in its tank and drove it home, leaving the car in a lay-by. Later that morning I unloaded the treasures and last of all, what did I find but a can of petrol hidden away! How my father must have smiled.

The two portraits which numbered among the treasures were in quite a state. I blew my financial inheritance on having them restored and repaired. This involved having the actual picture removed from its original canvas, put onto a new canvas and then cleaned. The picture of the gentleman when cleaned revealed that he was reading a book entitled "Speech Printing". This confirmed that he was indeed Peter Gedge (1758-1818) who was the founder of the Bury Post. His memorial in the great church of St. Mary, Bury St. Edmunds, bears the epitaph:

> *"Like a worn-out type he is returned to the maker,*
> *in the hope of being cast in a purer and better mould."*

The second portrait showed his first wife, Sarah Green (1762-1793), who had died shortly after giving birth to her second child, Robert Harvey Gedge, who himself died two months later.

My interest in the family portraits now became known and soon afterwards four more were passed on to me. Two were of Ann Johnson (1769-1840), Peter Gedge's second wife and while I kept the portrait painted when she was a widow, I passed on to my brother the portrait of young Ann because his daughter was named Ann. One of the remaining two portraits I had restored, but then the money ran out. By far the most interesting was the portrait I had not restored, which was believed to be of Dr. John Denny, who was Surgeon to the Tenth Hussars in the Peninsular War. Supposedly a good friend of the Prince Regent, he is reputed to have married one of the future King's ladies, the Prince Regent being Best Man at the ceremony. So John Denny became the legal father of Marianne Thomas Denny (1810-1897) and this fourth and final restored portrait shows her to have been an exceedingly handsome and buxom young lady. Later two more portraits reached me from as far away as South Africa: these showed Frederick George Peter Gedge (1880-1946) who had died in Durban and his wife, Enid Cleminson. A Major in the First World War, I could not understand why he had chosen to be painted in his Home Guard uniform, until I discovered that during the Second World War he had been Officer in Charge of the Wimborne Home Guard and that one of his medals was the D. S. O ... These are the only signed portraits, the artist being Alex H. Kirk. That of Enid Gedge portrays a very prim and proper lady, very much the Commanding Officer's wife.

My brother Peter had kept alive the "Denny" connection by naming his son John Denny Gedge, so eventually Hazel and I added another family name, Johnson, to the names of our son, but too late to add to his birth certificate. Later that year, 1968, Nicholas Paul Johnson Gedge was baptised by our dear friend Bishop Jack Thomas in Brecon Cathedral.

XXVI

The Cathedral choirboys as I first knew them could have come out of a Giles cartoon. So many of them were quite crazy! Most of them used to descend on the Cathedral for choir practices and services from the two Council Estates, Bryn de Winton and Coryton Close, returning there afterwards (if they had not already been ejected for some misdemeanour). To their credit, they worked exceedingly hard and put in far more effort than their Selby counterparts had done. The choir men - in Cathedral circles they are often given the grandiose title "Lay Clerks" - were an interesting bunch. Two in particular seemed to know my job better than I did. Initially I worried about this as they frequently told me how I should be controlling the boys and training them, yet invariably they themselves arrived late for practices, sometimes exceedingly so, continually complaining! However, there were two very special gentlemen in the choir, Len Hatton, a bass who had been singing since 1920 when St. John's was still a Parish Church, and Mel White, a tenor who was around ten years younger. They were kind, helpful and supportive and furthermore were continually grateful to me for being prepared to put in so much time with the choir and improve the quality of its singing. Len loved to potter around the Cathedral doing little jobs like cleaning brass; Mel devoted much time and energy to soccer in the community and later in life received a well-deserved award from the Football Association. Both worked as local government clerks and with Brecon being the county-town for Breconshire there were plenty of such jobs to be had.

Indeed, the town contained an interesting cross-section of people. There were county officials, town officials, Ministry of Agriculture officials, Inland Revenue officials, school teachers for a boys grammar school, a girls grammar school, a mixed secondary-modern school, three primary schools, a college of Further Education and a Public School (Christ College). There was also a Cathedral, which added a bishop to the community, along with a Roman Catholic Church (designed by no less a person than Joseph Hansom of Hansom Cab fame) and six Non-Conformist chapels. In addition there was the Assize Court and the Magistrates Court, a police headquarters, an important fire station, a county library plus all the supporting staff, solicitors, accountants and other professional people. Finally there was the surgery with six doctors, all of whom specialised in some branch of surgery so that various minor operations could be done at the local War Memorial Hospital. Even the army had an important presence in Brecon, because the gracious Regency barracks in The Watton housed the headquarters of the British Army in Wales, which brought with it the distinction of having a General living in the town. To all intents and purposes, Brecon was a garrison town and the presence of so many soldiers, some of whom married local girls and settled there, is one reason why there was not as much inbreeding in Brecon as might have been expected in a small country town of seven and a half thousand inhabitants, like there was in Selby and Howden back in the East Riding of Yorkshire.

With such a high proportion of professional people living in Brecon, why were there not more boys from these homes in the Cathedral Choir? I suppose part of the answer has to be that many children from such backgrounds were sent to boarding schools or went as day boys to Christ College. What did fascinate me was how these two council estates had been built in such a way as to be virtually invisible to the town and hidden away from the casual visitor. Such estates require much pastoral care but my suggestions to the Dean that one of the Minor Canons should live in a Council House were perpetually ignored.

As I had done at St. Mary the Virgin, Primrose Hill and at Selby Abbey, I soon organised a choir singing holiday to St. David's Cathedral, which was just ninety or so miles down the A40 road. Only one problem really seemed to concern the Lay Clerks: the fact that in Pembrokeshire on a Sunday the doors of the pubs were firmly shut. To solve this, therefore, Mel White ensured that his RAFA club membership was valid so that he could drink in the St. David's branch on the Sunday in question, signing in the other Lay Clerks as his guests. So we had a riotous time in this, the smallest city of Britain, working hard and playing hard. We enjoyed the sandy beach at Whitesands Bay by day and played wide games in the surrounding countryside in the evenings. By night, Hazel and I enjoyed the spectacle of a pair of socks regularly being hung out of the window belonging to the house where three of the Lay Clerks were lodging: apparently, one of them had such smelly feet that the other two had to remedy the situation.

On Sunday we sang two services in the nave of that fascinating Cathedral which rises upwards from the West End, so that the East End where the blue stone mediaeval arches lean outwards alarmingly and the wooden ceiling is covered with the most fantastic carvings, stands considerably higher. On most weekday evenings we sang Evensong in the magical miniature Quire while the angels carved into the organ case looked on silently. Here the choir occupied elaborately carved oak choirstalls where one of the Canon's stalls is set aside for the reigning monarch who, by tradition, is a member of the Cathedral Chapter. For our choirboys from the back streets of Brecon, this was a completely new and sobering experience. After Choral Evensong one day, the boys came rushing up to me calling out: "Mr. Gedge, Mr. Gedge, Ottie has peed on the floor." When they had calmed down a little, one of them explained that indeed young Calvin Ottewell had peed on the floor of the choirstalls. Apparently he had been taken short during the service and, being too shy and nervous to walk out in full view of the choir and congregation, had waited until everyone was on their knees for the prayers and then under the cover of his cassock had relieved himself onto the floor. Ottie was duly sent back to the choir stalls armed with a damp cloth, to remedy the situation.

Later that year the Cathedral Choir went to sing Evensong one Saturday afternoon at Worcester Cathedral. Given tea in the Cathedral café, they were bowled over by the smartly-dressed waitresses who served them at small tables. They had never met with such civility before. This was but a prelude to two trips further afield, to Lincoln Cathedral.

This stunning mediaeval cathedral had long been my favourite and in recent years I had helped Robert Crinall, the Organist of St. Wilfred's Church, Harrogate, run two Royal School of Church Music courses there. These had been held in the Old Bishop's Palace which possessed an old chapel that reeked of holiness. We worshipped here daily until the weekend when the course transferred to the majestic cathedral. While in Lincoln I had come to know well the kindly and hospitable Precentor, David Rutter, who had previously been a Minor Canon of St. Paul's Cathedral. Any service that he conducted had a timeless quality about it, helped by his effortless command of the English language, as perfect as his gentle speaking voice. His reading of the King James Bible was beautiful and could not be bettered. When he celebrated the Holy Communion nothing was hurried and the end result was worship that was unfussy but deeply meaningful and holy.

Sadly, however, such practices were beginning to be eroded by the modern brigade in their quest for popularising religion. In the eyes of such progressives, David Rutter was a relict of the past. However, here he was at Lincoln living in an ancient cathedral house, caring for his aged mother and dispensing hospitality liberally. He was very good for my soul: indeed, he made it his business to care for the souls of all who worked and worshipped at Lincoln Cathedral. When he visited all the homes of the Cathedral Lay Clerks, his reward was a letter from a local Vicar sent to the Bishop of Lincoln complaining that he was trespassing in someone else's parish. He devoted much attention to the RSCM course, ensuring that both staff and choristers were happy in all that they did. This was particularly important when the services were sung in the Cathedral, because the choirstalls there are massive and the experience must have been quite over-awing and intimidating to a young choirboy used only to worshipping in a small parish church. As Precentor of an old foundation Cathedral, David Rutter was one of the four Residentiary Canons who, with the Dean, made up the Chapter. They ran the Cathedral and his particular responsibility was the musical side of Cathedral life.

David took his duties so seriously that he even organised the organ recitals at Lincoln Cathedral, which must have irritated the Cathedral Organist immensely. This is how I found myself giving a rare performance. I was terrified, and remedied the situation by playing some unknown seventeenth-century music along with a modern Scandinavian organ sonatina by a certain Valdemar Söderhölm, which I loved, and so got away lightly! David loved to play piano duets and kept two upright pianos in a room in his house for that purpose: the fact that they were not always in tune, nor in tune with each other, did not seem to bother him unduly. His sense of humour was infectious and, as he and I packed up the large box of music which had to be returned to the RSCM after the course had ended, he included an empty beer bottle containing a sheet of paper bearing the message: "Regret empty"!

It was David Rutter who encouraged me to take Brecon Cathedral Choir to sing at Lincoln Cathedral when the resident choir was on holiday. The first visit was during the first week of August 1968 and, hospitable as ever, he had us accommodated in the Cathedral Choir School, ensuring that we were comfortable. The Brecon Cathedral choirboys used to rise early and usually by seven o'clock were to be heard shouting and bawling as they gleefully played soccer before breakfast in the shadow of the great cathedral on what passed for a soccer pitch. Afterwards David would bear the brunt of the complaints from residents of the Close who had been rudely awakened from their sleep, trying hard to attract their sympathy and understanding over having such wonderful, lively, young Welsh urchins around when Lincolnshire youths, by comparison, were usually so dozy and uninspiring.

He took the choir to sing at Lincoln Gaol, where there was a full house in the Chapel as one hundred and fifty prisoners attended of their own free will. The choir's rendition of the hymn "Cwm Rhondda" apparently inspired two inmates to volunteer to join the Prison Chapel Choir. When David told the assembled company that Hazel's and my sixth wedding anniversary was fast approaching, the prisoners cheered, wolf-whistled and stamped the floor. Of course they rarely saw a lady, yet here was Hazel playing the Chapel organ. Afterwards, the boys were given a tour of the prison cells which left them so quiet and thoughtful on the journey back to the choir school that I like to think that the visit may have acted as a deterrent and taught them that crime doesn't pay. David even took the trouble to invite a Welsh-speaking clergyman acquaintance to celebrate the Mass in Welsh for my choristers, little realising that not much Welsh was spoken in Brecon at that time and that none of my choristers or lay clerks was bilingual. That was another example of his thoughtfulness and of how he considered the Blessed Sacrament to be central to our lives. On our last Sunday he invited all the grown-ups to sherry before lunch and a small barrel was consumed in its entirety. This did not much help the anthem at "afternoonsong" (as Betty, wife of our Bishop Thomas, irreverently called an afternoon Evensong) which was a complicated piece by Herbert Howells.

When we returned to Lincoln Cathedral in 1971, we continued more or less as we had left off three years before: the Lay Clerks still drank in the "Adam and Eve" nearby, the boys still played soccer in the early hours of the morning or otherwise, in the words of the Psalmist, "ran about through the city". By now, there were more than ever of these unruly lads in the choir, which was good to see but made for a lot of hard work. Nor were matters made any easier by the fact that, having succeeded in persuading the father of my eighteen-year-old Head Chorister to allow him to come with us, the young lad, a butcher's boy who answered to the name of "Orrie" but was really called Christopher Morris, celebrated having got away from home for the first time in his life by vanishing into a Lincoln night club almost as soon as we had arrived, in the company of a young Lay Clerk aptly named Peter Boosey. The two lads then proceeded to slip out on three successive nights so that by the Sunday, when we were due to sing Morning Service not in Lincoln Cathedral but in Sheffield Cathedral, Orrie no longer sang treble! It was therefore necessary for the other trebles on Orrie's side of the choir, Cantoris, to do some work, and they did not take kindly to this.

One afternoon when the choir was rehearsing for Choral Evensong, I noticed that one of these boys was missing, so I went out to look for him. On finding him skulking in the Choir School, I dragged him by the scruff of his neck into the Cathedral and, as we crossed the South Transept through a crowd of tourists, he bawled at me to "F – k off"! Another afternoon it became necessary for me, Hazel and some of the Lay Clerks to run about through the city to find most of the boys and bring them back for a choir practice and Choral Evensong. Earlier that day they had divided into two camps, had a violent disagreement and then disappeared into the city to avoid hammering hell out of each other.

The Precentor, David Rutter, had invited Hazel to give an organ recital this time, so she was anxious to find practice time in between coping with Harriet and Nicholas and playing the organ for services. While the choir was practising one day for Evensong, one boy was being particularly obnoxious so I sent him to sit by the organ. He then devoted his entire efforts to seeing how far he could spit down the organ steps, which did little to help Hazel concentrate on her organ accompaniments. By now, the Organist of Lincoln Cathedral, Dr. Philip Marshall, and his wife had taken pity on us and invited us to supper. This was the last thing that Hazel wanted to do, as by now she was thoroughly fed up! However, Midge, Nick's godmother, who was cooking for everyone, persuaded her to go with me and took over looking after our children. The Marshalls could not have been kinder and cheered us up no end, telling us stories of their experiences when Philip had been Organist of Ripon Cathedral. On one particular occasion, they had taken their choirboys on an outing to a North Country seaside resort and on the journey back found them in a huddle comparing what they had pilfered from Woolworths! He also told us how, when he had begun to knock the Lincoln Cathedral Choir into shape with the result that Choral Evensong on a Saturday afternoon was starting to attract congregations of as many as two hundred people, the new Dean had come to him, saying, "I feel we should be giving them something", as if music was not enough and a sermon was required. At this, Dr. Marshall had rounded on him, saying in exasperation: "What do you want to give them – Green Shield stamps?" So we came away from dinner in a happier frame of mind, yet even with David Rutter's rock-like support it was an extraordinary time. Hazel continued to practice hard for her recital, but one day suffered the indignity of being reprimanded by a Verger for making too much noise. David, however, was equal to the situation and made the Verger present her with a written apology. The night before her recital, Hazel fell at the bottom of the organ steps, where her blood stained the cathedral floor for many years. Even so, at the recital she played well, leaving her happy and relaxed and with the distinction of being the first lady to give an organ recital in Lincoln Cathedral.

This had been an unusual year for Hazel, because only recently a 33 r. p.m. disc of her playing organ music at Brecon and Bangor Cathedrals had been released. This had come about through an old friend from the choir of St. Stephen's Church, South Dulwich, Michael Smythe, who had made a name for himself issuing records of organ music on the Vista label. He had sold Hazel's recording to the Decca Recording Company, which had issued it on its Qualiton label, Qualiton being a Welsh subsidiary based at Pontardawe. Travelling to Bangor in late November to make the recording there had not been a good idea. The morning in question was a frosty one and when we arrived in our car at the top of the icy one-in-three hill on the old Brecon to Builth Wells road, known as "Tumbledown Dick", there were problems. Hazel refused to travel down it in the car, so while I drove down the hill gingerly with two wheels in the ditch and arrived safely at the bottom, Hazel walked equally gingerly down the hill and fell over on the way.

This year, 1971, the National Eisteddfod was in North Wales and BBC (Wales) broadcast the Bangor side of the record on Radio Four, announcing everything in Welsh. Through this recording, we had the good fortune to meet Raymond Ware, a Decca producer who used to visit his mother regularly in the Rhondda Valley. He wanted to produce a record of Christmas Carols sung by Welsh choirs and we persuaded him to let us make it. So during the early summer months before the trip to Lincoln, we had set about the recording. In planning this, I realised that it was useless producing yet another recording of Christmas carols with organ accompaniment, as the market was saturated with them: this one had to be different. So the recording was anchored by four popular carols tarted up with noisy fanfares for trumpets and drums. As we were using adaptations of David Willcocks' superb versions, I had to seek his permission. Fortunately he was kindness itself in not only allowing this but also in being complimentary about the end result, which he had to pass. Then it was decided to include two readings and Bishop Thomas did these supremely well. Next, two of the Lay Clerks were bell-ringers, so some carols played on handbells were incorporated and space was also found for the bells of St. Mary's. When it came to the singing, not only were the Cathedral Choir required but also, in some carols, the Cathedral Singers and some of our chorister-friends from around the diocese, which made for a massive choir. This coupled to the organ and brass group made for a great sound and lots of variety. I was fortunate in discovering a fellow Royal Academy of Music student of my era living in Penclawdd on the Gower Peninsula close to Swansea, Tony Small, who duly organised three trumpeters and a timpani player for me.

Raymond Ware was exceedingly generous with his time and allowed for four three-hour recording sessions on weeknights, each including a break for refreshments provided by Decca. The Dean's vestry was transformed into a recording studio, complete with a television screen which allowed Raymond as producer to watch as well as listen. One night, when the choirboys were particularly wound up with the fun of it all, they came hurtling back into the Cathedral, running down the nave shouting and swearing at each other as was their custom. Unbeknown to them, the Dean was watching on the screen in his vestry, whereupon he rushed out into the Cathedral in pursuit of them, shouting: "Wash your mouths out, boys, wash your mouths out." The Decca engineers, who knew how hard the boys had been working and what lively characters they were, laughed uproariously as they in turn watched this performance on the screen!

Decca had sent down a wonderful team of engineers: Mike Mailes, Stan Goodall, Jack Law and David Frost. They were very experienced and had worked with the best orchestras and choirs throughout Europe, yet we all took to each other from the very outset. Furthermore, Mike Mailes and his wife Judy later brought down one of their sons for Minor Canon Peter Sims to baptise. So there was a wonderful atmosphere as the adults and the "Decca boys" socialised each night at The George Hotel. On the last night, Stan Goodall, considered by the choristers to be the double of Eric Morecambe in both looks and humour, ordered the first round of drinks but left David Frost to pay the bill which was not far short of £30! There remained a record sleeve to be devised, with the result that one day in the middle of June the choirboys could be seen plucking daisies from the grass in the garth outside the Cathedral in preparation for suitable Christmas photographs to be taken! After that, it was a question of waiting for the finished product to appear. The weeks passed slowly, but when the record "Christmas in Wales" finally did come out, it sold well. Sadly the national reviewers missed the point and, despite brass fanfares, readings, bells, handbells and also a carol in Welsh, called the programme "rather conventional". Only Kenneth Loveland in the South Wales Argus understood, realising that Christmas in Brecon was different and rather special.

And so it was. It all now began back in Advent, as the four weeks leading up to Christmas Day are called. Instead of Evensong in the Cathedral on Advent Sunday, there was a service of readings and carols for Advent, while on the second Sunday in Advent, the anthem at Evensong was J. S. Bach's Cantata 140, "Wachet Auf!" ("Sleepers, Wake!"), sung by the Cathedral choir with soloists and orchestral accompaniment. This was an idea that I had "stolen" from York Minster. Sometime after this, the Cathedral Singers visited the mental hospital at nearby Talgarth to sing carols to the patients. They also visited Crosfield House near Bwlch, which was a British Legion home for disabled servicemen, where in a beautiful oak-panelled room, they sang many more carols.

Then, on the Monday evening before Christmas Day, the Cathedral Choir joined up with the Cathedral Singers and St. Mary's Church Choir to give a carol concert in St. Mary's Church for the Mayor of Brecon's Christmas Fund for old people. This was attended by the Mayor and Mayoress of Brecon along with the Town Councillors. The highlight was the teaching of a new carol to the audience! Afterwards some of the Cathedral Singers moved across to The George Hotel to sing carols there in aid of the Breconshire Mentally-Handicapped while standing on the magnificent seventeenth-century oak staircase, happy in the knowledge that they were helping to enhance landlady Mrs. Jones's Christmas. Last of all and as near as possible to Christmas, the Cathedral Choir descended on the War Memorial Hospital to sing carols. The Matron was a specially lovely lady to whom this was important, particularly for those patients who could not go home for Christmas. So she liked to line up some of the nurses, give them lighted candles and get them to lead the procession around the hospital from the men's ward to the ladies' ward. Then, if there were any inhabitants in the maternity ward, the choir always went there to sing "Away in a manger" and the Czechoslovakian "Rocking Carol", "Little Jesus, sweetly sleep".

Meanwhile back at the Cathedral Edgar Hawkes, the Verger, had been painstakingly constructing the Crib behind the font, finishing it by Christmas Eve. On that day, by 3.30 p.m., around two hundred excited youngsters gathered into the Cathedral with their parents, for the blessing of the Crib. Later, in the evening I took the choirboys to Ely Tower to sing carols to the Bishop and his wife Betty. After this they entertained everyone to supper, much to the delight of the boys. This visit had come about as a result of a sad incident when the Bishop had been driving to a meeting in North Wales and a small boy had run out in front of his car at Llyswen and been killed. The irony of this tale is that because of bad weather, the Bishop would never have reached his destination and he was left thinking "If only ...". This affected the Bishop so much that I suggested to his wife that I should surprise him by creeping into the house with the boys and then launch into a carol. So began a tradition!

As I walked back with the boys to the Cathedral, we passed the Round Table float, all lit up with lights of many colours, carrying a larger-than-life Father Christmas around town to the accompaniment of loud canned music. By the time

I reached home, Harriet and Nick were tucked up in bed but wide-eyed and bubbling over with excitement, having seen Father Christmas pass by and wondering what he was going to leave them from his sack later that night. Midnight Mass followed at St. Mary's Church and while the vast congregation went to the altar during the administration of the sacrament, the church choir and a few of the Cathedral Singers sang Christmas carols in the South Aisle. The usual quaint custom found the Cathedral Lay Clerks singing at the eight o'clock morning Holy Communion in the darkened Cathedral, the building serene, peaceful and beautiful. One year we sang "In the bleak mid-winter" to end this service and indeed, outside in the lovely country churchyard, "snow was falling, snow on snow" as inside we enjoyed Gustav Holst's timeless melody. By contrast, the eleven o'clock Choral Communion was festive at last, and joyful, like a blaze of light, with a crowd of people enjoying lovely music and singing lustily the carols "O come all ye faithful", "While shepherds watched their flocks by night" and "Hark! the herald angels sing". At quarter to six in the evening a few of us would creep back and in a Cathedral lit only by candlelight would sing a plainsong Evensong ending with the hauntingly beautiful, plainsong, Nuns of Chester Carol, "*Qui creavit coelum*". Christmas in Brecon was always full of magic.

Afterwards, it was hard to return to normality. One year, at Ely Tower, Mrs. Kelly, who helped keep the house clean and tidy, called Bishop Thomas and his wife Betty into the sitting room to ask what had been going on. When she pointed to the ceiling and Betty looked up, it was patently obvious what had been going on: on Christmas Eve those Cathedral choirboys had been shaking up their cans of Coke and then spraying the ceiling with the dark-coloured liquid. Next Christmas they would have to drink from glasses! Next year, Christmas 1972, the choir of King's College, Cambridge, sang carols on the television directed by David Willcocks and for some of them he included, for the first time as far as I could recollect, brass instruments. I have often wondered if that was a back-handed compliment to our "Christmas in Wales" recording.

XXVII

When Nicholas Gedge had entered the land of the living back in 1968, it had become obvious that our Clergy House was too small for us. Quite by chance, the old Pendre School and School House had come onto the market at this time and the Dean and Chapter were able to purchase the lot for £2,000. We were immediately offered the School House, but when Hazel's mother saw it, she exclaimed: "You can't live here." She was quite right, of course. With running water in every room – down the walls – the one hundred year-old stone house was in a terrible state and much money needed to be spent on it. However, we had reckoned without Colonel Pryce, the Chapter Clerk, who told us that he would spend no more than £800 on the property. The house badly needed re-roofing but, knowing that this would have to be done sometime in the near future, we took a calculated gamble and asked instead for two rooms to be knocked into one, with the support of a girder, to give a good size kitchen, taking in also a larder which was so cold in the winter that eggs froze there of their own accord. Colonel Pryce himself, with no reference to us, had a cheap and nasty fire-grate installed in our sitting room and shortly afterwards, when a fitted carpet had been laid at our expense, he endeared himself further by standing in front of the fireplace smoking a cigarette and flicking the ash onto the carpet.

We paid for bookshelves to cover the longest wall in what became our music room, Hazel's teaching room, and here we housed our vast collection of music books which were important to our work. Colonel Pryce decreed that the walls of all the rooms be painted white or grey and that a painted strip do the job of skirting boards. Fortunately the builder saw Hazel's reaction to this edict, took pity on her and unofficially fitted proper skirting boards, but our attempts to secure decent living conditions resulted in a considerable amount of ill feeling. Bishop Thomas' wife, Betty, implored us not to move into the house until all the work had been done, otherwise it might not be done and we did not ignore this advice. As the Clergy House had been situated in the Cathedral Garth, Hazel wanted to call our new home "Garth Cottage" thereby implying a link with the ancient Priory Church. To our amazement, therefore, the Dean and Chapter solemnly discussed this for twenty minutes at their next meeting before allowing us to do so. This sorry tale was recounted to us some years later by dear Canon C. F. Jones, Vicar of Llanfrynach with Llanhamlach and Cantref, who admitted to feeling embarrassed at the Dean and Canons spending so much time discussing something so trivial.

Some months after this I received a letter from the Chapter Clerk asking me to word an advertisement to sell for scrap a derelict chamber organ that had stood for many years in the Cathedral. I was furious, because this organ had an interesting history and its dereliction was largely due to a lack of interest on the part of the Cathedral authorities. When the Guild of Cordwainers had paid for the installation of the wooden screen that completed the enclosure of their chapel, the Verger had been told to move the chamber organ out from where it had been standing for many years. So Mr. Hawkes had set about his task with the help of others. Such was the brute force used that part of the casework fell onto the pipes, seriously damaging some of them.

This chamber organ had been built by the firm of Henry Bevington and its claim to fame was that it is mentioned in the famous diaries of the Revd. Francis Kilvert. While this cleric was curate at the Radnorshire village of Clyro, he became a friend of the Revd. William Latham Bevan who was Vicar of Hay-on-Wye for more than fifty years and for some of these was Archdeacon of Brecon, then in the diocese of St. David's. On March 3rd 1870, the Revd. Francis Kilvert wrote in his diary:

> "Walked to Hay in rain ... at 2 went to the Castle. The 4 girls singing "Pilgrims of the Night" round the organ in the hall. Mary playing."

Again, on May 7th 1872, he wrote:

> "Some delightful music at the castle. All the young people, Bevans and Thomases, and Lucy Allen gathered round the organ in the Castle Hall and sang "Pilgrims of the Night" and some other beautiful hymns and music."

"Pilgrims of the Night" refers to one of Kilvert's favourite hymns, "Hark, hark, my soul". The organ remained in Hay Castle until 1901 when Archdeacon Bevan retired and moved to Ely Tower, Brecon, where the Bishops of Swansea and Brecon later lived. However, it seems that the organ did not follow the Archdeacon to Brecon, because it reappeared in 1907 in Pool House, Belmont Road, Hereford, where the Archdeacon's great-granddaughter, a Mrs. Mumford, lived. When she moved to Weymouth in 1923, the organ was moved to Brecon, where the Priory Church had become the Cathedral of the new diocese of Swansea and Brecon, with the Archdeacon's son, William Latham Bevan, its first Bishop.

So the organ had languished in the Chapel of the Guild of Cordwainers in Brecon Cathedral from 1923 until its disastrous move to the north-west corner of the Cathedral in 1963. As a result of my protestations, the Dean and Chapter allowed me to have a report made concerning the state of the organ with a view to its possible restoration. To this end I invited Robert Munns, Organist of Holy Trinity, Brompton, Hazel's former boss, to examine the remains. He was very excited by what he discovered and as a result of his report, the Dean and Chapter reversed their decision and invited me to obtain an estimate for the cost of restoration.

Not long before, I had given my final organ recital. By chance, this happened to be at the church of St. Mary, Bridgewater, where a fine Father Willis organ had been beautifully rebuilt by a local Somerset firm, Percy Daniel & Co. Ltd. of Clevedon. While the recital was not greatly inspiring, at least it gave me the opportunity of meeting the managing director of this firm, Walter Gulvin. He and I got on so well that I invited him to suggest a price for restoring the chamber organ. He, realising that in the not-too-distant future the main cathedral organ would need re-building, suggested the ridiculously low price of £800. The deal was done and a contract signed within a very short time. In due course, back from Somerset came a superb chamber organ mounted on a platform on wheels and with an electric blower, so that it could be used anywhere in the Cathedral. We had already known that the organ had a rare compass, stretching down to the low G, which made it an ideal instrument for playing late eighteenth- and early nineteenth-century music. Furthermore, all the pipework was enclosed in a swell box which made for added expression. It also had two combination pedals and two cancellers, which was most unusual. What we discovered during the rebuilding was that a soundboard contained the date 1789, which was odd, since Henry Bevington did not set up business until 1794, when he took over the premises of Ohrmann and Nutt in Soho, London, which had been used by the famous John Snetzler. Had Henry Bevington therefore used up some of his predecessors' materials? This suggestion was borne out by a member of The Organ Club who visited the Cathedral at a later date and suggested that some of the pipework was of foreign origin. Whatever the answer, the sound was superb and the stop list went right up to a two-rank mixture.

Soon afterwards, Hazel broadcast Samuel Wesley's "Twelve Short Pieces" (sometimes called "Samuel Wesley's Baker's Dozen" because there are actually thirteen pieces) on Radio Three. It was lovely to hear this music played on an organ which was in use when the composer was alive and which had such beautiful, unforced tone, not forgetting the essential low G compass of notes. Afterwards C. H. Trevor, our old teacher, wrote to Hazel:

> *"I enjoyed the Wesley recital. The whistles [sic] sounded well. It was interesting to hear all the pieces at one "go". Hope you are all fit and flourishing."*

We certainly were all fit and flourishing, but the main organ was not. During the previous summer when we had been on holiday in Kidwelly, we learned that while Mr. Hawkes' son-in-law, John Harrison, had been playing the Cathedral Organ, smoke started billowing out from the works behind the console. It was indeed fortunate that this had happened when John had been playing the organ, because he was such a good, upright, unimpeachable citizen that our alarm at the parlous state of the organ was made to seem all the more genuine when actually it was only a minor electrical fault! Even so, it was almost forty years since the organ had last been rebuilt, so perhaps it was time for some renovation work to be done to it. Unfortunately, the Dean and Chapter had not envisaged the amount of work that we wanted done. While it was tonally a lovely organ, built in 1886 by William Hill when he was one of the foremost organ builders in the land with instruments at King's College, Cambridge and Westminster Abbey to his credit, there could be no denying that it was ineffective. With no big mixture stops nor chorus reeds on the Great Organ, it was particularly hopeless in leading the singing of a large congregation and, believe you me, one thousand members of the Mothers' Union at a Festival Service took a lot of controlling, especially when singing hymns of the fervent Welsh variety.

Now did seem the right time to tackle the problem, because in 1973 the diocese of Swansea and Brecon would be fifty years old and, with Bishop Thomas planning great celebrations in his Cathedral, it was vital that the organ be able to do what was expected of it. Fortunately Bishop Thomas was an organist and he understood what Hazel and I were talking about. Therefore, when the Dean and Chapter said that no money was available to pay for work to the main organ (as even the Bevington Organ had only been restored largely because of four generous donations), the Bishop single-handedly set about raising the necessary money. In making the rebuilding of the Cathedral Organ the main project for the year 1973, the Bishop incurred the wrath of some people in the diocese, who considered such work an expensive luxury. Fortunately for us, however, he was one of the few people who appreciated worshipping through the medium of good music in cathedral services. Furthermore, he had a genuine love for this, knowing how it could be instrumental in bringing all heaven before the eyes of worshippers, some of whom might be least expecting such a reaction.

Hazel and I had definite ideas for the organ, but before anything could be done we needed to meet with organ builders, firstly to discuss what we had in mind, secondly to discover whether or not it was possible to put our ideas into practice and thirdly to price the work. By now we were good friends with Walter Gulvin, so we called in Percy Daniel and Co. Ltd. despite the fact that some of our organist friends thought us mad, as this firm was not fashionable. In addition we called in Hill, Norman and Beard, successors to the original builders and arranged to meet John Norman over lunch at Garth Cottage. Our plan was quite simple: to load the organ with mixture stops and put chorus reeds on the Great Organ so that more of its sound would reach the nave. We also wanted to move the Choir Organ from its remote position above the Swell Organ, where it was barely audible, take it out of its swell box, re-site it in the front of the organ case where the console used to stand and remodel it as a bright Positive division which, at that time, was a sign of the times, being part of the movement to popularise anything Baroque in music.

I must confess that my mind had been more or less made up as to who was to do the work before I met John Norman. Sometime earlier, when I had wanted the Cathedral Organ tuned for a Wednesday afternoon Choral Evensong programme on BBC Radio and for some reason the normal Hill, Norman and Beard organ tuner was unavailable, I had been told by the firm's Head Office to use the rival Willis tuner from Hereford. I took a dim view of this suggestion, as it left me with the distinct impression that the organ in Brecon Cathedral didn't really matter to the firm. The firm of Hill, Norman and Beard maintained a number of important cathedral organs and the organ here was one of their smallest. On the other hand, if Percy Daniel and Co. Ltd. took over the Brecon organ, it would be the firm's only cathedral organ and would become the "flagship" of the business, with the result that it would receive priority treatment. This point of view was further strengthened by the fact that on the day when John Norman was coming to lunch, Hazel had the meal ready by one o'clock, as arranged, but he did not arrive until half-past two, having made a detour to the more prestigious Bath Abbey where his firm was rebuilding the organ. When John then started expounding his ideas for our organ and suggested re-voicing the Swell string stops (salicional and *voix celeste*), Hazel's patience snapped and she told him in no uncertain terms that he was not to tamper with these lovely stops.

Thankfully, the contract was awarded to Percy Daniel & Co. Ltd. and with Walter Gulvin we worked out how the organ could be made brighter with its sound penetrating more of the building. He did just that, utilising the vacant space at the front of the organ case. We mourned the loss of the quiet solo reed stops on the old Choir Organ and the big solo Tromba on the Great Organ, but money was tight. Yet, to the credit of Bishop Thomas, he raised the necessary £11,580. So work started shortly after Christmas Day 1972 and continued throughout the first quarter of 1973. Late one night we wandered into the Cathedral to find Walter Gulvin painstakingly voicing the Open Diapason on the Swell Organ, remarking on the beauty of the old William Hill sound. As work progressed, it was good to see how the firm of Percy Daniel and Co. Ltd. did not stamp its own identity on the organ. Rather, it made sure that anything done to the instrument, any new pipework added to it, did nothing other than enhance the William Hill legacy. This was one of the joys of working with this firm; if we knew what we wanted, Walter Gulvin would see that we got it.

Meanwhile choral services continued in the Cathedral with Matins at 11 a.m. on the first and third Sundays of the month and Holy Eucharist on the other Sundays, Evensong being sung at 3.30 p.m. By now the choir was also singing Evensong on Wednesday at 5.45 p.m., usually with a congregation numbering Melville Thomas, the aged Secretary of the Friends of Brecon Cathedral and his equally aged wife Dorothy, who were great supporters of the Cathedral's musical activities. As they had ensured that the Friends of Brecon Cathedral had made a donation towards the restoration of the Bevington Chamber Organ, it must have pleased them enormously to find this fascinating instrument equal to the job of accompanying these services while the main organ was out of action.

Easter Day 1973 was the deadline for the completion of the work on the main organ, but all was ready by Passion Sunday, April 8th which, coincidentally, was Hazel's birthday. At Choral Evensong that day there was a Service of Thanksgiving for the Restoration of the Cathedral Organ. Jubilant music replaced the normally solemn music of the day and we hoped that God was understanding about the reason why. The Evening Canticles rang out to the glorious music from Sir Charles Villiers Stanford in C and the anthem was dear old Sidney Campbell's riotous "Sing we merrily unto God our strength". The organ pealed away merrily and filled much more of the Cathedral with sound from its new mixtures and Swell Organ reed chorus, not forgetting the Great Organ reeds. Afterwards, Hazel and I entertained to tea in Garth Cottage the Bishop and his wife, Betty, Walter Gulvin and his wife, Doris, along with some of the Percy Daniel and Co. Ltd. workers who had done such a marvellous job in so short a time and at so reasonable a price.

Later that year, Robert Munns returned to give a recital on the rebuilt organ. It was good to hear the instrument put through its paces in a programme that included some glorious French symphonic music. Recently we had discovered that Maurice Forsythe Grant, the controversial organ builder who had created the organ at New College, Oxford, had retired to live nearby on the Wales-England border at Rhydspence close to Whitney on Wye; he described his retirement home modestly as "only a bungalow with two bedrooms and an indoor swimming pool." Anyway, we invited him over to hear Robert Munn's recital and to stay to supper afterwards. He must have thought that Brecon Cathedral was in a farm yard, because as he emerged from his Range Rover, clad in an expensive suit but wearing

Wellington boots, he exclaimed: "I had no idea that the roads were so good to Brecon"! However, he proved to be marvellous company and a good evening was had by all, both musical and culinary. Furthermore, he proceeded to give my Cathedral Singers some welcome financial support.

Among other illustrious musical visitors at this time was the choir of Trinity College, Cambridge, with its director, my childhood friend Dr. Richard Marlow. His Canadian Organ Scholar was full of praise for the newly-created Positive Organ, but Richard wasn't so sure and said so! Not long after this visit, Dr. George Guest brought his famous choir of St. John's College, Cambridge, to sing at Brecon Cathedral. Their recital attracted an audience of around three hundred and fifty music lovers, which was good by Brecon standards. My five year-old son, Nicholas, spent the day with the young choristers and decided that this choir school was where he wanted to be educated. Hazel and I were fascinated by the care that George lavished on his choristers and Choral Scholars. We had arranged homestays for them all. However, one Choral Scholar was proving to be a problem and George insisted on this lad staying alone at The George Hotel under his personal supervision. A great Welshman, George included in his choir's recital programme a Welsh hymn which was sung in Welsh. That was my introduction to the wonderful "Cofia'n Gwlad", sung to the magnificently doleful melody known as "Rheidol". On the next morning, being Sunday, the choir sang Edmund Rubbra's "*Missa in Honorem Sancti Dominici*" at the 11 a.m. Holy Eucharist, but permission had to be sought from the Bishop for this to be done in Latin, as the Cathedral Choir was not allowed to sing Latin masses. Hearing the choir of St. John's College, Cambridge sing Mass in Brecon Cathedral was an unforgettable experience. It was pure magic, yet so different from the King's College, Cambridge, sound that I had idolised for years and always tried to copy.

There was an unexpected epilogue to the story of the 1973 rebuilding of the Cathedral Organ. Although admiration for the instrument was widespread, one person was far from happy and that was John Norman. He wrote to me requesting a copy of the stop-list, which I duly sent him. This resulted in my receiving a second, rather curious, letter from him in which he claimed that "Rumour had got around that the organ had been rebuilt to [his] stop-list, thereby infringing copyright." He continued: "I am glad to note however this is not so, though I am flattered that so many of my ideas have been adopted and am pleased to hear that the result is satisfying." This I found rather sad, because as a result of coping with the organ for the past seven years, it was Hazel and I who had formulated most of the ideas that were put into practice in the rebuild. Ideally, John Norman would have had the organ moved out of its restrictive chamber and placed in the South Transept, but even if there had been enough money to do this I would have opposed the idea most strongly, as it would have spoilt some of the lovely open space which appears to make the ancient Priory Church "speak" to people. Interestingly, not long after this, John Norman left the firm of Hill, Norman and Beard, exchanging work with pipe organs for work with computers, although he retained a lively interest in the "King of Instruments" and wrote much about them in magazines and books.

XXVIII

During these, my first years at Brecon, it had been my good fortune to meet a number of people who lightened my days. One of these was Kelvin Redford. Part of my income had been made up by some piano teaching at Christ College. I remember requesting a pay rise, as I received less that Musicians' Union rates, only to be told by the Headmaster, Dr. Sharp: "This is a public school, we do not pay union rates." However, it was at Christ College that I met Kelvin Redford, who taught French there and was a great lover of Cathedral music. He had been to the annual Choral Evensong attended by the Friends of Brecon Cathedral and had been surprised to find the Evening Canticles, Magnificat and Nunc Dimittis, sung to music by Daniel Purcell in such a way-out place as Brecon Cathedral. Being an Organist also, he soon offered assistance and his offer was eagerly and gratefully accepted because Hazel, my official Assistant Organist, was busily engaged in bringing up two young children and in earning some much-needed "pin money" by giving piano lessons at home. Now at all divine services I was free to devote my energies to directing the choir and so goad on the choristers to greater heights in their singing. Kelvin took his new task most seriously and worked hard to improve his musical contributions to services, particularly with regard to the organ voluntaries, only to be thwarted by the Verger and some clerics who, having been starved of real Cathedral music for so much of their lives, failed to appreciate that such musical offerings could be an integral part of the occasion.

With this is mind, it is not surprising that Kelvin used to get upset when Mr. Hawkes, the Verger, not only enticed the small congregation out of the Cathedral after the weekday evensong but also slammed shut and locked the main north door, even turning out the lights in the nave before Kelvin had finished playing his concluding organ voluntary. One Wednesday evening as Kelvin was playing a rather long final voluntary in the form of Hendrik Andriessen's fine "*Tema met Variaties*", "Hawkeye" had not only slammed and locked the north door and extinguished the nave lights, but was strolling noisily up the Chancel to turn out the lights there and so make off for home with all haste, there to enjoy his supper. That, at least, was his plan; unfortunately, however, as he passed between the choir stalls, near to the organ console, he shouted cheerfully across to Kelvin: "Enjoying yourself, Mr. Redford", whereupon the distracted organist flew into a rage, immediately stopped playing the organ, picked up a large hymn book, hurled it at the puzzled Verger, who was unaware that he had caused offence, then slammed shut the organ and stormed off home. It was some considerable time before Kelvin was talked round and normal service was resumed.

Sadly, before many months had elapsed, another crisis arose. On another Wednesday evening when Kelvin was playing a rather long, quiet, modern voluntary before Evensong, the kindly Archdeacon of Brecon, Elwyn Griffiths, a very dear friend to my family, wrongly thought that he was just playing around idling away a few moments. The Archdeacon had an eye for a tidy building and seeing some chairs out of line, he moved them noisily in line. Kelvin was far from happy about this, so he stopped playing his avant-garde voluntary, walked into the centre of the choirstalls, glared down the nave, saw the Archdeacon sitting down at the far end, went back to the organ and started up his voluntary again. The Archdeacon, seeing more chairs out of line, moved these also, just as noisily, whereupon Kelvin repeated his previous performance, walking to the centre of the choirstalls, glaring down the nave at the Archdeacon and returning to the organ and starting up once more. By now Kelvin was in a rage. Throughout Choral Evensong he slammed organ stops in and out noisily and when required to play a chord of E flat minor for the anthem to start missed out some of the flats, so that the resulting chord sounded like music for a horror film! That only succeeded in making Kelvin worse. When the service drew to a close, Kelvin slammed shut the organ console and played no voluntary. Rather, he stalked down the south nave aisle faster than the choir processed sedately down the nave from its stalls and vanished out into the night. No amount of pleading nor a written apology from the bemused Archdeacon (who was oblivious to what he had done, but most repentant when this was explained to him) brought Kelvin back to the Cathedral for some considerable time. Fortunately, however, Kelvin loved Cathedral Music too much to stay away for ever. He also enjoyed the company of the Lay Clerks, so one day he quietly returned to resume his important and much-valued contributions to our work.

Kelvin was only one of a whole host of characters who inhabited Brecon Cathedral at this time. The Cathedral is run by the Dean and Chapter. The Chapter consists of twelve Canons, who are appointed by the Bishop. They meet four times a year to discuss the affairs of the Cathedral. Each Canon comes into residence at the Cathedral for one month of the year and at this time they spent their month of residence living in the Canonry in the Close and saying the Holy Eucharist, Matins and Evensong daily so that the daily round of prayer in the diocesan church never ceased. Colonel Pryce fitted into this scheme of things by being secretary to the Chapter and given the grandiose title of Chapter Clerk, but he had no authority to make any decisions on his own. At least, that is how the system worked in theory.

In a diocese like Swansea and Brecon, Residentiary Canonries seemed to be handed out like Long Service medals. On the one occasion Bishop Thomas handed out a canonry to a clergyman on account of intellectual ability, there was much weeping, wailing and gnashing of teeth, not only by the clergy of the diocese but also by their wives, because the status of being a Canon and Canon's wife was highly prized. The Bishop had quite rightly thought that the Chapter would benefit from the new Canon's academic prowess. After all, he was Dean of the Faculty of Arts and a Senior Lecturer in History at University College, Swansea and in his spare time he was an unpaid Curate at St. Mary's, the Civic Church of Swansea. However, that cut no ice with either the clergy nor their wives, because the new Canon had not served time first as a Curate and then as a Vicar. They were indignant that he had not observed that unwritten rule: no clergyman in the diocese of Swansea and Brecon should have a "plum" living in Swansea, which represented civilisation, unless he had done time as the Vicar of a parish in Radnorshire or North Breconshire, which was equated with Outer Darkness. Strange to relate, some of the clergy when they were banished to a life of ministering to the farming communities and their livestock actually found the work to their liking and stayed put.

One of these was Chancellor Thornley Jones, so called because as Senior Canon he was entitled to use this exalted title. He had been Vicar of Cwmdauddwr for as long as could be remembered, Cwmdauddwr being a small attachment to the town of Rhayader. Indeed, it could be considered as part of Rhayader and its parish joined to the larger parish were it not for the presence of a formidable titled lady who expended an enormous amount of energy on ensuring that the parish retained its own identity. So Chancellor Trefor Thornley Jones ministered to a population of six hundred and fifty souls and enjoyed such preferment as Examining Chaplain to the Bishop of Swansea and Brecon back in 1940 and Diocesan Inspector of Schools from 1943 until 1963. The Chancellor was a large, rotund, benign gentleman of great charm, with a bald, egg-shaped head. It was said that he owed his canonry to his friendship with a previous scholarly Bishop, Edward William Williamson, but that must not be allowed to cloud the fact that he too was a scholar.

However, there was one little-known, surprising fact about the Chancellor. When he was a student at Oriel College, Oxford, he had sung countertenor in an early performance of Ralph Vaughan Williams's "Sir John in Love". If that sounds somewhat far-fetched, let me explain that there really was a performance of this opera at Oxford in 1930, the year when the young Trefor Thornley Jones took a second-class degree in Theology at that university and it was conducted by none other than a young Malcolm Sargent. Maybe the future Canon Chancellor being a countertenor could account for the fact that throughout his adult life he was the possessor of a high-pitched speaking voice. One weekend during one of his annual monthly residencies at the Cathedral, when Canon David Rutter was staying with us at Garth Cottage, Hazel telephoned the Canonry to invite him and his wife over for a sherry and a chance to meet David who, after all, held a similar position on the Chapter of Lincoln Cathedral. When a high-pitched voice answered the telephone, Hazel, without thinking, said, "Is that Mrs. Jones?", to which came the reply, "No, it's the Chancellor speaking"!

The Chancellor's acquisition of Mrs. Jones was legendary. This lovely lady had been his housekeeper for many years but when, unexpectedly, she inherited a goodly sum of money, it is said that she presented him with the ultimatum: "Marry me or I'm off" although she was too gracious a lady ever to have put it as bluntly as that. So they married and lived happily ever after and our lives in Brecon Cathedral were enriched by their annual monthly sojourn among us at the Canonry.

The second most senior Residentiary Canon was grandly entitled "The Treasurer", but his appointment had nothing to do with the financial affairs of the Cathedral; these were looked after by the Chapter Clerk. The Treasurer at this time was one more clerical character who had settled for Radnorshire and the northern extremities of Breconshire and who answered to the name of Ken Evans. For many years he had been Vicar of Knighton, a small town close to Offa's Dyke, but nearing the age of retirement he had opted for lighter duties and had moved to the small parish of Llanigon with Capel-y-Ffin on the outskirts of Hay-on-Wye. There he looked after two small churches, a large chunk of the Black Mountain, two hundred and eighty-two parishioners and a multitude of sheep. He was a delightful character, the possessor of a grating voice, a wife and a number of cats that prevented her from joining him for his annual monthly periods of residence at the Cathedral.

His final residence before retirement coincided with the rebuilding of Ely Tower, which meant that the Bishop and his family had taken over the Canonry while the Canons had to slum it in the Clergy House. When the Treasurer, Canon Ken Evans, drew up in his car outside the Clergy House he entered the venerable building, found the kitchen and put the kettle on the gas stove to brew himself a cup of tea. However, in this he was distinctly unsuccessful, as the kettle steadfastly refused to boil. Puzzled, he wandered out into the Close where he met Joan, wife of Archdeacon Griffiths, to whom he complained about the lack of gas pressure on the Clergy House cooker. Immediately Joan went into the kitchen to find out what was wrong, only to discover that the Canon had been trying to boil the kettle on the pilot light. So Ken, now able to boil water for his cups of tea, set about enjoying his last month as a Canon of the Cathedral that he loved so dearly.

Daily the milkman would deliver a bottle of milk to the front seat of the Canon's car and daily the Canon collected this as he shuffled back from saying the statutory early morning services in the Cathedral. Come the last Sunday of the month's residence, the Canon was so busy at the Cathedral that he enlisted the help of Archdeacon Griffiths to take his eleven o'clock service at Llanigon Church. This was possible because the parish of Bronllys in which the Archdeacon ministered was mid-way between Brecon and Llanigon. If the Archdeacon finished his service in Bronllys Church at 10.45 a.m., he could be at Llanigon by 11. So the Canon Treasurer started the day by officiating at the 8 a.m. service of Holy Eucharist in the Cathedral, then he collected his pint of milk from the car and returned to the Clergy House where he made himself a pot of tea and enjoyed a leisurely breakfast. Afterwards he tidied up, packed his bag, walked over to Garth Cottage to chat with my wife, Hazel, gave her what remained of the bottle of milk, wandered back to the Clergy House, loaded up his car and finally set off for Bronllys Vicarage, driving at a speed of twenty to thirty miles per hour. So ended his busy morning at Brecon Cathedral! Meanwhile at Bronllys Vicarage, the Archdeacon had leapt into his car at 10.50 a.m. and made off at great speed for Llanigon Church to take the Canon's service for him. While he was doing that, the Canon, after enjoying a gentle drive from Brecon, arrived at Bronllys, let himself into the Vicarage, helped himself to a large glass of sherry, sat down in a comfortable armchair in the sitting room and set about reading the Sunday paper, awaiting the return of the Archdeacon from taking his service. What a character!

It was fortunate that he and the Archdeacon were good friends, but then the Archdeacon of Brecon, Thomas Elwyn Griffiths, was very much loved and appeared to have no enemies. He had spent almost all his ministry in the wilds of Radnorshire and North Breconshire, as well as some time in Bronllys Sanatorium recovering from tuberculosis. He, Hazel and I used to make regular forays into his archdeaconry for hymn-singing evenings, when congregations were encouraged to sing some good traditional hymns along with a few newer or unknown hymns which we thought they ought to know and hoped they would adopt into their own church services. We were desperate to counter the pop-hymn explosion which was sweeping across Great Britain at this time, perpetuating music of little or no value and words of no literary worth. Wherever we went, Elwyn was treated like royalty and it was obvious that he was held in high regard and great affection by both the clergy and laity alike.

Eventually he became full-time Archdeacon with no parochial responsibilities, which was good and sensible because it left him free to officiate in churches where clergy were either ill or on holiday, or where there were vacancies due to retirement. So he moved into the Almonry in the Cathedral Close with his family to live within the shadow of the Cathedral that he loved so dearly. Convinced that behind the lovely slate fire-surround in the Almonry sitting-room was an even lovelier large open fireplace with a huge stone lintel, he invited his builder brother up from Ammanford to do the necessary work, which indeed did prove him right. Now he was able to enjoy a magnificent, huge open fireplace in his sitting room while Hazel and I had the pleasure of installing the now-redundant slate fire-surround in our sitting room at Garth Cottage, to replace the miserable fireplace chosen by Colonel Pryce.

By now it had become obvious to us that everyone in Wales was related to everyone else so it came as no surprise to discover that Elwyn had an Uncle Tudor living in Kidwelly, of all places, who was married to the very Grace Jones, Organist of St. Mary's Church, who had played the organ at our wedding. What did come as a surprise was one more coincidence: Gracie was trained as a school teacher and the first job she could obtain when she left college in 1938 had been teaching in Selby Abbey School before she could obtain a similar appointment back in her beloved Carmarthenshire. Our two families, Gedges and Griffithses, became quite close. Elwyn became Nicholas's Godfather and his three boys always were great fun with Harriet and Nicholas, while Hazel and his wife Joan found much to chat about. Elwyn worked tirelessly for Church Schools in the diocese and nothing delighted him more than the building of the new Priory Church in Wales County Primary School, where the five windows of the school hall echo the five lancet windows above the High Altar of the nearby Cathedral. It was good and right, therefore, that his name be perpetuated in the new Primary School he had built in Llyswen where later his eldest son, Mark, became Head Teacher before eventually following his father into the sacred ministry.

Elwyn's predecessor as Vicar of Bronllys had been John Davies, who had gone on to be Vicar of Holy Trinity, Llandrindod Wells and, eventually, a Residentiary Canon of Brecon Cathedral. The choirboys looked forward greatly to his appearances at the Cathedral because his sermons always began in the same delightful way. Having climbed up into the pulpit, he would take a deep breath and say in loud and staccato tones, every syllable being delivered with identical weight: "Inthenameofthefatherandofthesonandoftheholyghostamen", whereupon he would clear his throat with a great deal of noise. This extraordinary syllabic performance plus his gaunt facial appearance and his balding head resulted in the choirboys calling him "THE DALEK", after some strange mechanical characters on the famous futuristic television serial "Dr. Who". His wife explained to me one day that he was petrified of preaching in the Cathedral, but that didn't matter to us as he was always kind and appreciative of our musical efforts. Furthermore his chirpy daughter was a very useful double bass player who generously helped in the orchestra at many Cathedral Singers concerts.

It must not be thought that the northern end of the diocese alone was the preserve of the most interesting of the clergy characters, because plenty were still to be found at the southern end around Swansea. Canon Thomas Clifford Bowen, Rector of Loughor, was one. His parish was the westernmost part of the diocese and the bridge over the Loughor Estuary linked the diocese of Swansea and Brecon with its mother diocese of St. Davids. This bridge also had an important function on Sundays at this time as it linked "dry" Carmarthenshire, where all the pubs were firmly shut, to "wet" West Glamorgan, where all the pubs were invitingly open. It even provided a direct link between Swansea and Kidwelly, some fifteen miles away. Canon Bowen, knowing of Hazel's connections with that nearby town, delighted in telling her, with his eyes twinkling, how Kidwelly people were always boasting that anything grown in their gardens, be it carrots, runner beans or cabbages, was always twice as big as anything grown in Loughor gardens! I can still remember that highly-emotional sermon which he preached in St. Mary's Church, Brecon, on the Sunday after the dreadful Aberfan disaster, for this unfortunate village was but twenty miles away and the sufferings felt close to home. On this sad occasion, he was the archetype of the emotional Welshman, and quite rightly so, but normally he was the bright-eyed Welshman, short in stature and full of fun, with a homely wife and an attractive oboe-playing daughter.

Nearby lived likeable, easy-going Canon Garfield James, Vicar of Sketty, that part of Swansea with a posh accent all of its own, where "sex" is what coal is carried in (i.e. "sacks"!). His son was a choirboy at Westminster Abbey while his daughter was such a beauty that she set fluttering the hearts of the older choirboys whenever her dad came into residence at Brecon Cathedral. Many times on a Sunday evening did I see Orrie (Christopher Morris) and his cousin Dilwyn sitting on the ground at the entrance to the Choir Room desperately hoping to catch a glimpse of her walking out from the Canonry.

Another of the Swansea Canons was endowed with a wife who, when she tried to pull rank, was reduced to size in true Welsh fashion by mention of the fact that her mother used to sell cockles on Swansea Market. Then there was Canon Hubert Hughes, who was endowed with such a fine tenor voice that he shared the stage as a soloist with the renowned soprano Jennifer Vyvyan in a concert at the Alpha Chapel in Builth Wells. Later, as Vicar of Morriston, part of his ministry included producing Gilbert and Sullivan operas with his parishioners. When he came into residence at the Cathedral he would tell me in great detail all about his latest production.

However, chief among the Swansea Canons was Harry Craven Williams, Vicar of St. Mary's, the great church in the heart of Swansea, which at that time was joined with St. James's Church in the Uplands to form one huge parish. One day he remarked to a colleague how, since disestablishment, all the previous Vicars of St. Mary's had become bishops, only to be reminded that someone had to be the first ... and it was Harry! When Dean Gwynno James died, Harry, apparently, quickly put his parish into order, awaiting the summons to the Deanery, which never came. The pinnacle of his career was the call to be Archdeacon of Gower, but never to the bench of bishops. In a way this was sad, as Harry was a priest of the old order who believed in caring for his flock. Furthermore he had been decorated for his war service and before that had been a notable athlete. It seems that he trained his curates well and they in turn thought the world of him. Every Friday he had a staff meeting when each curate was presented with a list of parishioners to visit. Then, at the meeting on the following Friday, each curate would be called to account for his labours. Sometimes, however, while the spirit was willing the flesh was weak and many a time on the next Thursday curates would be found wanting, with a long list of calls to make and little time in which to make them. So they would trudge the streets of Swansea hoping against hope that a few of their clients would not be at home and valuable time thereby saved.

Some of his curates at this time went on to positions of eminence. David Evans, a former Minor Canon of Brecon Cathedral, eventually succeeded Chad Varah as Organising Secretary of the Samaritans, becoming also an Honorary Canon of Peterborough Cathedral. Brian Jones rose through the ranks of the clergy in the diocese of Swansea and Brecon to become Chancellor of Brecon Cathedral and Tony Pierce went further to become the eighth bishop of Swansea and Brecon.

I always got on well with Harry and liked him, but others fared less well, particularly Haydn James, the gifted Choirmaster of St. Mary's Church, Swansea, who left, taking most of the choir with him, after a dispute over BBC Choral Evensong fees which, it seems, Harry tried to divert to other, parochial use. Harry actually encouraged my Archdeaconry choirs into St. Mary's to take part in the service which began the month-long prestigious Swansea Festival, but his new resident choir was not very happy about this and eventually took over. Most fascinating was his attempt to bring me to Swansea as City Director of Music with responsibility for the Festival and as Organist and Choirmaster of St. Mary's Church with the assurance of a choir-school type of link to one of the private schools in the area. I must admit to being tempted, as the church had a wonderful acoustic, very similar to that of Southwark Cathedral. The thought of a school supplying captive choirboys was also most appealing. I applied, but after agonising about the move countless times as I walked my dog around leafy Brecon lanes and having been shortlisted for the city appointment, I withdrew at the last minute and stayed put in lovely Brecon.

Two other Canons were of more than passing interest. Josiah Jones-Davies was a very special person and an Honorary Canon of the Cathedral, which meant that he did not have a seat on the Chapter even though he had been singled out for recognition. During the Second World War he had served as a Chaplain in the Royal Navy, then from 1947 he was Vicar of two rural parishes, Llywel and Trianglas, near to Trecastle on and around the A40 road mid-way between Brecon and Llandovery. This was his only living and he remained here until he retired. To him went the distinction of creating an interesting and enterprising museum in Brecon, housed in an old chapel in Glamorgan Street, opposite the Ursuline Convent School. He devoted so much of his spare time to this that it was right for him to be rewarded with not only an honorary degree of M. A. from the University of Wales but also an M. B. E. from Queen Elizabeth II. Many people, including Hazel and me, wondered how such a lovely old man could remain unmarried. He was particularly kind to us and very appreciative of our work with the Cathedral Choir. Indeed, his ancient church at Llywel was the first venue outside of the Cathedral in which the choir sang.

One day, in the depths of an old-fashioned snowy and bitterly cold winter, I called at his Vicarage on the way to Kidwelly. Before I could drive off, he gave me a cup of steaming hot coffee laced with whisky "to fortify me against the weather for the remainder of my journey", so he said! When he was awarded the M. B. E. his many friends were delighted, a delight which was soon tempered by sorrow when the beginning of Parkinson's Disease unexpectedly became apparent. Yet there was a surprise in store for everyone. Unexpectedly a young French lady appeared at Llywel Vicarage; she had come to claim the Vicar as her father. Out tumbled the Canon's sad secret: after the war he had married a French lady and brought her to Llywel Vicarage but she had found it so isolated and remote that she had returned to France taking with her their only child. However, now that the Canon and his daughter were back in touch with each other, they became good friends for the time that remained to him.

Finally there was Canon Owain Jones, Vicar of Builth Wells, to which was attached the parish of Llanddewi'r Cwm, two miles away on the old Brecon Road that crosses the remote Mynydd Eppynt that I used to travel along regularly on my way to and from school. A former curate of Dean Gwynno James at St. Martin's Church, Roath in Cardiff, it is said that he never recovered from being told that he was a bishop-in-the-making. Had he worked for the Church of England he might well have found his niche as a residentiary canon at a Cathedral like Lincoln or Ely, where he would have been "in residence" for three months of the year and for the other nine months he could have indulged in his passion for writing biographies, which was his gift. The Church of England had money to pay for such specialised ministries but the Church in Wales had not, so Owain worked as a parish priest, became a Residentiary Canon of Brecon Cathedral and wrote in his spare time two biographies, the first about the nineteenth-century Welsh-born Tractarian priest and hymn-writer, Isaac Williams, the second about Glyn Simon, Archbishop of Wales and a former Bishop of Swansea and Brecon.

Owain did me a great favour in drawing my attention to the story of Dr. Joseph Pring who had been Organist of Bangor Cathedral from 1793 until 1842. Dr. Pring had been courageous enough to sue the Dean and Chapter for misappropriating the Tithes of Llandinam, using this money to build a church in Bangor for Welsh services when part of it should have been used for the maintenance of the music at the Cathedral. In those days, Cathedral Organists were lesser mortals: consequently, while the Bishop accumulated an annual salary of £4,464 and the Dean enjoyed an annual salary of £858, the Organist, Dr. Pring, had to make do with £75 per annum. Some difference! Dr. Pring won his case but was irked that the person who did best out of the pay rises awarded to the Cathedral musicians as a result of this legal victory was the Precentor who received two such increases, one by virtue of being Precentor, the other because he also numbered among the Vicars Choral. Furthermore, the Precentor was the Bishop of Bangor's son-in-law and had therefore profited from nepotism. This did not please Dr. Pring, although it seems that he had conveniently forgotten how, back in 1793, a relative of his had conveniently resigned from the position of Organist to make way for him.

Owain wrote up this story and I persuaded the editor of the Musical Times to publish it in his magazine. The editor then asked me to prepare for publication one of Dr. Pring's "Twenty Anthems" and I chose the shortest, which he duly published as the monthly supplement. So I came to produce Joseph Pring's setting of "O Lord, We Beseech Thee", which used the words of the Book of Common Prayer Collect for Trinity XVI and while the Canon was paid £15 for his article, I received little over one penny (1/2 p) for each copy of my anthem that was sold. As I was hardly likely to make a fortune from my labours, the Canon took pity on me and gave me a bottle of sherry! In due course I went on to edit more of Dr. Pring's anthems and four of them were published by the Anglo-American Music Publishing Company. Over the years these were sung at Brecon Cathedral *ad infinitum* until one day one of my Lay Clerks, Paul Jackson, had a sign made which read: "The Pring Room". This he fixed to the door leading into the Lay Clerks' toilet.

XXIX

One summer's evening while in the Cathedral, I was drawn into conversation with a visitor, as so often happened. This one turned out to be a professional violinist. Like so many of his kind he had started out in his youth full of idealism, fired by the desire to make music in a great orchestra, but before long reality had set in. So often when the British public attended a concert it wanted the same old music and, before long, what had started out as a great musical adventure had turned into a boring chore and within a few years one more orchestral player had bit the dust. By now the violinist had married a sympathetic primary school teacher and they had two children to care for along with a mortgage to pay on a house somewhere in London, as that was where most of the regular orchestral work was to be found. By "regular work", the violinist did not necessarily mean playing classical music in a major orchestra, but making session music in an "orchestra" backing pop records. After all, not very long before, the Beatles had backed the song "Yesterday" with a string quartet. It was the money earned from this sort of work that had enabled the violinist and his wife to keep their two sons at Christ's Hospital, a public school in Horsham, providing them with a better and more musical education than they would have obtained in a London comprehensive school.

Eventually the London violinist and his wife had purchased a holiday home, a "bolt-hole", where they and their children could escape from London and their work. This turned out to be a small stone cottage in Ffrwdgrech Road in Llanfaes, at the western end of Brecon. By now the violinist was desperate to make real music: he had reached that stage in life where "real music" meant chamber music and "chamber music" implied string quartets. So he had a proposition which he made to me as we wandered around the peaceful, gentle cathedral in the cool of an afternoon out of the summer sun. He suggested that if I could find the money to pay the Second Violin, Viola and 'Cello players, while he gave his services as First Violinist, his Quartet could play Joseph Haydn's "Seven Last Words from the Cross" on the evening of next Good Friday. The more we discussed this, the more excited I became, especially when we both agreed that the best way to do this was to invite Bishop Thomas to preach for a few moments on each of the Seven Last Words before the relevant music was played by the Quartet. After all, this was how the music was first performed in Cadiz Cathedral on Good Friday in 1787.

With Bishop Thomas being so musical, it was hardly surprising that he needed no persuasion, with the result that on the evening of Good Friday, April 9th 1971, Joseph Haydn's "Seven Last Words" was performed in Brecon Cathedral. Bishop Thomas's sermons were perfection, as was the playing of the string quartet which was hardly surprising when joining my friend Eric Bowie (first violin) and Australian Reg Larner (second violin) were musicians of the calibre of Maxwell Ward (viola) and Peter Halling ('cello), whom I had last seen tutoring the 'cello section of the London Schools Symphony Orchestra. Max Ward was a particular delight, as he so obviously enjoyed the occasion and remarked on how much at home he felt, as the A40 road which wound its way to Brecon also passed his home in Shepherd's Bush, West London.

The following year the quartet repeated the experiment, with slight changes to the personnel but with no lowering of the musical standards, and took it one stage further by giving an additional recital of string quartets on the evening of Easter Day. This was blissful. It also acted as a spur to my Cathedral Singers activities, because I vowed to complete the musical Easter weekend with a performance of J. S. Bach's "St. John Passion" on Holy Saturday. Already I had set about teaching this to the Singers, but they found it tough going, particularly the six stunning choruses at the centre of the work. Indeed, some of them initially did not like the music, probably because it was so hard to learn. Anyway, on Saturday June 19th 1971 we tried out J. S. Bach's "St. John Passion" in a concert and all went well. We were particularly fortunate that John Hugh Thomas, who conducted the Swansea Bach Choir, had directed us towards the rising star Rogers Covey-Crump, a tenor who sang the taxing part of the Evangelist so well. The part of Jesus was sung by Graham Sorrell, who had been a bass Lay Clerk during my last days at Southwark Cathedral and now was a Vicar Choral at St. Paul's Cathedral. So I was ready to organise a musical weekend, with the concerts complementing the services that were sung on Good Friday and Easter Day and which were the mainstay of this great religious festival.

However, J. S. Bach's "St. John Passion" could not be performed without an orchestra and where did one find an orchestra that we could afford out in the wilds of Mid Wales? When I had been Organist of Selby Abbey, I had heard about J. S. Bach's Cantata 140, "Sleepers, Wake!", being performed at Choral Evensong on Advent Sunday in York Minster under the direction of the legendary Dr. Francis Jackson. I had been anxious to do this at Brecon Cathedral, because it seemed right to perform such works in a liturgical setting. So this was when I set about searching out orchestral players. First I enlisted the help of the Breconshire Education Authority peripatetic violin teacher, but this proved to be a disaster as not only did he know nothing about playing baroque music, but he also had an unfortunate habit of tapping one rhythm with his feet while playing another on his violin.

Fortunately, two people made me persevere with my search. One was oboe-playing Hugh Davies, an intriguing character who had been ordained as a Church in Wales priest but then, after preaching a sermon at the church where he was Curate, in the course of which he listed all the problems of working for the Church, had promptly resigned and become a Religious Education teacher at the local comprehensive school in Abergavenny. By chance, he was married to Ann Vines, who played the flute and had been a fellow member of the graduate course at the Royal Academy of Music when Hazel and I had been there. The other person was John Roberts who, like so many Welsh-born teachers, had gone to a university in England but then had set about working his way back to his homeland. At that time he taught mathematics at a comprehensive school in Newport, but eventually he returned home as Head of the Mathematics department at Ebbw Vale Comprehensive School. He was no ordinary violinist, as not only had he played in the National Youth Orchestra of Wales but when he had been an undergraduate at Brasenose College, Oxford, he had led the Oxford University Students' Orchestra. Together we managed to assemble enough players, one to a part, to put on annual performances of J. S. Bach's Cantata 140, "Sleepers, Wake!", during Advent, even if it did mean having the third oboe part played on a clarinet.

The quest for a suitable orchestra to accompany the Cathedral Singers in performances of large-scale choral works came to an end when I met Morgan Lloyd one day in the Cathedral Close. He was on a visit to one of the Swansea Canons who was in Residence, maybe Garfield James, Vicar of his local church at Sketty or Canon Harry Williams, Vicar of St. Mary's, Swansea, where his wife was Organist. Morgan and his wife, Dilys, soon numbered among the delights of our life. Morgan Lloyd was a legend in Swansea musical circles. According to hearsay, he was the youngest of nine children from somewhere around Swansea and from an early age he had given every indication of being a talented violinist. Unfortunately, his family had little money, so the future looked bleak until the local community took the matter in hand. A concert was organised, reputedly at the Brangwyn Hall, and the proceeds provided enough money to keep Morgan at the Royal Academy of Music in London for two years. The proceeds of a second concert kept him there a little longer, whereupon he joined the orchestra of the Royal Opera House in Covent Garden.

Three years later he gave up this and returned home to Swansea as if to repay his debt to the community that had done so much for him. So he visited schools to give violin lessons and also gave violin lessons privately. Most importantly, he brought together sufficient musicians to provide an orchestra for every conceivable occasion. Such was his good nature that he held together this itinerant band of instrumentalists for years and years. The Neath, Swansea and Llanelli area contains countless local choral and operatic societies and whenever an orchestra was needed by one of them, the conductor usually turned to Morgan to provide it. Moreover, Morgan often provided more than just orchestral players. Many of these conductors were self-taught, with the result that often at their concerts Morgan directed the performance from his violin while the conductors followed him. So on one famous occasion as the conductor stood with his baton raised and Morgan sat with his violin at the ready, nothing happened until the embarrassed conductor leant across to Morgan and whispered: "When the hell are you going to start?", whereupon Morgan and his orchestra began to make music and "off" went another performance.

When Hazel and I went to an opera at Craig y Nos, once the home of the famous soprano Adelina Patti, Morgan's orchestra was playing very loudly, as was reported later in the Western Mail, yet it was obvious that Morgan was having to play loudly to hold the performance together. Unfairly, once again, he became cannon-fodder for a journalist. The first time Morgan led his orchestra at a Brecon Cathedral Singers concert he started to lead with his violin, overplaying in this way until he realised that I did know what I was doing and he sat back, relaxed and played his violin like an angel, wearing that seraphic expression of contentment which I came to know so well. On one of Morgan's more significant birthdays, friends and associates made him a present of the car number-plate MLIIII. Sometime afterwards, late at night while returning from playing the violin at a concert, he was stopped by a young policeman who asked him what he did for a living, to which he replied disarmingly: "I'm on the fiddle"!

Morgan's petite wife, Dilys, was unbelievably glamorous, always beautifully dressed and made up. Indeed, Hazel and I never saw either of them when they were not impeccably turned-out. One Monday evening we were invited to be Guests of Honour at the Annual Dinner of the Swansea and District Organists Association, a collection of organists of all shapes and sizes and all known religious denominations, which was organised by two kindly gentlemen answering to the names of Reg Blundell and Miner Crocker. That day our car was misbehaving, so we enlisted the help of one of the Cathedral Lay Clerks, Malcolm Johns, who worked at a local garage, in the hope of being mobile in time to drive to Swansea. Getting prepared to go was a fraught operation, as early in the evening I had a choir practice with the unruly boys, which was anything but relaxing, while Hazel had a few piano pupils to teach as well as Harriet and Nicholas to prepare for bed. Furthermore, the car caused more trouble than was expected and was ready only at the last moment. When finally we set off for Swansea, neither of us felt particularly relaxed and we had not really had the time to make ourselves as presentable as we would have wished. Imagine our dismay when at the Dinner we went to sit on either side of the President to discover an immaculate Dilys between us. Later, worse was to follow. After I had given my speech, Reg Blundell rose to his feet, thanked me and then unexpectedly added: "I am sure that Mrs. Gedge would like to say something." Mrs. Gedge, however, was quite sure that she would not like to say anything at all, but unfortunately that would have appeared rather ungracious, so she had no choice but to rise to her feet and say something.

Dilys was always pleasant company, asking after the children and about our work and our plans for the future. Indeed, considering the disparity in our ages and the fact that Hazel could have become a musical rival, she was never patronising, never anything but completely genuine and kind. A remarkable lady, she was an FRCO and had been Organist of St. Mary's, Swansea, for many years. In her earlier years she had been a noted piano and organ accompanist. The dispute between Haydn James as Choirmaster and Archdeacon Harry Williams, the Vicar of St. Mary's, which had resulted in Haydn and many of the choristers walking out, had been fuelled by the fact that both Dilys and Haydn had equal status, a situation that was of Bishop Thomas's making when he had been Vicar of St. Mary's Church. Experience tells me that someone had to be the boss, but the unanswerable question then had been: who? This had left the Archdeacon in the middle, trying to keep the peace yet being fair to both musicians. This situation had been further exacerbated but the fact that Haydn James was a brilliant choir-trainer with progressive ideas while Dilys Lloyd was a brilliant organist but with more traditional ideas, so that occasional musical collisions were inevitable. Dilys, however, never got worked up about this but always laughed off any suggestion of conflict, seeming not to want to cause any offence. As always, in this again, she was so gracious.

Another fascinating church musician in South Wales was the aptly-named Frank Tallis. He was Organist and Choirmaster of St. Paul's Church, Porth, in the Rhondda Valley and was the brains behind the Rhondda and Pontypridd Organists and Choirmasters' Association. Every year he organised an annual Dinner for this Association at Gambarini's Restaurant in Porth, to which he invited the Organists of Brecon, Llandaff and Newport (St. Woolos) Cathedrals, along with their wives. These occasions were very precious, never failing to sparkle and reflect the radiant and bubbling personality of this genial man. He worked hard for the Royal School of Church Music and for church music in general in the Rhondda and I helped him on a few occasions, when I experienced at first hand his unbounded enthusiasm which I could not but admire. The RSCM rightly recognised his labours on its behalf by presenting him with one of its awards. It was sad that his untimely death also brought about the end of such activities as no-one came forward to continue his valuable work in that rather special corner of Wales, once a bastion of non-conformity but where the Church in Wales never lost its grip.

Many other interesting musicians came our way through the activities of the Associated Board of the Royal Schools of Music, which used our music room in Garth Cottage with its Bechstein Grand Piano as a centre for its practical examinations in the Brecon area. One of the first examiners to visit us was a Professor at the Royal Academy of Music whose name eludes me. On completing his stint at Garth Cottage, he was in a hurry to catch the bus to Abergavenny from where he would return to London by train and thence home to his house and Steinway grand piano. As I drove him through the narrow streets of Brecon he thanked me profusely for driving him around the village, not realising that this "village" was the county town of Breconshire. Some years later, the point was made to me that if the population of a Welsh town is multiplied by seven, the resulting figure is the population of the equivalent English town. So, interestingly, if the population of Brecon (7,500) is multiplied by seven, the resulting figure (52,500) is around the population of Hereford, the county town of Herefordshire.

Another examiner who made his mark was Sssydney Wwwatson, the recently-retired Organist of Christ Church Cathedral, Oxford, who was delightful company but endowed with an extraordinary stutter which amazingly vanished when he was taking a choir practice. He made his base in The George Hotel and on the Thursday evening the Brecon Cathedral Lay Clerks joined him to reminisce about cathedral music and cathedral musicians, during which on one occasion he made almost ten attempts to start a word.

Perhaps the most fascinating of these examiners, one who managed to be sent to Brecon on a few occasions, was the redoubtable George Heath-Gracie, the elderly, outspoken, retired Organist of Derby Cathedral. For some reason he had taken an interest in my work since hearing the BBC Choral Evensong from Selby Abbey and we had corresponded regularly since then. Frequently the Lay Clerks sat around him at The George Hotel while he drank Gin and Tonics, recounting to them countless tales about his days as a Cathedral Organist. So fascinating and outrageous were some of these recollections that to this day I have lamented the loss in the post of the manuscript of his autobiography. Had it been published it would surely have been a best-seller, although this loss may have spared him many a libel action. How he announced his retirement from his post at Derby Cathedral is legendary. Apparently he marched into the Provost's office on September 25th at 12 noon and demanded to see the Provost's Secretary. (In those days the chief clergyman in a Parish Church Cathedral was entitled "Provost", not "Dean".) Handing her a letter, he said: "My dear, this is three months' notice of my retirement, in writing. Now, my dear, I want you to take note of today's date and the time now, because if on December 25th, Christmas Day, at 12.05 p.m., that bloody Provost is still preaching, I shall get up from the organ, lock it, go home and not return."

In due course, George Heath-Gracie and his artist wife, Marjorie, retired to a cottage named "Shawms" out in the wilds near to Honiton in Devon. Whenever we visited them they were always gracious hosts. Sadly, however, towards the end their eyesights faded and neither of them could see the state of the food which they put in front of us; nor, fortunately, could they see where we were putting it. Old age can be cruel; it was so sad, as they were such kindly people. The end was disgraceful. They moved into an Old People's Home and during the move some of their valuable antique furniture mysteriously disappeared. They did not live on for long, as institutional life was not for them, so they slipped away within a very short time, leaving the world all the poorer a place.

The George Hotel was the magnet for another extraordinary lover of cathedral and organ music, a wealthy businessman from Oxford answering to the name of Sansom Fenn. He was decidedly an amateur organist but, for all that, was not without ability. He loved to play the Cathedral Organ and one Sunday lunchtime, after he had consumed a few gin and tonics at The George Hotel, he walked up to the Cathedral and did just that, entertaining himself and any visitors who happened to call, for an hour or so. Afterwards, as he staggered down the south nave aisle he came face to face with Mr. Hawkes, the Verger. Said Hawkeye: "You've had too many sherries"; said Sansom Fenn: "You're jealous", then on he went back down Priory Hill to the George Hotel for a few more. One evening, when some new Canons were being installed during a Choral Evensong at the Cathedral, Sansom Fenn decided to entertain the congregation to half-an-hour of organ music before the service while I rehearsed the Cathedral Choir in the Choir Room. This time, he drove up to the Cathedral in his car, but after passing through the narrow archway into the Cathedral Close, his car jerked to a stop as it ran out of petrol. Getting out of his car, he left it just where it had stopped so that no-one else could drive a car in or out of the Close. Then he marched up to the Lay Clerks' vestry and, being unable to find a cassock that would fit him, merely donned a surplice and then went downstairs into the Cathedral to play the organ. Chaos reigned out in the Close, while he who had caused it calmly entertained the congregation as it assembled for divine service.

One Saturday, I drove down to a church near to Merthyr Tydfil to play the organ at a choral festival evensong, when choirs from the neighbourhood were to be directed by Dr. Gerald Knight, Director of the Royal School of Church Music. While I was looking forward to meeting Gerald Knight, as I had not seen him since my days at Southwark Cathedral, I was also apprehensive as I now played the organ so little that I was afraid I might do something wrong and so incur his wrath! Sansom Fenn decided to come along with me, as he too was an acquaintance of Dr. Knight and, like me, had not met him for a few years – so he said! Anyway, on arriving at the church we were ushered towards the Clergy Vestry and as we approached the door Sansom Fenn took over. Putting on his most confident manner (after all, he had consumed a few gin and tonics earlier in the day), he brushed me aside, lunged into the vestry and heartily shook a hand, saying: "Dr. Knight, how lovely to meet you again after all these years." Unfortunately the hand belonged not to Gerald Knight but to the local Vicar!

XXX

Bishop Thomas was right to make the rebuilding of the Cathedral Organ his priority for the fiftieth anniversary of his diocese of Swansea and Brecon, because during that year of 1973 there were special services galore. One was attended by Representatives of Civic Life in the diocese; another was attended by the Mayor and Mayoress of Brecon along with the Aldermen and Councillors of the Borough of Brecon, Her Majesty's Lieutenant for the County of Brecknock, the High Sheriff, the Member of Parliament for the constituency of Brecon and Radnor, the Honorary Freemen of the Borough, H. M. Justices of the Peace, Civic Heads and representatives of the Army, the Chamber of Trade and Local Organisations. How grand it all read on the special service sheets that were printed by the Brecon and Radnor Express: yet these people were all merely "mortal too like us"! So many members of the Mothers' Union wanted to attend their special Jubilee Service that two such services had to be held; Hazel's quiet opening organ voluntaris were rendered inaudible by the ceaseless round of chatter but the congregational singing was magnificent.

There was also a Diocesan Missionary Festival and a Young Wives Diocesan Festival, not forgetting a Commemoration Service attended by members of the Kilvert Society, the usual annual service attended by the Friends of Brecon Cathedral and a United Service attended by members of churches belonging to other religious denominations. (How ironic that my Uncle Michael, now a Roman Catholic priest, should choose this time to publish an article in 'The Times' suggesting that the road to unity between the Roman Catholic and Anglican Churches was well and truly closed.) In the round of services to commemorate the fifty years of the diocese, children were not forgotten. Indeed, the Archdeaconry of Brecon's Children's Festival on Ascension Day served as a reminder of the days earlier in the century when there used to be a procession of clergy and laity through the town to its Cathedral to mark this great religious festival.

Two Archbishops preached at services in the Cathedral during the course of the year: on Easter Day it was the Archbishop of Wales and on Holy Cross Day, September 14th, it was the Archbishop of York, Donald Coggan. Why Holy Cross Day? Historically this was an important day for Brecon Cathedral because it is believed that the ancient Priory Church of St. John the Evangelist, Brecon, was consecrated on this day. For that reason, it was on this very day back in 1923 that Edward Latham Bevan had been enthroned as the first Bishop of Swansea and Brecon.

The Diocesan Choral Festival gave me the opportunity to invite the Bishop of Birmingham to preach; this was Laurence Brown who some twenty or so years before had been Precentor of Southwark Cathedral while I was a choirboy there. As Canon Brown, he had chaired the committee that had closed Holy Trinity Church, Lambeth and so had been the first subject to be ridiculed in the poem that graced the opening page of my father's final Church Magazine. Naturally, he and his wife stayed with Hazel and me at Garth Cottage and as they were not averse to socialising with what our local Brecon and Radnor Express called "Brecon Natives", we took them down to The George Hotel for a drink after supper. At 10.55 p.m., five minutes before Closing Time, Kelvin Redford rushed in from Christ College, as was his wont, and ordered a pint of his beloved Guinness – a legacy of his student days at Trinity College, Dublin. By now, Kelvin had acquired the reputation of being the "Limerick King of Brecon" so when he had obtained his Guinness, I said to him: "Kelvin, tell my friend here the limerick about the Bishop of Birmingham." Kelvin needed no second bidding and launched into:

> *"The dirty old Bishop of Birmingham,*
> *Who used to…"*

Then, suddenly, he stopped and, remembering the next day's Choral Festival, looked my friend up and down and asked, "You aren't, by any chance, the Bishop of Birmingham?" to which, with a wry smile, the Bishop nodded his assent. So Kelvin said no more, which, I suppose, was fortunate, as this particular limerick is exceedingly disgraceful and unprintable. We all enjoyed the joke, as, in any case, it was hardly likely that we should have the company of the Bishop of Birmingham in The George Hotel again. The Festival Service on the Saturday afternoon was fun. The diocesan choristers had come on a long way in six years of working with Hazel and me, so the "menu" reflected this: The *Magnificat* and *Nunc Dimittis* from the Service in C by C. V. Stanford and the *Te Deum* from his service in B flat, with the anthem "How lovely are thy dwellings fair" by Brahms. This, plus a sermon from the Bishop of Birmingham, added up to a great occasion.

Two weeks later, however, I took the plunge and directed a Choral Festival sung through the medium of Welsh in St. Peter's Church, Pontardawe. Although this was only a Parish Evensong, which meant that the canticles were sung to simple chants and fewer singers attended, not a word of English was uttered throughout the entire service. The fact that we had made the effort was greatly appreciated by the Welsh-speaking choristers. Hazel had learned to speak Welsh at school and so coped well. I, being hopeless at languages, did my best and managed phonetically: my only previous experience had been singing the occasional hymn in Welsh at the Cathedral and taking my school choirs to compete at the annual Urdd (League of Welsh Youth) Eisteddfod when everything, whether it was a folk song or music by Mendelssohn, had to have Welsh words.

Meanwhile the Cathedral Choir had taken its music out into the diocese. On Sunday June 17th, the choristers sang a Holy Eucharist at Holy Trinity, Llandrindod Wells in the morning and an Evensong at St. Edward's, Knighton, in the afternoon, which was followed by a second Evensong at St. Clement's, Rhayader. The Cathedral congregation had the better part of this bargain, because its services were sung by the eminent choir of Trinity College, Cambridge, directed by my great friend from Southwark days, Richard Marlow. A fortnight later, on Sunday July 1st, while the Madley Festival Choir from Herefordshire sang the Cathedral services, the Cathedral choir went out again to sing a Civic Service at St. Edmund's, Crickhowell, and Evensongs at St. Gwendoline's, Talgarth and St. James, Llanwrtyd Wells. Such jaunts were always entertaining. The choristers travelled in a local Williams bus and enjoyed each other's company, not forgetting the overwhelming hospitality at each port of call, which left them to cope with more food or drink than they could possibly consume. It was like going on safari, but the very act of sharing our cathedral music with congregations which had hardly ever witnessed such worship was of inestimable value and I like to think that we helped bring "all Heaven before [the] eyes" of many people who lived in the wilds of Breconshire and had never before experienced this.

Even before these visits, the Cathedral Choir had aready sung a Festal Evensong for the Golden Jubilee of the Diocese of Swansea and Brecon for the benefit of del-gates attending a Meeting of the Governing Body of the Church in Wales at Llandrindod Wells. Now it joined Swansea choristers to sing the annual service for the Swansea Festival of Music and the Arts at the bidding of Archdeacon Harry Williams. Yet the choral highlight of the year was undoubtedly an Evening of Music and Readings which the Archdeaconry of Gower and the Cathedral Choristers gave in the Brangwyn Hall on the evening of Saturday November 24th. In the organising of this novel event I was greatly assisted by the Archdeacon, not forgetting Morgan Lloyd, who brought along his orchestra, his wife Dilys, who played organ solos, and my wife Hazel, who played the organ for the choral items. My admiration for the Swansea choristers knew no bounds, for most of them came from parish churches in the area where few had the opportunity to sing such music with any regularity. That night they sang their hearts out in John Joubert's "O Lorde, the maker of al thinge", G. F. Handel's "Zadok the Priest", Vaughan Williams's "O how amiable are thy dwellings" and his coronation arrangement of "All people that on earth do dwell", Brahms's "How lovely are thy dwellings fair" and G. F. Handel's "Hallelujah Chorus", much of it with orchestral accompaniment. My only disappointment on this magnificent occasion was that so few people came to support their local choristers. The great hall was barely a quarter full, even though hymns had been included in the programme for everyone to sing together.

At the Cathedral that year the Cathedral Singers had put on two major concerts with solists and Morgan Lloyd's orchestra. The first was a "first", the first time that J. S. Bach's "St. John Passion" had been sung in Brecon Catehdral on Holy Saturday. Some people asked why it was sung then and not on Good Friday: the answer was simply that most of the chief soloists, like Rogers Covey-Crump who sang the important part of the Evangelist, were booked on Good Friday at venues that could afford to pay their correct fees, whereas on Holy Saturday we could obtain their services at considerably reduced fees. This resulted in the establishment of two strange traditions which survived for a few years. The first concerned dear Mr. Hawkes the Verger. During the morning on Holy Saturday as we prepared the Cathedral for the St. John Passion, we noticed that he was busily putting the fin-ishing touches to the Easter Garden. With great aplomb he added the figure of the risen Lord, ignoring the fact that at that time Jesus should still have been lying in his tomb. However, such liturgical improprieties did not worry Hawkeye who, with his Easter Garden completed, then set off for home to enjoy his day off, not to reap-pear until Easter morning itself, when his creation was always the source of much admiration. No sooner had he gone from the Cathedral than we whisked away the figure of Jesus from the Easter Garden, safe in the knowledge that Hawkeye would not return to the Cathedral that day. By the time he arrived on Easter morning we had returned the figure of the risen Lord to its rightful place and he was none the wiser, blissfully unaware of our antics on the day before. The second tradition was established by Mike Thomas, a bass Lay Clerk and Cathedral Server who always signed himself "Mike the Light" in his Christmas cards in true Welsh fashion, because he worked for the Electricity Board. He also sang bass in the Cathedral Singers and now took it upon himself to make a habit of exchanging the sober Holy Saturday High Altar frontal for the festive Easter Day frontal while the final chorus of the St. John Passion was being sung, safe in the knowledge that he could not be seen by the audience because the choir was lined up on staging in front of the sanctuary, thereby covering his actions.

The second major Cathedral Singers concert that year found them singing the Brahms "Requiem" which was preceded by Morgan Lloyd's orchestra playing the Academic Festival Overture, with the Singers adding the words of the student song *"Gaudeamus Igitur"* in the final section. This was a fun event with everyone enjoying themselves and having a good time, so much so that we were all devastated to read a detrimental letter in the local "Brecon and Radnor Express" on the following Thursday morning. This had been written by a certain Mrs Gwanwyn Evans, who complained at great length that, seated in the nave, she could neither see the performers properly nor hear the music adequately. Back came a number of letters in support of the concert. One from Kidderminster stated that "we were able to see and hear everything" despite sitting at the back of the Cathedral. Another, from the wife of one of the Singers, suggested that next time, Mrs. Evans brought "a pair of opera glasses with her." Someone from Hereford wrote to say that he had come away from the Cathedral "enchanted, yet sorry that not more people were present to enjoy the results of the hard work which led up to this enterprising performance." Another letter writer, from Potters Bar, offered the consoling opinion that he had "never heard the work performed so near to perfection".

I have long puzzled over this difference of opinions, during which time I have not only come to know and like Mrs Gwanwyn Evans, but also to admire her for her good works in the community and for her outspoken comments on council matters. Being older, wiser and more tolerant, I now offer this explanation. From an early age, I had been brought up performing in concerts in Cathedral and Churches where performers were often unsighted to the audience in certain parts of the building, where seats were hard and uncomfortable, where arctic conditions sometimes prevailed - I nearly froze to death listening to J. S. Bach's "St. John Passion" at York Minster - yet always the atmosphere and acoustic of these buildings added a gloss to the musical proceedings which made all this physical discomfort bearable. Furthermore, interestingly, applause was frequently discouraged in these venerable surroundings, notably as a result of utterances by such famous conductors as Sir Adrian Boult and Sir Malcolm Sargent. It had come as a shock to me when my friend John Kent, not at my request, actively encouraged applause in concerts at Selby Abbey. In Wales, however, a different tradition had prevailed for the last one hundred and fifty years or so: the performance of oratorios in non-conformist chapels. When Hazel and I had gone to hear the Plough Augmented Choir sing Handel's "Messiah" in the Plough Chapel during our first week in Brecon, the choir had been ranged around the organ, high up in the gallery at the front of the building with everyone clearly visible to the audience, while the soloists and conductor had occupied the pulpit, one tier below but still clearly visible to the assembled multitude. Such chapels adapted well as concert halls and, furthermore, possessed concert hall acoustics. This was what many Brecon music-lovers were used to, while I was accustomed to, and adored, the booming, resonant, echoing acoustic of a cavernous mediaeval cathedral. There was some considerable difference!

Meanwhile Hazel and I had noticed another non-conformist trait infiltrating our music-making. Choral Evensong had been broadcast a few times from the Cathedral on Radio Three and we had noticed how the BBC (Wales) producers liked to place a separate microphone close to the organ so that they could control the balance between the choir and the organ. The Head of Religious Broadcasting was a non-conformist and had what we called "non-conformist ears", with the result that he liked the singing to dominate and the organ noises to be confined to the background. This was contrary to what we had been used to and liked, but we were unable to do anything about it as our opinions were always disregarded and we were rarely allowed into the BBC control van to listen to the sound during the rehearsal for the broadcast.

The difference between Anglican and Non-Conformist, English and Welsh traditions reared its head once again later that year when a BBC TV "Songs of Praise" was broadcast on Suday November 25th. To the usual collection of hymns were added the chorus "How lovely are thy dwellings fair" from the Brahms "Requiem", sung by the Cathedral Choir and the Cathedral Singers, along with R. Vaughan Williams's coronation arrangement of "All people that on earth do dwell." All appeared to go well, so imagine our surprise when the following letter, written by a listener in Harrow Weald, Middlesex, was published in the Western Mail:

> "Sir – It was *Songs of Praise* from Brecon Cathedral on BBC Wales on Sunday, November 25, so I settled down for a breath of what I thought would be some real Welsh "hwyl" from the very heart of the land of St. David. This, I thought, would be not only a spiritual tonic but also a stimulus to the Welsh language receiving succour from a Church that owes it so much.
>
> What a terrible disappointment it was, as one dreary un-Welsh rendition gave way to the next right up to the very last, which I thought would surely be a rousing Welsh hymn – but no, this, of all things, was of German extraction. As far as I can remember, not a single word of Welsh was uttered.
>
> If this is the best that the Church in Wales, and in Brecon in particular, can do for the spirit of Wales, then for goodness sake decline the next offer and leave it to the chapels who know how to do both jobs well."

This led to a letter from a reader in Tredegar:

> "Sir – Having read the letter written by Mr D. H. Griffiths regarding *Songs of Praise* from Brecon Cathedral, I feel I must comment.
>
> Firstly let me say that this was televised for the whole network of the Bristish Isles and not a *Dechrau Canu* programme which we hear sometimes

at this time from Wales.

I thought the singing from Brecon was magnificent and how pleasing to hear *How lovely are thy dwellings* Brahms and Vaughan Williams's arrangement of *The Old Hundredth*.

Surely our minds are centred around the Holy Spirit and not the spirit of Wales during a half-hour such as this.

Brecon Choristers and conductor can feel very proud of their performance. Congratulations."

One more letter, from a reader in Swansea, read:

"Sir - Mr D. H. Griffiths of Harrow wants the BBC *Songs of* Praise left to the chapels.

However, I found it an agreeable change when the singing came from Brecon Cathedral and the hymns were not Welsh. It was not so doleful as Welsh chapel singing.

When are we going to get rid of Welsh dirges and get back to the spirit of the old Welsh songs prior to the advent of the cold hand of Nonconformity?"

However, an unexpected letter written by Lionel Dakers, the recently-appointed Director of the Royal School of Church Music, helped to assure us that perhaps, after all, we were on the right track with our work:

"I was away for the Associated Board all last week and consequently happened to look in on Songs of Praise. I felt I must write to say how much I enjoyed this particular prigramme. Out of interest I often look in at that time on a Sunday night and am often very depressed or bored or both. Yours by contrast was so vital. A special word of congratulation to your wife who I thought, played the organ most admirably and so rhythmincally, if I may say so. Many congratulations to you both."

A month before, a service of Holy Eucharist had also been broadcast on BBC TV from the Cathedral so it was good to hear from our old organ teacher, C. H. Trevor, who wrote in his Christmas card:

"We much enjoyed "Songs of Praise" on Sunday: also the previous celebration which was a model of what this sort of thing should be. Pefect ceremonial.

On Sunday we were allowed a brief glimpse of Hazel at the whistles at the opening of the Brahms. The organ sounded fine as did the brass and timps."

The loveliest letter was written by Bishop Thomas on New Year's Eve, December 31st 1973, and it was typical of his thoughtfulness:

"My dear David,
I write before the year goes out to say how grateful I am to you,

Hazel, and all the choristers for a magnificent contribution to our Jubilee Celebrations. It has been a most inspiring year and will remain a very happy memory, with so many "highlights", made even higher by the fine music which accompanied services and other events. I am deeply grateful.

Yours Very Sincerely,
John Swansea & Brecon."

But the Bishop went further. He and his wife Betty invited all the Lay Clerks along with Hazel and me to have supper with them at their home in Ely Tower sometime in the New Year, and a most enjoyable evening was had by all.

XXXI

I was as "happy as a sandboy" - one of my mother's phrases, in my Cathedral music making. It was as if my work was my hobby. However, Dean Jones had been quite right back in January 1963 when he said that the Cathedral Organist's pay could not support a married man with a young family, for without my school teaching work I would have been in desperate financial straits. As it was, even with this work, I was frequently short of cash. To help motivate the enthusiasm of the Cathedral Lay Clerks who did so much voluntarily for the Cathedral, not forgetting the Cathedral Singers (many of whom now travelled great distances to sing), nor the church choristers who were making so much music with me in the diocese, involved me in a considerable amount of social drinking with a wide variety of people. This was fun and did wonders for the morale of the singers, but cost me much money.

Part of my school work involved piano teaching at Christ College, which was not the most exciting of occupations even if it did result in my singing alto alongside Simon Hughes, the future Liberal Democrat MP for Bermondsey. When the School Chapel Choir broadcast a service on BBC Radio, he mischievously took out his transistor radio to listen to the concluding voluntary which was being played by Hazel on the organ at the other end of the mediaeval chapel. (Apparently this is the oldest school chapel still in regular use.) My piano teaching was undertaken on the second floor of a dilapidated building called "The Bridgend", named after the old pub that it once was. Below me was the Music Room, while on the ground floor was a primitive Woodwork Room where, according to legend, a local undertaker had once taught boys to make pencil boxes in the shape of coffins. So I would sit in a grim little room listening to a succession of boys making noises on an upright piano that had seen better days, trying to stay awake! What made the work bearable, apart from the end-of-term cheque, was the occasional talented pupil, like Hefin Owen, a future Producer of music programmes for BBC Wales. While the pupils sat on my left, the River Usk flowed below on my right, with the occasional salmon catching the sun as it leapt. Indeed, I once watched a man catch one by lying on the bank and tickling it in shallow water, which, of course, is highly illegal.

Yet my main income as a teacher came from the Secondary School in Builth Wells where I went in the daytime on Tuesdays, Wednesdays and Thursdays by the bus that left Brecon at 7.30 a.m. and wound its way through Llanfihangel Talyllyn, Llangorse, Llyswen and Erwood, following the route of the recently-closed railway line, arriving in Builth Wells at 8.35 a.m. and finishing up at Newtown two hours or so later. It was, I suppose, a substitute for the train as this particular bus service received some sort of financial subsidy from, I believe, British Railways. When David Verey published his Shell Guide to Mid Wales in 1960, his remark that Builth Wells was "a busy but rather ugly little town" did not endear him to the locals, although such a description certainly suited the Secondary School which was my destination. Called then a Bilateral School, it consisted of the original stone building dating from the 1890's, to which had been attached on one side a grim, two-storied red-brick building that contained science laboratories, an art room, some changing rooms and two dirty, smelly loos, while on another side had been added a long succession of wooden classrooms with non-existent sound-proofing, beyond which was a more solidly-constructed metalwork room. At this point a road intervened on the other side of which stood one more row of wooden classrooms, in the middle of which was a more substantial woodwork room. That conglomeration of buildings was called the "modern", i. e. Secondary Modern School, as opposed to the more extensive buildings on the other side of the road which were grandly labelled the "Grammar School".

So, with one side of the site a "Grammar School" and the other a "Secondary Modern School", a "Dives and Lazarus" situation prevailed across the intervening road: any child who passed the dreaded eleven-plus examination was educated on the "Grammar" side, while those who failed were educated on the "Modern" side. Rarely did any child cross that narrow divide. That the teaching staff were so high-powered for such a small school was simply because Breconshire Education Committee, in its wisdom, paid Heads of Department very generous allowances. As one such explained, "Why move to a larger school to work harder and take more responsibility only to be paid the same amount of money?"

Among the departmental Heads was W. R. Nicholas, known as Nick. He was the Head of the Classics Department for, amazingly, Latin, Greek and Ancient Roman History were still taught in this extraordinary little school. His colourful past included a spell of running the Palestine Police in Ramallah shortly after the Second World War, hence the name of his house in Builth Wells. He explained to me one day that out in Palestine the atmosphere was so tense that you fired your gun first to make sure that you were alive to ask the questions afterwards. The Head of English, Eric Corfield, was also an interesting character. Like "Nick", he had come to the school in those heady days immediately following the War, when he quickly became esteemed as an opening batsman in the town cricket team. An amateur mathematician of some ability, he must have had a charismatic personality, because he swept a sixth-form girl off her feet and made her his wife. Even so, his greatest days at the school were yet to come and were to be largely of my making. Now, however, I revelled in his cantankerous behaviour. Throughout my entire first term at Builth Wells Bilateral School, he uttered not a word to me. On the first day of the second term, he offered the explanation that he had thought I was going to be like my predecessor. What Bryan Hesford had done to offend him I never did discover. At the end of my seond term I witnessed another of his claims to fame. Both the summer and the autumn terms ended with examinations. These always began with English, as Eric had the most marking to do. On the first day, at lunchtime, he would march into the staff room and sweep everything off the huge table onto the floor, whereupon he would fill the newly-created space with his examination papers and start marking. Woe betide anyone who interrupted him.

Head of Physics was Roy Baynham, who was of such size that watching him lower himself into the driving seat of his car, a Mini, provided regular entertainment. A kindly man, he was an excellent churchman. This was surprising, as his father, Cyril Baynham, had been Organist of St. Mary's, Swansea, at the time when the church had been destroyed during the devastating bombing of Swansea. The Vicar, a future Bishop of St. David's, ignoring his many years of service, had terminated his contract, without any thought for his future. Roy was bitter about this, but intrigued to learn that Hazel's father had been writing to his father in retirement in Devon, hoping to glean information about the old Thomas Warne organ which had stood in St. Mary's, Swansea, from 1762 until 1904, but now stood in St. Mary's , Kidwelly. Roy had married the daughter of the Vicar of Cwmbach, commonly called Builth Road, in which parish were two remarkable stations. One was for the LMS railway line from Swansea Victoria to Shrewsbury, which then went on to Crewe and Manchester, while the other served the GWR line from Talyllyn – which, from Brecon, crossed beneath its rival's tracks and on to Llanidloes and Newtown. Now that the parish of Cwmbach had been united with its neighbouring parish, Roy lived with his wife in the former Vicarage where she had been brought up. She was headmistress of the tiny village primary school. A few miles down the road to Brecon lived her brother, who was Vicar of Llyswen. In Brecon lived another relative: the following information is the reason why one should always check on their family tree before passing comment about any person in Wales. Roy Baynham's father had succeeded his uncle, Arthur Hey, as Organist of St. Mary's Swansea, in 1919. Later, Arthur Hey's granddaughter, Margaret Hey, turned up at the youth club attached to the Church of the Good Shepherd, Tadworth, which Richard Marlow and I had attended sometimes on Saturday evenings. When Hazel and I had arrived in Brecon, one of the first people we met had been Margaret Hey, who was lecturing at the local Rural Technical Institute. She was sharing a flat with a fellow lecturer, Imogen "Midge" Hollingdale who became a good friend and, later, Godmother to our son, Nicholas. What a series of coincidences!

Another coincidence concerned one of the few photographs hanging on the wall of the Choir Room in Brecon Cathedral, which showed the choirboys' football team of 1935. One of the non-playing members of this team, resplendent in a raincoat and school cap, was Walter Scott, whom I met at Builth Wells Bilateral School, where eventually he became a legendary figure with an unsurpassable record. Not long after that photograph had been taken, Walter moved away from Brecon with his family, to reappear at Builth Wells Bilateral School which he left aged eighteen in 1945 at the end of the Second World War. However, he never actually left, because such was the shortage of teachers after the War that he was kept on as a Student Teacher. Superb as a teacher, a model for discipline and classroom control, he never did leave the school until he retired at the age of sixty, having been continuously a pupil for seven years and a teacher for forty-two.

Another who almost never left the school was Bryngwyn Griffith, who became Headmaster's Secretary not long after ceasing to be a pupil and remained in that job until retirement many years later. His office was small and often so chaotic that the Headmaster sometimes made him give up a day or two of his holiday to bring about some semblance of order and normality to his surroundings. A fount of local historical knowledge, he was a staunch member of Horeb Chapel, a pillar of local society, the possessor of a magnificent pair of eyebrows and also had a propensity for pouring a mountain of salt over the first course of his lunch!

Another fount of local knowledge was the Physical Education teacher, Martin

Davies. Young, fiery and with a fine head of red hair, he was a great sportsman, particularly at soccer and table tennis, and was another magnificent disciplinarian. His first teaching job was at a secondary school in Leominster and, when an unruly pupil tried to get the better of him, he cornered him alone in the changing room, held him up against the wall, put his fist to his face and said: "You step out of line again and this is what you'll get. It'll be your word against mine and I know who'll be believed", or words to that effect. A crude treatment, yet it procured the desired result. He could vamp well on the piano and I envied him for the way in which he could get the second and third form louts on the "Modern" side to sing folk songs lustily and with obvious enjoyment. Thursday lunchtimes were Martin's moments of glory with the staff, for having read the local Brecon and Radnor Express he would tell us all the local scandal over the lunch table, filling in missing information and adding historical background as he had been born and bred in Builth Wells and also educated in the school. For obvious reasons, this became known as "Screws News".

Another rugged character on the staff was Ian Ingles, who taught gardening and a variety of other subjects to the less academic pupils. Yet another superb disciplinarian, he was seen more than once ejecting an unruly boy from his classroom, picking him up by the scruff of his neck and the seat of his trousers to deposit him on the path outside his classroom to cool off. Indeed, one naughty boy was held out of a window in this way! A fellow gardening and horticultural teacher whose name eludes me, but who had played the clarinet in the Welsh National Youth Orchestra, achieved immortality by writing on one pupil's gardening report just one sentence: "And some fell on stony ground ..."! "Ev the Rev" was another teacher, so named because once upon a time he had been a Vicar until he had run off with his Organist, a soprano of some repute who had been a Blue Riband winner in the National Eisteddfod. Known as "Popeye" to his pupils because he was rarely seen without a pipe in his mouth - even in the classroom, his forte was setting the class some work so that he could sit behind his desk to read the daily newspaper. His undoing came on the day when, lulled into a false sense of security, he was called over to a large cupboard by some pupils and then gently pushed into it, whereupon the rascals locked the door, leaving him inside, protesting!

History on the "grammar" side of the school was taught by Harold Bicknell. A native of Wisbech, about which he would talk with great affection, he had come to the school originally to teach P. E., but when he had passed the age of unlimited physical energy he transferred to History. He had two famous lessons which were listened to with great glee not only by the class he was teaching but also by anyone in the surrounding classrooms within earshot, courtesy of the non-existent sound-proofing. The first concerned the great local Nonconformist preacher, Hywel Harris, whom "Bick" would imitate declaiming a sermon in loud, sonorous tones. The second, and best, was the slaughter of Prince Llewelyn, the last true Welsh prince, at Cilmery, two miles away, by English soldiers. Apparently, the Prince hid for a night at nearby Aberedw, where he had his horse shod with the horseshoes put on backwards to confuse the pursuing soldiers. Unfortunately, they tortured the blacksmith and gleaned from him this vital piece of information so that they were able to follow the prince and eventually do their worst. So dear old

"Bick" would deliver this story in detail, acting all the parts right down to the cries of the dying Prince, all with great relish, while his pupils and anyone else who was able to listen-in hung on every word. By chance, late in life, "Bick" married Sally, Headmistress of a little school at Cilmery. Legend had it that they made love once a year, on Boxing Day. It is easy to imagine the unruly hilarity that this led to in the little staffroom as the momentous day approached. However, this was no ordinary staffroom.

Amazingly, there were three staffrooms dotted around the school: one on the "modern" side for the few teachers that catered for the needs of these pupils; one at the top of the stairs in the original stone building which was the preserve of the few lady "Grammar" teachers and was presided over by "Aunty", as the Senior Mistress was called. Her real name was Joan Spoonley and she was married to Ron, who had been the last Station Master at Builth Wells Railway Station. She was a very dear, gushing lady, who taught art and class music (mostly singing) at the school. On Sundays she played the organ at Alpha Chapel in town. Very old-fashioned, I remember well the look of horror on her face when a particularly obnoxious girl swore at her, using the word f—k for the first time. I remember too the day she was given a sum of money to spend on some pictures and she returned with two examples of modern art, one of which she hung upside-down for almost six months until she realised her mistake. The third staffroom was the first room in the long row of wooden hovels that formed the heart of the "grammar" side, and here hung out the motley collection of male grammar teachers, including myself. It was the happiest staffroom that I was ever to know. Sometimes it was so rowdy that messages had to be sent by staff teaching in the other, non-soundproofed, rooms along that row asking us to quieten down and to watch our language, as we were disturbing their lessons. Initially this room was presided over by Rog, Mr Rogers, a very gentle man who taught French but was so mild that he had no control over the goings-on in the staff-room. Furthermore, he had a formidable wife who ruled the roost both at home and out and about.

This incredible collection of teachers was held together by the most fascinating Headmaster, J. Ewart Davies, a striking man, very clean shaven, with a fine head of silvery-white wavy hair. He was always immaculately dressed in a smartly-pressed suit, never anything but outspoken, who knew his own mind and refused to tolerate fools or indiscipline in any way, who never failed to address members of staff by their title, "Mr., Mrs. Or Miss" and who never entered any of the three staffrooms without first knocking on the door. Everyone knew just where they stood with him. I certainly did. For reasons unknown, he held me in great regard: maybe because I was Organist and Choirmaster of Brecon Cathedral, but more likely because Hazel, my wife, heralded from Wales and could speak Welsh (if only a little) as well as being a better organist than me. I remember how on one Sports Day, the day when a new Archbishop of Wales was due to be elected, and an aeroplane flew at great speed over the Sports Field in the direction of Llandrindod Wells where five minutes later the Electoral College was to start its deliberations, he clutched my arm and exclaimed loudly: "Mr. Gedge, Mr. Gedge, the Holy Spirit on his way to Llandrindod!" adding wickedly, "I wonder if he speaks Welsh". My only disagreement with him had nothing to do with the school but came about simply because he insisted that Tonic Sol-fa was an invention of the Welsh. I never could convince him that this, with its movable "doh", was in fact an English creation, developed by Sarah Glover, a Sunday School teacher in Norwich.

When first I started teaching at the school I was given just two girls to teach, with the command that they pass O level and then A level. There was no music room and the only piano was a broken-down affair in a classroom which could not be timetabled for me to use as it was only separated from next door by a thin, movable, wooden partition. So we worked in the canteen and when that wasn't available we went down to the small room in the Church Hall where there were two awful pianos and the large room did duty as a PE room. One winter, it even provided refuge for a swarm of bees which came to life during a PE lesson when the heating was switched on. Both girls were good pianists, so I arranged lessons for them with Hazel, which is how the Associated Board of the Royal Schools of Music came to use Garth Cottage as an Examination Centre, as it was realised that if Hazel taught to Grade VIII standard then she must possess a good piano. I did all that was required of me, with the result that Marian, daughter of Brynmor Thomas, Headmaster of Llanwrtyd Wells Primary School, duly went off to the Guildhall School of Music, graduated, returned to teach music in Herefordshire, became Secretary of Hereford Choral Society and is now a family friend. The other girl began as Cynthia Bloxham, but became Cynthia Williams when she moved in with relatives in Llangammarch Wells and after going off to a teacher training college she disappeared without trace.

As I got sucked into the life of the school, so I began to help with the School Eisteddfod and excelled myself by heading a notice with the spelling "SCHOOL EISTEDDFORD", which betrayed my English origins. What amazed me was the amount of talent that was revealed in these competitions. This was probably nurtured by Young Farmers' Clubs activities in the area, with which some of the school staff were involved. Nevertheless the Eisteddfod was good for the school, especially as it involved other creatve activities in addition to music, such as drama, cooking woodwork, metalwork and needlework, which meant that a large proportion of the school pupils were actively involved. This in turn led me to the Urdd (League of Welsh Youth) Eisteddfod and I began to prepare school choirs and vocal groups for the competitions. These began at county level early in the year, before moving on to national level when the Eisteddfod was held during the Whitsun (Spring) Bank Holiday, one year in North Wales, the next year in South Wales. All singing had to be in Welsh, which was a nightmare as far as I was concerned, although eventually it helped me to understand the language enough to sing the occasional Welsh hymn at the Cathedral.

Fortunately, I was able to enlist the help of the Welsh teacher, Gwynfor Evans, who was one more interesting member of staff. If he was not wholly enthusiastic about the English race, this was understandable, because in his childhood, while playing near his home in the hills of Montgomeryshire, he had picked up some explosives left unintentionally by soldiers and blown off bits of two fingers. However, over the years, the more I became involved in Urdd Eisteddfod activities, the more I became disenchanted, because time after time my choirs and choral groups were criticised for their Welsh pronunciation and rarely given credit for trying: after all, Builth Wells was not exactly a Welsh-speaking area. I noticed also how the same choirs succeeded all the time. Because all adjudications had to be given in Welsh it was vital for the adjudicators to be Welsh-speaking, with the result that the same adjudicators kept on appearing at the National competitions. In the end I became convinced that it would be fairer if adjudicators sat behind a screen and the competing choirs were identified by numbers only so that the assessors had no idea of who was singing: some results might then have been very different.

This was not all that worried me about local and national eisteddfodau, as these seemed to breed competitors with a "pot-hunting" mentality. There were singers who did nothing other than compete in eisteddfodau, following from eisteddfod to eisteddfod any adjudicator who liked the sound of their voices and often refusing to compete if other adjudicators were presiding. Few of these people could cope with the real challenge of singing as a soloist in an oratorio, performing with an understanding of historical style and with orchestral accompaniment. Fewer still were prepared to sing in a choir, as this appeared to be beneath their dignity. Some who succeeded at local level and went on to succeed at National level sometimes ended up by prefixing their name with the unofficial title "Madam" and thereafter expected to be treated almost like royalty. The Headmaster and I arranged for one girl at the school, who possessed a fine voice and had already started on the pot-hunting trail, to have fortnightly singing lessons at the Welsh College of Music and Drama in Cardiff, where she was given as a pupil to one of Wales's finest teachers. Imagine our horror when, two months later, we discovered that the girl had stopped attending these lessons without notifying either the college or us; worse still, she had returned to her local teacher and resumed her pot-hunting activities on the mid-Wales eisteddfodau circuit. However, at school, all this had led me to an activity which I came to realise was much more musically valuable: Gilbert and Sullivan Operas.

For years I had despised Gilbert and Sullivan operas and also some nineteenth-century English Church music. Indeed, at Selby Abbey I had destroyed volume after volume of such ditties. It was Cyril Simkins, a Lay Clerk at St. George's Chapel, Windsor Castle, who had opened my eyes to the fact that some of this music was rather special. Apparently, when my idol Dr. Campbell had arrived at St. George's Chapel as Organist, he had dumped much of the nineteenth-century repertoire into the castle dustbins, from where Cyril Simkins had rescued some choice numbers. Copies of some of these he had sent to me and I remember being very moved when playing through "O pray for the peace of Jerusalem", written out in Cyril's beautiful handwriting. Here was some beautifully expressive music in sonata form, which led me to reflect on how its composer, John Goss, had been a pupil of Thomas Attwood who, in turn, had been a favourite pupil of none other than W. A. Mozart. As for Arthur Sullivan, had not he been a chorister at the Chapel Royal, come from my part of South London and been a pupil of John Goss – so perhaps his music was not that bad! So I was sucked into the Builth Wells Bilateral School tradition of Gilbert and Sullivan operas. It had not taken long, for within two years of arriving I was in charge of the music for a production of "Pirates of Penzance", a job which Rog, the Senior Master, was only too happy to pass on to me as my success in the Breconshire Urdd Eisteddfod had impressed him!

It all began with the Headmaster going on a progress around the school. He entered every room, surveyed the inmates, pointed out which boys and girls had parents or grandparents who could sing and then nominated them for the chorus. In no time at all, there was a large, if unwilling, chorus as none of the nominated singers dare defy the Headmaster. As for soloists, they were easy to find as the local YFC activities had successfully produced a number of good singers who were used to performing in public. Indeed, one girl in particular, with an ambition to be an air hostess, has no problem at all with the high "D" required for the star solo part of Mabel. I was quite unprepared for what happened next. Firstly the Headmaster timetabled the opera, starting with one lesson on each of the three days that I was in the school, moving on to one lesson on each of two days and a double lesson on the third day, ending up with two weeks (i. e. six days) of nothing but rehearsals. What bliss! At least half, if not two-thirds of the school was involved. The metal-work, woodwork and art departments created the scenery and lighting, the needlework department created the most lovely costumes, Bryngwyn the Secretary organised the make-up, while "Bick" took charge of the ticket sales. In addition, four members of staff took important solo parts: John Thomas, the Chemistry teacher, was the Major-General, Gwynfor Evans was Frederick, Rhian Owen, another Welsh teacher, was the Pirate King and finally Eric Corfield was the producer. My pupil Marian, now in the sixth form, supplied such an admirable piano accompaniment to the singing that it came as no surprise four years later when she was encouraged to stay on at the Guildhall School of Music to develop this specialised art.

The four performances in Builth's Strand Hall were a delight. What was lacking in finesse was more than compensated by the enthusiasm of everyone involved, and what it all did for the morale of the school is beyond belief. It was an amazing team effort, quite humbling to behold. It was also most gratifying, a year later, to discover that two members of the chorus had been so overcome by the fun of it all that, on arriving as students at University College, Cardiff, they had soon set in motion a student performance of their own. One later returned to work in Builth Wells, married one of the chorus sopranos - George Bradley's granddaughter - and joined Builth Wells Male Voice Choir. Indeed, through learning to sing the catchy melodies with their basic supporting harmonies, many a Builth youngster unsus-pectingly came to a realisation that classical music could be as much fun as "pop".

By now, I was hooked, with the result that two years later, "The Gondoliers" fol-lowed. This was a tougher nut to crack and as the performance dates drew nearer, so the rehearsals became increasingly intense. One morning, when the Duchess of Plaza-Toro removed herself from the lap of the Duke of Plaza-Toro (Mr. Thomas, the chemistry teacher), a wet patch was found there! Again, the magic worked and there were scintillating performances. One was enlivened by a young male mem-ber of the chorus who had a tiny solo to sing at the start of the opera but at the crucial moment suddenly spotted his parents in the audience and forgot to sing. The piano accompaniment also had a new dimension, as a clarinet part had been added, courtesy of the Breconshire Education Committee. Having discovered, at last, the vast amount of instrumental teaching that was going on in other English and Welsh counties, the Committee had appointed its first-ever woodwind teacher. Afterwards, the following poem appeared in the school magazine:

"Sing a song of Gondoliers,
Bringing Mr Gedge to tears?
And then in all those tra-la-la's,
In Sullivan's long-quavered bars,
His plastered glasses come undone.
Now, quipping and quaffing, here's some fun.
The arm of his specs has gone without trace,
But still he sings on in soprano and bass.
He's found it and started to stick it on
While shouting "Where have all the tenors gone?"
List and learn what Gedge has said
To the roses white and red.
"Sing it high and sing it low,
You dainty rose - you so-and-so!"
So sing a song of Gondoliers,
You'll not bring Mr. Gedge to tears."

XXXII

Inevitably "Mikado" made its appearance at Builth Wells Bilateral School and shot Eric Corfield to stardom, for not only did he produce the opera, but, also sang the lead part and stole the show. As he rattled off his patter songs, what words he could not remember he made up and the results were often disastrously funny. However, the fact that our production of "Mikado" was in direct line to the D'Oyly Carte productions came about in the following, most unexpected, way.

My "reward" for the success of the Decca/Qualiton recording "Christmas in Wales" was the opportunity to make a record of the nineteenth-century Cathedral Music that I had grown to love and champion. Although this recording also was on the Qualiton label, the same superb team of Decca recording engineers was in residence in Brecon and once again we teamed up for a riotous four days of recording and fun, working hard and playing hard. Wisely, producer Ray Ware had brought along with him a certain Jimmy Walker, who was not only a very experienced and very knowledgeable musician but also a very lovely person, so from the beginning we all got on famously. One by one we recorded a sucession of anthems by worthy cathedral musicians of the nineteenth-century. There was the extraordinary "He maketh the snow to fall apace" - another discovery of Cyril Simkins, which was the product of an Organist of Norwich Cathedral, John Christmas Beckwith, so-named because he had been born on Christmas Day. This little aria is an extract from the unlikely-titled anthem "The Lord is great and terrible", and it ended with the exquisite line, "The eye marvelleth at the whiteness thereof", which I have long wished could be made into a washing-powder advertisement.

Then there was another Cyril Simkins "find", William Russell's beautiful musical setting of the Collect for the Second Sunday in Advent: "Blessed Lord, who has caused all Holy Scriptures to be written for our learning". How that had remained undiscovered I shall never know. There was also music by Thomas Attwood, the famous Organist of St. Paul's Cathedral, who had conducted many early London performances of Beethoven symphonies for the Philharmonic Society and who had befriended Felix Mendelssohn on his trips to this country. Also included were anthems by the Revd. Canon Professor Sir F. A. Gore Ouseley, Bt., founder of St. Michael's College, Tenbury, including his exquisite "How goodly are thy tents, O Jacob", which he composed as a result of seeing Cologne Cathedral by moonlight while on a tour of Europe after being caught up in London's "No Popery" riots; that anthem the Choir nicknamed "The Camper's Anthem"! More profound was his wonderful eight-part setting of the words "O Saviour of the World", which is sung in Brecon Cathedral at the "Veneration of the Cross" service every Good Friday morning. Another of the Revd. Sir Frederick's anthems that we recorded was the ever-popular "From the rising of the sun", which we dubbed "The Japanese National Anthem".

Not forgotten was the little "O Lord, we beseech thee", a setting of the collect for the sixteenth Sunday after Trinity by Dr. Joseph Pring, which I had edited for the music publisher Novello & Co. and which at that time earned me a few pounds in royalties, a source of beer money which soon dried up. Why this happened I do not know, because I happen to think this anthem worthy of consideration. Indeed, it was sung in the diocese of Peterborough's annual choral festival at around this time. We also recorded Dr. William Crotch's "Lo! Star-led chiefs", an extract from his oratorio "Palestine", which once appeared in a cathedral music list somewhere (not Brecon) as "Lo! Startled Chefs". Coupled with this was Dr. Crotch's shorter anthem "How dear are thy counsels unto me", which in Brecon Cathedral is known as "The Lawyers' Anthem".

When we came to record John Goss's "Praise the Lord" in its entirety, which includes the gem "O pray for the peace of Jerusalem" that originally brought C. F Simkins to Brecon, Jimmy Walker proved his worth. I could not get the fugal final movement, "As the mountains are round about Jerusalem", to gel. "Try it twice as fast", he suggested, and he was right; the music went off with great gusto with Hazel playing the loud organ part with much aplomb. When the record finally reached the shops it was entitled "Praise the Lord", while on the cover were reproduction photographs of four of the worthy musicians whose music we had sung: William Crotch, Thomas Attwood, John Christmas Beckwith and the Revd. Sir Frederick Ouseley. Unfortunately they did not look a particularly inspiring lot: worse still, underneath their pictures were the words "The Choir of Brecon Cathedral"! The music critics were patronising to say the least, asking "Why Brecon Cathedral Choir?" and "Why this music?" At that time, as far as I can remember, only one similar record had been issued and that was by the superlative choir of St. John's College Cambridge, which had included S. S. Wesley's great anthem "The Wilderness" (which was the name given to his garden when he was Organist at Gloucester Cathedral). Purposely I had omitted all music by this fascinating composer from our record as this would have begged comparisons and, without doubt, we would have come off worst. However, time has proved that our record was on the right track, as nineteenth-century cathedral music has made a comeback as the twentieth century has drawn to a close.

Jimmy Walker had steeped himself in nineteenth-century British music of a different sort. For several years in the past, he had conducted Gilbert and Sullivan operas for the famous D'Oyly Carte company for which they were composed. As I was preparing "Mikado" at school I had the temerity to do the obvious; I asked him to come over to Builth Wells and show me how to do the job properly. Jimmy was only too happy to oblige, not just once but twice, and his engaging manner not only mesmerised the pupils but impressed greatly the Headmaster who was inclined to regard professional musicians as a race apart. However, Jimmy had that rare gift of communication, not forgetting the humility that oozed from him. Not surprisingly, he struck up a wonderful rapport with the youngsters and treated them like true musicians, with the result that their performances gained immeasurably.

At this time there were some especially musical youngsters at Builth Wells Bilateral School, ten of whom had been persuaded by the Headmaster to pursue the "O" level music course. When Ray Ware asked me to follow up "Christmas in Wales" with another record of Christmas music which was to be issued on a full Decca label, I decided to enlist their help. Three of them, Enfys Hill and Heather

Masters from Llanwrtyd Wells along with Glenda Evans from Llanafan, not only had good singing voices but also were excellent guitar players. So we decided to record two of Sidney Carter's folk carols, "Lord of the dance" and "Every star shall sing a carol", with the three girls not only joining forces to sing with the cathedral choirboys but also to add guitar parts to Hazel's organ accompaniments. However, the 'icing on the cake' was the two-part descant that they composed for the final verse of "Every star" and actually sang themselves, very beautifully. Again, I had permission to add trumpet parts to three of David Willcock's carol arrangements; these, along with the brass in Martin Shaw's "Fanfare" which led into the hymn "Christians Awake", were used to open and close each side of the record. The inclusion of three carols by Peter Warlock led to a letter of appreciation from the Peter Warlock Society, while the entire record, with its lovely sleeve showing the Cathedral covered in snow, brought from the Gramophone magazine an A1 rating, which was a just reward for our labours.

Not long after the music for "Sing Noel" was recorded during the summer of 1973, the Cathedral Choir embarked upon its first-ever tour across the English Channel. This came about through a young German named Dieter Edel, who had fallen in love with Brecon and had begun to spend more and more of his holidays there. A very determined character, used to having his own way, Dieter soon moved onto the Cathedral Choir and Singers scene, which led to his deciding to take our music to his homeland. So, towards the end of July we found ourselves on a Williams bus heading for Dover and the ferry to Ostend, from where we embarked upon a thirteen-hour drive across Europe. For the youngsters this was a first venture into foreign lands, giving them new and valuable experiences which they would never forget. So the smelly public toilets in Metz are indelibly printed on many minds, as is the discipline of crossing main roads in Pforzheim at the same time as other pedestrians or else be in trouble with the police. Most off-putting was watching delectable fish swimming around in a large tank outside a restaurant in Maulbronn knowing that selection would result in the fancy-free creature being fished out, killed, cooked and served up to a hungry customer. Yet apart from this, Maulbronn was a delightful town, little bigger than Builth Wells. It was the proud possessor of the finest remaining monastic complex in Germany that somehow had remained unscathed by any conflict. This boasted a most elegant fountain in its cloisters, a rood bearing an almost life-sized image of Christ that I found strangely moving, wonderfully-carved old oak choirstalls with indentations in the wooden floors made by countless monks and then parishioners kneeling in prayer over the centuries; it also contained a fine three-manual tracker action Walcker organ which was a revelation to play, aided by a stunning resonance that produced a five-second echo, helped by there being no unnecessary furniture or carpet. There was, furthermore, no electric light in the building except at this organ! It was a stunning ecclesiastical edifice that cried out for the daily round of prayer that is the lot of such buildings in England and Wales, as well as a choir school and daily choral services, but that was not the way of the Lutheran Church in twentieth-century Germany. Instead alongside it stood an ancient school, thoroughly modernised, where we stayed in great comfort. The restoration work had been done by the state, so painstakingly that we were each forbidden to hang so much as a wet towel out of a dormer window to dry in the constant warmth of the summer sun, which never seemed to disappear except in the occasional violent storm. Never before had I seen a school so immaculate, so well kept and having so many grand pianos; but then it was a school that catered for specialist musicians.

Experiencing what to me seemed to epitomise prosperity, at such close quarters, left me wondering who actually had lost out through the Second World War. Outside the school and church was a beautiful cobbled forecourt, while the area around was littered with delightful half-timbered buildings that looked as if they had come straight from the pages of Grimm's fairy tales. What also struck us, as we were driven around to give our concerts and sing services, was the complete absence of the hedges that we were so used to back home in Breconshire.

We sang at churches in Pforzheim, a largish modern city which had been rebuilt after heavy bombing during the Second World War; in once-fashionable Wildbad in the stunning Black Forest, where long ago springs had made it a spa for sufferers from rheumatism, gout and nervous troubles; in Freudenstadt, another popular tourist centre in the Black Forest, where the stone town church was strangely built in the shape of a gigantic V during the early years of the seventeenth century, with the altar sited at the point of the V, while ladies sat in one arm and gentlemen in the other.

One day we made the long journey through the Black Forest of Württemberg and out the other side, driving onto Blaubeuren, near to Ulm, which was Brecon's twin town. There we spent a happy day hosted by local inhabitants, gave a concert in the town church and afterwards enjoyed a civic reception. One host had been introduced to his two guests as "Herr Pouffe" and when they smiled gently, in the belief that language differences would protect their indiscretion, he also smiled as he explained that the word meant the same in German as it did in English. As usual, I had laced all the concert programmes with a liberal sprinkling of nineteenth-century items and, as such Anglican Cathedral music was largely unknown in this part of Europe, press reviews were, happily, appreciative. So while we taught the Germans about our sort of music we also taught our own youngsters a thing or two. Three of them slipped out of the school at Maulbronn one night, intent on sampling German *bier*. When they returned, they were violently sick in their beds! Having made sure that they were otherwise all right, we left them to sleep. Once they awoke the next morning, feeling the worse for their escapade, we made them clear up their mess, in exchange for not telling their parents. It was a long time before they drank beer of any sort again!

Only the journey home was problematic. We had intended to leave Maulbronn at 6 a.m. to make the thirteen-hour journey to Ostend, but we had reckoned without Dieter. On our arrival at the school, the wash-basin in every bedroom had been equipped with a tiny piece of soap and a small sponge. As we waited to depart, he went from room to room ensuring that the soap and sponge were still in place. Worse than that, he made us unpack all the rubbish bags and re-pack the contents into bags containing remains of food, now evil and smelly, and bags containing empty bottles and tins. Meanwhile the bus driver was becoming frantic and when Dieter finally uttered "You may go now" we had lost almost an hour. Nevertheless we arrived at Ostend in time for the boat, only to find that departure had been delayed because a force-eight gale was raging and because the great luxury liner the Queen Elizabeth II was in the vicinity. As the ferry left the harbour, the youngsters excitedly searched the mountainous seas for the Queen ELizabeth II; one of them, wearing spectacles, was promptly sick into the wind and so succeeded in covering his clothes, his face and his glasses with the evil-smelling mixture!

The autumn brought with it a crisis. Pupil numbers had been steadily dropping at Builth Wells Bilateral School and this made even more remote any possibility of a new school being built. Suddenly serious mention began to be made of closing the school and moving its pupils to Llandrindod Wells High School, while taking away pupils from that school who lived in Rhayader and transferring them to Llanidloes High School. This would have been disatrous for me as not only would I have had to commute an extra seven miles each way but, worse still, being only part-time I would have had to work under another teacher and would no longer have been boss of my own department. By chance, just at this very moment the Organist of Llandaff Cathedral, Robert Joyce, chose to resign and his job became available."Go for it, 'Edgie," said Bick in the staff-room one day at school (Mr. Bicknell had called me that ever since, in his capacity as Business Manager for the School Opera productions, he had plastered Builth Wells and its surrounding villages with posters for the Mikado, bearing by mistake the legend "Musical Director: Mr. D. G. Edge"!). After careful consideration, I went for it.

I was shortlisted along with Harry Bramma, Assistant Organist of Worcester Cathedral, Paul Morgan, Assistant Organist of Exeter Cathedral, and Michael Smith, Assistant Organist of Salisbury Cathedral. Two of these I knew well: Michael Smith had been Organist of Pontefract Parish Church and Director of Music at Kings School, Pontefract, when I had been Organist at nearby Selby Abbey, and Harry Bramma was in the habit of taking refuge in The George Hotel, Brecon, with two clerical friends after certain major church festivals. We were all summoned to interviews shortly after Christmas Day.

I went with a heavy heart, as I was not the least bit attracted by Llandaff Cathedral. As I drove out of Brecon with Hazel, Harriet and Nick accompanying me, Harriet protesting loudly that she did not want to live in Cardiff, the car ground to a halt in sympathy in Llanfaes, leaving us to limp back home and transfer to the car that Hazel used for local journeys like shopping, taking the children to school or for getting to St. Mary's Church to play the organ at funerals. Our second car succeeded in getting us to Llandaff however much as we didn't want to go there. While the remainder of the family spent the day with Mary, the widow of Dean Gwynno James who had appointed me to Brecon Cathedral, I went off to the interviews which began with each candidate taking a practice with the Parish Choir and then playing the organ. When my turn came play the organ, I thought to myself about Llandaff Cathedral: how I hated the modern choir stalls, the work of George Pace in his most angular and restless style; how I hated the four concrete supports which ruin Jacob Epstein's magnificent statue of Christ in majesty; most of all, how much I hated the cathedral organ, which was an awful mongrel of instruments. So, thinking of it being Christmas and how much I loved Breconshire, where sheep outnumbered people, I extemporised exceedingly badly on "While shepherds watched their flocks by night". Afterwards I talked with the Dean and his interviewing committee before setting off for home, hoping that if I got the job I would not have to stay for long. However, I need not have worried. No sooner had we arrived home than the telephone rang and the Dean of Llandaff told me that he had appointed Michael Smith, adding that had Michael not accepted the job then he would have appointed me. Moments later there was a second phone call, this time from Bishop Thomas inviting us to join him and "Betty Bish" at a Christmas party in Ely Tower. As we crossed the threshold of Ely Tower, he said to Hazel and me with a smile: "Welcome Home!"

XXXIII

The year 1974 opened with an event of national importance which was disastrous to Brecon – local government re-organisation. This was supposed to save money, but seemed to do the opposite. In mid-Wales it resulted in the three counties of Montgomeryshire, Radnorshire and Breconshire being lumped together to form one new and unwieldy county of Powys, with the result that to travel from Brecon to Bristol was a shorter journey than to travel from one end of the county to the other. In any case, it was a marriage of unlikely and unwilling partners, because the people of Montgomeryshire were more like North Walians while those of Breconshire were closer to South Walians. I could never understand either why the opportunity was not taken to move Ystradgynlais in the south-western tip of Breconshire into the Swansea Valley and South Glamorgan. As for the people of Radnorshire, stuck in the middle of these unlikely partners and like neither of them, they were a race apart with speaking voices that pointed to Herefordshire. Perhaps all that united the people of Powys were sheep and there were thousands upon thousands of them.

Two items on the amalgamation agenda interested me greatly. Firstly, the old Breconshire County Council was reputed to possess forty-seven snow-clearing vehicles and these had assured road users that, no matter how much snow fell, main roads in the county invariably remained passable. These vehicles now had to be shared among the three counties that formed Powys, so this safety could no longer be taken as a matter of course. Secondly, Montgomeryshire had been renowned for its school music and especially for its county youth orchestra. But instead of places in this orchestra being made available to musical pupils living in other parts of the new county, the orchestra was re-named "The North Powys Youth Orchestra" and remained a Montgomeryshire organisation, based at Newtown, the old county town of the area. The biggest blow to Brecon itself was its loss of County Town status. As Llandrindod Wells, the capital of Radnorshire, was sited in the very centre of the new county, it was obviously placed to become the strategic county town. David Verey in his Shell Guide to Mid Wales was as rude about Llandrindod Wells as he was about Builth Wells, stating that the town contains some "Ruabon red brick buildings of peculiar hideousness" and that it is "pretty dead now all the year round." Because of the large number of buildings suitable for providing hotel accommodation, all of red brick, he added: "Round every corner one expects to find the sea; but there is no sea, only rain." So this Victorian spa town had greatness thrust upon it, but from that moment onwards my daughter Harriet hated it, because it had usurped her beloved Brecon.

The reorganised three-tier system of local government put the county of Powys at the top with Brecknock Borough Council – the old Breconshire – next, leaving little for Brecon Town Council to do. As a result there was now a Mayor of Brecknock and a Mayor of Brecon, which was really rather confusing to anyone who did not know the difference between Brecon (town) and Brecknock (borough). On Sunday, March 31st 1974, a special service at Brecon Cathedral marked the last day of the Corporation of Brecon. Afterwards the Mayor and Mayoress of Brecon, Councillor and Mrs Tony Elston, held a reception in the Guildhall to emphasise the sadness of the occasion.

Yet the creation of Powys eliminated the anomaly of young people being educated only in a school situated within the county in which they lived, no matter how much the inconvenience. The Vicar of Clyro's son, for example, having passed the eleven-plus examination was subjected to a daily journey of twenty-six miles each way to attend Llandrindod Wells Grammar School in his county of Radnorshire, passing through Breconshire's Builth Wells on the way where he could have received the same education and saved himself seven of those miles. For pupils less able than the Vicar of Clyro's son, Radnorshire provided secondary modern education at Clyro Court, where there was an extraordinary school with less than one hundred pupils, yet only five miles away on the other side of the River Wye (and therefore in Breconshire) was a more viable secondary modern school at Gwernyfed with around three hundred pupils. Now the creation of Powys gave the young people of Clyro the chance to attend this school, or even to go on to Brecon High School, while Clyro Court school could be closed. Similarly, this is what had made possible the idea of moving Breconshire's pupils at Builth Wells Bilateral School into Radnorshire's Llandrindod Wells High School and Radnorshire's Rhayader pupils into an enlarged Llanidloes High School in Montgomeryshire. However, an economic crisis in Britain that soon followed put paid to that plan, with the result that my teaching job in Builth Wells remained secure.

While all this was going on, the Cathedral Choir broadcast another BBC Choral Evensong in which I took my championing of nineteenth-century Cathedral music a stage further by including the Revd. Sir Frederick Ouseley's Evening Service in B minor, that he had composed in the style of the seventeenth-century composer Benjamin Rogers, whose music was much admired by the Tractarians for its purity of style. However, it was not this that resulted in my receiving a flood of letters but the fact that the hymn "Abide with me, fast falls the eventide" was sung to a very lovely tune by S. S. Wesley, which was published in the Oxford Hymn Book but which no-one appeared to know. Hazel too was heard to good advantage on the radio and television at this time, both accompanying the Cathedral Choir for the radio Choral Evensong and the Treorchy Male Voice Choir for a television programme and giving a solo organ recital on BBC Radio Three. This recital moved our organ-builder friend Maurice Forsyth-Grant to write in a letter to Hazel:

> "Now I do know that you are a proficient Organist! I did enjoy your recital this morning, especially the Reger and the modern pieces. They came off very well."

Dear old Dr. Campbell, in the course of answering a letter containing our enquiries about his choir school at St. George's Chapel, Windsor, wrote in his own inimitable way:

> "How kind you people are in what you say – There was that Ian White playing viola d'amore here in J. S. B. St Matthew on April 5 and he too was so nice. I

most certainly listened to Hazel Davies who acquitted herself with flying colours in a very interesting programme. I once played the Soderholm in S'wark. The organ too sounded splendid: how clevah you all are."

Another recital which gave Hazel particular pleasure at this time was given before Evensong at St. John's College, Cambridge. Afterwards George Guest, the eminent College Organist and Choirmaster, wrote in a letter:

"Many thanks for a very fine recital; I heard a number of most flattering comments after you had gone."

By this time we were looking for a suitable choir school for Nicholas. We knew that in his heart of hearts he wanted to be a chorister at St. John's College, Cambridge, as he had enjoyed his time with the choristers when they had made their two visits to Brecon Cathedral, but to us that seemed to be reaching out for the moon. However, Hazel wrote to George Guest in her own inimitable hand-writing to ask him of the necessary requirements and in reply he wrote:

"Thank you very much for your long letter, the bulk of which I was able to decipher!
It is very difficult to know what to advise about Nicky, not having heard him do his stuff musically, but I shall be glad to do anything which you might feel to be helpful.
I should certainly advise you to write to Mr. Alan Mould, Headmaster of St. John's College School, about the academic questions which you raise. He has the whole thing at his fingertips and is, in addition, a very nice and helpful person. But I believe you will find that he will tell you that, at the age of 8, it does not greatly matter where a boy has been to school previously – but that it does over the age of 8. Meanwhile, I will send you what information I have on the school."

There was always the possibility that Nick might fail to get to St. John's, as the school was popular and the demand for scholarships was great, hence our letter to Dr. Campbell asking about the choir school at Windsor. For me the attraction there was Nicholas being with Dr. Campbell, but for how long? The great man must have been nearing the age of retirement and in his letter he had written:

"Impossible to say whether I shall be here or elsewhere on this earth in five years' time."

Did he know what we later learned, that there was a move afoot to ease him out from his job? He had done wonders with the choirboys but had achieved little with the Lay Clerks because so many of them were old and set in their ways and, having freehold of office, could not be removed. Apparently he himself was so unhappy that at the start of every term he had run away to Ely to spend a few days with his old pupil and assistant Arthur Wills and his wife, Arthur now being the Cathedral Organist there, to summon up strength to endure the new term. God moves in mysterious ways, however, for within a few weeks Dr. Campbell died in his sleep and we crossed St. George's off our list.

Next we went to Westminster Abbey, a favourite haunt of my childhood days when I had lived but a stone's throw away at Holy Trinity Vicarage. While we quickly struck up a rapport with the Headmaster of the Choir School and Nick fell in love with the roof-top soccer pitch which was encased in wire netting to prevent footballs from being despatched to various parts of the neighbourhood, the Organist, Dr. Douglas Guest, proved to be more elusive. This reminded us of our friends at Selby, John Barnett and Bruce Robinson, who had both been pupils at Uppingham School when he had been Director of Music there; they had told us how he had insisted on being addressed as "Major Guest". We went to Choral Evensong and then tried to see Dr. Guest, but he seemed not to be interested, so we crossed Westminster Abbey off our list.

One school half-term holiday, Hazel, Harriet, Nick and I went to Cambridge to take a good look at St. John's College Choir School. While there, we searched for a Choral Evensong on the Monday at King's College and St. John's College and found none, so we drove over the fens to Ely. On entering the Cathedral we were waylaid by a burly Verger who said gruffly: "There's Evensong now!" and we explained that we were there to join the congregation. It seemed very appropriate to worship in this stunning Cathedral where my great-uncle had been Organist some forty years before and where Dr. Campbell had begun his career as a Cathedral Organist. It was bitterly cold, so much so that the words of the service almost froze as they left the choristers' mouths. Indeed, the brains of the choristers may well have done just that, as they almost succeeded in capsizing the anthem, a routine one by Thomas Tallis – "O Lord, give thy Holy Spirit into our hearts", because when they came to start the second part, one side of the choir started before the other side and chaos reigned briefly until the Lay Clerks sang and order was restored. The next evening found us enjoying Evensong at King's College, Cambridge, with the choir singing the fiendishly difficult unaccompanied "Norwich" Service by John McCabe, very well too; however, when it came to the anthem, another routine one, Gibbons's "Almighty and Everlasting God", unaccountably some of the trebles slipped up in the final cadence. A brisk walk got us to St. John's College Chapel in time for Evensong, allowing us to hear this great choir sing as only it could, in its very distinctive style, yet for some reason the second set of responses began with the Choral Scholars on one side of the choir singing different music from the Choral Scholars on the other side. George Guest, directing the musical proceedings, did not look very happy! However, to an Organist and Choirmaster of a small country cathedral, this was all most reassuring, with all three premier division choirs, two of world renown, slipping up within the space of twenty-four hours.

Afterwards we set off for home. On the way, while driving through Northampton, trundling along in our Morris 1000 Traveller, I had a fleeting glimpse of a car shooting out from a side road on the right, then there was a mighty crash, the sound of jangled metal and broken glass; by the time we had come to a standstill the car was facing the wrong way with its shooting-brake doors forced open and our luggage strewn all over the road. As Hazel and I staggered out from our wrecked car, a man got out from his now-stationary car, blurting out "Thank

God you weren't a lorry, I might have been killed!" Hazel was not amused! What he had done was to put his foot by mistake on the accelerator instead of on the brake as he approached the main road, which meant that his car had been accelerating when it struck our car. What had frightened us afterwards was the realisation that had this happened two evenings before, when we were on our way to Cambridge with the back seats down so that Harriet and Nicholas could sleep in their sleeping bags, they too would have been thrown out of the car with our luggage. Needless to say, they never slept like that again in the car. Meanwhile, with John and Betty Barnett living nearby, we telephoned them and they came to our rescue as our Morris 1000 traveller was a write-off. Yet despite the accident spoiling the trip, our minds were made up: St. John's College, Cambridge it had to be and we took a chance in having no reserve school. Already Nick was learning to play the violin with me and the piano with Hazel; now, in addition, he started singing with Brecon Cathedral Choir. Normally I refused to take a boy into the Cathedral Choir if there was any hint of his going-off to a private school later, just when he was about to be useful to my choir, but Nick was family so an exception was made for him.

It was during this August that the Cathedral Choir was dragged home from its customary holiday to sing at the morning service on Sunday, August 11th, which was the sixth Annual Reunion of the Royal Regiment of Wales. There had to be a reason for this summons and it turned out to be the presence of a special guest. Amidst considerable security, Charles, Prince of Wales, attended Matins at the Cathedral. I had booked my trumpet-playing friends, led by Tony Small from the Gower, to enable the service to begin rather splendidly with Ralph Vaughan Williams's Coronation arrangement of The Old Hundredth, "All people that on earth do dwell" and later to hot up C. V. Stanford's *Te Deum* in B flat. As the anthem was Dr. Campbell's exuberant "Sing we merrily", the choir also had a good time. Afterwards Prince Charles came to talk with the choirboys in the Close, outside the Vestries, and chatted to Nick about his two front teeth which had recently gone missing. That afternoon, Evensong was sung by the Madley Festival Choir, which left the Cathedral Lay Clerks free to relax and play a cricket match against a team representing the Sergeants' Mess from the Barracks. The Lay Clerks were on a high after the service, but the soldiers were exhausted after having given lunch to all the Old Comrades and their guests, so the musicians won the game and the barrel of beer which was the agreed trophy.

By this time there was such an excellent spirit among the Lay Clerks that, as a result of a concert given in the Cathedral by Michigan's Music Youth International from Saline, Brecon's twin town in the U. S. A., they had decided to organise a return trip by Brecon Cathedral Choir. They had set about fund-raising with a vengeance, their target being £5,000, which was a considerable sum of money in those days. Led by John Evans, a bass, and Tonlas Evans, a tenor, who were not related but who both had moved to Brecon to work for the Ministry of Agriculture Advisory Service, they started by whipping up enthusiasm among the choirboys for collecting newspaper on Saturday mornings. Fifty tons was collected and initially it fetched £18 a ton until the bottom fell out of the market and the price dropped to £5 a ton, whereupon a lot of paper was left standing around in John's barn and Tonlas's cellar with no ready market available. Nevertheless, the Lay Clerks were equal to the situation and not short of ideas. Their ingenuity knew no bounds. They opened a shop in the centre of town in which they sold second-hand household articles, clothing and jewellery; they organised a fashion show, a garden fete, an autumn bazaar and a barbecue; they set up innumerable jumble sales and coffee mornings, not forgetting a barn dance, as there were plenty of barns in the area which John and Tonlas came into contact with in the course of their work. However, one item on the agenda had not been sorted out: the itinerary for the tour. They need not have worried as the Almighty appeared to have that under control. One Sunday morning after the Cathedral Service, the lay clerks gathered in The George Hotel for a lunchtime drink as was their wont. On this particular Sunday we were visited by Hazel's and my friends from Aberystwyth, Joy and Michael Cooke, who had lived for a few years in Canada. They in turn had brought with them two friends from Canada, Fred and Judy Pile and, believe it or not, at this very moment, Fred, seeking a career change, was setting up as a tour operator. Our trip became his first challenge and he responded by organising an eighteen-day tour for the choir which took in Toronto, Saline, Ann Arbor, Detroit, Washington, New York, Utica and the Niagara Falls. It was a fantastic proposition which could not have been bettered.

Meanwhile the Cathedral Singers had taken on a project of their own: learning to sing J. S. Bach's monumental "St. Matthew Passion". This was a tough proposition which resulted in eighteen months' hard labour and was achieved around the usual round of concerts and carol-singing jaunts. Morgan Lloyd had been over-joyed at the prospect of renewing acquaintance with this great work, as he had not played it for more than thirty years, To be sure of adequate preparation, an extra full rehearsal was arranged one Tuesday evening in the Church Hall at Pontardawe. I brought my singers down from Brecon in a bus, he brought his orchestra up from Swansea in cars and we spent a happy evening running through the choruses. The Performance in Brecon Cathedral on Holy Saturday, March 29th 1975, went off hap-pily, with Rogers Covey-Crump the usual faultless Evangelist, and my old friend Graham Sorrell from Southwark Cathedral days, now a Vicar-Choral at St. Paul's Cathedral, singing the part of Jesus. Of that historic performance, what always stands out in my mind is the picture of Morgan Lloyd contentedly playing the vio-lin solo in the lovely aria "Have Mercy Lord on Me", beautifully sung by talented local contralto Pauline Desch, with a cherubic smile on his face, looking as if he hadn't a care in the world. Sadly, however, this turned out to be his swan-song. On the following Saturday, as his orchestral players were preparing to rehearse "Messiah" with a local Swansea choir, someone asked: "Where's Morgan?" When they found him, he was sitting slumped over his violin case having suffered a stroke. The St. Matthew Passion that he had so dearly wanted to play had turned out to be the last major work that he ever did play.

This provided the cue for John Roberts, who by now had married and was liv-ing in Beaufort on the other side of the Llangynidr Mountain, close to the infamous "Heads of the Valley Road". For a long time he had helped me find orchestral players for the J. S. Bach cantatas, the Christmas music from Handel's "Messiah" or Vaugham Williams's "Fantasia on Christmas Carols", all of which had been performed in recent years at Choral Evensongs on Sunday afternoons during Advent. Very soon he was to lead the string trio needed for Joseph Haydn's "Missa Brevis de Sancti Joannis de Deo", the "Little Organ Mass", which was to be performed liturgically for the first time in Brecon on Whitsunday, May 18th, at the 11 a.m. Holy Eucharist. Indeed, so worried was I about the reception of an Orchestral Mass and Latin words that I duplicated a grovelling explanatory note for members of the congregation! Now John suggested that we start our own orchestra. So the Gwent Chamber Orchestra was born, so-named because rehearsals were held firstly at Nantyglo Comprehensive School where his wife Judith taught, then at Ebbw Vale Comprehensive School where he himself was Head of the Mathematics Department, both schools being in the new county of Gwent. Most of the founding members had played together in the National Youth Orchestra of Wales: John Roberts himself, with David Walker, a music student at University College Cardiff, and Phil Stokes, a peripatetic teacher from Gwent, played violins; John Watkins, Head of German at Blackwood Comprehensive School and Paul Jenkins, a BBC (Wales) Sound Engineer, played violas; Steve David and Frances Mason, peripatetic teachers in Gwent, played 'cellos. Because we wanted to give talented youngsters the chance to experience good orchestral music, we invited two schoolgirls to join us: Julia Watkins, who eventually was to play violin in the Philharmonia Orchestra, and Jane Tunley, who went on to play in the Opera North Orchestra and to marry the principal Horn player of the Hallé Orchestra! The new Gwent Chamber Orchestra made its debut in Brecon Cathedral on Saturday, June 21st, when it played the Elgar "Serenade" and Schubert's fifth symphony and accompanied the Cathedral Singers in Schubert's melodious "Mass in G".

Another "first" was on the horizon. In previous years I had helped on Royal School of Church Music residential courses at Lincoln Cathedral and St. David's College, Lampeter. Now I was offered the chance to run my own course at St. Elphin's School, Darley Dale in Derbyshire. The person who should have been in charge had suddenly become unavailable. I was therefore given the job and, furthermore, allowed to choose my own musical staff. As it was a girls course, with ages ranging from around nine to nineteen, I enlisted the aid of five highly-experienced school teachers who acted as Housemistresses. Obviously I asked Hazel, my wife, then our friend Penny Croke, who was now in the exalted position of Deputy Head at Morriston Senior Comprehensive School, and our former pupil from Builth Wells, Marian Thomas, who was now teaching music at the Bishop of Hereford Bluecoat School. From our Royal Academy of music days I also invited fellow student Valerie Dove, who as Mrs. Hill was now a very experienced Head of the Music Department at Chiswick School in London, along with the violinist of our Selby days, Sheila Pigott, who was a visiting tutor at Bretton Hall College and at Queen Elizabeth Grammar school in Wakefield. To these were added David Hatton of Brecon Cathedral Choir, who acted as Librarian; a delightful Irish lady called Mrs. Carberry, who worked at St. Elphin's School and who was great fun in her capacity as Course Matron; and Timothy Ganz, Chaplain to University College Swansea, who acted as Course Chaplain. (Interestingly, he came from an old Swansea family of clockmakers and jewellers; indeed an old "Ganz of Swansea" grandfather clock stands in the entrance hall of Bridgend House, Kidwelly.)

The five houses contained one hundred and twenty girls belonging to choirs ranging from Gateshead to Whitstable and from the Gower Coast to Bury St. Edmunds. Four houses contained the juniors, while one house contained the thirteen senior choristers who, fortunately, were led by our old friend Janet Morris from the choir of All Saints' Church, Oystermouth. Perhaps because she had experienced some of the Brecon Cathedral Choir trips and so knew well our ways, she appeared at the Staff Room door on the first night to ask if the seniors could all go out to a nearby public house. I consulted the Head Chorister, a seasoned RSCM campaigner from Grantham who knew all the rules and regulations and was determined that everyone should abide by them; she said a very definite "No"! However, after a quick consultation with the Housemistresses, Hazel and I ended up going out with the Senior Choristers to find a pub and a good time was had by all. By the next day we had also opened up the staff room to the seniors, again much to the disgust of the Head Chorister. Even she had to agree, reluctantly, that this contributed much to the good of the atmosphere, as staff and seniors began to pull together wonderfully well and everyone became more relaxed in their work.

Meanwhile the weather had become unbearably hot and as the Chapel (where all the rehearsals were held) was a funnel of a building, the atmosphere inside became so heavy that some of the younger choristers began to wilt. Immediately I dispensed with wearing robes and let the choristers wear light clothing instead. In so doing, I earned another black mark from the Head Chorister, as this had never been done before. Every day before lunch, a regulation half-hour was allocated to the younger choristers as a rest period when they had to lie down on their beds, yet none of them seemed to need this, so we did a little more singing. Similarly, one and a half hours were set aside in the early evening for instruction, but as far as I was concerned there were more practical ways of learning, so we did still more singing. To the credit of these one hundred and twenty choristers, they learned to sing all of the Benjamin Britten "Missa Brevis", some of Kenneth Leighton's "Easter Sequence", Herbert Sumsion's Evening Service in G, plus lots more music.

Finally, because of the calibre of the Senior Choristers, I enticed to Darley Dale some of the younger Brecon Cathedral Choir Lay Clerks and their friends who brought up sleeping bags and copies of the Orlando Gibbons "Short Service" and Joseph Haydn's "Little Organ Mass", plus two violins and a 'cello. So at eight o'clock on Sunday morning, instead of a Holy Eucharist, there was a fully choral Matins sung by a choir made up out of the staff, the Senior Choristers and the younger lay clerks of Brecon Cathedral. What an experience for the Senior Choristers to sing the Benedictus and Te Deum from the Gibbons "Short Service" in this way! At eleven, the entire course sang Benjamin Britten's *Missa Brevis* for the Holy Eucharist and at 6.30 p.m., everyone sang Sumsion in G for Evensong. So, on that day, Morning Prayer, Evening Prayer and the Holy Eucharist were all fully choral, which was an amazing achievement for this collection of choristers who had never worked together before. More was to follow, because on the evening of the next day, Monday, the final day of the course, the Senior Girls again joined with the staff and Lay Clerks to sing all but the Credo of Haydn's "Little Organ Mass" with a string trio; Penny Croke sang the solo *Benedictus* and Hazel supplied the organ solo which gave the Mass its name.

Spirits were high after this, but we were brought down to earth when late that night we discovered one of the Senior Choristers, a rather rough diamond with a heart of gold, not tucked up in bed as she should have been but sitting on the stairs at the top of the school, weeping. She sang in a church choir in Sheffield and loved her church music, but having had the time of her life for the past week and having glimpsed so much more, she did not want to return to her council estate and broken home. Hazel was marvellous with her and by the next morning had arranged for the girl to spend more of her holiday with us in Brecon and Kidwelly. So Shelagh Worthington entered our lives and became like an adopted daughter; but the Royal School of Church Music never again let me loose on one of its courses.

XXXIV

Shelagh came to Brecon for the following Christmas and the usual riotous time was had by all, even if we were just a little preoccupied. Nicholas's hour of reckoning had arrived, as the Voice Trials for the choir of St. John's College, Cambridge, were due to take place in the New Year, on Saturday January 3rd 1976. Hazel, Nick and I set off in our car on the day before, leaving Harriet in the care of friends. We drove across the Cotswolds, through Stow-on-the-Wold, past signposts pointing the way to Broadwell, where Grandma Middleton first saw the light of day, and on to Cambridge. When we arrived, we found our lodgings where we had booked Bed and Breakfast, settled in and then walked the city dreaming dreams and looking for somewhere to have supper. The night was stormy and near Trinity College we watched a corrugated iron sheet gently float down to the road having been blown from its moorings high up.

The next morning we rose bright and early, ate our breakfast and set off for the Voice Trials, which actually began with some mathematics and English tests. These were as important as the singing tests simply because, when boys came to the end of their time at the choir school some five years later, it was important for the prestige of the school that all the boys should win valuable scholarships to Public Schools for the next part of their education and this involved passing the Common Entrance examination in which mathematics and English featured prominently. After these tests came the singing tests, when Nick had to sing his hymn "Ye watchers and ye holy ones" and, more importantly, succeed at the difficult aural tests, the climax of which was to pick one note from a cluster of four and sing it correctly; that, for an eight-year-old boy, was a tall order.

There were as many as thirty-six candidates for six places, so it was fascinating meeting all the other boys and their parents. Some took it all in their stride and were pleasant and amiable company; some were tense and strung-up, said little and smiled even less; some did nothing other than discuss the achievements of their own offspring and compare the merits of other choir schools; one particularly obnoxious boy spent much of his time telling other boys which ones would number among his friends when he was at St. John's College School and his parents looked on proudly. By early afternoon, a short-list of twelve had been announced, which included Nick but not the boy who had been busily distributing friendships. The final round involved each of the twelve boys singing their solo with organ accompaniment. This turned out to be all the more intriguing, because it transpired that a few of the candidates experienced some difficulty in staying in tune with the organ, but here Nick had benefitted from his experiences of singing with Brecon Cathedral Choir and all went well. When the results were announced, Nick was "in", and wasn't he overjoyed! We telephoned Harriet and he began by telling her in mournful tones that he had been unsuccessful but suddenly, unable to contain himself any longer, he shouted gleefully down the telephone: "I've got one", referring to the six vacant choristerships. After the triumphal journey home, we had to keep him happy for a year until he could take up his place at St John's

College School next January, but at least there was the Cathedral Choir trip to Canada and the U. S. A. to distract him.

One sad event quite soon distracted Hazel and me: the imminent retirement of Bishop Thomas. This was exceedingly sorrowful to contemplate, as he had been such a support to matters musical in the Cathedral as well being such a good friend to us. He was a wise counsellor, as also was his wife. A few years before, when we had been trying to move into Garth Cottage amidst all the chaos of building works and the arguments over what could and could not be done, "Betty Bish" had said to Hazel: "My dear, don't you think of moving in until everything has been done for you; once you move in they will not do another thing for you." She had realised the problems that we had been having with the Dean and Chapter, not the least with the Chapter Clerk, and had taken our side. She said this forcibly, quite unlike the way her husband was wont to speak, for while he obviously adored her and loved her dearly, he was very much her opposite in his manner of speech, always gentle, purposeful and wise, with a quiet determination when necessary. Legend had it that Bishop Thomas's wisdom was well-founded, because he had always set aside up to two hours daily for reading. Certainly, his erudite sermons were proof of this, being more often than not models of their kind. Whomever I invited to preach at the Diocesan Choral Festival was always expected to call at Ely Tower to spend time talking with him. Canon David Rutter of Lincoln Cathedral was one who liked calling, because he too read widely and enjoyed learned discourses. Bishop Thomas and his wife Betty were certainly going to be greatly missed."Come and visit us, dear," Betty would say, and as they were retiring to Tenby, she would continue: "We shall be at Woodbine Cottage, close to the Parish Church, but do call it "Fag End"", Woodbines being the cheap and nasty cigarettes that many of my generation had smoked secretly under the cover of darkness in cinemas during our youth.

Not long after the departure of Bishop and Mrs. Thomas, one more sad event distracted Hazel and me still further: the death of dear old C. H. Trevor on June 16th 1976. In recent years we had come to know him so well and had visited him and his wife, Joan, regularly at their Highgate home, always taking them a leg of Welsh lamb from a local Brecon butcher, safe in the knowledge that they would appreciate this enormously. As Harriet and Nicholas increased in years, so he enjoyed their company all the more and on our last visit he had suddenly and quite unexpectedly begun producing coins from their hair. Only then did we discover that he had a great aptitude for performing conjuring tricks in addition to being a world-class organist. For the last fifteen years of his life he had kept the promise that he had made to his students and had given no organ recitals. Instead, he had spent many a day seated in the British Museum producing a succession of valuable, instructive books of organ music containing many exceedingly fine but unknown miniatures, always giving suggestions as to finding the right sound.

Hazel and I had made great use of these books and valued them exceedingly, with the result that when "C. H." approached his eightieth birthday, she had a brainwave. She persuaded BBC (Wales) to let her broadcast a recital on Radio Three as a tribute to him, playing pieces from these books on a small church organ to shows that this could be done satisfactorily and that a cathedral organ was not necessary for such music. The organ we chose for the recording was the historic

Thomas Warne organ of 1762 in St. Mary's Church, Kidwelly. It had recently been rebuilt by Percy Daniel & Co. Ltd of Clevedon, Avon. Grace Jones, the Organist and the Vicar, Douglas Walters, had successfully raised £5,000 for this work to be done, while Hazel and I had worked out the scheme of work with Percy Daniel & Co. Ltd. and it was a joy to hear the lovely unforced tone of this instrument. Fortunately C. H. Trevor lived long enough to hear this recital before he departed from this earthly life. How amused he would have been had he known that, when Hazel recorded the programme, the R.A.F. had decided on a gunnery practice nearby at the same time. So it became essential for Hazel to start recording an item while the jet was turning around to start its fly-in over Kidwelly so that the organ music could cover the sound of the plane screaming across the nearby Burry Port estuary on its way to firing its guns at its target on the Gower coast before turning around to start all over again.

A musician of C. H. Trevor's standing deserved an obituary in The Times newspaper, but I waited in vain for one to appear. In the end I picked up my pen, wrote one myself and sent it to the Editor; to my amazement it was published. It read:

"The death occurred on June 16 of the organist Caleb Henry Trevor. C. H. Trevor was born at Much Wenlock, Salop, in 1895. He was organist at St. Paul's Cathedral, Calcutta, sub-organist at Wells Cathedral, director of music at Sherborne School, organist at St. Peter's, Eaton Square and, finally, organist to the Honourable Society of Lincoln's Inn. For many years he was Professor of Organ at the Royal Academy of Music.

C. H. Trevor was a fine recitalist. Although he specialised in early music, it was his series of five broadcast recitals in 1935 which attracted attention in Britain to the organ music of Max Reger. In that year he was recitalist at the Brussels Exhibition. His recital to the International Congress of Organists at St. Sepulchre's, Holborn, in 1957, was widely acclaimed. C. H. Trevor was a great teacher, numbering among his pupils some who have reached the top of their profession. Perhaps his methods were somewhat ruthless as he insisted on points simple, obvious but not always acceptable to many organists – correct notes and correct rhythms, pouring scorn on flamboyant mannerisms found in many second-rate organists."Don't play like an organist," he would tell pupils, "play like a musician."

Nearing the age of 65 he stopped giving recitals. Instead he began to produce a large number of fine books of organ music suitable for both amateur and professional organists. Through these and his recently-published 'Organ Music for Beginners' he has done much to revolutionize the organists' repertoire, something which badly needed doing. Always impeccable in appearance and in what in old-fashioned terms is called manners, his gruff exterior belied a heart of gold. He is survived by his wife and by one son – his grandchildren will doubtless miss his endearing conjuring tricks!"

Hazel and I had written to Mrs. Trevor to express our sorrow at this inevitable but unexpected event. She in turn had explained how C. H. had spent the last two weeks of his earthly life in a hospital bed with leg and feet pains caused by circulatory problems. She also said how much he had appreciated Hazel's broadcast recital and how he had asked her to give some of his books to former pupils. He had earmarked for us John Klein's "The First Four Centuries of Music for Organ". Two weeks later she wrote again: "I am anxious to know if it was you who sent the excellent appreciation to "The Times". It seemed like you and there can't be many people who knew about the conjuring tricks. Many people have said how much they liked it." Naturally I owned up and back came a card: "I thought I guessed right! I am so pleased that you took the initiative about the Times." In answer to my comment that I had only done this because I was cross that no-one had bothered, she wrote: "It does seem rather odd that it didn't occur to anyone else." She added: "Your saying you got cross makes me think of your grandmother, who used the word "vexed" a good deal - influenced by Holy Writ, I expect."

There was yet a third event to distract me that year before the Cathedral Choir set off for Canada and the U.S.A ... That occurred at Builth Wells Bilateral School, which by now had become Builth Wells County Secondary School. I had already begun planning a production of Gilbert and Sullivan's "H. M. S. Pinafore" when I was called into the Headmaster's office to be told unexpectedly that this was not to be. Mr. Davies went on to explain sadly that this wife had been diagnosed as suffering with cancer. He therefore did not feel able to give me his full support as he might be called away at any moment to help at home. This saddened me also, because Mrs. Davies was the most lovely lady, with beautiful complexion and such kindness. Indeed, I had never heard her speak ill of anyone. Utterly devoted to her husband and her two sons, both of whom had taken part in my Gilbert and Sullivan operas at school, she supported them in all that they did. In their home there was no television, but there was regular attendance at Horeb Chapel and full attention to school work. The boys may have been the Headmaster's sons, but I admired them for the way in which they maintained popularity among the other pupils without compromising their loyalty to their father. The older brother did what no pupil of the school had done before and became a student at Cambridge University. Allowed to live his own life at last, he returned home for the Christmas holiday after his first term with hair down to his waist, wearing a hippy-style long coat, much to the distress of his father. His loving mother, however, kept the peace at home and carried her husband through his humiliation, after all that he had stood for, preached about and insisted on at school, knowing also that certain members of the school staff who lived in the same small community were only too happy for a weakness to appear in the Davies family's moral armour. J. Ewart Davies was going to miss his wife dreadfully; it was the beginning of the end of his reign at the school.

The final weeks before the long-awaited trip took off were spent in getting passports sorted out and visas collected from the American Embassy in London. We also learnt to sing some folk songs to add to our repertoire of Cathedral Music. Eventually on the evening of Tuesday October 12th 1976 the Cathedral choristers left Brecon and made for Gatwick Airport, staying the night in a hotel nearby. The party did not consist of the Cathedral Choir alone but included some parents who came along to look after the youngsters and help them overcome homesickness. In the event, the only person to suffer from this complaint was one of the mothers! Among the party of eighty-two people were the Mayor and Mayoress of Brecon (Councillor and Mrs. Denzil Griffiths), some of the town and borough councillors including Tony Elston and his wife Liz, a former Mayor and Mayoress of Brecon, not forgetting Brecknock Borough Secretary, Franklyn Jones, and his wife Evelyn (who were great supporters of our music) as well as the Chief Reporter from the

Brecon and Radnor Express, John Augustus, and his wife Marilyn. Much amusement was caused by the Canon in Residence for October at the Cathedral, my friend Owain Jones, Vicar of Builth Wells, who decided to complete his statutory month's residence by accompanying the choristers to Canada and the U. S. A., bringing with him his wife Margaret. Being a good Rotarian, the Canon provided a useful link with Rotary Clubs as wherever we went, he dined with Rotarians.

Early on Wednesday morning, October 13th, the party left the hotel and arrived at Gatwick Airport at 9 a.m., flying off at 12 noon, safely ensconced in a 180-seater Boeing 707 belonging to Wardair, a small Canadian company which had the distinction of providing free drinks as well as the customary free refreshments. Flying over Greenland, the choristers gathered together to sing folk songs to the other passengers. At 7.30 p.m. British time, 2.30 p.m. Canadian time, we arrived at Toronto airport. Strangely, as our luggage was unloaded we ran into difficulties with the airport authorities, who for some reason tried to impound our music. Maybe they thought we were going to sell it! When finally we retrieved it, we set off in two buses for St. James' Cathedral, where we attended Choral Evensong sung by the resident choir. Afterwards everyone was introduced to their hosts and dispersed to their homestays. By chance, Hazel and I stayed at the home of an old fellow chorister of Southwark Cathedral, Anthony Sanguine, who sang alto in St. James' Cathedral Choir and who with his wife made us very welcome. As Anthony had been living in Canada for some fifteen years, we had a lot of catching up to do and talked well into the night.

Our first full day in Toronto found the choir rehearsing in St. James' Cathedral in the morning; afterwards we walked into a "Tom Jones Tavern" nearby, but beer was expensive. Later that day we discovered just how large a city Toronto is, as we travelled by subway (underground train) into a city suburb where lived the Toronto Welsh community. First we rehearsed in their Eglwys Dewi Sant (St. David's Church), then we were given supper and in return gave a concert - only forty-eight hours after leaving Brecon. However, this was the first of the few occasions when we sang to audiences made up predominantly of Welsh exiles. Such people expected rather more emotional renderings of Welsh hymns and arias than we were prepared to give, as our speciality was disciplined Anglican Cathedral Music, which must have come to them as something of a cultural shock, being so different.

The next day, Friday, started with a free morning, when many of the party inspected what Toronto had to offer in the way of shopping. Afterwards, the choristers rehearsed in St. Paul's Church, Bloor Street, where they were to give a concert later that day. This church is enormous. It is reputed to be the largest in Canada and to have the same floor area as Westminster Abbey. The organ is also massive, having not only two thirty-two feet pedal stops but also boasting four manuals (keyboards), a floating tuba stop and stops for chimes and a harp. We had taken with us on our tour an excellent string quartet: Julia Watkins and Jane Tunley, the two young violinists in the Gwent Chamber Orchestra, along with Tony and Liz Elston's son Chris, who was studying the viola at London's Guildhall School of Music, and Andrew Healey, a 'cellist from the Royal Academy of Music. This enabled us to give as authentic as possible performances of verse anthems by Henry Purcell and his teacher Pelham Humfrey to add interest to our programmes.

The choir was amazed when six hundred people graced the church for their concert but here, unlike the concert on the previous evening, the inclusion of an occasional rousing Welsh hymn added icing to the cake for an audience that was expecting nothing but Anglican Cathedral Music.

Saturday was full of surprises. At lunchtime the choristers assembled at St. James' Cathedral to rehearse, as at two o'clock they were to sing at the wedding of Fred and Judy Pile's daughter, Kathryn. During the signing of the register, the choir sang S. S. Wesley's exquisite anthem "Thou wilt keep him in perfect peace", while for the nuptial mass they sang the *Kyrie* and *Gloria* from Joseph Haydn's exuberant "Little Organ Mass" and the *Sanctus, Benedictus* and *Agnus Dei* from G. P. da Palestrina's sublime *Missa Aeterna Christi Munera*. It was a lovely occasion, followed by a gorgeous reception at the nearby Harbour Castle Hotel. Afterwards, in the evening, everyone attended an ice-hockey game, when the Toronto Maple Leafs played a team from Philadelphia at Maple Leafs Gardens. One player set a club record by scoring three times in two-and-a-half minutes. Added entertainment was provided by two players who had a fight during the game and adorned the ice with their blood, not to mention an organist who, whenever there was a lull in the proceedings, chimed in with some appropriate music on a loud electronic organ. It was great!

The next day, Sunday, was our last in Toronto. At eleven o'clock we sang at the Holy Eucharist in St. James' Cathedral, then had lunch in the crypt. Afterwards we made our fond farewells, boarded two Greyhound buses and set off for Saline. As we travelled through the suburbs of the city, our curiosity was aroused by a propeller aeroplane flying low. Closer inspection revealed that it was trailing behind it a long banner bearing a message which read something like: "Good-bye Brecon Cathedral Choir, Thank You and Good Luck"! By 6.30 p.m. the buses were crossing the border from Canada into the U. S. A. and by 8 p.m. they arrived at Saline, Brecon's twin town in the state of Michigan, where we were greeted by the local High School Band, a Flag Raising Ceremony and a crowd of people.

If our time in Toronto had bordered on the hectic, our time in Saline was the opposite: very relaxed and laid back. Much was accomplished, but at such a leisurely pace that the locals coined a phrase "Brecon Time", which meant anything up to an hour late. We visited a farm and compared farming methods; we toured the local hospital; as for the local High School, that was a revelation, especially for me to discover in the Music Department a room set aside for choir practices with tiered seating for the singers and another room for band practices. Such luxuries were unknown to me at Builth Wells High School, where I did not even have an official Music Room. More surprises were in store for us at this school: a fully equipped library staffed by a full-time librarian, a luxury which also had yet to reach our part of Wales, and an incredible indoor sports arena complete with running track, football pitch and tiered seating which could be pulled down from the ceiling. I was gobsmacked, all the more so when I discovered that the pupils were locked into the building from the moment they arrived in the morning to the moment they left in the afternoon, because if they were let out at the mid-morning break or at lunchtime, some would, as likely as not, disappear into the horizon.

The choir and some of the parents gave a concert to the town in the enormous, well-equipped theatre that was another of the school's amenities, singing both religious music and folk songs. I had included among our musicians a pupil of Builth Wells High School who went on to become a family friend, young Eleri Davies from Llanwrtyd Wells; she now earned her keep by contributing to the programme some solo songs which she sang in Welsh to her own expert guitar accompaniments. Further Welsh flavour was added by the sight of young Harriet Gedge and Hilary, daughter of Tonlas and Nerys Evans, parading around dressed in traditional Welsh costume, right up to the black stove-pipe hat.

Later in the week the townspeople entertained us to a sumptuous banquet at which there were copious speeches. We were given many gifts, including a Michigan State Flag that is now framed and hangs on the wall of the Cathedral Choir Room back at Brecon. Meanwhile, Brecon's civic party also made its contribution to the visit by attending a Saline City Council meeting, at which there was a warm exchange of greetings and gifts. Particular amusement was caused by the Mayor of Brecon when he presented to Saline's Police Chief a British policeman's helmet, a set of handcuffs used in Wales at the turn of the century, a photograph of the Brecon Constabulary taken in 1911, and a Brecon police whistle.

However, the most extraordinary event in Saline was the takeover of Big Daddy's Den, the town's nearest equivalent to Brecon's "George Hotel", a saloon bar and dining room. Mine host, Larry, found his premises taken over by a Welsh invasion which the locals found hard to understand, as most social drinking in the U.S.A. is done at home, as indeed initially it had been that week, with countless homes hosting cocktail parties. However, by the end of our time in Saline the Brecon invaders had enticed many of their hosts into Big Daddy's Den, where the atmosphere was tremendous and the electronic organ was put to excellent use accompanying the singing of folk songs and, inevitably, Welsh hymns, "Blaenwern", "Calon Lân" and "Cwm Rhondda" becoming great favourites.

While at Saline, the Cathedral Choir gave a concert at St. Andrew's Church in the city of Ann Arbor, home of Michigan's enormous state university. There Hazel and I met Marilyn Mason, the famous organist whose playing I had much admired at the International Congress of Organists in London back in 1957. While discussing matters ecclesiastical, she told us a story which I still find hard to believe. Apparently, someone donated a small chalice to the First United Church of Kentucky, Maine, but as there was not enough room to engrave the church's name on the chalice, the first letter of each of the principal words was used. When the letters "ME", the abbreviation for Maine, were added, the result was unfortunate and far from ecclesiastical!

During our week in Saline the choristers also spent a fascinating day in nearby Detroit, visiting Greenfield Village and the Henry Ford Museum, where we enjoyed a special Bicentennial exhibition to mark the two-hundredth anniversary of the British being thrown out of the U.S.A ... At this museum also I shed a tear for an Antonio Stradivarius violin which was marooned inside a glass case, never to make glorious music. Our day continued with a visit to the famous Ford Motor Car plant and ended with the choristers singing a particularly eventful Evensong in St. Paul's Cathedral. The Dean was a Liverpudlian Welshman of great character, who revelled in the distinction of having been mugged inside his own cathedral. A fount of fascinating stories, he told us how at Choral Eucharist one Sunday morning the collection had been taken as usual by the sidesmen, who then passed the contents of their offertory plates back to the two sidesmen at the far end of the line so that they could process with the money to the High Altar. However, rather than do this, the two sidesmen turned about and walked straight through the West Door and out of the Cathedral, disappearing into the city with the proceeds: far from being sidesmen, they had turned out to be local villains who had infiltrated the ranks of the sidesmen. So the choristers were warned not to stray away from the Cathedral for fear of being mugged and this was not an exaggerated warning. Later, while some members of our civic party were enjoying a quiet smoke outside, when the choir was rehearsing, they were approached by an elderly lady who asked if they would walk her home, as she was afraid of making the short journey alone. Our rehearsal had been enlivened by Hazel who, when accompanying Ralph Vaughan Williams's anthem "O how amiable are thy dwellings", pressed a piston to bring out more stops and make more noise, only to find that, while stops did come out, the resulting noise actually became quieter. At this the resident Cathedral Organist, standing alongside, roared with laughter and explained kindly that, as the organ was incomplete, "some stops were for show while others were for blow."

I was fascinated by the fact that this organist was paid an annual salary of $19,000 (approximately £10,000) for producing the music at just one choral service each week, on a Sunday morning. Apparently, Evensong had not been sung in the Cathedral for around three years because the choir did not consider that the size of the congregation warranted their turning-out to sing it. So much for "When two or three are gathered together, there am I in the midst"! However, our choristers were only too happy to sing Evensong in St. Paul's Cathedral, Detroit, especially as it was to be of the solemn variety, with vast quantities of incense pervading the atmosphere. The Dean, too, was excited at the prospect of this service, so on we went with our practice. However, when Choral Evensong began that night, the Dean was nowhere to be seen. I was puzzled, until during the singing of Psalm 121, I spied him lying stretched-out on the chancel floor, filming the service with his video camera! During the office hymn, an aged, wizened-looking thurifer, wearing a black skull-cap, entered alongside his boat-boy, and in no time "the house was filled with smoke" – a considerable amount of smoke indeed, which added to the difficulties of singing unaccompanied the twenty-eight intricate pages of Thomas Weelkes's *Eighth Service*. However, the choristers survived and went on to complete a lovely Evensong by singing the entire "Ascribe unto the Lord" by S. S. Wesley. The atmosphere was magical. When the final voluntary had ended and I was clearing up, I suddenly noticed someone taking down a microphone and from him I learned that, unknown to me, Choral Evensong had been recorded by Radio Detroit and was to be broadcast on the next morning!

Inevitably our time at Saline drew to a close and early on the Saturday morning there were many fond farewell and few dry eyes. Our departure could not be delayed for an instant, however, as we had to travel five hundred and fifty miles before the day was out. Our two buses were to drive us along the Ohio and Pennsylvania turnpikes to Oxon Hill on the outskirts of Washington, travelling at no time more than fifty-five miles-per-hour. It was a long and tiring drive, compensated by the scenery, especially the trees and the bright changing colours of their countless leaves which, with the chill in the air, left us in no doubt that the time of year aptly called by Americans "The Fall" had arrived. Late that evening we drove into Oxon Hill, but there was little time to socialise as we had an early start the next morning. Wisely, Fred Pile had arranged for us to set off at 8 a.m., allowing an extra hour to reach Washington Cathedral, because our bus drivers became hopelessly lost. While the magnificent, gleaming white, stone building stood like a beacon at the top of a high hill in this great city, they couldn't get us there until minutes before we were due to sing the Prelude at 10.30 a. m … It became rather a panic as we rushed into the Cathedral, robed, lined up and processed into that glorious building which was so much a replica of Canterbury Cathedral but for the unfinished West Towers. Indeed, the great Nave had only been completed that year, 1976.

As we took up our positions on the chancel steps, we were not only immediately mesmerised by the gleaming white, pristine condition of the wonderful stonework, but we were also overawed to see more that two thousand people, so we were reliably informed, sitting in preparation for the service which followed our Prelude. One of my tenor Lay Clerks, Maurice Parry, still occasionally wakes up at night in a cold sweat remembering this moment. Oh that the bus drivers had done their job properly that morning and arrived in time for the choristers to get mentally prepared for their singing! Our programme consisted of three of the loveliest examples of Tudor Church Music, starting with "*Ave Maria*" by Robert Parsons. We continued with the Lay Clerks singing the first part of Thomas Tallis's "Lamentations" and ended with William Byrd's sublime "*Sacerdotes Domini*". We did not do justice to this great music and I was left hoping that the aura of the building and the uniqueness of the occasion may have taken people's minds away from the imperfections of our offering.

Choral Eucharist followed, sung by the resident Cathedral Choir, which is one of the few American cathedrals to have a choir school. To this service, Brecon Cathedral Choir contributed two more sixteenth-century motets at the Offertory: the famous, anonymous "Rejoice in the Lord alway" and Adrian Batten's "O praise the Lord". Having by now settled into the proceedings these performances went along much more happily. Afterwards we had time to admire the interior of the Cathedral, whereupon the youngsters were taken to a Roy Rogers Fast Food Restaurant. To the older members of the party, Roy Rogers was a childhood cowboy hero who rode a horse called Trigger, so when one of the choristers consequently asked for a "Triggerburger", his request met with a frosty reception. The Lay Clerks and those wives who had come with us, however, had been taken in tow by two of the Washington Cathedral Lay Clerks, who seemed anxious to please. We found out why when they produced copies of our record "*Praise the Lord*", which we were all asked to sign. They remained kindness itself and took us all to a local bar for lunch, where for two hours we ate, drank and swapped stories about Cathedral Music in Britain and the U. S. A.

Afterwards, back on the buses, we toured Washington, passing by an area where statistics indicated a regular weekend tally of twenty-five murders before returning to Oxon Hill. I never did discover the full story of what happened next. The Vicar was a rebel priest and a firebrand with whom I got on famously, yet who reduced Judy Pile to tears in a dispute with Fred, about what I do not know, while our two friendly Washington Cathedral Lay Clerks threatened to report him to the Bishop over something that happened that evening. I remember that he had re-written various of the American Prayer Book services, because he gave me copies of these to take home to study.

We pushed our luck to a certain extent at Evensong when, rather than use an electronic organ donated by a local worthy, we chose instead to coax into life an old nineteenth-century chamber organ. With this instrument, what could be better than to sing the Evening Canticles to the doleful music of Daniel Purcell, brother of the more famous Henry Purcell? We continued with other suitable musical offerings and, if my memory serves me correctly, finished by singing some folk songs and Welsh hymns, which the congregation loved. Afterwards there was a "Pot Luck Supper", followed by various parties around the parish, especially at the home of the Church Organist, Peter Ulrich, where Hazel, Harriet, Nick and I stayed. He and his wife had taken out a second mortgage so that they could grace their home with a large electronic organ, and as a result some of the choristers who had stopped by with their hosts regaled them with more music until well into the night.

The next morning a large number of bleary-eyed choristers settled down in the buses to sleep through a return journey to Washington, where we toured the Capitol and had a group photograph taken outside it, before setting off for New York. The visit to New York passed like a dream. We saw so much in so short a time. For the youngsters to stay in a huge city hotel was paradise itself as they raced around long corridors and played in express lifts. One young lad even celebrated his sixteenth birthday there, but was decidedly ill on the next day. To see this great city and its huge skyscrapers from a boat in Manhattan Harbour was breath-taking, reminiscent of the opening of the film "West Side Story", but to experience the hustle and bustle of its life from the streets was even more exhilarating, although the occasional presence of a real live beggar sitting morosely on the sidewalks did provide an occasional dampener. St. John the Divine Cathedral was, and still is, fantastic. Six hundred and one feet in length, it is the largest Gothic Cathedral in the world, so extensive that it takes a guide book of two hundred and thirty pages to do it justice. The width of the great West Front alone equals the entire length of Brecon Cathedral and its nave roof is one hundred and seventy-seven feet from ground level. Only the entire expanse of St. Peter's, Rome, is larger, while its ground area is two-and-a-half times that of Westminster Abbey.

The Organist, David Pizarro, was a larger-than-life character. The main Cathedral Organ at which he presided was a magnificent creation. As he demonstrated it to us, he played a fanfare on a state-trumpet stop situated at the far end of the Cathedral and Jim Morris, father of one of the young Lay Clerks, who was selling Brecon memorabilia beneath these pipes, dropped everything in a state of shock! When the choristers sang Evensong along with the St. John the Divine choirboys, we set off at a good speed in singing a hymn to the famous Welsh tune *Hyfrydol*, only to be hauled back by David Pizarro playing the melody on one of the many loud solo trumpet stops in order to dominate the proceedings, with a broad grin on his bearded face as he did so. Despite Choral Evensong being advertised in various New York daily papers and being attended by many of the New York Welsh community, the congregation was small. That was hardly surprising, however, as the Cathedral is surrounded by the slums of Harlem and muggings were commonplace. Indeed, only recently had one of the St. John the Divine Lay Clerks been relieved of his wallet as he walked through Cathedral grounds to attend a choir practice. Naturally, the neighbourhood had seen better days and David Pizarro kept us enthralled by his stories of the past. The best concerned a certain Cathedral cleric of dubious sexual orientation, who instituted the Kiss of Peace at the Holy Eucharist one Sunday; when he turned to kiss the server on his left, the gentleman in question took one step backwards and gesticulated towards his fellow server on the other side, saying, "Not me, buddy: try him." Among the other sights that we were taken to in New York was the United Nations building and we earned the distinction of being the first choir to sing in it, while Harriet and Hilary Evans dressed in their Welsh costumes again became objects of curiosity.

We left New York at 8.30 on Wednesday morning and spent much of the day driving through New York State to Utica, arriving there early in the evening. We were entertained to supper by the local St. David's Society in a hall attached to a chapel where services had been conducted through the medium of Welsh until barely fifty years before. A short drive took us to a comfortable motel at nearby Rome where we were to spend our last two nights in the U. S. A ... Next morning we returned to Utica, the home of the first-ever Woolworth's store and also of the famous Utica Club Brewery, which many toured, as this provided the opportunity to stock up with cans of beer for the evening's entertainment. Grace Church, where the choir was to sing Evensong that night, was very mindful of its musical traditional, its boys choir being only the second to be formed in the U. S. A ... I was given a one-hundred-and-thirty page hardbound book telling the history of this church, which made fascinating reading. Inside the building was a monster of a pipe organ, built in a French style, with a *trompette en chamade* and, believe it or not, a sixty-four-foot pedal *bombarde* that had pipes only for the bottom four notes, C, C sharp, D and D sharp, along with a silver stop knob! A "must" that night was for the choristers to sing the famous setting of the *Magnificat* and *Nunc Dimittis* in D minor by Thomas Attwood Walmisley, because the words "For he that is mighty" are prefaced by a solitary note D at the bottom of the organ pedals: with this stop available, the note could be mighty indeed – and it was! This service was the last music of the tour, and that pedal D provided the highlight.

Afterwards we returned to the motel at Rome and partied through the night. Early in the morning, the first snow of that autumn fell and the last sight I saw through my bedroom window before falling asleep was one of the young Lay Clerks prancing around in this snow wearing only his underpants! At a more respectable hour we dragged ourselves and our luggage onto the Greyhound buses for the last time. Early in the afternoon we were tipped out to experience the fantastic Niagara Falls. The next stop was then Toronto Airport, where we said our thanks and good-byes to our two bus drivers and to Fred and Judy Pile. Our plane left at 9 p.m., which was 2 a.m. British time. Propelled along even faster than normal by a following wind, we were flying over Brecon by around 7.30 a.m., shortly before landing at Gatwick Airport. By mid-afternoon we were back home with countless stories to tell, but desperate for sleep.

Over the next few weeks there was a considerable exchange of letters between

Wales, Canada and the U. S. A ... Among those that I received was a kind letter from Richard W. Dirksen, Musician-in-Residence at Washington Cathedral, thanking the choir for its "excellent singing" on Sunday morning (October 24th), ending with: "I did hear some of your prelude and it was most lovely", although I myself still wasn't so sure about that. Another letter, from Canon G. Alexander Miller of St. Andrew's Episcopal Church, Ann Arbor, stated that the Cathedral Choir's visit had been "a very great treat". David Pizarro wrote to say how he was overwhelmed by what music was produced at Brecon Cathedral "with such limited resources and so little funding". Nicest of all came from Carl Zwinck of Ann Arbor, who had taken a great interest in our trip to the extent that he had given some help with making arrangements. He wrote to say that he had "never had a group on tour which left behind a better impression," adding: "Not only was the music appreciated but the people also." He ended with: "Your group made a better impression on their hosts than any other foreign group I have had in the U. S. A.".

Meanwhile, it was back to work as usual and at Builth Wells High School the annual Christmas Carol service sadly became a farewell to the Headmaster, J. Ewart Davies, who had decided to devote himself to nursing his wife to her grave. I gave him a special send-off by including Advent and Christmas music from Handel's "Messiah", with a small string ensemble and soloists. Among the soloists was a male alto from the Cathedral Choir, Dudley Palmer, who created something of a sensation, because I had forgotten that Builth Wells had not experienced this type of voice before. Indeed, the Headmaster himself was quite amused by the comments generated by the performance. The next day he wrote to me:

> "Dear Mr. Gedge, [he never called any of his staff by their Christian name]
>
> Thank you very much for a delightful "send-off". By a strange coincidence when I first came to Builth in 1956, I attended in the July of that year a performance of "The Messiah" when the late Mr. George Bradley conducted the Builth Wells Choral Society accompanied by a section of the B.B.C. orchestra. Last night 3 of his children were in your choir + one granddaughter. And again it was The Messiah.
>
> And what a wonderful performance. Had I been allowed (and I was not as you well know) to plan my own departure from this post I could not have thought of a better programme.
>
> Please express my gratitude and that of my wife to our friends from Brecon who came along last night to help the school ...
>
> And my thanks to your wife – my wife never fails but admire her.
> Yours sincerely,
> J. Ewart Davies.

And so ended an eventful year.

XXXV

On Sunday, January 9th, 1977, Nicholas started at St. John's College School, Cambridge. That lunch-time Hazel, Harriet, Nick and I all ate with the Cathedral Lay Clerks in the George Hotel after Choral Eucharist, whereupon Nick was photographed standing outside the main door, resplendent in his new school uniform: red cap, red blazer, white shirt, red tie, grey short trousers, grey socks with a red band at the top and black shoes. Off we then went in our car, experimenting with what became a well-tried and much-loved route from Brecon through the centre of England to Cambridge, our main object being to avoid large towns and busy roads. Leaving by the A470, which after six miles or so became the A438 we made for Hereford and Ledbury, arriving at Tewkesbury where we joined the B4077 shortly afterwards at Toddington. This took us on to lovely Stow-on-the-Wold, then Chipping Norton, from where we transferred briefly onto the A363 and turned right onto the B4031, which wound its way through the Oxfordshire villages of Hempton and Clifton, past a lovely old pub called the Duke of Cumberland which eventually became our regular eating and watering hole. Next came the villages of Aynho and Broughton where we joined the A421 to Buckingham (which was soon given a welcome time-saving by-pass).

Continuing on to Milton Keynes (eventually, we found a way around this monstrosity) and then down the A5 for a short way, past the Brickhills with their tall chimneys and distinctive smell, we soon turned left down a narrow, windy lane that took us briefly through a wood and out into Woburn with its attractive antique shops. On we drove, skirting the Duke of Bedford's famous estate, down the A4012 to Husborne Crawley, down the A507 to Ridgmont, then Ampthill and so on to Shefford, where a bridge carried us over the River Hit, although the road sign announcing this inevitably carried an additional letter "S" added by some local street-artist. Henlow followed, where the A6001 took us through another Clifton and across the A1, which was often like dicing with death, so fast, furious and heavy could be the traffic. Once safely on the other side, the B1063 directed us through Edworth and Eyeworth, with the graceful spire of Ashwell Church dominating the skyline on our right, then through Tadlow, past Wendy, across the A1198 and on to the A503. The end was nigh now as this took us through Orwell, past some University telescopes and into Cambridge itself, a total of some 185 miles that eventually we regularly accomplished in four-and-a-quarter hours, including our stop at the Duke of Cumberland. So much of this journey was through lovely countryside that we never tired of it, although on many a Saturday night we were tired by it.

Our initial mistake, however, was to listen to a friend who said: "Don't visit Nick for three weeks," because after we had left him on that Sunday evening, excitedly playing snooker at the school, the realisation that he was on his own suddenly hit him and he cried daily for those three weeks. Yet he knew that he wanted to be there. After this we visited him regularly on alternate Saturdays and all of us eventually became as "happy as sandboys". He grew to love his school and singing with the College Choir in the College Chapel, we grew to love Cambridge and experiencing Choral Evensong, not forgetting the joy of spending time with him.

Soon there developed a regular routine: leaving Brecon at five in the morning, arriving at Cambridge at around 9.30 when Hazel, Harriet and I would enjoy wandering around the lovely shops, especially those of the large departmental variety which we did not have in Brecon. At around 12 noon we would collect Nick from school in Grange Road and take him to a Berni Inn for lunch before driving out to somewhere like Ely or Saffron Walden. There we would have tea and return him to school in time for the choir practice before Evensong. At this point in the proceedings and unknown to him, we often took up a hidden vantage point to watch the "crocodile" of St. John's College Choirboys walk in a double line, shepherded by the Head Chorister, from the school, across the playing fields, through the College gardens to the Backs, over the Bridge of Sighs that spanned the sometimes smelly River Cam, into St. John's College and on to the Choir's Practice Room by the College Chapel. Dressed in their flowing black cloaks and wearing their mortar boards, the sixteen full Choristers and the four Probationary Choristers presented a wondrous sight resembling a vision from the past, especially on a dark and misty autumnal evening, much photographed by foreign tourists. Choral Evensong was always a disciplined and dignified affair, following to a word the Book of Common Prayer with no emotion. Beautiful music beautifully sung, it was Cathedral-style worship at its best, so much so that frequently I could not bring myself to join in the singing of the hymn that ended the proceedings, choosing instead to let this wash over me just like the other music. The psalms in particular were always magical. Invariably, Hazel and I left the Chapel feeling that "All Heaven" had been brought "before our eyes". Never did I understand why countless multitudes of visitors flocked to Evensong down the road at that other place, King's College, for here was something infinitely finer.

Not long after we had set Nicholas up in Cambridge I received an unexpected letter from the Royal Academy of Music, informing me that I had been awarded an A.R.A.M., a "distinction" reserved for past Academy students who had supposedly distinguished themselves in the musical world. Apparently my cause had been pleaded by Hugh Marchant whose Aural Training classes I had attended. He was a fellow Organist, at St. Mary's, Bryanston Square, close to Hazel's flat in her final year at the Academy and who had lived in King Henry's Road close to the Church of St. Mary the Virgin, Primrose Hill, where I had been Organist. I was flattered!

This was but a pleasant prelude to an extraordinary incident which I would not have believed could have happened had I not been there. At about this time the Vicar of St. Edmund's Church, Knighton, in Radnorshire but close to the English border, wrote to me inviting me to take charge of a BBC "Songs of Praise" service that was being recorded in this church. I needed no second bidding, as a healthy fee was involved and money was tight at home because Nick's scholarship at St. John's College School only provided two-thirds of the fees, leaving us to find the remainder, not forgetting the cost of our fortnightly visits to Cambridge. As Hazel and I were used to working together, I asked if she could play the organ, only to be told by the Vicar, Roy Luther Thomas, that he had already invited his resident Organist to do this. My heart sank and, as it turned out, justifiably so. At the first rehearsal it became patently obvious that I had a potential disaster on my hands because while the singing had possibilities, the Organist, a very dear lady who was obviously quite at home playing for the normal church services, was not up to the tensions involved in playing for a televised service.

Fortunately the Vicar had invited the local Silver Band to take part and as the musicians were well up to the musical demands which were being made of them, I spent the next few days writing out parts for them. At the same time I persuaded the BBC Sound Engineers to place their microphones in such a way as to allow the band to dominate the accompaniment to the singing. On the night the programme was televised, Hazel came with me to Knighton to give any necessary help. Little did either of us know what form this help would take. As the recording progressed, so Hazel found herself occasionally guiding the hands of the dear Organist from one manual to the other on the organ, even lying on the floor at one point in the proceedings to lift her feet from one pedal note to another. Fortunately, the actual programme was a success and was broadcast on Sunday May 15th. As a result, I received another of those promises so freely made by BBC Producers but so rarely kept; that I must be used again. Needless to say, I wasn't - at least not by BBC (Midlands) which had made this programme.

A few days later, Hazel and I helped commemorate the life and work of C. H. Trevor in an evening of music at the Chapel in Lincoln's Inn where he had been Organist for so many years. Organ solos were contributed by four former pupils: Hazel, Roger Wibberley, Aldeburgh conductor Steuart Bedford and David Robinson, who was now in charge of the Graduate Course at the Royal Academy of Music. Christopher Regan, who had succeeded C. H. as Organist of the Chapel, also played, while I supplied programme notes. Hazel's contribution comprised a typical C. H. Trevor "find", three dances which he had put together to form a short Suite, composed by an unknown eighteenth-century Bohemian composer Frantisek Tuma. To these pieces she added a Chorale Prelude "Built on the rock the church doth stand", which had been composed by the Czechoslovakian composer Bedrich Janacek in 1966 and dedicated to the great man himself.

However, there was a commemoration of national importance that year, 1977, it being the twenty-fifth anniversary of Queen Elizabeth II's accession to the throne. This was marked by a Civic Service in Brecon Cathedral on Sunday, May 22nd, when the Cathedral Choir sang music associated with her Coronation Service, which I remembered so vividly. So we contributed G. F. Handel's anthem "Zadok the Priest", which had been sung at every coronation since that of King George II in 1727; C. Hubert Parry's "I was glad" which had been composed for the coronation of King Edward VII in 1902 and sung at all subsequent coronations and R. Vaughan Williams's arrangement of the "Old Hundredth", the hymn "All people that on earth do dwell", which had been made for the Queen's own coronation. This drew from the Mayor of Brecon an unexpected letter of appreciation, which showed that unlike many of his predecessors, he indeed did realise "that the standard achieved must represent a great deal of hard work" and wanted us to know that he appreciated it, which was a refreshing change.

Interestingly, early the next month there was another service, only much more magnificent, in St. Paul's Cathedral, which led to my being drawn into some correspondence published in the *Church Times*. It was a wonderful service, the Church of England at its best, yet it provoked a reader to suggest that such wealth, pomp and ceremony was "hardly symbolic of an institution whose leader was the friend of outcasts and sinners". So the reader went on to ask "What impression of the Church of England a T. V. viewer from a poor underprivileged country in the Third World felt when he saw the splendidly-dressed congregation?" Remembering my upbringing in a back-street South London parish among poor and underprivileged youngsters, some of whom had glimpsed heaven in my father's church, while others had glimpsed it in middle-class Southwark Cathedral and its choir, I wrote that as "the original leader of the Church, Jesus Christ, was able to mix with high and low, rich and poor", would the writer "really have been happy to see the congregation turn out dressed like tramps just to please the poor, underprivileged countries of the Third World?"

Strangely, much of this was made a lot more relevant to our times in a "round-robin" letter sent by my Uncle Michael almost a year later.

The letter announcing his retirement from his Roman Catholic parish made fascinating reading:

"Dear David & Hazel,

Please forgive a duplicated letter: I simply haven't the energy to write to all those to whom I owe a word about my future.

I am "retiring" on Sat: July 1st ... to what?

For a long time I have felt that the homeless are "swept under the carpet" in this country. To give two examples: 1. there is not a single reception centre (formerly called Casual Ward) on the south coast route between Southampton and Lands End. 2. if you are entitled to the Old Age Pension you cannot draw it unless you have a permanent Post Office for ten weeks out of every twelve, i. e. those on the road can't get it. I have been arguing this case with the Ministry of Health and Social Security - and finally with the Ombudsman. The answer is "There are 7,000,000 pensioners in this country; we cannot arrange the system to cope with every minority group. Mr Gedge represents only a small minority." This is another way of saying: "We can't help those in greatest need of help".

There are two possible explanations - or more: 1. there are very few people on the road in these prosperous times, 2. a modern welfare state doesn't like to admit that anyone falls through the net. Both of these might be true.

Anyhow, I want to find out. So ... I am leaving everything behind me to the Parish here except to leave one suitcase with friends in Southampton and I shall carry what is left on my back - including a sleeping bag with a water-proof cover. On July 1st I shall start walking down to my god-daughter's home in Cornwall, sleeping rough and seeing what I can see. Unfortunately (for me) that will mean keeping more or less to the main roads whereas I much prefer paths; but then the homeless keep to the more obvious roads because they haven't got maps, or good shoes. When I am too dirty I may put in a night at a Youth Hostel to get a shower - though that is really "cheating". I do not propose to beg - even from the clergy! - I shall take a cheque card with me, and leave enough in my bank to cover a couple of months.

I shall come back to Southampton some time at the end of August – or there-abouts – and I hope to live in the Church Army Home – for the homeless -. The boss of this (C. of E.) establishment tells me that about half his shifting popula-tion of inmates are usually R.C.s. Would he like to take me in as one of them and let me minister to my co-religionists as best I can? He would be delighted. They have a chapel in the House and my own (R.C.) Bishop says I may say Mass there. And from there I shall be able to stand in for the Southampton clergy occasion-ally when they want an extra priest; and I want to study the under-world of Southampton in the autumn and winter.

Beyond that I have no plans ... until the days when I become a geriatric patient myself.

From 1 July for some weeks I shall have no known address – except that any letters sent to NATIONAL WESTMINSTER BANK, 77 LONDON ROAD, SOUTHAMPTON *will be kept for me. As that bank is about 200 yards from the Church Army home it can remain my address until further notice. There is a Post Office just down the road where – when I get back – I can draw my pension. If I find out any facts which are worth broadcasting I shall do what I can to get on to the Media through our man on the Southern I.T.V ...*

If by any chance you are living on my route I may turn up without notice, wearing a beard. I shall not necessarily want a bed – only a space where I can lay my sleeping bag – under cover, if wet; outside if fine.

With all good wishes, Ever yours
Michael.

Michael did exactly what he said he would do, but such an unusual life-style led to his health giving way and caused a group of nuns to give him sanctuary and take him into their care, making him their Chaplain. However, he had always been an independent soul, unable to bear being fussed and pampered in any way, so quite soon he moved on, obtained a single-bedroomed flat near to his birthplace at Havant and there ended his days many years later. His funeral service at the local Roman Catholic Church in the autumn of 1996 took place in a very different Havant from the one that he had grown up in more than ninety years before. A large congregation of priests and people sang a rousing plainsong Requiem Mass accompanied on the organ by me and the moving ceremony was made all the more endearing by a scintillating eulogy from the Roman Catholic Bishop of Portsmouth; he had the entire congregation chuckling at stories of Fr. Michael's eccentricities all of which, however, seemed to centre around a rock-like faith and a rock-like discipline with no compromises. As usual it was impossible to get away from the influences of the old Southwark Cathedral Choir, for among the Roman Catholic priests in the congregation was an old chorister who had at some time "changed sides" and recently been appointed Administrator of the Roman Catholic Cathedral in Michael's diocese of Portsmouth.

Strangely, that summer of 1978, while Michael had been planning his social-security fact-finding walk from Southampton to Cornwall, back in Brecon the Cathedral Singers had been planning their first trip, taking Anglican Cathedral Music to Germany. Like the Cathedral Choir before them, this project also was masterminded by Dieter Edel who, having been mesmerised by a performance of the Vaughan Williams "Mass in G minor" had asked for it to be included in at least three of the six performances that were planned. Much of the travel arrangements had been in the capable hands of Ivor and Dorothy ("Dotty") Phillips, the couple whom I had met some years before at my first Diocesan Choral Festival rehearsal in Pontardawe and it was they who were mad enough to make the sixty-mile round trip to Brecon and back every Tuesday evening for Cathedral Singers rehearsals. Ivor booked a bus for the trip from Morris Bros. of Swansea, which really was quite cunning as it resulted in him and Dotty, along with their soprano friend Annie and her retired miner husband, Will, from Abercraf, getting free transport to Brecon before the trip and home after it.

The bus left Brecon at 2.30 on the morning of Thursday July 27th and made good time to Dover. We enjoyed a perfect crossing on the English Channel, all sun plus smooth sea, and by early evening we were comfortably ensconced in a hotel in Brussels. Throughout the next day the bus took us on the long journey to Schmie, close to Maulbronn, giving the driver ample time to tell us his story. Apparently, when he had arrived back at his Swansea depot from another European trip, he was immediately told that he was driving us to Germany on the next day. When he discovered that we were a church party, he told his boss angrily that if he was still unhappy after four days he would leave us and his bus just where it was and fly home; as a precaution he had packed a bottle of whisky in his suit-case. One night with us in Brussels was enough to convert him to Brecon Cathedral Singers and by the next morning he had become an integral part of the group, with his wicked sense of humour and infectious laugh making him popular with everyone. He had arrived as Russell Beare, but by now he was known as Russ the Bus, and what a great acquisition he came to be. When we arrived at Haus Schmie and were busy unpacking, he was out and about exploring, so that in next to no time we knew where to find the local Bier parlour (and that it didn't close until midnight) and that, according to a local, the good weather had just arrived.

Haus Schmie was a well-appointed Youth Hostel with ample accommodation, a lovely garden with a huge outdoor chess set, tennis courts and a gorgeous swimming pool. What more could we want? All this combined with temperatures in the eighties and everyone was soon enjoying themselves thoroughly. Indeed, it was not long before we were requested to make less noise during the night! The idea of rehearsing at half-past nine in the morning was to help the Singers to come to after their nocturnal exploits and then to have done with singing by the time the village Bier Parlour opened at 12 noon.

Our first concert, in the village church at Bauschlott, created a sensation for the simple reason that never before had an audience there been moved to applaud. Having brought with us four members of the Gwent Chamber Orchestra - John Roberts and Philip Stokes (violins), Paul Jenkins (viola) and Frances Mason (cello), it was possible for Hazel to play Organ Concertos by G. F. Handel and John Stanley and for the choir to sing Henry Purcell's Verse Anthem "Rejoice in the Lord alway" with orchestral accompaniment. John Blow's "*Salvator Mundi*" and four unaccompanied motets by Peter Tchaikovsky were also sung, while the orchestra in addition played the Chacony in G minor by Henry Purcell. A newspaper report on the concert commented on the way the Cathedral Singers put across their joy and skill at singing. It seems also that that at the local Bier Parlour they were equally successful at putting across their joy of life and drinking. By Tuesday evening the local choristers had made themselves known to us in the Bier Parlour; so everyone sang folk songs of their own countries to each other and with each other.

On Wednesday evening the Cathedral Singers gave a concert at the nearby town church of Bretten, but it was like a Turkish Bath, so hot that Tony Wainwright, one of the basses, could not stand the pace and had to sit down while the concert progressed, hidden from the audience by his fellow tenors and basses. Afterwards he was revived at the Schmie Bier Parlour, where Singers met members of the local gymnastic club whom they challenged to a volleyball match on the next evening. Unbeknown to us, this was fortunate, because on a Thursday the Bier Parlour was closed. We were not supposed to be able to play volleyball, but 6'2" Russ the Bus along with John Evans, Chairman of the Tour Committee and Ivor Phillips (who by now was known in jest as "Whoppa") succeeded in hurriedly organising an excellent team, which included me. Despite looking like tramps – after all, we had come equipped to give concerts, not to play volleyball – and not being all that conversant with many of the rules, we lost by only 8-15 in the first game, then much more closely 13-15, which was not bad for amateurs playing a beautifully-turned-out German team, which had begun to get quite nervous about the eventual outcome of the second game. Afterwards, five-a-side soccer was enjoyed by everyone before we were entertained to free food and bier; by the end of the evening, much had subconsciously been accomplished for Anglo-German relations.

The next evening found the Cathedral Singers giving a prestigious concert in the Stiftskirche at Stuttgart, which was notable for three reasons. Firstly, Dieter had told us that we were singing at 8 p.m., but fortunately in consulting a poster outside the church, some of the singers had discovered that we were to sing earlier, at 7 p.m. Secondly, our items had actually been incorporated into a service which contained a congregational chorale that was introduced by the resident organist extemporising a very fine prelude, which the Singers admired greatly. Thirdly, when Dieter finally arrived shortly before 8 p.m., he found the concert almost over and "ze Vaughan Williams Mass" sung, he was not amused! As we were back at Haus Schmie early after the concert, we had time to change out of our formal clothes into something more casual before setting off for a night-cap at the Bier Parlour. While changing, two of our teenage sopranos complained that some German boys were up in a tree watching them through a gap in the curtains. Tony Wainwright was equal to the situation. He worked his way round the copious undergrowth until he had reached the tree, whereupon he leapt out, shouting loudly "Achtung!" At this, two lads tumbled out of the tree, one running off into the undergrowth, the other lying in a crumpled heap to be ministered to by Tony who was, after all, a doctor!

On Saturday, the Cathedral Singers made that long journey to Brecon's twin town Blaubeuren. While travelling along an autobahn, Russ overtook a lorry by driving at little more than 1 m.p.h. faster. As the two drivers' cabs slowly drew up alongside each other, Russ being a right-hand drive and the lorry driver being a left-hand drive, the opportunity arose for Russ to offer the German a cigarette. He, on taking it, indicated that he had no matches, whereupon Russ threw him a box, then roaring with laughter, put his foot down hard on the accelerator and pulled ahead. At Maulbronn, a concert was followed by the inevitable Civic Reception, at which I became Mr. Jedge, while Judith, the German-teacher wife of John Roberts, became a star interpreter. Small wonder that she later became Chief Examiner in German for the Welsh Joint Education Committee "O" level examination. Later that night we returned to Haus Schmie, because next morning the Cathedral Singers were to sing the Vaughan Williams Mass liturgically in a Roman Catholic Church near to Schmie. Happily, on this occasion, the Roman Catholic Father allowed the Anglicans to share the sacrament, which was a pleasing sign that religious barriers were being removed.

That night, the Singers gave a concert in the wonderful monastery church, the Klosterkirche, in Maulbronn. This was lit by candlelight for the occasion and, again, was memorable for three reasons. The opening part of the concert was admired by the five-hundred strong audience for the Henry Purcell Verse Anthem "My beloved spake" and for the "unique beauty" of the Vaughan Williams Mass. Secondly, as a central item, Hazel and Hugh Thomas played the long Organ Duet by Samuel Wesley, which so suited the Monastery's mechanical action Walcker Organ, while I sneaked out for a quick drink in the Bier Parlour close by. When I crept back into the Klosterkirche, up the side of the candlelit Nave, through the solid stone screen and into the Quire, while Hazel and Hugh were playing the final movement, a Gavotte, there, in the unlit gloom between the ancient dark oak choir stalls, many of the Singers were dancing in pairs to the graceful music, unseen by the audience. Thirdly, in the final part of the concert, when the Singers came to perform the "Two Psalms" by Gustav Holst, their impeccable tuning which had added distinction to the first part of the proceedings, deserted them, leaving me very puzzled. Afterwards John Evan's wife, Jill, whispered to me that seven of the sopranos had started their "monthlies" during this music: by chance, only a month later, an article published in some scientific journal explained how such a phenomenon could happen when a group of ladies were living together in abnormal circumstances. However, the evening ended with a wonderful reception that continued until well into the night, with exchanges of gifts and pleasantries that kept Judith Roberts very busy translating and ended with both Germans and British linking arms to sing "Auld Lang Syne".

Monday was a much-needed "Rest Day" except for the instrumentalists who, as a favour for Dieter, gave a concert at nearby Schloss Konigsbach, where he lived in a small flat. When we arrived in the dusk of a warm summer's evening, it seemed like fairyland, with lanterns illuminating the castle walls and grounds. Once inside, I, as *Leitung* (Musical Director) was taken in to the "Holy of Holies" to meet the lady who owned this impressive pile in her private apartment, which resembled a mausoleum to the memory of her dead husband, who had been a noted fighter pilot in the Second World War. The concert was fun: the three Mozart *Divertimenti*, K136-8, between each of which was sandwiched a J. S. Bach Harpsichord Concerto played by Hugh Thomas, first in F minor, then in D minor. Afterwards, just as we had settled down to enjoy the wine that was flowing freely, Dieter breezed in saying: "You vill go now!" We had no intention of going - after all, we had worked hard all evening as a favour and now were busily reaping our reward, at the same time, it was pointless arguing with an insistent Dieter. So we made Frances take her 'cello out to the car without its hard case, then we filled this with several bottles of wine, hid one more each within our clothing, said our farewells and left as requested. The party that followed at Haus Schmie that night beggars description, but we paid the price the next morning, particularly Frances who was very unwell and, further- more, lost a contact lens which, fortunately, was found in time for the next concert. Meanwhile Dieter was furious because, unfortunately and unknown to us, the Lady of the Castle had counted the number of bottles before the concert and then had counted them again after the concert and so found some missing, which led her to complain to Dieter. For the second time, Dieter was not amused!

That afternoon there were tennis tournament finals in the grounds of Haus Schmie before Russ could drive the Singers to nearby Stein to rehearse for the final concert, As we left, a still smouldering Dieter ordered: "You vill sing ze Vaughan Williams" as so far, through his own fault, he had missed all the performances. When I saw the inside of this delightful church, however, I knew that we would not be singing the Vaughan Williams Mass as there was no resonance at all in the build- ing. After the rehearsal we left our music in the church hall and used the loos before returning to Haus Schmie for tea and a clean-up, as it was still very hot. I was last out and, unexpectedly, found Russ waiting to walk me to the bus. He explained that, as he had been leaving the Church Hall, he had noticed Dieter hanging around outside the gents toilets as if to set about me when I came out, to insist on his Vaughan Williams. Russ had never liked Dieter because of his dictatorial man- ner, so he too had waited for me and, as Dieter was afraid of Russ, Dieter just quietly melted away and left me alone.

That night we did not sing the Vaughan Williams, but we did sing what had become known as "Russ's Anthem", "There shall a star from Jacob come forth", from the opening of Felix Mendelssohn's unfinished oratorio "*Christus*". The Singers loved singing this, with its opening soprano recitative telling of Jesus being born in Bethlehem, followed by the trio for men's voices asking: "Where is he, born the King of the Jews, for we have seen his star and are come to worship him?", after which the entire choir sang the magical "There shall a star from Jacob come forth", which would reduce pop-music-loving Russ to ecstasy. God moves in a mysterious way!

So the tour was coming to end, but not before we had one more opportunity to reduce Russ to tears, only these were tears of laughter. After a final happy barbecue arranged by our Sports Club friends in the clearing of a wood out in the cool of the night, we went on a shopping spree to Pforzheim the next morning. Unknown to Russ, Ivor and Tony W. had written a "fun" letter to his boss at Morris Bros. Swansea, complaining about his drinking, swearing and womanising. When Russ stopped his bus by a letter box, Tony and John Evans suddenly held him to his seat while Ivor held the letter for him to read, but on the other side of the windscreen, then folded up the letter, put it in an envelope, sealed it and dropped it in the letter box. So much for Russ's Church Party!

The long journey home took us through Luxembourg where Russ told us how, on a previous trip when he had been short of time, he had taken his bus on a short-cut along a road forbidden to coaches, only to be stopped by the police. The litigation that followed he had taken care of by having all his answering letters translated into Welsh by a friend, so that in the end the Luxembourg police gave up bothering him. We spent one more night in Brussels, where for the first time ever we paid £1 for a pint of beer. Then, on the next day, we crossed the English Channel and in next to no time were speeding up the M4 towards Wales.